V&R

Refo500 Academic Studies

Edited by
Herman J. Selderhuis

In Co-operation with
Christopher B. Brown (Boston), Günter Frank (Bretten),
Bruce Gordon (New Haven), Barbara Mahlmann-Bauer (Bern),
Tarald Rasmussen (Oslo), Violet Soen (Leuven),
Zsombor Tóth (Budapest), Günther Wassilowsky (Linz),
Siegrid Westphal (Osnabrück).

Volume 53

Simon J.G. Burton/Michał Choptiany/
Piotr Wilczek (eds.)

Protestant Majorities and Minorities in Early Modern Europe

Confessional Boundaries and Contested Identities

Vandenhoeck & Ruprecht

Bibliographic information published by the Deutsche Nationalbibliothek:
The Deutsche Nationalbibliothek lists this publication in the Deutsche Nationalbibliografie; detailed bibliographic data available online: http://dnb.de.

Typesetting: 3w+p, Rimpar
Printed and bound: Hubert & Co. BuchPartner, Göttingen
Printed in the EU

Vandenhoeck & Ruprecht Verlage | www.vandenhoeck-ruprecht-verlage.com

ISSN 2198-3089
ISBN 978-3-525-57129-3

Contents

III. Refugee Reformation

IV. Marginal Reformation

V. Confessional Identity and Otherness

Simon J.G. Burton/Michał Choptiany/Piotr Wilczek

Introduction

This volume contains papers drawn from the international RefoRC colloquium on "Reformed Majorities and Minorities: Confessional Boundaries and Contested Identities". This took place in the Faculty of *Artes Liberales* at the University of Warsaw on September 22–24 2014. It was organised by the then Commission for the Study of the Reformation in Poland and East-Central Europe (now the Centre for the Study of the Reformation and Intellectual Culture in Early Modern Europe) in collaboration with RefoRC, the Johannes a Lasco Bibliothek, Emden and the Tolle Lege Institute, Warsaw. The organisers of the colloquium, who are also the editors of this volume, are especially grateful to Professor Jerzy Axer, the former Dean of the Faculty of *Artes Liberales*, for permission to use the Faculty buildings and for financial support, to Professor Herman J. Selderhuis and Dr Karla Apperloo-Boersma of RefoRC for administrative and financial support, and to Dr Dariusz Bryćko of the Tolle Lege Institute for the generous financial contribution of his organisation.

This volume is intended as a companion volume to *Reformed Majorities in Early Modern Europe* (Göttingen: Vandenhoeck & Ruprecht, 2015), edited by Herman Selderhuis and J. Marius Lange van Ravenswaay. This marked the principal output of an earlier international RefoRC conference "Reformed Majorities and Minorities in Early Modern Europe", organised by the Johannes a Lasco Bibliothek, Emden in co-operation with the Faculty of *Artes Liberales* of the University of Warsaw, which took place in Emden in 2013. As originally envisaged the Warsaw colloquium of 2014 was intended to cover Reformed minorities and to consider the way in which Reformed institutions and individuals dealt in theory and practice with the relation between doctrine and tolerance. In fact, as indicated below, the colloquium and resulting volume ended up embracing a wider inter-confessional and even (to some extent) inter-religious scope. For this reason the decision was taken to change the name of the volume to *Protestant Majorities and Minorities in Early Modern Europe: Confessional Boundaries and Contested Identities.* Nevertheless, the identity and experience of Reformed minorities, in both a strict and broad sense, remains central to this volume. Likewise, there are many important thematic continuities which bind the two volumes together, providing a linking narrative on minority and refugee experience to complement the earlier focus on Reformed majorities.

The volume itself is organised into five sections: I) Intellectual Culture and Confessional Freedom, II) Clandestine Reformation, III) Refugee Reformation, IV) Marginal Reformation and V) Confessional Identity and Otherness. Each of these presents a different aspect of the relation between religious majorities and minorities in early modern Europe, while cumulatively they offer a view of the complex intellectual, social, economic, political, and, of course, theological and ecclesiastical factors that shaped the dynamics of intra- and inter-confessional encounter. While by no means comprehensive in scope or intention, the different chapters in the volume cover a wide geographical area and interact with an impressive array of confessions.

The first section explores intellectual trajectories, especially those which promoted confessional unity or sought to break down confessional boundaries. The second section, taking the neglected Spanish Reformation as an important case-study, examines the clandestine aspect of minority activities and the efforts of majorities to control and suppress them. It also highlights the way in which Reformed minorities could be empowered through their connections to an international movement. The third section pursues a similar theme but examines it through the lens of Flemish and Walloon Reformed refugee communities in Germany and the Netherlands, demonstrating the way in which confessional factors could lead to the integration or exclusion of minorities. The fourth section examines marginal Reformations, whether geographically or doctrinally understood, focussing on attempts to implement reform in the shadow of the Ottoman Empire. Finally, the fifth section looks at confessional identity and otherness as a principal theme of majority and minority relations, providing both theoretical and practical frameworks for its evaluation.

I. Intellectual Culture and Confessional Freedom

Gábor Ittzés' chapter "From Bullinger to Specker and Garcaeus: The Reformed Origins of the Lutheran Doctrine of the Immortality of the Soul in the Sixteenth Century" considers an important theme of philosophical debate in the early modern period and the way in which it crossed confessional boundaries. While Martin Luther's own views of the soul's immortality were often viewed with suspicion, the doctrine later became a central tenet of Lutheran orthodoxy. Ittzés' paper examines this transformation by means of a detailed textual study of the work of two lesser known sixteenth-century Lutheran theologians: Melchior Specker and Johannes Garcaeus Jr. He demonstrates that both of these authors drew extensively on a sermon by Heinrich Bullinger, the influential Swiss Reformed theologian. As Ittzés suggests, at a time when Lutheran and Reformed theologians were increasingly at odds confessionally, their common stance with respect to the immortality of the soul shows the ongoing potential for philosophical and theological cross-fertilisation between rival communities.

Questions surrounding the soul are also at the heart of Alessandra Celati's chapter "A Peculiar Reformed Minority: Italian Protestant Physicians between Religious Propaganda, Inquisitorial Repression and Freedom of Thought". This focusses on the reception of the Reformation in the sixteenth-century Italian medical community and its impact on the wider horizon of the European Reformation, especially in its radical streams. Celati shows that the physician's office as doctors of body and soul, gave them an important spiritual role in their communities, frequently causing them to come into conflict with the Inquisition. The records of the Inquisition show that many Italian doctors were attracted to Reformed doctrine. However, their own education and especially its radical Aristotelian (Averroistic) tenor, often led these same doctors to unconventional views of the soul and its relation to God. In advocating an unprecedented freedom of thought, Celati shows how they sought to overcome religious boundaries at the very moment when the different confessions were entrenching themselves, ever more deeply, in positions of doctrinal rigidity.

A similar desire to break down traditional boundaries, albeit towards a very different end, was in evidence in early modern Ramism, which is the subject of Simon Burton's chapter "From Minority Discourse to Universal Method: Polish Chapters in the Evolution of Ramism". Burton examines aspects of the complex evolution of Ramism in the seventeenth century, examining especially the tension between its increasing marginalisation and its universalist aspirations. In particular, he considers the way in which both pragmatic and theological considerations motivated the adoption of Ramism in minority contexts and fuelled its ongoing transformation. The first case-study focusses on Bartholomäus Keckermann, one of the leading intellectuals of the early seventeenth century. Keckermann's own desire to relieve the embattled Reformed community of his native Danzig, under siege from a hostile Lutheran majority, led him from being a critic of Ramist educational methods to becoming a pioneer in their adaptation. This leads into discussion of Jan Amos Comenius, the visionary Czech philosopher and theologian. Even more than Keckermann, Comenius saw the potential of Ramism to contribute to the reform and reunification of divided Christendom. From Keckermann to Comenius (via Johann Heinrich Alsted) we can therefore chart the way in which different minority experiences, within the broader Reformed community, shaped the evolution of Ramism and prepared the way for universal reformation.

II. Clandestine Reformation

Christopher Matthews' chapter "A Reformed Hiding Place in Sixteenth-Century Seville: The Significance of the Monastery of St Isidore" provides a window onto the history of an influential Spanish monastery, that of St Ididore's in Seville, from its early origins and expansion during the Reconquista to its startling transformation in the sixteenth century from a Catholic beacon of reform into a secret Protestant seminary. In doing so Matthews demonstrates the deep and surprising roots of Spanish Protestantism in the intellectual and spiritual reforms of Isidore of Seville and of the Hieronymite Order of observant monks who followed in his footsteps. He offers an account of the clandestine life these monks led in their efforts to spread the Gospel among Spanish clergy and academics and to promote Bible study and translation. Ultimately, however, their close connections with the underground Protestant Church in Seville led to their discovery by the Inquisition, causing many to become refugees and to make their abodes in Protestant centres across Europe. However, while today the Monastery of St Isidore stands empty, its legacy lives on in the Spanish churches, both Catholic majority and Protestant minority, which have benefitted from its monks and especially their work of translation.

In "*Sola Scriptura:* The Rationale behind the Early Protestant Translations of the Spanish Bible", José Moreno Berrocal reminds us that in the early modern period Bible translation could often be a minority pursuit in the face of a very hostile majority. Through a detailed examination of the lives and witness of three brave Protestant translators – Francisco de Enzinas (Francis Dryander), Juan Pérez de Pineda and Casiodoro de Reina – he shows the way in which the minority attempt to provide a Spanish translation of the Bible, which had its beginning in Catholic reform circles, became an international endeavour, eventually involving Reformed intellectual and printing networks across Europe. Even more importantly, however, Moreno Berrocal examines the theological roots of this endeavour in Protestant convictions about the authority of the Word of God and the internal testimony of the Holy Spirit. In doing so he demonstrates the way in which these translators sought to appeal to the hearts and minds of their Spanish brethren in an effort to turn their minority position into a majority one.

Matthews' and Moreno Berrocal's accounts are nicely complemented by Frances Luttikhuizen's chapter "Clandestine Protestant Literature Reaches Spain", which examines in more depth the underground book trade which nourished the Spanish Protestant Church and particularly the reforming intellectuals of St Isidore's. In the process Luttikhuizen also highlights censorship as an important instrument which was frequently used by early modern majorities in their efforts to control and suppress minority viewpoints. In the

Spanish context this tightening of regulations affected not only the Protestant minority but also the increasingly marginalised reforming Catholics, who early in the sixteenth century had looked set to become a dominant majority. Nevertheless, Luttikhuizen shows how, by exploiting their connections with international networks of Reformed printers and booksellers, Spanish Protestants were able to smuggle into Spain a remarkable number of Bibles and religious books. Once again the minority situation of a beleagured Protestant community is shown to be more complex than it might appear at first sight.

III. Refugee Reformation

Barbara Kaminska's chapter "A Religious Minority between Triumph and Persecution: Frans Hogenberg's *Hedge-Preaching outside Antwerp* and the Flemish Community in Cologne" examines the remarkable phenomenon of Protestant hedge-preaching during the Dutch Wonder Year of 1566–1567, and its intriguing afterlife in the engravings of Frans Hogenberg, himself a Protestant refugee from the Low Countries. By comparison with official documentation of the hedge-preaching, Kaminska shows how Hogenberg subtly manipulated the facts in his own representation of a famous outdoor sermon which took place outside Antwerp in order to legitimate his own, minority, interpretation of the events. In sharp contrast with the triumphant tone of other contemporary Protestant accounts, Hogenberg chose to emphasise the divisive potential of the field-preaching, especially its role in splitting the Walloon Reformed, Flemish Reformed and Lutheran Churches. At the same time he sought to neutralise the radical political elements of the preaching and to present it as a necessary reaction against the corruption of the Catholic Church. In doing so, Kaminska suggests, he aimed both to stimulate reflection and reconciliation among newly divided Protestant communities and to secure Cologne and other German cities as a safe-haven for the refugees by convincing sceptics of the legitimacy of their revolt.

Leon van den Broeke's chapter "Acceptance and Organisation of the French Protestants in the Northern Netherlands: A Reformed Minority within the Reformed Majority" presents us with another unusual encounter between majority and minority. Focussing on the French-speaking Walloon Church he examines the circumstances and conditions of their acceptance and integration into the Reformed Church of the Netherlands. Van den Broeke argues that while the Walloons were welcomed into the Netherlands on both compassionate and economic grounds, it was their shared Reformed faith which allowed them to integrate so well. For this allowed them to develop their own Church order, with their own French pastors, liturgy and even academy, but at the same time to slot into the established synodical system of Church government. In this way they retained their own distinct identity as a community, which was for a long time protected by generous privileges granted by the Dutch government, and also gained an important voice in Dutch affairs. Ultimately, however, their very success led to their almost complete assimilation into Dutch culture, leading to the Walloon Church today having become a near invisible minority.

IV. Marginal Reformation

Traditional research on early modern relations between Catholics and Protestants has focussed on the European context, in which one of the two confessions almost invariably exercised a dominant majority role over the other. Felicita Tramontana's chapter "An Unusual Setting: Interactions between Protestants and Catholics in the Ottoman Empire" presents an alternative, non-European, perspective, drawing our attention to the fortunes of the early modern Protestant and Catholic communities of the Ottoman Empire. In this unusual setting both groups were minorities under Muslim rule and the majority Christian group was the Orthodox Church. Through detailed consideration of the correspondence between Catholic priests and missionaries and the Holy Office in Rome, Tramontana provides us with an on-the-ground account of the dynamics of Tridentine Confessionalisation. In particular, she examines the tension between Rome's recognition of the pragmatic reality of Catholic life in the Ottoman Empire, in which amicable contact between Protestants and Catholics was both inevitable and essential for the survival of both communities, and their desire to establish a robust oriental Catholic identity as an effective counter-measure against the incursions of Orthodox Christianity.

Mihály Balázs' chapter "Aus der Mehrheit in die Minderheit: Der Weg des siebenbürgischen Antitrinitarismus im 16.–17. Jahrhundert" focusses on the Anti-Trinitarian community in Transylvania, a principality on the edge of the Ottoman Empire, and their journey from influential majority to marginalised minority. While many scholars have blamed the Anti-Trinitarians for their own demise, especially due to their internal theological dissensions and radical views, Balázs takes a different view. He argues that the Transylvanian Anti-Trinitarians, despite their prevalent and highly controversial Non-Adorantist stance on Christ, had a surprisingly international and inclusive perspective. This was markedly different from the Sabbatarians, with whom they are usually compared, who dwindled into a sect. Rather, like the Polish Anti-Trinitarians, with whom they were closely connected, the Transylvanian Anti-Trinitarians shared the view that they had been given a special role by God for the renewal of all Christendom. Drawing on the writings of the Polish-Lithuanian Anti-Trinitarian Szymon

Budny and the Transylvanian Anti-Trinitarian György Enyedi, Balázs reveals their theological arguments for a universal Christianity, which were for the latter even capable of embracing both Trinitarians and Anti-Trinitarians, and their openness to political involvement and alliance. However, he concludes that political changes in Hungary and Transylvania, a rising Anti-Ottoman sentiment and increasing confessionalisation during the seventeenth century left no room for this kind of radical irenicism.

Borbála Lovas' chapter "On the Margins of the Reformation: The "Local" and the "International" in György Enyedi's Manuscript Sermons and Printed Works" complements Balázs' chapter in providing a detailed account of the struggle of the Anti-Trinitarian minority in Transylvania against Catholic and Reformed opposition. She focusses on György Enyedi, who was actually bishop of the Anti-Trinitarians, and the complex legacy of his published works and manuscript sermons. Enyedi's sermons were preached at a time when the Anti-Trinitarians, following the death of their patron Prince John Sigismund Zapolya, were in danger of losing their majority position. In them, Enyedi attacks the princes for deserting the Anti-Trinitarian cause and calls on the Transylvanians, as a chosen nation, to establish the true Christian religion in Europe. Later, however, as Lovas establishes, the sermons were adapted to become a principal source for Enyedi's *Explicationes*, his major theological work against the Trinity. In the seventeenth century this became a target not only for Catholic, Reformed and Lutheran theologians across Europe but the centre of an inter-confessional battle between the new Reformed majority, sponsored by the Calvinist princes, and the now embattled Anti-Trinitarian minority. In this we see how sermons delivered to a minority in a marginal principality could have Europe-wide repercussions.

V. Confessional Identity and Otherness

Magdalena Luszczynska's chapter "Inter-Faith Disputation, Christian-Hebraism or a Leadership Campaign?: The Multi-Dimensional Character of Marcin Czechowic's Anti-Jewish Polemics" presents an account of the way in which Marcin Czechowic, a theologian of the Polish Brethren, exploited the "otherness" of the Jewish faith in order both to distance himself and his Anti-Trinitarian views from accusations of "Judaising" and to position himself as the natural leader of the Anti-Trinitarians. Examining in detail Czechowic's Anti-Jewish polemics, which were written in the form of dialogue with a Jewish Rabbi, Luszczynska shows how Czechowic's inter-faith discussion with a Jew became the implicit framework for intra-faith discussion with his Anti-Trinitarian rivals. In particular, by presenting himself as a deeply-learned Christian Hebraist – a veneer, as Luszczynska demonstrates – he was able to cleverly address the issues of pre-existence and adorantism which were at that time beginning to divide the Polish Anti-Trinitarians. In this way Czechowic sought to unify the Polish Brethren, as well as to defend their own minority understanding as the true meaning of Christian Scripture.

Joanna Partyka's chapter "British Protestants and Women's Freedom to Write", which focusses on female writers from a Puritan and Quaker background, offers a compelling account of a minority within a minority. The early modern period saw a dramatic rise in female literacy, leading to a significant number of women becoming writers. Partyka, like other scholars before her, links this trend to the Protestant, especially Puritan, habit of writing a spiritual journal which took off in the sixteenth century. She argues that this task, perceived by many as a spiritual duty, provided an outlet not only for religious sentiment and ideals but also for female creativity. Indeed, in writers such as Lucy Hutchinson and Anne Dudley Bradstreet we see a flowering of early modern female literature and poetry. Writing therefore became an important way for this particular minority to express themselves, and voice their own female *and* Puritan views of the world. While in the sixteenth-century Puritan movement female writing largely remained within the bounds of societal norms and expectations, the seventeenth century saw the rise of the Quakers. Taking advantage of their opportunity to write, Quaker women like Margaret Fell used it to promote controversial female preaching and leadership roles. Paradoxically, therefore, the Puritan minority, which many scholars have simplistically viewed as oppressive and patriarchal, gave rise to important expressions of feminine spirituality and freedom.

Paweł Rutkowski's chapter "Papists, Frogs and Witches: Representing Quakers in Seventeenth-Century England" also centres on the Quakers, but this time from the perspective of their hostile Anglican and Puritan opponents. He shows how in their struggle to understand and contain this new, revolutionary spiritual movement, which was perceived as deeply threatening both to key Protestant doctrines and English societal norms, Anglicans and Puritans alike turned to stereotypical views of the "other". In particular, Rutkowski argues that portraying Quakers as Catholic conspirators, witches and even beasts was a way of making sense of their unusual theological views and social radicalism and justifying their ongoing persecution. For many these images were not mutually exclusive but rather fit together into a master narrative according to which the Pope was using an alliance of counterfeit Protestants and unholy powers to undermine the Protestant Church in England and bring it back under the thrall of the papacy. It was only when the Quakers toned down their radical views in the later seventeenth century that they could be accepted and tolerated as a religious minority and absorbed into the new Protestant pluralistic settlement.

Jakub Koryl's lengthy chapter, "Sources of Community: Mythical Groundwork of Early Modern Identities", stands out in terms of its theoretical nature and comprehensive scope. At the same time it goes to the heart of the question of confessional identity and otherness, and thus provides an illuminating perspective on many of the themes covered in both this section and the volume as a whole. Drawing on case-studies from both the Lutheran and Catholic Reformation, Koryl seeks to offer a new account of confessional-identity building from the late Middle Ages through to the Enlightenment. In particular, he argues that in the early modern period the theme of myth – and especially the rival German and Roman "myths" of Reformation – became the driving force for the creation of new confessional identities, harnessing and uniting into one powerful synthesis, social, intellectual, political and religious forces. Then, following in the footsteps of Hans Blumenberg, Charles Taylor and others, Koryl traces the roots of the modern conception of identity to late medieval Nominalism and its overturning of the medieval analogical and hierarchical understanding of reality. According to Koryl, it was this philosophical move which helped release the creative – and destructive – interplay of forces that shaped the early modern confessional landscape for the next two centuries. Importantly, this situation gave minority views a new voice in European affairs, allowing them eventually to construct their own (secular) myths and take on the dominant, majority role they exercise in the world today.

Edinburgh/Warsaw/Washington, D.C.,
19 December 2018

Simon J.G. Burton
Michał Choptiany
Piotr Wilczek

I. Intellectual Culture and Confessional Freedom

Gábor Ittzés

From Bullinger to Specker and Garcaeus

The Reformed Origins of the Lutheran Doctrine of the Immortality of the Soul in the Sixteenth Century

1. Introduction

In the second half of the sixteenth century, German Lutheran theologians developed a robust doctrine of the immortality of the soul. The body of literature they produced covers a broad range in geographical, cultural, and temporal terms.[1] Yet the teaching was quite consistent, which may in part be due to the fact

1 Abbreviations

ADB	Allgemeine Deutsche Biographie, 56 vols. (Berlin: Duncker & Humblot, 1875–1912), online, www.deutsche-biographie.de.
BBKL	Biographisch-bibliographisches Kirchenlexikon, gen. eds. Frierich-Wilhelm Bautz and Traugott Bautz, 36 vols. to date (Hamm/Herzberg/Nordhausen: Bautz, 1990–), online edition: www.bbkl.de.
DS	Heinrich Denzinger, Peter Hünermann and Helmut Hoping (eds.) (2005), Enchiridion symbolorum definitionum et declarationum de rebus fidei et morum / Kompendium der Glaubensbekenntnisse und kirchlichen Lehrentscheidungen, German trans. by Peter Hünermann and Helmut Hoping, 40th edition, Freiburg: Herder. English trans. from the 30th edition: The Sources of Catholic Dogma, trans. Roy J. Deferrari, St. Louis: Herder, 1957.
NDB	Neue Deutsche Biographie, 25 vols. to date (Berlin: Duncker & Humblot, 1953–), online edition: www.deutsche-biographie.de.
VD16	Verzeichnis der im deutschen Sprachbereich erschienenen Drucke des 16. Jahrhunderts (www.vd16.de).
WBIS	World Biographical Information System (WBIS) Online (Munich: Saur), http://db.saur.de/WBIS.

The works, in chronological order, include but are not limited to Melchior Specker's Vom Leiblichen Todt (Strasbourg, 1560), Andreas Musculus' Gelegenheit/Thun vnd Wesen der Verstorbenen (Frankfurt a.d.O., 1565), Basilius Faber's Tractetlein von den Seelen der verstorbenen (Leipzig, 1569), Johannes Garcaeus, Jr.'s Sterbbüchlein (Wittenberg, 1573), Martin Mirus' Sieben Christliche Predigten (preached in Regensburg, 1575, first printed in Erfurt, 1590), David Chyträus, Sr.'s De morte et vita aeterna (Wittenberg, 1581–1582, German trans. by

that these works constitute an intricate web of interconnected texts. Later authors not infrequently quoted or paraphrased, usually without acknowledgement, earlier writings from the corpus. To prove that claim would require complex philological arguments, which I cannot pursue here. What I offer in this paper instead is an analysis of some formative influences on two, interrelated, early examples of this tradition.

My contention is that Zurich Reformer Heinrich Bullinger's work, especially his sermon "Of the Reasonable Soul of Man; and of His Most Certain Salvation after the Death of His Body" (Bullinger: 1849–1852, 3:365–408) is a tangible source of both Melchior Specker's 1560 florilegium *Vom Leiblichen Todt* and Johannes Garcaeus, Jr.'s *Sterbbüchlein* (1573). If that claim can be substantiated, which I will hope to do in this paper, and if my larger thesis about Lutheran eschatological thought holds, which I will assume rather than argue here, then Bullinger's significance extends far beyond the works which absorbed its impact initially. Through their transmission, the Swiss Reformed theologian's influence ultimately informed the development of North German Lutheran teaching about the *Zwischenzustand*, the soul's immortality and the interim state between the body's death and resurrection.

The doctrine of the immortality of the soul is not a central tenet of the Reformation, but it can offer an interesting case study for the process of confessionalisation. On the eve of the Reformation, Lateran V (1512–1517) declared the immortality of the human soul.[2] Luther's polemic against the council is well known, and his opposition is often interpreted as a rejection of that doctrine.[3] Calvin, on the other hand, was a staunch supporter of the immortality of the soul against the Anabaptists. He dedicated his theological maiden work to this issue,[4] and it has been suggested that an unnamed but implied opponent of his on this point was Luther himself (George: 1987, 310–311). Luther's views need careful evaluation, especially as Melanchthon also produced a forceful defence of the doctrine of immortality in the last chapter of his *De anima* commentary (1544, 303–315), which was first published in Luther's lifetime in Wittenberg, hardly without his knowledge and consent. Be that as it may, after mid-century there

Heinrich Rätel, Berlin/Frankfurt a. d.O., 1590–1591), Moses Pflacher's Die gantze Lehr Vom Tod vnd Absterben des Menschen (Frankfurt a.M., 1582), and Georg Weiser's Christlicher Bericht (Bautzen/Eisleben, 1583). All works were reprinted, some many times and well into the seventeenth century, often at different places.

2 Apostolici regiminis, 19 December 1513; cf. DS 1440 (English trans. #738).

3 A major twentieth-century theological debate swirled around Luther's views and resulted in a flood of contributions. For the origins of the debate, see Stange: 1925 and 1926, and Althaus: 1926 and 1930; for more recent positions, see, e. g., Heidler: 1983, and Thiede: 1982 and 1993; and for a helpful overview, cf. Lohse: 1999, 325–329.

4 The Psychopannychia was written in 1534 although its publication (1542) postdates the first edition of the Institutes in 1536.

emerged a full-bodied doctrine of immortality among Lutheran thinkers. Its critical edge was directed against Catholic teaching, especially the doctrine of purgatory, but it proved non-divisive between the Swiss and the German branches of the Reformation. Whatever the apparent distance between Luther's and Calvin's positions in this matter, the gap was narrowed rather than reinforced or widened in the course of the century, despite the Crypto-Calvinist controversies, which were arguably the bitterest of all intra-Lutheran disputes. By the time the minority status of Reformed positions was sealed with the ascendancy of the *Book of Concord* (1580) in Lutheran lands, the Swiss impact had been absorbed so widely and deeply by the evangelicals of the North that it had become part and parcel of the majority view. Bullinger's teaching as mediated by Specker and Garcaeus, which I will explore on the following pages, probably played an important part in that process.

2. Authors and Texts

Heinrich Bullinger (1504–1575) is best known as Zwingli's successor in Zurich after the latter's death at the Battle of Kappel in 1531, which also forced the former to flee his native Bremgarten, where he had been an evangelical pastor for two years. It is often lamented that his recognition does not match his importance, although he has been called "an architect of the Reformation" (Gordon/Campi: 2004) and, already in his lifetime, a "father of the Reformed church" (Blanke: 1990). The 500th anniversary of his birth in 2004 spurred renewed interest in his work, and the literature produced in recent years has to some extent rectified that undervaluation.[5]

Bullinger left a copious oeuvre, comprising well over 120 works. His correspondence, estimated at 12,000 letters, exceeds not only Melanchthon's but also Luther's, Calvin's and Erasmus' *combined.*[6] Of his theological writings, a collection of fifty sermons arranged into groups of ten, and hence called *Sermonum decades quinque*, is widely considered the most important. Written in Latin, they were first published as a series of "decades" from the late 1540s onwards, and translations already began to appear then. Vernacular versions became known under the title *Hausbuch/House Book*. The first full Latin edition was issued in Zurich in 1552 (VD16: B 9696), and the work not only proved an immediate and

5 Basic information has long been readily available on him in standard handbooks, cf., e.g., ADB 3:513–514, NDB 3:12, BBKL 1:809–811. See also Gordon: 2002, with a helpful short bibliography of major contributions from the second half of the twentieth century. Of recent book-length re-evaluations, see especially Campi/Opitz: 2007.

6 Cf. the project website on the homepage of the Institute of Swiss Reformation Studies at http://www.irg.uzh.ch/hbbw.html.

exceptional publication success[7] but has remained in print ever since.[8] It is a bulky work of some 1,800 pages in which Bullinger treats fundamental loci of Christian theology such as the Word of God, faith, justification, the Ten Commandments, the Apostles' Creed, the Trinity, offices, prayer, the Church, sacraments and many more.[9] My main concern will be with Sermon 40 (the tenth and last sermon in the fourth decade) on the rational soul and its immortality (salvation), but I will also reference another influential sermon cycle by Bullinger, his homiletic commentary on Revelation (VD16: B 9635).[10]

Melchior Specker (?–1569) was a pastor and professor in Strasbourg. Only the basic outlines of his life are known, and even those only fragmentarily. A native of Isny im Allgäu, he was a student of the great Hebraist Paul Fagius (1504–1549) and ended up teaching, first, logic and metaphysics, and later, theology at the Strasbourg Academy.[11] Half a dozen of his works are still extant,[12] and only one of them was reprinted (shortly) after his death. This piece was first published under the title *Vom Leiblichen Todt* in 1560, issued again the next year and finally for a third time, posthumously, in 1571. Consisting of over six hundred pages, it is a bulky book divided into three parts.[13] It is essentially a collection of thematically arranged quotations taken from the Bible and 1500 years of theological reflection, including the Church Fathers, medieval theologians and Reformation divines, whose names Specker carefully lists at the end of the volume (1560, GG3$^{r/v}$).

7 A quick bibliographic search in VD16 and major library databases shows that by 1600 there existed, in addition to six Latin printings of the complete series (1552, 1557, 1562, 1567, 1577, 1587), numerous editions of translations into major European languages: four in German (1558, 1568, 1597, 1598), five in Dutch (1563, 1567, 1568, 1582, 1595), three in French (1559–1560, 1564, 1565), and four in English (1566, 1577, 1584, 1587). Taken together, these are over twenty editions within half a century, covering most lands where the Swiss Reformation exerted significant influence.

8 For the Latin and German versions there is now a new critical edition (Bullinger: 2008 and 2006, respectively) which appeared as vol. 3. (parts 1–2) of div. 3 of Bullinger's Werke and as vols. 3–5 of his Schriften, respectively. The English translation was edited for the Parker Society by Thomas Harding in the mid-nineteenth century (Bullinger: 1849–1852), which is still available in reprint (New York: Johnson Reprint Corp., 1968 and Grand Rapids, MI: Reformation Heritage Books, 2004).

9 For a theological interpretation, see Opitz: 2004.

10 Its publication history follows a similar pattern to that of the *Decades.* It was written in Latin (1557), in which language it was printed four more times by the very early seventeenth century (1559, 1570, 1590, 1601), but it was also published in German (1558b, 1560, 1587), Dutch (1567, 1581), French (1558, 1564, 1565), and English (1561, 1573) translations.

11 For details, see Archives Biographiques Françaises [ABF], I:966.317, citing Édouard Sitzmann, Dictionnaire de biographie des hommes célèbres de l'Alsace: Depuis les temps les plus reculés jusqu'à nos jours, 2 vols., Rixheim 1909–1910, available through WBIS.

12 Cf. VD16: S 8164–8172 and ZV 29061.

13 Pt. 1 (19 chapters, c. 250 pages) on bodily death and its names; pt. 2 (13 chapters, c. 180 pages) deals with the corpse and burial while pt. 3 (12 chapters, c. 140 pages) with the souls and their place and state until judgement day.

Citations appear under a complex system of logically organised rubrics, which provide the material with a four- or five-level structure. I will examine the role Bullinger's sermon plays in the third part of Specker's work.

The third author to be discussed is Johannes Garcaeus, Jr. (1530–1574). His name recognition, commensurate with his oeuvre and impact, falls between the first two authors.[14] His father belonged to Melanchthon's circle. After growing up in Hamburg, Garcaeus returned to Wittenberg, where he had been born, to study theology with the Reformer. Later he accepted positions in Greifswald and Neubrandenburg, became a professor of theology and a superintendent, and also earned a theological doctorate. His literary output exceeds fifty titles, and extends to topics beyond the scope of theology. His works remained in print till the early seventeenth century. His most successful theological piece is the *Sterbbüchlein*, a 300-page octavo volume on the post mortem state of the human soul, which, as I have argued elsewhere, drew in large measure on Specker's *Vom Leiblichen Todt.*[15]

3. Bullinger Cited

Turning now to the question of Bullinger's influence upon the two later works, the basic point is easily gained. Specker repeatedly quoted Bullinger and acknowledged him by name, even if he did not always identify the precise locus from which he took his citation. In fact, Bullinger's series of a hundred sermons on Revelation (1557) in Ludwig Lavater's German translation (1558b) is one of Specker's most frequently cited sources. It is mostly used for exegetical purposes as commentary on the relevant biblical verses quoted for a given topic. Its significance is largely "local", pertinent in the narrow context of the scriptural prooftexts in question. I will, therefore, not discuss it much further than to provide an overview of some correspondences illustrating Bullinger's pervasive presence in *Vom Leiblichen Todt.* It is worth noting that in the passages marked with an asterisk (*) in *Table 1*, soul sleep is mentioned, but always with a critical edge.

14 For his biography, see ADB 8:370–371.

15 For details, see my essay (Ittzés: 2015b), in which I also argue, on the basis of a dedication dated to 24 June 1568 (Garcaeus: 1573, A4^{r}) and evidence from Garcaeus' pre-1900 biographers, that we should reckon with a no longer extant editio princeps of 1568, augmenting the available editions (1573, 1577, 1581) and bringing the total number of the Sterbbüchlein's printings to four.

Table 1: Specker (1560) and Garcaeus (1573) citing Lavater's translation of Bullinger's commentary on Revelation (1558b)

Revelation	*Bullinger (1558b)*	*Specker (1560)*	*Garcaeus (1573)*
2:7	21^{v} (Sermon 8)	261^{v}	–
2:17	29^{r} (Sermon 11)	$262^{r/v}$	$O2^{r}$
3:4	37^{r} (Sermon 16)	264^{r}	$O3^{v}$
4:4	48^{r} (Sermon 23)	264^{v}	–
6:9–10	65^{v} (Sermon 32)	223^{v} (*)	$C8^{v}$–$D1^{r}$
6:9–10	66^{v}–67^{r} (Sermon 32)	275^{r}	$P7^{r}$
6:9–12	67^{v} (Sermon 32)	264^{v}–265^{r}	[$O4^{r}$]
7:9–10	75^{r} (Sermon 35)	265^{r} (*)	–
7:15–17	$77^{r/v}$ (Sermon 36)	263^{r}	–
14:3	154^{r}–155^{v} (Sermon 65)	250^{v}–251^{r} (*)	$K5^{v}$–6^{v}
14:4–5	149^{v} (Sermon 62)	269^{v}–270^{r}	$P3^{r}$
20:4–6	203^{r} (Sermon 88)	224^{r} (*)	$D1^{r}$

On two occasions, Specker cites Sermon 40 of the *Decades.* The first passage is on how souls come to their place upon leaving the body (*Table 2*):

Table 2: Specker (1560) citing Haller's translation of Bullinger's Sermon 40 (1558a)

Bullinger (1558a, 323^{r})	*Specker (1560, 253^{v}–254^{r})*
Wie das zůgange /	Wie diß zůgehe /
kan ich nit anderst sagen /	weiß ich nit anders zůsagen /
dañ das dasselbig Gott volkom[m]enlich bekañt /	dañ das solches Gott vollkom[m]en wisse.
vns aber allein so vil vns zů wüssen gnůg ist in der geschrifft ewntworffen seye /	Vns aber ist in der schrifft souil dauon entworffen / uñ furgebildet / so vil Gott / das es genůg sey / erkennet hat /
nam[m]lich /das daß gescha[e]he in schneller eyl vnd bewegung / durch die Engel so die seelen dahin fürend.	nemlich / das wir durch die heyligen Engel / auff das aller schna[e]llest hingefu[e]ret vnd entzuckt werden.
Dann es spricht der Herr im Euangelio / dz die seel Lazari von den Englen in die schoß Abrahe seye getragen wordē.	
Von welchen handel ich auch daobē geredt hab / da ich disputiert von den gůten Englen.	
Was aber das für ein bewegung seye /	
ein natürliche oder eine vnnatürliche / wil ich nit erforschen.	Ob diß natürlicher / oder vber natürlicher weise geschehe / daruon will ich nit grüblen.
Jch glauben das Gott thu[e]ge vnd volbringe was er verheißt.	Jch glaub / das Gott vollendē vnd leisten kann / was er verheissen hat.
Das hatt er aber verheissen /	Nůn hat er verheissen /
Dañ er spricht / Der ist von dem tod zum la[e]ben hindurch trungen:	wir seien schon durch den todt ins leben hindurch gedrungen.
Jtem zum mo[e]rder /	Vnd zům Mo[e]rder spricht er /
Luce am drey vnd zweintzigsten /	
Hüt wirst du bey mir sein im Paradeiß /	Heut warstu bey mir sein im Paradeiß.

(Continued)

Bullinger (1558a, 323^{r})	*Specker (1560, 253^{v}–254^{r})*
da er gleich als inn einem augenblick das gantz hinfu[e]ren begreifft.	Jn welchen worten er die hinfu[e]rung vnd tragung begreifft / als geschehe sie augenplicklich.
Doch ist hie auch notwendig zůmerken /	Das soll man aber hie nit aussen lassen /
das wir es für ein gůthat Christi erkennen so[e]llend /	das solches allein Christo vnd seiner erlo[e]sung ist zuzuschreiben /
das wir in die him[m]el gezuckt werdend /	das wir in den Himmel entzucket werden /
dann er ist die türen vnd das la[e]ben.[16]	Dann er ist allein die thür / vnd der weg.

The second passage offers a refutation of the doctrine of soul sleep (*Table 3*):

Table 3: Specker (1560) citing Haller's translation of Bullinger's Sermon 40 (1558a)

Bullinger (1558a, $323^{r/v}$)	*Specker (1560, 257^{r})*
Dei schla[e]ffer habend nichts /	Die Dormitantianer / das ist / dis Seelschla[e]ffer sect / haben nichts /
damit sie jhren lethargum vnnd schlaff schirmind /	damit sie jre Schlaffsucht ko[e]nnen beweysen /
dann das die geschrifft	dann das die Schrifft /
an etwan mengem ort /	
wenn sie das sterben der glo[e]ubigen beschreibt /	wann sie den Todt der Heyligen beschreybet /
deß schlaffs vnnd entschlaffens gedenckt.	so brauchet sie die wort schlaffen vnnd entschlaffen /
Als: Er ist entschlaffen	Er ist entschlaffen /
vñ zů seinē va[e]tteren versam[m]let.	vnnd zů seinen Va[e]ttern versam[m]let /
Vñ das Paulus spricht / Wir wo[e]llend euch nit verhalten von denen die da schlaffend. Da er aber von den sterbenden redt.	vnnd der heylige Apostel / da er redet von den Abgestorbenen / nennet er sie schlaffenden / j. Thessa. iiij.
Aber wie die seelen dieweil sie noch bey disem hinfelligen leyb gewesen sind /	Seytenmal aber dei Seelen / solang sie in disem bauwfelligen leyb seind /
nie geschlaffen habend /	nie geschlaffen haben /
auch nit habend mo[e]gen schlaffen /	noch schlaffen ko[e]nnen /

16 "Touching the manner, I can say nothing else but that it is fully known unto God; and that, so far forth as seemeth sufficient for us, it is shadowed out in the scriptures; namely, that it is brought to pass by angels carrying up our souls with a most swift flight or moving. For the Lord saith in the gospel, that the soul of Lazarus was carried by angels into Abraham's bosom: of which thing also we spake before when we preached of God's angels. But what manner of moving this is, whether natural or supernatural, I mean not to make search. I believe that what God promiseth, the same he performeth and accomplisheth; and he promising saith, 'He is passed from death to life'. Again, he said to the thief, 'To-day shalt thou be with me in paradise', comprehending that his passage as it were in a moment. Hereunto we also necessarily add this, that it must be attributed to the merits of Christ that we are taken up into heaven; for he is the door and the way" (Bullinger: 1849–1852, 3:388–389).

(Continued)

Bullinger (1558a, 323r/v)	*Specker (1560, 257v)*
also ist vil minder zůglauben das sie schlaffind / nach dem sie vonn dem last dises leybs entlediget sind.	wie vil weniger so sie nůn von dem last des leybs entlediget seynd / solle man glauben / das sie schlaffen.
Darumb so wirdt das schlaffen von dem leyb verstanden /	Derha[e]lben so geho[e]ret das schlaffen dem leyb zů /
dann der entschlafft im Herren /	Dan der entschlafft im Herren /
der im waren glauben stirbt.	der im waren glauben stirbt.
Wie aber die so entschlaffend /	Gleich sie aber die schlaffenden /
nach dem die glider durch den schlaff erfrischet sind /	wann sie jre glieder durch den schlaff erquicket haben /
bald widerumb erwachend /	er wachet /
vfstond vñ arbeitend /	stehen auff / vnnd gehen an jre arbeyt /
Also wirt der leyb durch den tod	Also würt durch den Todt der leyb
nicht sogar außgemacht /	nit gantz vertilget /
das er nit etwan widerumb la[e]bendig werde /	das er nimmermehr wider lebendig werde /
sonnder er wirt jetzund inn die rûw genom[m]en /	sondern bleybet jetzt in der rûge /
auf den tag aber deß gerichts	Aber am Jüngsten gericht
stat er widerumb auff vnd la[e]bt.	stehet er wider auff / vnd lebet.
Darum[m] stat in der geschrifft /	Vnnd darumb sagt die schrifft /
das die glo[e]ubigen entschlaffind vñ nit das die sterbind /	das die Heyligen nicht sterben / sondern schlaffen /
vff das die geheimnuß der vrstende vnnsers fleischs damit bedeütet werde.[17]	das dardurch das geheyinnuß der aufferstehung des fleysches angezeyget werde.

In both cases, Specker identifies not only Bullinger but the specific sermon as his source, and we can be fairly certain from the circumstances[18] and the correspondences that he uses Johannes Haller's (1523–1575) translation, but he treats

17 "These sleepy-heads have nothing to allege for this their lethargy or imagination of the sleep of the soul, but that the scripture oftentimes, describing the death of the saints, maketh mention of sleeping and laying to sleep; as, 'he fell asleep, and was gathered unto (or laid by) his fathers'; and Paul saith, speaking of those that die, 'I would not have you ignorant concerning them which are asleep'. But even as souls, when they were joined to these frail bodies, never slept, neither could sleep: so being delivered from the burden of the body, they are much less to be thought to sleep. To the body therefore is sleep to be referred. For whosoever dieth in a true faith, he sleepeth in the Lord. And as they that sleep, when their limbs are therewith refreshed, do immediately awake, rise, and labour; even so the body is not altogether extinguished by death, that it should not live again any more, but now verily it is received into rest, and at the day of judgment it riseth again and liveth. And for this cause holy men are said in the scriptures to sleep, not to die, that thereby the mystery of the resurrection of our flesh may be signified" (Bullinger: 1849–1852, 3:389–390).

18 When he cites Latin sources, Specker includes the original first and then provides his own German translation. When he gives no Latin, as in these cases, it is quite obvious that he is quoting a German source.

the original with considerable liberty.[19] The insistence on the soul's wakeful existence, at any rate, is a strong thematic link between the *Decades* and *Vom leiblichen Todt.*

Garcaeus also incorporates over half of the Bullinger passages, but his case is somewhat different. Instead of a florilegium, he produces a smoothly flowing text into which quotations, biblical and otherwise, are seamlessly incorporated. He usually provides references for scriptural passages cited, but often omits the identification of non-biblical sources altogether. Such is the case with Bullinger. Garcaeus offers the Swiss Reformer's commentary on verses from Revelation (introduced as prooftexts for particular points) without any indication of alien authorship. Given that he only includes passages that can be found in Specker and that they appear in structurally similar positions (*Table 1*), we may reasonably infer that he was actually using Specker and appropriating Bullinger through the mediation of the Strasbourger rather than consulting the *Hundred Sermons* directly.[20] The same seems even more obvious in the case of the *Decades.* Garcaeus also adopts both passages from Sermon 40, again without identifying Bullinger (or Specker) as his source, and in the citations he stays closer to the Strasbourger's German than to Haller's published translation:

> WJe dis zugehe / ist Gott allein bekant / vns hat Gott dauon so viel geoffenbaret / als uns zu wissen gnug vnd zum tro[e]stlichsten no[e]tig / als/das wir durch die heilige Engel / auffs aller schnellst hingefu[e]ret vñ entzu[e]cket warden. Ob das netu[e]rlicher oder vbernatu[e]rlicher weise geschehe / das wollen wir nicht gru[e]blen. Wir gleuben / das Gott vollenden vnd leisten ko[e]nne / das er vns gnediglich verheissen hat / nemlich / das wir schon im Glauben durch den Tod ins ewige leben hindurch gedrungen / vnd nicht weniger Christus vns das Paradis zugesagt / als dem Mo[e]rder / vnd die heimfu[e]rung erwarten vnsers Geists / wie dem heiligen Lazaro widerfaren (Garcaeus: 1573, L2^{v}; cf. *Table 2*).

> Vnd sein in vor zeiten gewesen sonderliche sectarij, Dormitianer genant / das ist die Seelschlaffer sect / welche geleret / dz die Geister schlaffen/vnd in eine schwere Schlaffsucht / profundissimum lethargum, geraten in der andern Welt. Solche opinion zu erweisen haben sie gar keinen grund / allein dis / das die Schrifft sagt/wenn sie den tod der Heiligen beschreibet / sie schlaffen oder sie sind entschlaffen / Er ist entschlaffen / vnd zu seinen Vetern versamlet. Lazarus schlefft / Jtem das S. Paulus 1. Thess.4. die abgestorbenē die schlaffenen nennet (Garcaeus: 1573, M4^{r}; cf. *Table 3*).

19 While faithfulness to the letter was certainly not an established norm of citation in the early modern period, Specker is noticeably closer to Lavater's German in citing the Revelation commentary (Bullinger: 1558b) than to Johannes Haller in quoting the *Decades* (Bullinger: 1558a).

20 This, of course, provides strong grounds to argue for Garcaeus' familiarity with and dependence on Vom Leiblichen Todt.

Taken together, it is clear that both Specker and Garcaeus quote Bullinger. The former routinely identifies his source, including Sermon 40 of the *Decades.* Specker's citation technique thus provides clear evidence that he knew the work of the Swiss Reformer. Garcaeus, on the other hand, seems to rely on Specker for his knowledge of (or at least for his quotations from) Bullinger. Given the Strasbourger's conscientious approach, Garcaeus must also have known from where he was tacitly borrowing ideas, but it is impossible to tell from what we have seen whether he knew the *Decades* and the Revelation commentary directly or only through Specker's mediation. To answer that question, we will have to look further.

With this, an essential connection is established, through *Vom Leiblichen Todt,* between a major representative of the Swiss Reformed tradition and the emerging German Lutheran teaching on the soul's immortality, but little is yet gained in terms of determining the nature and significance of the Swiss influence on the doctrinal development among the Lutherans. I will want to go further and ask to what use Specker and Garcaeus put their Bullinger. My claim is that it was much more than borrowing an odd citation here and there or taking over particular details in local contexts.

4. Borrowing on a Larger Scale

To answer the broader question, it is helpful to note that in the case of both passages borrowed from the sermon on the rational human soul, Specker essentially takes over all of Bullinger's relevant text as part of a larger discussion in which other authorities are also cited and further considerations weighed. This is quite typical of Specker's overall strategy in that he seems to take his hints from Bullinger and then develop them. That happens on two levels, first on the level of overall topics (*what* needs discussion) and, second, on the level of individual discussion points (*how* the matter is discussed).

In terms of particular issues, the thrust of Bullinger's and Specker's reasoning is not identical. Though taking fewer pages, the former makes a broader sweep and covers the field of early modern psychology. The latter, by contrast, has a narrower question in mind, focussing on the place and state of departed souls. Consequently, several aspects of Bullinger's theological reflections are irrelevant for Specker's enquiry. These differences notwithstanding, many if not most of the Strasbourger's chapter topics can be detected as major discussion points in the Zurich Reformer's sermon. They include definitional questions (soul and spirit), the fundamental thesis of immortality, the interim abode of departed souls between the body's death and resurrection, and are complete with such problems as how and when they come to that place, and the life of righteous souls (*Table 4*).

Table 4: Thematic parallels between Bullinger (1558a), Specker (1560), and Garcaeus (1573)

Topic	*Bullinger (1558a)*	*Specker (1560)*	*Garcaeus (1573)*
Soul and spirit	316^r–318^v	Ch. 1	Ch. 1
Immortality of the soul	320^r–322^r	Ch. 2	Ch. 2
Place of souls	$322^{r/v}$	Ch. 3	Ch. 9
When souls come to their place	323^r	Ch. 4	Ch. 12
How souls come to their place	323^r	Ch. 5	Ch. 12
Life of righteous souls	$328^{r/v}$	Ch. 6	Ch. 16

It is true that parallels in the second half of Specker's twelve chapters are less close, but issues raised there are also germinally present in the material already covered. The overarching concern in those sections is the life of disembodied souls, with individual chapters devoted to such specific questions as what righteous souls know (ch. 7) and what they do (ch. 8). Three further chapters (10–12) are allocated to corresponding issues in the case of damned souls. The basic pattern of how the two texts interrelated is thus, again, that Specker takes his clues from Bullinger and develops them at greater length and with a somewhat different methodology.

We have seen in *Table 4* that the *Sterbbüchlein* is in concordance with Specker's book in appropriating topics for discussion from Sermon 40. That, however, may simply reflect Specker's influence on Garcaeus, rather than Bullinger's direct influence. However, the picture changes considerably if we examine the rest of the *Sterbbüchlein.* That work consists of 25 chapters, as against Specker's twelve. Much of the surplus is given to topics that have their counterparts in Bullinger. These mostly relate to ontological and soteriological questions, including purgatory, which Specker treats elsewhere (*Table 5*).

Table 5: Thematic parallels between Garcaeus (1573) and Bullinger (1558a) against Specker (1560)

Topic	*Bullinger (1558a)*	*Garcaeus (1573)*
Origin of the human soul	316^r–318^v	Ch. 3
The powers of the human soul	320^r–322^r	Ch. 5
Death as separation of body and soul	$322^{r/v}$	Ch. 6
Whether souls come to purgatory	323^r	Ch. 9
Proofs against purgatory	323^r	Ch. 10
Redemption only through Christ	$328^{r/v}$	Ch. 11

This thematic correspondence between Garcaeus and Bullinger (against Specker) is not easily dismissed. It amounts to at least fifty per cent of the difference between the two Lutheran works.

5. Argumentation Adopted

To illustrate Bullinger's influence on the later authors in terms of specific lines of reasoning, let us first look at their treatment of the place of departed souls.[21] The Swiss Reformer's argument exhibits three key features. First, it advocates the thesis that souls are either in heaven or in hell. The argument is biblically grounded but operates on the principle of the excluded middle. Second, Bullinger discusses the righteous souls' abode under different names including: Abraham's bosom, heaven, God's hand, Father's house, under the altar, and heavenly house. Third, he supports his argument with a set of biblical prooftexts.[22]

Specker develops this into the most complex and longest of his chapters in the last major section of his book, which alone fills roughly a third of the pages in part 3. He creates a catalogue of biblical names for the souls' post mortem abode. He arranges individual terms into a fourfold structure, first dividing them according to their referent (place of righteous or damned souls) and secondly according to their origin (Old or New Testament). Under each rubric (name) within each of the four categories, he then supplies relevant passages, both biblical and otherwise, to illustrate the given title. All but one of Bullinger's names appear in the "New Testament names for the abode of righteous souls" category, which also includes three further appellations not found in the *Decades* passage. The remaining designation (God's hand) is categorised under the Old Testament. Almost all of Bullinger's scriptural prooftexts appear in the corresponding places of *Vom Leiblichen Todt*, which, naturally, includes many more. Not only do we see a fundamentally biblically-based argumentation in Specker (a general Protestant characteristic), he implicitly also adopts the law of the excluded middle, which he employs more evidently elsewhere. In short, all of the main features of Bullinger's text have a counterpart in Specker's. The Strasbourg theologian seems to be inspired by his more distinguished Swiss colleague and to develop ideas he found in the latter's work more systematically, using his own method of thematic compilation.

We also find similar correspondences between Garcaeus and Bullinger, but those have to be treated with caution because they may have been mediated by Specker and may reflect the Northerner's reliance on him. It is again instructive to examine those parts of the text that have no parallel in *Vom Leiblichen Todt*. Bullinger begins the passage with a reflection on the local circumscription of the soul. Specker, working with a catalogue of names, has neither need nor room for such introductory material, but we encounter a similar line of thought in Garcaeus' second paragraph in the "names" chapter. His version is significantly

21 Bullinger: 1558, 322$^{r/v}$; Specker: 1560, 229^{v}–236^{v}; Garcaeus: 1573, G3^{r}–7^{r}.
22 E.g. Luke 16:22–23, Phil 1:23, John 14:2–3, 2 Cor 5:1, etc.

shorter than Bullinger's (77 words as compared to 149), but the logic of his argumentation is essentially the same. Ten of his twelve major semantic units (roughly, clauses) are identical in meaning with Bullinger's, and they follow the same pattern. What he leaves out is little more than circumlocutions and repetitions of points adopted in simpler form, and he only adds an aside (italicised in *Table 6*). Overall, that constitutes a correspondence rate of over 80%, which exceeds, in my estimation, a degree that could be ascribed to mere coincidence. I present the passages in a parallel format that visually renders their thematic correspondences (*Table 6*).

Table 6: Parallel reasoning in Bullinger (1558a) and Garcaeus (1573)

Bullinger (1558a, 322^{r})	*Garcaeus (1573, G3^{v})*
Dieweil sie bey den lyben warend /	DEnn dieweil die Seele
	mit dem Cörper vereiniget /
bewoneten sie dieselbige[n]	regieret vnd gebrauchet sie
als jre gehüset / also /	jre wonung /
das wiewol man nitt von jnen sagē kan/	
das sie mit gewüssem ort vmschriben seyend /	
so sind sie doch nit	vnd verlasset nicht den alten kercker /
aussert jren lybē um[m]ha[e]r gfaren /	hat nicht aussen dem Cörper
sonder in den selbigen / als in gfencknussen	jrgend eine wirckung.
biß vff die zyt jrer vflösung	
verschlossen wordē.	
Diewyl nun a[e]ben die selbigen /	Aber da der leibliche tod
nach dem sie jetzund vō dē lybē abgescheidē /	ein scheiden macht /
jre siñ / jr art / vñ jr gantze substantz	
la[e]blich behaltend /	behelt sie je lebendiges wesen /
wiewol man auch jetz nit von jnen sagen kann /	
das sie mit gewüssem ort	
vm[m]schriben werdind /	
so zerfliessend sie doch nit /	verschwindet nicht /
vñ verdend nit vffgelo[e]ßt /	
das sie nienē mee seyend /	vnd wird nicht zu nicht /
sonder bleibenb nochmals	
in jrem wa[e]sen vnzerteñt /	
vñ habend wol nit nüwe lyb	hat nicht einen newen Cörper /
(dañ sie sind fry biß zum gericht /	*wie die Pytagorici geschwermet /*
deñ zůmal werdend sie jrē lyben	*in welchen die Seele widerumb feret /*
widerum[m] vereinbaret)	
aber doch gewüsse ort vñ herbergen	sondern lebet
	in einer gewissen wonung /
von Gott bereitet /	die Gott dazu verordnet
in denen sie sind vñ bleibend.[23]	vnd bereitet hat.

23 "While they were coupled to the bodies, they used them as their dwelling-houses; so that, though they be said not to be limited in place, yet they do not wander out of their bodies, but they are as it were shut up in them as in prisons, until the time they be dissolved and set at liberty. Those same souls therefore being now dissevered from their bodies, since they retain

To give one more example of analogous reasoning in the different authors, I will briefly consider the discussion of the souls' appearance on earth before judgement day.[24] Bullinger introduces the topic in the context of refuting proofs of purgatory, while the Lutherans, operating along somewhat different lines, dedicate an independent chapter to the question, evidently deemed worthy of attention for its own sake as part of the immortality locus. The Swiss Reformer starts with evidence and authorities of the old faith marshalled by its proponents in support of Roman doctrine, which he counters with the parable of Lazarus and Dives (Luke 16). This leads to the articulation of the thesis that souls cannot appear. Three moves follow. First, Bullinger quotes Tertullian's *De anima*; then he brings in a long passage from Chrysostom's 28th Homily on the Gospel of Matthew. Finally, he turns to the biblical story of Saul's visit to the Endor sorceress (1 Sam 28:7–25) and argues that the apparition is not really Samuel's soul but rather the devil's deception, since necromancy is forbidden by God's law and righteous souls are not allowed to participate in it. The discussion is then rounded off with some further authorities and a repetition of the central claims.

Both Specker and Garcaeus include other elements in their treatment such as extensive passages from Luther or closer attention to biblical texts, whether those embedded in the Chrysostom passage or external to it (esp. Judas' dream from 2 Macc 15 and the transfiguration from Luke 9 and parallels). Yet it is also clear that the very same excerpt from Chrysostom's homily and the Endor scene constitute crucial parts of their chapters. In later texts of the Lutheran tradition, the two (Homily 28 and 1 Sam 28) will be separated and the former relocated to a different context for good reasons.[25] Their initial proximity, justified in Bullinger's line of thought but unmotivated in that of the Lutherans, suggests, however, that they may indeed have been adopted from the Swiss Reformer's work.

Yet once more we find here some details that connect Garcaeus with Bullinger without Specker's mediation. For one thing, the former also includes a paraphrase of Tertullian's argument from *De anima* (ch. 57), and that in a structurally similar position to Bullinger's text. For another, Specker omits the number of Chrysostom's sermon, which is supplied by both his colleagues. In fact, they both

their sound senses, their nature or disposition, and their whole substance in lively manner, albeit they are said, no, not even now to be limited in place, yet they are not let loose and run astray, having their abiding in no place; but being compact and set fast in their own essence or being are in some place again, having no new bodies, (for the souls are free even till the judgment-day, when they shall be joined again to their bodies;) howbeit certain abiding-places are prepared for them of God, wherein they may live" (Bullinger: 1849–1852, 3:386).

24 Bullinger: 1558a, 326^{v}–327^{v}; Specker: 1560, 275^{v}–278^{v}; Garcaeus: 1573, L4^{v}–M3^{v}.

25 For a full discussion of Lutheran treatments of the possible return of departed souls' in the later sixteenth century, see Ittzés: 2015a.

identify it as the 29th although the citation is actually taken from Homily 28. While none of my arguments may be fully convincing on its own, the combined effect of all evidence is such that it strongly suggests, first, that Garcaeus had direct access to Sermon 40 of Bullinger's *Decades* and not only had mediate knowledge of it through Specker. Second, Bullinger's influence on the Lutheran authors extended well beyond supplying a few quotations.

6. Conclusion

Did Lutheran theologians know and use Bullinger, especially the fortieth sermon of his *Decades*, on the human soul? The answer is "definitely" for Specker and "probably" for Garcaeus. Given the Strasbourger's foundational role in the later development of Lutheran doctrine,[26] his mediation is sufficient to secure Swiss Reformed influence on the emerging German Lutheran teaching, but Garcaeus likely provided an independent secondary tributary to that stream, while he surely transmitted the Bullinger material that had reached him via Specker.

The influence of Zwingli's successor can be detected in several areas, and its extent is not negligible. It seems to have informed both the choice of topics and the way particular arguments were developed. Many local points and details of lines of reasoning seem to have been adopted from Bullinger, who also supplied examples of authorities to cite in a given context. His Lutheran colleagues borrowed a great many references, biblical and otherwise, from him. It would, of course, be a mistake to overstate the case, and assign too exclusive a role to the Zurich Reformer. The development from Luther to later sixteenth-century Lutheran doctrine was a complex process with Melanchthon and others also providing crucial impulses.

The position of the Wittenberg Reformers' followers on the immortality of the soul was not per se irreconcilable with Lateran V (DS 1440), yet in the broader context of doctrinal development even this question became a Church-dividing issue between Protestants and Catholics. Caught up in the debates about purgatory and the invocations of saints, the immortality locus developed "rough edges", such as the problem of the return and appearance of souls, that prevented rapprochement (Ittzés: 2015a).

Between Lutherans and Calvinists, by contrast, it was a Church-uniting teaching. In principle, that was not inevitable either. In the light of the distance between the notion of soul sleep, often attributed to Luther, and the Reformed

26 Cf. n. 1, above. I have explored the thematic unity of the wider Lutheran corpus elsewhere, going significantly beyond the two works discussed in this paper; see, e.g., Ittzés: 2014 and 2015a.

position forcefully articulated in Calvin's *Psychopannychia*, a convergence of the Swiss and German traditions might also be surprising. In this paper, I have sought to demonstrate that Bullinger was a major link in the chain that ultimately connected Reformed and Lutheran teachings on this issue and helped turn what might have been a minority position into an established part of the majority view.

Bibliography

ALTHAUS, PAUL (1926), Die Unsterblichkeit der Seele bei Luther, Zeitschrift für systematische Theologie 3, 725–734.

ALTHAUS, PAUL (1930), Unsterblichkeit und ewiges Sterben bei Luther: Zur Auseinandersetzung mit C. Stange, Gütersloh: Bertelsmann.

BLANKE, FRITZ (1990), Heinrich Bullinger: Vater der reformierten Kirche, Zurich: Theologischer Verlag Zürich.

BULLINGER, HEINRICH (1558a), Haußbůch: Darinn begriffen werdend fünfftzig Predigen, trans. Johannes Haller, Bern: Samuel Apiarius/Christoph Froschauer, Sr. (VD16: B 9701).

– (1558b), Die Offenbarung Jesu Christi Anfangs durch den heiligen Engel Gottes / Joanni dem säligen Apostel vnd Euangelisten geoffenbaret / vnd von jm gesähen vnd geschriben / jetzvnd aber mit hundert Predigen erklärt, trans. Ludwig Lavater, Mühlhausen: Peter Schmidt/Johann Schirenbrand (VD16: B 9639).

– (1849–1852), The Decades, trans. H.I., ed. Thomas Harding, 4 vols., Cambridge: Cambridge University Press.

– (2006), [Dekaden 1549–1551], ed. Peter Stotz/Emidio Campi/Detlef Roth, 3 vols., vol. 3–5 of Schriften, Zurich: Theologischer Verlag Zürich.

– (2008), Sermonum decades quinque: De potissimis Christianae religionis capitibus (1549–1552), ed. Peter Opitz, vol. 3 (parts 1–2) of div. 3 of Werke, Zurich: Theologischer Verlag Zürich.

CAMPI, EMIDIO/PETER OPITZ (eds.) (2007), Heinrich Bullinger: Life – Thought – Influence, 2 vols., Zurich: Theologischer Verlag Zürich.

GARCAEUS, JOHANNES, JR. (1573), Sterbbüchlein Darin Von den Seelen / jrem ort / stande / thun und wesen / aller Menschen / bis an den Jüngsten tag / aus Gottes wort vnd der lieben Veter Schrifften / warhafftiger bericht, Wittenberg: Peter Seitz (VD16: G 461).

GEORGE, TIMOTHY (1987), Calvin's *Psychopannychia:* Another Look, in: Edward J. Furcha (ed.), In Honor of John Calvin, 1509–1564: Papers from the 1986 International Symposium, McGill University, Montreal: Faculty of Religious Studies, McGill University, 297–329.

GORDON, BRUCE (2002), Heinrich Bullinger (1504–1575), in: Carter Lindberg (ed.), The Reformation Theologians: An Introduction to Theology in the Early Modern Period, Oxford: Blackwell, 170–183.

GORDON, BRUCE/EMIDIO CAMPI (eds.) (2004), Architect of Reformation: An Introduction to Heinrich Bullinger, 1504–1575, Grand Rapids, MI: Baker Academic.

HEIDLER, FRITZ (1983), Luthers Lehre von der Unsterblichkeit der Seele, Erlangen: Martin Luther-Verlag.

Ittzés, Gábor (2014), Somnus mortis imago: Az alvás mint a halál metaforája a 16. század második felének német evangélikus teológiájában, Theologiai Szemle 57, 196–205.

– (2015a), Szellemjárás a késő 16. századi német evangélikus teológiában: Visszatérhetnek-e a földre a holtak lelkei?, Egyháztörténeti Szemle 16, 20–39.

– (2015b), Text and Subtext: Johannes Garcaeus' *Sterbbüchlein* and Melchior Specker's *Vom Leiblichen Todt:* A Study in Early Modern Literary Borrowing, German Life and Letters 68, 335–355.

Lohse, Bernhard (1999), Martin Luther's Theology: Its Historical and Systematic Development, trans. Roy A. Harrisville, Minneapolis, MN: Fortress.

Melanchthon, Philipp (1544), Commentarivs de anima, Strassburg: Kraft Müller, 1544 (VD16: M 2753).

Opitz, Peter (2004), Heinrich Bullinger als Theologe: Eine Studie zu den "Dekaden", Zurich: Theologischer Verlag Zürich.

Specker, Melchior (1560), Vom Leiblichen Todt. Was er sey / waher er kom[m]e / vnd wie man sich darzů bereyten solle / Auch Von der Begräbniß vñ Begäncknussen / vnd wie man sich der Abgestorbenen halben trösten vnd halten solle. Jtem Von der Selen vnd jrem ort / stand / vnd wesen / biß auff den Jüngsten tag. Alles auß H. Schrifft / vnd der Vätter außlegung / fleyssig zůsam[m]en gebracht, Strasbourg: Samuel Emmel (VD16: S 8169).

Stange, Carl (1925), Die Unsterblichkeit der Seele, Zeitschrift für systematische Theologie 2, 431–463.

– (1926), Zur Auslegung der Aussagen Luthers über die Unsterblichkeit der Seele, Zeitschrift für systematische Theologie 3, 735–784.

Thiede, Werner (1982), Luthers individuelle Eschatologie, Luther Jahrbuch 49, 7–49.

– (1993), Nur ein ewiger Augenblick: Luthers Lehre vom Seelenschlaf zwischen Tod und Auferweckung, Luther: Zeitschrift der Luther-Gesellschaft 64, 112–125.

Alessandra Celati

A Peculiar Reformed Minority

Italian Heretical Physicians between Religious Propaganda, Inquisitorial Repression and Freedom of Thought

1. Introduction

In this paper,[1] I will try to define the role physicians played in the religious turmoil which occurred in Italy over the course of the sixteenth century. The high acceptance of reformed doctrines among those involved in the cure of the body, above all physicians, has been pointed out by historical research,[2] but so far it has not been deeply examined. However, because of the social and cultural role of physicians in the community, the analysis of religious dissent among medical doctors seems entirely relevant. Examining original archival sources, my research seeks to go some way to filling this historiographical gap, trying to investigate the specific link between medicine and the Italian Reformation. In order to achieve this, my work follows three major guidelines. First, I aim to determine the extent to which Italian physicians' religious non-conformism was exposed to repression by the Inquisition. Secondly, I examine what was specific to medical religious dissent with regard to social practice and intellectual elaboration. Thirdly, I consider whether the medical profession had any kind of impact on the wider horizon of the European Reformation.

This article will be structured in two sections. In the first I will narrate the experience of several medical doctors, describing their reformed activity and

1 This paper presents results of research I have been carrying out for my Ph.D. and during my Marie Skłodowska-Curie post-doctoral fellowship at Stanford University and the University of Verona.

2 In particular Aldo Stella has suggested a sort of continuity between medical-philosophical research and religious non-conformism focussing on the Venetian area. See Stella: 1969. Stella's thesis has recently been complemented by Silvia Ferreto's works, see in particular Ferretto: 2009. A relevant resource on the more general connection between heterodoxy and early modern science is Brooke/Maclean: 2005. This connection has also recently been suggested in Addante: 2010. For the impact of the Reformation and above all Counter-Reformation on medical institutions, see Pastore: 1993; Pastore: 2006.

their relationship with the Inquisition.[3] In the second I will sketch the most relevant characteristics of Italian medical religious dissent and look at two case studies in detail. Finally I will summarise my conclusions.

2. Healing the Body, Healing the Soul, Spreading Heresy

In order to provide some necessary context, it is important to recall the extent to which early modern society perceived the body and the soul as strictly connected. This entailed the contiguity, even identity, between the physical and the spiritual dimensions of the medical *cure*,[4] and certainly put physicians in a peculiar position in the community. This in turn led the Roman hierarchy to pay special attention to the activities of this profession.

This was probably the reason why the papal bull *Super gregem dominicum* was enacted in 1566, which allowed the Roman Church to compel doctors to stop providing care to those who did not confess within three days of the physician's first visit. A similar rule had already been enacted in the mid-thirteenth century in a *decretale* by Innocent III. However, during the Counter-Reformation, this rule was reinforced, since the *Super gregem dominicum* implied the charge of heresy for those who did not respect it, with the additional penalty of a large fine and expulsion from the College of Physicians (Pastore: 2006, 136–137; Prosperi: 2009, 469–470). Referring to John 8:1–11 and to Innocent III's *decretale*, the bull directly connected the physical and the spiritual dimensions of sickness, describing it as due to both sin and natural causes (Cocquelines: 1745, 281). This made physicians responsible for the souls of the sick as much as for their bodies, and required that they persuade their patients to confess.

Historical sources in the Venetian Archives tell us that physicians were not willing to passively accept this interference in their work.[5] In particular, a file significantly named *Contra medicos* reveals the controversy which broke out between the Inquisition and the College of Physicians once doctors were caught neglecting the instructions of the Church. In 1571 a Venetian priest denounced "all physicians" in Venice to the Inquisition, asserting that "in their own interest"

3 For the relationship between heretical physicians and the Inquisition in Venice see Palmer: 1993, which is an essential starting point for my research. My paper aims to develop and integrate Palmer's work, considering Venice but also moving to other cities.

4 This link has been broadly analysed by historiography. See in particular Ziegler: 1998, Henderson: 2006, Agasse: 2008.

5 On this topic see also Palmer: 1993, 120–121. In these pages I am accepting his argument and I am taking it further by examining unpublished primary sources from the archives in Venice. The attempt to resist interferences by the Inquisition and to counteract the effects of the papal bull was not limited to Venetian physicians: see the reformation of the statuti of the College of physicians in Modena examined in Weber: 2011, 97–121.

they did not make any effort to convince patients to confess, letting them die without receiving the sacraments.[6] The Inquisition reacted by summoning the Prior of the College, Aloiosio Bagnolo, reminding him of the bull and of his religious duties, and compelling him to tell his colleagues to respect the ecclesiastical rule, with the threat of being marked out as potential heretics if they did not. It is significant that reading the *Libro dei Priori* itself, which collects all the news related to the activity of the College, we can see that the Prior positioned himself against the bull, which he considered as conflicting with its medical mission. Exactly what he told the Inquisitors is not reported in the files of the Inquisition, nor in the *Libro dei Priori*, which only vaguely mentions his attempt to oppose Church interference. Eventually, however, he did gather all the physicians and ask them to respect the Inquisition's request. However, we know that in 1579 and in 1589 another Prior of the College was again summoned and that he again tried to protect his colleagues from intrusion by the Inquisition.[7] Over the course of the century, physicians kept trying to slip out of the control of the Holy Office.

Indeed, the *Contra medicos* file also tells us that in May 1572, eight months after the denunciation of all physicians and the summons of Prior Aloisio Bagnolo, Prospero da Foligno, a member of the College, failed to insist that his dying patient receive the sacraments. Denounced by the priest of the San Zuan Grisostomo parish, Prospero was promptly summoned by the Inquisition and interrogated. The interest of the Judges in the medical activity carried out by the accused and on the frequency of Prospero's visits, as well as their inquiry into the kind of illness from which the patient was suffering, confirm the Inquisitors' desire to keep medical practice under control. On the other hand, the physician tried to justify his conduct by putting forward pragmatic arguments. Since his patient was German she was not obliged to confess and, since sick people were usually inclined to associate the arrival of a priest with the approach of death, Prospero decided to avoid scaring the woman. However, the Judges were not impressed by such flimsy arguments and replied that Prospero should have informed the ecclesiastical authorities about the woman's denial of the Catholic sacraments in any case. When directly asked why he had not done so, the physician simply replied: "I do not know" ("*Io non vi so rispondere a questo*").[8] Unsurprisingly, the Inquisitors were not convinced and established that he should be interrogated again a week later. Unfortunately, we do not know what

6 Archivio di Stato di Venezia (hereafter ASV), Sant'Uffizio, Contra Medicos, Busta (hereafter Bu.) 35.

7 A first summons had occurred in 1558. See: Notizie Cavate dalli libri dei priori, Biblioteca marciana. Ms Ital VII 2342=9695, 9v. After the one reported in the Inquisition file in 1571, two other summons followed: one in 1579 (Ibid. 17v); and one in 1589 (Ibid. 21r).

8 ASV, Sant'Uffizio, Contra Medicos, Bu. 35, 10th May 1572.

happened next, as the file is interrupted. However, reading the *Libro dei Priori*, we can see that, in this and subsequent years Prospero was a regular attendee at the College's meetings. Therefore, we can assume that, even if he was put on trial, he was quickly released. We may surmise that this is due to the relationships that Prospero, as a member of the College, might have formed with important gentlemen in the city.

Practicing with all sorts of people, medical doctors were able to form relationships with powerful patricians in the city, who often interceded on their behalf before the judges, and sometimes shared the same heretical views.[9] It is certain that the protection of influential gentlemen helped Girolamo Maccagno, an important physician from Cremona well-known for his Calvinist ideas, to be discharged after the Inquisition had caught him in 1552.[10] His value as a physician was mentioned as the main reason why he had to be released (Cf. Fumi: 1910, 361): he was considered as indispensable to the community. Instrumental for his liberation was the support of Count Ulderico Scotti (Chabod: 1971, 358) and, once free, Maccagno was allowed to practice his art in the city of Cremona and elsewhere, due to the help of Hieronimo Bosio, who spoke on behalf of the important people he wanted to please.[11] Not only is the case of Maccagno interesting with respect to his influential protectors, but also because of his defensive assertion that: "the physicians in Cremona are all heretics" ("*a Cremona tutti i medici sono eretici*") (Chabod: 1971, 357). This declaration highlights the considerable role physicians played in the mid-century religious turmoil which swept through Italy. Despite his patrons' claims, Maccagno's case, namely the attention the authorities paid to him[12] and his explosive statement about the religious orientation of physicians in Cremona, shows that reformed ideas could indeed be spread easily by doctors. After all, we know that the radical heretical physician from Casalmaggiore, Pietro Bresciani (Tedeschi: 1972), was working in the same area. He was considered, in the words of the village's preacher, "the pope"[13] of the citizens who had embraced the Reformation. Bresciani himself admitted in front of the Inquisitors that two colleagues of his had provided him with prohibited books. A certain Maestro Cristoforo had given him Luther's *Babylonian Captivity* and Maestro Pietro had supplied him with Calvin's *In-*

9 This is apparent when one examines the names of the witnesses who testified in physicians' favour in Inquisition trials. For the general involvement of patricians in the heretical movement in Venice see Ambrosini: 1999.

10 See the letter from Giovanni Battista Rainoldi to the "presidente del Senato", in Archivio di Stato di Milano (hereafter ASM), Culto, 2104, 29th June 1552.

11 ASM, Carteggio cancellerie di Stato, 1st July 1553.

12 See again the letter from Giovanni Battista Rainoldi to the "presidente del Senato", in ASM, Culto, 2104, 29th June 1552.

13 See the letter from Fra Giovan Piero Celso da Capodistria, Inquisitor of Istria and preacher in Casalmaggiore, to Ferrante Gonzaga, 27th March 1548. ASM, Culto 2104.

stitutio Christianae Religionis. Also, we know that Anabaptism was introduced in Gardone by a physician from Cremona, called Stefano de Giusti.[14] These elements show how effective heretical activities carried out by physicians could be.

One of the possible reasons for this might be found in the specificity of the medical professional mission. Physicians' presence at deathbeds, when the most delicate rite of passage was going to take place, and their contact with patients suffering from serious illness and fearing death, created the deepest intimacy between the doctor and the sick person (Palmer: 1993, 120). The physician was the patient's counsellor on all matters relating to the latter's *salus*, which was not regarded as merely physical in nature.[15] The case of Teofilo Panarelli, the leader of a secret heterodox group in Venice, reveals something about the medical professional and religious practice carried out by non-Catholic physicians.[16] It also sheds light on the nature of the bond formed between doctor and patient when common religious views were at stake. Panarelli told the Inquisitors that, as a physician, he had assisted his dying colleague and comrade in faith, Giuseppe Moscardo, at the time of the latter's mortal illness. Teofilo said that he used to visit Moscardo at his sickbed every day, reading some Protestant books to his sick friend and talking with him about religious matters:[17] the cure of the body and that of the soul were indeed being perceived as one. Panarelli confessed that, when death was about to arrive, he had encouraged Moscardo to die "merrily sticking to his heretical opinions and being aware that they were good and true".[18] Moscardo did so and died without confession. This episode demonstrates that, at the most delicate moment of the Christian "cycle of life", physicians sometimes deliberately advised their dying patients to reject Catholic rituals. As Richard Palmer has suggested, this must have posed a serious threat to the Roman Church: "The gravest source of danger, from the point of view of the Inquisition, was the Protestant physician" (Palmer: 1993, 121). Indeed, having been arrested, Panarelli was sent to Rome to be tried by the Roman Inquisition, showing that the ecclesiastical authorities considered his case particularly serious. Despite his recantation, Panarelli was eventually sentenced to death and executed in Rome in 1572. The leading role the physician played in the reformed movement in Venice

14 Paschini: 1959, 48; ASV, Sant'Uffizio, Girolamo Allegretti, Bu. 8, November-December 1550.

15 The choice of being healed by a particular physician could already be representative of the patient's religious views: see the case of Cardinal Girolamo Seripando and doctor Donato Antonio Altomare, in Conforti: 2008, 13–32.

16 I owe to Palmer: 1993, 121 the discovery of this interesting case. The trial of Panarelli is not only relevant from the point of view of the relation between medical and heterodox activities, but it is a precious source with respect to the daily religious life of heretical groups in Venice: see ASV, Sant'Uffizio, Contro Teofilo Panarelli e Ludovico Abioso, Bu. 32; further information on Panarelli can be found in ASV, Sant'Uffizio, Contro Paolo Moscardo, Bu. 23.

17 ASV, Sant'Uffizzio, Ludovico Abioso e Teofilo Panarelli, Bu. 32, 6th December 1571.

18 ASV, Sant'Uffizzio, Ludovico Abioso e Teofilo Panarelli, Bu. 32, 6th December 1571.

certainly had an impact on the harshness of his punishment. When considering it, we must not forget the special attention that Rome was paying precisely at this time to the medical context.

A heterodox sickbed conversation between two physicians, Francesco Severi and Marcantonio Florio, also took place in Ferrara at the time of the former's illness. As his care provider, Florio used to visit Severi regularly, checking his health and keeping up his spirits by reading for him the *Libro Grande*, the masterpiece by the radical heretic Giorgio Siculo.[19] In Counter-Reformation Italy, where intellectual debate had to be secret and sharing ideas in an overt way could lead straightaway to a charge of heresy, books represented one of the few means of keeping in touch with the cultural life of the country. Hence they were a priceless vehicle for nourishing one's own *intellectus.*[20] It is arguable that this had to be even more the case when involving men of science. Considering this, and bearing in mind the strong connection between the body and the soul, one can suggest that, in this episode, the reading of the *Libro Grande* could even have been conceived as a ritual to help in recovering from physical illness.[21] As a matter of fact, according to his own words, Severi had been attracted to Giorgio Siculo's doctrine by reading another book, Giorgio's *Trattatello sulla justificatione.*[22] Wanting to know something more about the author of a book he had loved, Severi got in touch with Siculo himself. For the physician, this event triggered a spiral of growing involvement in heterodoxy and secret propaganda, although conscious Nicodemism[23] always underlay all of his heretical activity. Severi's trial provides convincing proof of his religious involvement. It also highlights the special spiritual connection the physician developed with his colleague and comrade in faith, Marcantonio Florio, when sharing with him Giorgio Siculo's books. Francesco said that Don Giorgio had asked him to give the *Libro Grande* to Marcantonio. Over the next fifteen years the two men read the book together several times, mutually reinforcing their heterodox views. Besides the episode of the sickbed, we know that, in 1561, seven years before the trial and ten years after Siculo's death, Marcantonio gave the book to Francesco again, piece by piece, until Severi re-read it all. The two men also used to meet in the very early morning

19 Archivio della curia patriarcale di Venezia (hereafter ACPV), Archivio Segreto, Inquisizione, bu. 2, 83r.

20 On the centrality of books in Italian clandestine heretical groups see Seidel Menchi: 1990, 286ff.

21 Something similar has been suggested in Proseperi: 2000, 271, who speaks about the "mystic value of reading" and deals with Severi on pp. 267–277.

22 ACPV, Archivio Segreto, Inquisizione, Bu. 2, 83r.

23 ACPV, Archivio Segreto, Inquisizione, Bu. 2, 82r.

in a chapel close to the Chiesa degli Angeli in Ferrara, where Marcantonio would read the book aloud.[24]

In addition to Severi and Florio, Giorgio Siculo's secret heretical group gathered together other men of culture and other physicians, such as Pietro Giudici, Niccolò Beccaro and Pietro Bresciani (Prosperi: 2000, *ad indicem*, 280; Belligni: 2008, 239, 241). An effective original synthesis between mysticism and rationalism, predestination and Pelagianism (Belligni: 2008, 241), Siculo's doctrine had attracted those who, aware of the doctrinal boundaries which were dividing Christian Europe, were looking for a convincing doctrine to be embraced in the spiritual crisis that Italy was experiencing. Furthermore, as Adriano Prosperi has suggested, a possible reason for the popularity of Siculo's radical doctrine among physicians might be found in Giorgio's speculations on the origins of the human soul and in his stress on the *power* of human nature (Prosperi: 2000, 265). According to Siculo, God had only created the soul of Adam, while all the other souls had been generated by "*i parenti per propagazione*", so that the human seed was considered the only agent involved in the generation of both the body and the soul. It is likely that these sorts of speculations appealed to physicians, who were humanists and men of culture familiar with such issues since they had studied them at university.[25] However, in Counter-Reformation Italy this kind of intellectual curiosity could become very dangerous. After the Inquisition had repressed this radical group in 1568, all the physicians involved faced a horrendous fate. Marcantonio Florio was sentenced to life imprisonment,[26] to row at the *galera* until he died; Niccolò Beccaro was sentenced to the *galera* as well, for seven years; Pietro Giudici and Francesco Severi were sentenced to death: one was executed at the stake in 1568, and the other was beheaded and burnt in 1570.

Intellectual curiosity also got the physician from Orzi Nuovi, Girolamo Donzellini, into trouble. He faced the same doom as the executed medical doctors who belonged to Siculo's sect. Girolamo was a physician of great renown, acting in the Venetian Republic and put on trial by the Venetian Inquisition five times before being sentenced to death in 1587.[27] His case confirms that doctors and

24 ACPV, Archivio Segreto, Inquisizione, Bu. 2, 83r.

25 The debate about the origins and destiny of the human soul had been raging in Italian universities since the fifteenth century. Considering the medical curriculum, we can be sure that physicians found themselves involved in this kind of discussion. For the medical education see Grendler: 2002.

26 In 1574, the Inquisition allowed Florio to go back to his medical profession, Prosperi: 2000, 281, 448.

27 The figure of Girolamo Donzellini as an Italian Protestant doctor has been examined in Palmer: 1993. For further information about Girolamo Donzellini see Schutte: 2001; Pastore: 1993. I also take the liberty of quoting my own article on Girolamo Donzellini's religious and medical orientations, Celati: 2014.

patients built up long-lasting relationships, and this bond could be established and strengthened by sharing the same religious views. Reading Donzellini's file I found evidence of his conscious attempt to carry out reformed activities as part of his medical work. For instance, he was using his professional role to share Protestant doctrines and books with some of his patients;[28] and he even promoted reformed doctrines in a Catholic nunnery. In the deposition a woman gave to the Inquisitors in 1575, concerning the flight of two nuns from the monastery of Santa Lucia in Venice, she said that Donzellini, who was allowed to enter the nunnery in his professional capacity, had taken advantage of that. He had passed his heretical ideas on to the nuns, providing them with prohibited books and convincing them to escape.[29] Quite predictably, Donzellini denied that he had ever encouraged the nuns to escape. However, being a man of culture, who had travelled across Germany and Switzerland and was in touch with Protestant scientists there, he was indeed very active in the spread of banned books.[30]

According to his own words, his intellectual commitment, which derived from his humanistic education and his professional status, was the main reason why he had found himself involved in theological debate.[31] The same commitment had played an essential role in shaping his religious attitude. Donzellini was hostile towards the contemporary tendency of erecting religious boundaries between different denominations, and advocated a tolerant, inclusive idea of Christianity. This kind of conception stemmed from his adherence to the idea of *docta religio*, the *sapientia* which, since the age of antiquity, had spread without interruption and still connected intellectuals of different religious beliefs and different cultural tendencies all over Europe. This concept derived from Agostino Steuco's *philosophia perennis*, which in turn recalled Marsilio Ficino's *prisca theologia* (Schmitt: 1966; Muccillo: 1996; Vasoli: 1999; Perini: 2002, 69–70). Examining Donzellini's works, we understand that this idea must have been extremely important to him and that he was keen to spread it. He expressed the concept of *docta religio* twice. First, in his introduction to Themistius' *Orations*, which he prepared a renewed edition of in 1559, and then again 27 years later, in his treatise on anger, when he significantly said: "for we judge there to be one unique and true philosophy, thoroughly in agreement with true and germane religion, of which the end is sincere truth, knowledge and worship of God".[32] It is important

28 See in particular his relationship with Gasparo and Pantasilea Parma, ASV, Sant'Uffizio, Girolamo Donzellini, Bu. 39, 134r–135v, 151r–153v.

29 ASV, Sant'Uffizio, Girolamo Donzellini, Bu. 39,123v.

30 On Donzellini's role in the smuggling of banned books see Baldini/Spruit: 2009, tome I, 683–704.

31 ASV, Sant'Uffizio, Girolamo Donzellini, Bu. 39, 48r, 182r.

32 Donzellini: 1586, 2: "Arbitramur enim unam solam, ac veram philosophiam esse, cum vera ac

to underline that in 1559 Girolamo was in Basel, where he was part of the tolerant and open-minded group of intellectuals who had taken shelter there. This shows that, just as different confessions started to erect the dogmatic boundaries that separated them from each other, Donzellini advocated a religious conception which implied tolerance and which, grounded in humanistic culture, aimed to overcome religious antagonisms. Then, when the confessionalisation of Europe had become a fact, the physician decided to express his irenic ideas again in his philosophical treatise. Later in this paper, I shall comment in more detail on the open-minded approach to Christianity that physicians took, but it is significant to stress Donzellini's intellectual commitment to religious peace already at this point. He was sentenced to death by the Inquisition one year after the publication of this irenic piece of work.

Other similar stories could be told, but this would go beyond the scope of the present paper. We have seen that due to their unique situation in society and in their role as learned humanists favouring a rationalistic approach to religion, physicians played a special role in the Italian Reformation. What is left to be examined is the nature of their religious dissidence, the intellectual context in which they worked and their potential influence on the wider horizon of the European Reformation.

3. Radical Religious Views among Italian Physicians: Two Case-Studies

In order to carry out a thorough examination of Italian medical religious dissent, I have worked on the collection of as many cases of religiously non-conformist physicians as I could find. Searching for material in archives[33] and studying bibliographies[34] I have selected a rather significant sample. I have found evidence of 200 physicians who, over the course of the century and across the whole of Italy, grew distant from conventional Roman Catholicism.

germana religione penitus consentientem, cuius finis sit veritas sincera Dei cognitio et cultus".

33 In particular, I have been conducting research at the Archivio di Stato di Venezia, Archivio di Stato di Modena, Archivio di Stato di Milano, Archivio di Stato di Trento, Archivio Vescovile di Belluno and Archivio Diocesano di Pisa.

34 Particularly useful has been the study of the big and important trials that took place in the 1550s, which in many respects can be thought of as the crucial years of the Counter-Reformation. These historical sources have been edited and published: see Manelfi's trial in 1551 (Ginzburg: 1970), Morone's trial in 1557 (Firpo/Marcatto: 1981–1995), Carnesecchi's trials 1557–1567 (Firpo/Marcatto: 2000), Soranzo's trials 1551–1558 (Firpo/Pagano: 2004).

The individuals I am considering are those whose professional and religious experience took place in the first century of the Reformation and the last century of medical humanism, before the Scientific Revolution; that is to say in the sixteenth century. Within that time frame two processes appear to lend support to one another: the gradual shift of medicine from the reliance on tradition to a personal search for new theories and solutions and a hands-on attitude toward the sacred. The fact that Italian universities were the epicentre of the reformation of medicine in the sixteenth century has to be put in relation with the high number of physicians who, at exactly that time, developed non-Catholic ideas. Investigating the deep epistemological reasons which supported this relation exceeds the scope of this paper. Yet, when focussing on Italian medical religious non-conformism, it is essential to bear in mind this general scenario.

The fact that 200 physicians across the whole peninsula developed non-conformist religious opinions gives us an idea of the extent to which physicians were involved in the Italian Reformation. The specific link between a new conception of medicine and a free-thinking attitude toward the sacred was a relevant cultural phenomenon. An examination of the doctrinal positions embraced by Italian physicians leads to the emergence of a varied picture. Only a few of them could be labelled as strict followers of the Lutheran or Calvinist Reformation (and, in this respect, the latter seems to have been more appealing to them). In many cases, without consciously perceiving themselves as Protestants, they developed an interest in theological debate and in the reading of reformed books, matched with more or less radical forms of anticlericalism and hostility towards Catholic ceremonies and precepts. As far as the great majority of them are concerned, it might be appropriate to speak about a sort of religious individualism which made them shift across religious denominations, including radical ones. As a result, they sometimes crossed the doctrinal boundaries of both the Roman Church and the Reformation, in Italy as well as in their migration *religionis causa*. Antitrinitarianism, Anabaptism, the heretical sect of Giorgio Siculo and Valdesianism[35] were the main groups counterbalancing the magisterial Reformation among Italian physicians (Cantimori: 2009, Caccamo: 1970; Stella: 1967, 1969, Ginzburg: 1970). In a few cases, the religious path these doctors followed, stimulated by their ongoing search for personal theological solutions, spanned the whole range of reformed doctrinal positions.[36] In some other cases, in the

35 Firpo: 2013. On the radical outcomes of the Valdesians' theological research see Addante: 2010.

36 See, for example, the case of Pietro Bresciani, the physician from Casalmaggiore, that I have quoted above. A leading figure of the Reformation movement in the Duchy of Milan, he migrated to Chiavenna in the early 1550s where he came into contact with the radical heretic Camillo Renato. On returning to Italy, Bresciani recanted and then joined Giorgio Siculo's sect. See Chabod: 1971, Tedeschi: 1972, Prosperi: 2000.

second half of the century, physicians even moved on from theological debate as it had been practiced in previous decades, putting forward an a-confessional criticism of dogmas and religious boundaries, which can be interpreted as an early form of libertinism.[37]

This doctrinal fluidity and complexity has been pointed out by historiography as a general trend of the Italian Reformation, but it is striking how significant it was in the religious experience of physicians. What seems to be common to all the 200 individuals I have selected is their attitude as men of culture: the possession and distribution of prohibited books;[38] their eagerness to get in touch with all the most relevant cultural developments, including religious news; the primacy of the moral and spiritual sides of religion; and the rationalistic aspects of their rejection of Catholic rituals. Moreover, Nicodemism, a rather common doctrine in the Italian Reformation, was particularly widespread among them. This was not merely a practical strategy to shelter from the Inquisition, but it involved a specific conception of religion and a special way to conceive one's own relation with God (Ginzburg: 1970; Prosperi: 2000). Based on tolerance, anti-dogmatism, interior freedom, subjectivism and a sense of elitist distance from the masses, it seemed to be particularly appropriate for men of science who were developing a personal approach both to the sacred and to medicine. This is confirmed by historical sources. It is not only the number of recantations that was rather high (48 % of the total number of physicians who had been put on trial, which suggests a certain "carefree" attitude towards recantation), but some doctors even overtly asserted in front of the judges that they had been supporters of the idea that one *should* dissimulate one's real religious beliefs.[39] In one case, it is even obvious that an attempt had been made to promulgate religiously non-conformist propaganda while attending Catholic rituals.[40] Physicians were men of science: they were humanists, culturally curious, even eclectic, and they tended to underrate the importance of religious boundaries. It is therefore not surprising that Nicodemism, understood as a conscious theological theory, appealed to them.

It is not possible here to describe all the individual religious paths these non-conventional reformed physicians followed. In order to endow the data provided with more particularity, I will briefly narrate the experience of two significant

37 See discussion below.

38 Some texts regularly recur in the lists of books physicians confessed to having read. Here are some titles: Bernardino Ochino's Prediche, Francesco Negri's Tragedia del Libero Arbitrio, Urbanus Rhegius' Dottrina Vecchia et Nova, Philipp Melanchthon's Loci Communes, John Calvin's Institutio Christianae Religionis, Juan de Valdés' Cento e dieci divine considerationi, and a long series of commentaries on the Holy Scripture, especially on the Gospel of John, some Hebraic versions of the Bible, and some restored Latin versions of the New Testament.

39 ASV, Sant'Uffizio, Contra Teofilo Panarelli e Ludovico Abioso, Bu. 32, 6th December 1571.

40 ASV, Sant'Uffizio, Contra Agostino Modenese Medico, Bu. 17, 16th October, 1563.

individuals. Their religious experience can give us an idea of the extent to which physicians' heretical dissent could easily result in further radical theological elaborations.

The first interesting case to be quoted is that of Ascanio Schrattemberg, an illustrious physician from Trent put on trial in 1568. In his experience, the strong connection between medical-philosophical studies and the development of highly radical theological views is quite evident. As a follower of Pietro Pomponazzi's, Schrattemberg used to maintain that "when the body dies, the soul dies" ("*morto il corpo, morta era anchor l'anima insieme*"). What is more, he also asserted that many physicians in Trent shared the same opinion "*in via Aristotelis*" (Zanolini: 1909, 81). Witnesses testified that the doctor used to lampoon religious ceremonies. The same witnesses also reported that, when referring to Jesus Christ, Schrattemberg would say "Christ, that poor man" ("*quell pover'homo de Christo*") lashing out against religion and grounding this conception on the thought of Heinrich Cornelius Agrippa.[41] Schrattemberg's habit of neither confessing nor receiving communion, and the fact that he did not abstain from meat on Fridays, point in the same rational, anti-superstitious and radical direction.[42]

The overt references to Pomponazzi and to Agrippa are highly significant as they allow one to clearly pinpoint the intellectual framework within which the physician was working. On the one hand, Schrattemberg's views can be classified as belonging to the stream of radical Aristotelianism; on the other hand, the nature of Agrippa's thought makes it possible to interpret the physician's orientation as consciously anti-authoritarian. When quoting Agrippa, Ascanio was probably referring to *De incertitudine ac vanitate scientiarum declamatio invectiva*, which enjoyed an outstanding European reception.[43] In this text, the German magician and humanist attacked the sciences, the clergy and the Inquisition, addressing them in an overtly aggressive way. Besides the undoubted importance of *De incertitudine*, it is useful to underline that, reading between the lines of Cornelius Agrippa's *De nobilitate atque praecellentia foemini sexus*, one can also find a strong criticism of ecclesiastical authority. Since Agrippa would "*parle d'une chose feignant de parler d'une autre*" (Wirth: 2003, 43), his feminism can be considered a means of attacking any form of authoritarianism. In this light, it is not surprising that Ascanio advocated religious freedom, not only by referring to Agrippa, but, for instance, also by praising the French Calvinist

41 Archivio di Stato di Trento (hereafter: AST), Archivio del Principato Vescovile (hereafter: APV), sezione latina, capsa 4, 3r.

42 AST, APV, sezione latina, capsa 4, 4v.

43 For the circulation of Agrippa's texts in Italy, and especially among Italian heretics, see Adorni Braccesi: 2004; 2007.

Prince of Condè for having rebelled against the King in order to preserve his faith and the "*freedom* to live accordingly" ("*la libertà di vivere secondo quella*").[44]

The mortality of the soul "*in via Aristotelis*", the denial of Christ's divinity, and the advocacy of religious freedom epitomise the most radical ideas developed by sixteenth-century Italian heretics (Addante: 2010.). However, despite his dangerous approach to theology, Schrattemberg was eventually liberated. Once more, it is likely that the intercession of influential noblemen, in this case the South Tirol authorities, helped the physician to get away with his religious crimes.[45] We do not know what happened to him afterwards; Salvatore Caponetto suggested that his case was resolved through his voluntary exile (Caponetto: 1997, 204). Even if he did not go into exile, it should not be a surprise that Schrattemberg did not run into the charge of heresy again.

Schrattemberg's rationalism, his desire for intellectual and religious freedom, his lampooning of theological boundaries and his discrediting of religious ceremonies can be interpreted as a form of sixteenth-century early libertinism. It is not possible to sum up here the wide-ranging historiographical debate about the concept of libertinism. But it should be noted that, when using this term, I refer to Jean-Pierre Cavaille's definition, which puts "the matter of freedoms" at the core of the views of early modern libertines, and underlines their "a-confessional" questioning of any kind of dogmas and theological barriers.[46] In this sense, although we must be aware that any attempt to pigeonhole sixteenth-century ideas into too strict definitions runs the risk of being misleading, Ascanio's thought can fall into this category. Moreover, considering the physician's assertion that faith in Christ was nothing but "a fairy-tale invented to dupe humanity" ("*fabule trovate per ingannare li homeni*"),[47] we would not be entirely mistaken if, going beyond the concept of libertinism, we even categorised

44 AST, APV, sezione latina, capsa 4, 4r.

45 In 1569, Schrattemberg was still in Trent. In the same year, he published his most important book, De indicationibus curativis libri X, in Brescia. This does not mean that the ecclesiastical authorities were not aware of how dangerous the spread of Ascanio's ideas was. This is the reason why Schrattemberg's file was sent to Rome to be examined by the Roman Inquisition, see Paris: 2010, 174.

46 For an accurate synthesis of the extensive historiographical debate about the concept of libertinism, see Addante: 2011. Here I am using the term in a broad sense, based on Cavaillé's suggestion of softening the "diachronic" differences between sixteenth- and seventeenth-century libertinisms and the "synchronic" ones between "libertinism of thoughts and libertinism of mores; philosophical libertinism and practical libertinism; libertinage flamboyant and libertinage erudite" (Cavaillé: 2012, 13). In this way, the libertine becomes an early modern defender of radical freedoms. Cavaillé also wrote the entry "Libertinismo" in the Dizionario Storico dell'Inquisizione (Prosperi/Lavenia/Tedeschi: 2010), a definition to which I refer in this paper, see Cavaillé: 2010, vol. II., 904–905.

47 AST, APV, sezione latina, capsa 4, 4v.

Schrattemberg's ideas as a form of sixteenth-century atheism.[48] Now, many sixteenth-century libertines and atheists, taking Averroism (which was a well-known philosophical theory among physicians) to extremes, saw intellectual orientations as the result of a very personal philosophical search for the truth. In contrast, they attributed to religion the mere role of instructing the masses and maintaining the political order. The willingness to recant and to dissimulate one's own real opinion, and to formally take part in official religious rituals, was therefore implicit in these highly individualistic doctrines.[49] In an aristocratic manner, most[50] libertines and atheists thought that the truth could be discovered by only very few people, and they gave up any intention of proselytism. They were inherently Nicodemitic[51] and affirmed the specific intellectual function of recantation. It is, then, not surprising that, after being liberated, Ascanio decided to refrain from further overt manifestations of intellectual anti-conformism. Thus, he managed to retain his freedom and, by doing so, he was able to keep pursuing his philosophical research.

If the case of Ascanio Schrattemberg hovers on the border between radical Aristotelianism, radical reformation, libertinism and atheism, that of the physician from Piacenza, Pier Paolo Malvezzi[52], has been interpreted as an example of conscious libertinism (in the sense of behaviour that ignores accepted morals). This judgement has been grounded especially on Malvezzi's arguments in favour of sexual promiscuity and on his actual *libertine* sexual behaviour. I will try to show that his thought was far more complex than this.

Pier Paolo was born in Piacenza and, like many of his colleagues, travelled around Italy, living in Rome, Ferrara, Bologna (where he graduated), Florence and Venice. In Venice, he was put on trial twice by the Inquisition. In his second

48 When considering the concept of atheism within sixteenth-century society, one should not forget that this term referred, often in an accusatory way, to different positions: Zanobi Acciaioli defined atheists as "Deum negantes". The Suida Lexicon described them as those who denied the immortality of the soul; in the Strasbourg synod in 1535, atheists were stigmatised as "tous ceux qui prètendent que Dieu ne se souicie pas de nos actes et qui nient toute autre vie pares celle-ci". On early modern atheism see Davidson: 1992, 55–86; Barbierato: 2006, Frajese: 2010, vol. I, 114–118.

49 Frajese: 2010, vol. I, 118.

50 Most, but not all of them: libertinism was not necessarily an elitist movement. Historiography has shown the existence in the 1530s, in Siena and Florence, of some republican libertines who would fire up crowds using radical tones in their public speeches. Barthas: 2008 quoted in Addante: 2011, 979.

51 In addition to the points I have already made in the text, it is necessary to underline the strong link between Calvin's attacks against libertines, in 1544–1545, and his own polemics against Nicodemites in 1544: this strengthens the connection between libertines and Nicodemites. Addante: 2010, 132.

52 ASV, Sant'Uffizio, Contro Pier Paolo Malvezzi, Bu. 46. See also: Palmer: 1993, 119, 129; Dall'Olio: 1999, 431–432.

trial, it is precisely for sexual crimes that he was denounced – in particular, for incest. The obscenity of his crime has perhaps distracted scholars from the fact that, by the time Malvezzi was charged with promiscuity in 1589, he had already been put on trial for religious crimes in 1578. Also, already in the first trial he was charged with being an atheist.[53] These elements make Malvezzi's a relevant case-study which cannot simply be labelled as a form of libertinism in the sense of moral indecency.

Reading the *constituti* of the first trial, we encounter a man of culture who, probably moving from the widespread premises of the Reformation, developed such an extreme interpretation of the "free examination" of the Holy Scripture that he reached the point where he considered his reason as the only parameter for theological understanding. Considering the outcomes of his religious views and bearing in mind that he had been studying and working between Bologna and Venice, we can be rather confident that he had had the chance to come into contact with heretical ideas. In these two cities, the religious debate was extremely lively and Malvezzi seems to have been curious enough to take an interest in these debates.[54] He certainly developed his ideas in a highly radical way, since, for instance, he denied the authenticity of the four Gospels. He claimed that all the Apostles had written holy texts, but that the Roman Church had only kept those which were most useful in its project of spiritual and worldly domination.[55] Moreover, based on a rationalistic approach to the Holy Scripture, Malvezzi asserted that, in its least verisimilar scenes, the Bible and the Gospel had to be interpreted in a "spiritual" (allegorical) and not "corporal" (literal) way.[56] In particular, he was puzzled by the Gospel passage which maintained that Jesus had been carried into the desert, where he was to be tempted, by the Spirit. He also had doubts regarding the literal truth of the passages of the Old Testament which describe "wars between sheep and other animals" ("*guerre di pecore e altri animali*").[57]

These considerations are important because, as research has shown, according to Calvin's polemics, one of the main characteristics of libertines was precisely their tendency to advocate the allegorical reading of the Holy Scripture. This resulted in the extinction of any belief in the supernatural (Wirth: 2003, 37). Therefore, the concept of libertinism again seems useful in defining the radical theological achievements of these Italian physicians. When considering the extent to which Malvezzi's intellectual research strayed far from orthodoxy, I think that it is necessary to put forward an interpretation which goes beyond confes-

53 ASV, Sant'Uffizio, Contro Pier Paolo Malvezzi, Bu. 46, 14th October 1578.
54 On the spread of the Reformation in Venice, see Martin: 1993; for Bologna, see Dall'Olio: 1999.
55 ASV, Sant'Uffizio, Contro Pier Paolo Malvezzi, Bu. 46, 7th December 1578.
56 ASV, Sant'Uffizio, Contro Pier Paolo Malvezzi, Bu. 46, 9th December 1578.
57 See the text of Malvezzi's recantation in ASV, Sant'Uffizio, Contro Pier Paolo Malvezzi, Bu. 46.

sional identities. Accordingly, it is appropriate to describe Malvezzi's intellectual elaboration by referring to the category of libertinism, and by broadening the meaning of the latter term beyond the sphere of sexual behaviour. Bearing this in mind one should also consider that, according to witnesses, Malvezzi's radicalism developed into a sort of conscious profession of atheism after the recantation and in the ten years following. In his last trial, Pier Paolo openly admitted to having replaced the law of God with his own. He also asserted that, in this shift, he had made *morality* assume a new meaning: from a reliance on an absolute external and eternal religious precept to the free action of the individual. For instance, when giving help to a desperate beggar in the street, Malvezzi claimed that this good action was the outcome of his free will. It was not the result of the grace of God as reflected in human actions, and he expected no heavenly reward for it. He had not helped the girl in order to please God, who "doesn't care about human things", but because of his own generosity.[58] Perhaps this does not correspond to an absolute denial of God's existence. However, it definitely amounts to a conception of the divinity which comes very close to that of those who were charged with atheism in early modern society, or with that of seventeenth-century libertines. Forcing sixteenth-century men's radical intellectual accounts into a rigid category would be entirely mistaken: Inquisition sources are always to be interpreted "elastically" and we cannot know the actual extent to which Malvezzi's denial of the existence of the Christian God had gone. Considering this, if the concept of modern atheism might appear too strong and therefore not appropriate to describe his ideas (as the physician still speaks of some sort of God "who doesn't care about human matters"), the concept of sixteenth-century atheism or proto-libertinism could indeed suit his case.

The justification Pier Paolo gave for his promiscuous sexual behaviour might, at first glance, seem to be going in a different direction. Witnesses testified that Malvezzi grounded his incestuous behaviour on the fact that "God says be fruitful and increase in number" ("*Iddio dice crescete e moltiplicatevi*"), which could be taken as the physician's "corporal" interpretation of the Genesis passage. However, according to all the other information we have about him, it is most likely that Malvezzi was not only taking to extremes the reformed concept of universal priesthood, advocating a definitely non-conventional way of interpreting the biblical passage; he had also utterly abandoned any religious precepts on morality.

We do not know where and how Pier Paolo came to develop his radical ideas. He only mentions a preacher from Arezzo as a possible source of influence on his rationalistic interpretation of scriptural passages.[59] Malvezzi was not in touch

58 ASV, Sant'Uffizio, Contro Pier Paolo Malvezzi, Bu. 46, 17th December 1578.
59 ASV, Sant'Uffizio, Contro Pier Paolo Malvezzi, Bu. 46, 9th December 1578.

with the members of the College of Physicians, who had marginalised him because he had practiced medicine without submitting his professional qualifications. Also, his reputation as a heretic was widespread: a witness testified that he had discouraged people from employing Malvezzi as their medical doctor because of his religious views.[60] In addition, I am not aware that he was part of any heretical clique. It is therefore arguable that Pier Paolo's religious path was quite an individualistic one. This lack of religious guiding reference and his isolation suggest that his extreme radicalism had to be the result of something the physician had been experiencing in his life. In this context, it is useful to recall some of the characteristics of the "Reformation of physicians" I discussed above: medical doctors' open-minded search for some form of religious and philosophical *truth*, their frequent abandonment of any confessional belonging and their tendency to develop extreme, sometimes a-theist, views. In this light, I suggest that Malvezzi's approach might have been grounded on his education and practice as a man of science, which made him drift away, in the first place, from Catholicism, and then from any other forms of orthodoxy.

Despite the inherent specificity of individualistic non-conventional understandings, it is possible to draw a general trend: the connections between the most extreme philosophical currents in the Renaissance (such as radical Aristotelianism or the thought of Cornelius Agrippa – possibly mixed up in an eclectic way) and the radical Reformation (to be thought of in a broad sense) found a fertile ground in the medical context. In the second half of the century, this sometimes developed into further radical ideas, such as rising libertinism. The humanistic education physicians received was instrumental in shaping a strong connection between medicine and heresy. Historiography has already noted how deep the connection was "between heretical and humanistic culture, and between heresy and Renaissance" (Addante: 2011, 983–984). In this paper, I have tried to show the role medicine played in this scenario. Medical attention to the philological accuracy of classical works shared the same ground and aims as the primacy of biblical exegesis and individual scriptural interpretation in the Reformation. Medicine and religion being so closely interconnected, it was natural for physicians to apply the humanistic method from the medical to the theological context. Moreover, because of the coeval spread of radical philosophical theories, of physicians' familiarity with the philosophical debate and of their intellectual liveliness, they were apt to absorb and mix in an original way the most radical ideas of the sixteenth century. Natural philosophy was indeed an essential part of the medical curriculum in Italian universities. For example, the research and teaching on the origin and destiny of the human soul tended to be based on a "naturalistic or functional" approach (Grendler: 1996, 32), which resulted in

60 ASV, Sant'Uffizio, Contro Pier Paolo Malvezzi, Bu. 46, 14th October 1578.

radical philosophical solutions. The step from this sort of independent theoretical research to the development of outright heretical doctrines was evidently a small one. In times of religious turmoil, physicians played an important role in the radicalisation of the doctrinal debate. Accustomed to speculating on the most delicate philosophical issues as well as yearning to slip out of the control of the Church, they were eager to gain freedom for both their professional activity and their intellectual research.

In this section, I have referred several times to the concept of libertinism because I think it is particularly suitable to describe these non-conformist (a)theological experiences. It echoes opinions and behaviours whose common matrix was the independent search and need for religious, intellectual and moral liberty. The concept is also fluid enough to apply very well to men of culture whose intellectual elaborations cannot be clearly labelled or pigeonholed in rigid categories. Moreover, we must not forget the spread of Nicodemism within the medical context, a theory which implied the uselessness of rituals, ceremonies and dogmas, and which was linked to libertinism too. Its spread suggests that, although they followed different paths and adopted more or less radical views, most of the physicians I have discussed can be considered, to a certain extent, as free-thinkers. Thus, this term could be applied not only to those whose emblematic cases have been quoted in this section.

What is common to all the individuals with whom I have been dealing is their eagerness for a rational investigation into theology, their intellectual curiosity, their claim for religious, and also scientific, liberty, as well as their anti-dogmatic character. As men of culture who had the chance to get in touch with all sorts of people and, in many cases, embraced a rationalistic approach to theology, physicians were essential actors on the stage of the Italian Reformation, and they were so in a rather peculiar way.

4. Conclusion

At this point, I would like to sum up the main points I have made in this paper and draw some conclusions. Overall, what the cases I have quoted in the first section show, is that reformed activities carried out by those dealing with patients' *salus* could be particularly pervasive because of the social role that physicians occupied. Not only could they act at highly opportune moments, but they were also influential and practised on all sorts of people, allowing them to spread non-conventional religious ideas far and wide. The Inquisition tried to keep physicians under its own control. In some cases, the relationships medical doctors were able to develop with influential gentlemen in the community helped them get away with light sentences even before recantation. However, the special attention that the ecclesiastical authorities paid to physicians is undeniable. Often, as in Girolamo Donzellini's fourth trial, punishment was directly meant to prevent the *reo* from continuing to carry out his medical activity;[61] the *Contra medicos* file suggests an attempt at subordinating the whole professional category; and the death sentences of Teofilo Panarelli, Francesco Severi, Pietro Giudici and Girolamo Donzellini suggest that, when physicians' reformed propaganda had gone too far, the most severe punishment could be the only option for the Inquisition. The strong connection between early modern medicine and religion meant that the very role of physicians - dealing with pain, suffering and death – acquired a spiritual dimension. In this way, they shared common ground with religion. The step from this to finding themselves involved in the theological debate, and running into repression by the Inquisition, was evidently a small one.

Living in a Catholic context, religiously non-conformist physicians could not but represent a reformed minority. The cases I have analysed in the second section demonstrate how peculiar this minority was. In the second half of the century, led by their rational approach and their intellectual curiosity, physicians were inclined to take to extremes the premises of the Reformation. That Italian doctors who adopted Nicodemism, developed radical theological ideas, advocated religious freedom and peace, and travelled all over Europe, shows that some physicians were trying to overcome religious boundaries. They did so at the very moment when different confessions were entrenching themselves in positions of doctrinal rigidity. Right at the time when Europe was being torn to pieces by religious wars, some medical doctors were instead moving to a position of religious relativism, questioning the very importance of belonging to a specific confession.

The cases of many of these non-conformist physicians need to be investigated in more detail, and much more could be said about the few examples discussed in this article. However, with this contribution, I hope to have suggested a new research perspective by focussing on the medical context in order to examine the religious transformations that occurred in the age of the Reformation.

61 This happened as a result of the trial Donzellini endured in 1578, when he was charged with complicity in the escape of his patient and former cellmate Nascimbene Nascimbeni. ASV, Sant'Uffizio, Contro Nascimbene Nascimbeni, Bu. 30.

Bibliography

ADDANTE, LUCA (2010), Eretici e Libertini nel Cinquecento Italiano, Rome-Bari: Laterza.
- (2011), «Parlare liberamente»: I Libertini nel Cinquecento fra Tradizioni Storiografiche e Prospettive di Ricerca, Rivista Storica Italiana CXXIII, 3, 927–1001.

ADORNI BRACCESI, SIMONETTA (2004), L'Agrippa Arrigò e Ortensio Lando. Fra Eresia, Cabbala e Utopismo. Ipotesi di Lettura, Historia Philosophica, an International Journal 2, 97–113.
- (2007), Fra Eresia ed Ermetismo: Tre Edizioni Italiane di Enrico Cornelio Agrippa di Nettesheim, Bruniana e Campanelliana 13, 11–29.

AGASSE, JEAN-MICHEL (2008), Girolamo Mercuriale. Humanism and Physical culture in the Renaisaance, in: Concetta Pennuto (ed.), Girolamo Mercuriale, De Arte Gymnastica, Florence: Olschki, 861–1133.

AMBROSINI, FEDERICA (1999), Storie di Patrizi e di Eresia nella Venezia del Cinquecento, Milan: Franco Angeli.

BARBIERATO, FEDERICO (2006), Politici e ateisti. Percorsi della miscredenza a Venezi fra Sei e Settecento, Milan: Edizioni Unicopli.
- (2012), The Inquisitor in the Hat Shop. Inquisition, Forbidden Books and Unbelief in Early Modern Venice, Farnham: Ashgate.

BALDINI, UGO/LEEN SPRUIT (eds.) (2009), Documents from the Archives of the Roman Congregations of the Holy Office and the Index. Volume I. Sixteenth-Century Documents, Vatican City: Libreria Editrice Vaticana.

BELLIGNI, ELEONORA (2008), Evangelismo, riforma ginevrina e nicodemismo: l'esperienza religiosa di Renata di Francia, Cosenza: Brenner.

BROOKE, JOHN/IAN MACLEAN (eds.) (2005), Heterodoxy in Early Modern Science and Religion, Oxford: Oxford University Press.

CACCAMO, DOMENICO (1970), Eretici italiani in Moravia, Polonia, Transilvania (1558–1611): Studi e documenti, DeKalb, IL: Northern Illinois University Press.

CANTIMORI, DELIO (2009), Eretici italiani del Cinquecento e Prospettive di storia ereticale italiana del Cinquecento, Turin: Einaudi.

CAPONETTO, SALVATORE (1997), La Riforma Protestante nell'Italia del Cinquecento, Turin: Claudiana.

CAVAILLÉ, JEAN-PIERRE (2010), Article "Libertinismo", DSI 2, 2010, 904–905.
- (2012), *Libertine* and *Libertinism:* Polemic Uses of the Terms in Sixteenth- and Seventeenth-Century English and Scottish Literature, Journal for Early Modern Cultural Studies 12, 2, 12–36.

CELATI, ALESSANDRA (2014), Heresy, Medicine and Paracelsianism in Sixteenth-Century Italy: The Case of Girolamo Donzellini (1513–1587), Gesnerus 71, 1, 5–37.

CHABOD, FEDERICO (1971), Lo Stato e la vita religiosa a Milano nell'epoca di Carlo V, Turin: Einaudi.

COCQUELINES, CHARLES (1745), Bullarum, privilegiorum ac diplomatum Romanorum Pontificum amplissima, Rome: Mainardi.

CONFORTI, MARIA (2008), Girolamo Seripando e Donato Antonio Altomare: note sulla medicina a Napoli a metà Cinquecento, in: Marco Santoro (ed.), Pomeriggi rinascimentali, Rome-Pisa, Fabrizio Serra, 13–32.

Dall'Olio, Guido (1999), Eretici e inquisitori nella Bologna del Cinquecento, Bologna: Istituto per la Storia di Bologna.

Davidson, Nicholas (1992), Unbelief and Atheism in Italy, 1500–1700, in: Michael Hunter/David Wootton (eds.), Atheism from the Reformation to the Enlightenment, Oxford: Clarendon Press, 55–85.

Donzellini, Girolamo (1586), Remedium Ferendarum Iniuriarum Sive de Compescenda Ira, Venice: Francesco Ziletti.

Ferretto, Silvia (2009), Il "caso" Pomponio Algieri. Appunti di una Ricerca in Corso, Bruniana & Campanelliana 15, 43–57.

Firpo, Massimo (2013), Valdesiani e Spirituali. Studi sul Cinquecento Religioso Italiano, Rome: Edizioni Storia e Letteratura.

Firpo, Massimo/Dario Marcatto (eds.) (2000), I processi inquisitoriali di Pietro Carnesecchi, 1557–1567: Il processo sotto Pio V, 1566–1567, Rome: Archivio Segreto Vaticano.

– (eds.) (2011), Il Processo Inquisitoriale del Cardinal Giovanni Morone. Nuova Edizione Critica, Vatican City: Libreria Editrice Vaticana.

Firpo, Massimo/Sergio Pagano (eds.) (2004), I processi inquisitoriali di Vittore Soranzo: (1550–1558), Rome: Archivio Segreto Vaticano.

Frajese, Vittorio (2010), Article "Ateismo", DSI 1, 2010, 114–118.

Fumi, Luigi (1910), L'Inquisizione Romana e lo Stato di Milano, Saggio di Ricerche nell'Archivio di Stato, Archivio Storico Lombardo 37, 5–124.

Ginzburg, Carlo (1970), I Costituti Di Don Pietro Manelfi, DeKalb, IL: Northern Illinois University Press.

– (1970), Il Nicodemismo, simulazione e dissimulazione nell'Europa del '500, Florence-Chicago, IL: Sansoni-The Newberry Library.

Grendler, Paul F. (1996), Intellectual Freedom in Italian Universities: The Controversy over the Immortality of the Soul, in: Jesus M. De Bujanda (ed.), Le Contrôle des Idées à la Renaissance, Geneva: Droz, 31–48.

– (2002), The Universities of the Italian Renaissance, Baltimore, MD/London: Johns Hopkins University Press.

Henderson, John (2006), The Renaissance Hospital. Healing the Body and the Soul, New Haven: Yale University Press.

Martin, John (1993), Venice's Hidden Enemies. Italian Heretics in a Renaissance City, Berkeley and Los Angeles, CA: University of California Press.

Muccillo, Maria (1996), Platonismo, Ermetismo e Prisca Theologia: Ricerche di Storia Filosofica Rinascimentale, Florence: Olschki.

Palmer, Richard (1993), Physicians and the Inquisition in Sixteenth-Century Venice: The Case of Girolamo Donzellini, in: Ole Peter Grell/Andrew Cunningham (eds.), Medicine and the Reformation, New York: Routledge.

Paris, Alessandro (2010), Dissenso religioso e libri proibiti nel principato vescovile di Trento tra fine Quattrocento e inizio Seicento, Ph.D thesis, Università degli Studi di Trento.

Paschini, Pio (1959), Venezia e l'Inquisizione Romana da Giulio III a Pio I, Padua: Ed. Antenore.

Pastore, Alessandro (1993), L'Onore della Corporazione. Il Collegio Medico di Verona fra Tardo Quattrocento e gli Inizi del Seicento, in: M. Zangarini (ed.), Studi di storia per Luigi Ambrosoli, Verona: Cierre edizioni, 7–28.

– (2006), Le Regole dei Corpi. Medicina e Disciplina nell'Italia Moderna, Bologna: Il Mulino.

Perini, Leandro (2002), La Vita e i Tempi di Pietro Perna, Rome: Edizioni di Storia e Letteratura.

Prosperi Adriano (2000), L'Eresia del Libro Grande. Storia di Giorgio Siculo e della Sua Setta, Milan: Feltrinelli.

– (1996), Tribunali della Coscienza. Inquisitori, Confessori, Missionari, Turin: Einaudi.

Prosperi, Adriano/Vincenzo Lavenia/John Tedeschi (eds.) (2010), Dizionario Storico dell'Inquisizione, 4 vols., Pisa: Edizioni della Scuola Normale Superiore.

Schmitt, Charles B. (1966), Perrenial Philosophy: From Agostino Steuco to Leibniz, Journal of the History of Ideas 27, 505–532.

Schutte, Ann Jacobson (1992), Article "Girolamo Donzellini", DBI 41.

Stella, Aldo (1967), Dall'anabattismo al Socinianesimo nel Cinquecento veneto, Padua: Liviana.

– (1969), Anabattismo e Antitrinitarismo in Italia nel XVI secolo, Nuove Ricerche Storiche, Padua: Liviana.

Tedeschi, John (1972), Article "Pietro Bresciani", DBI 14, 1972.

Vasoli, Cesare (1999), Il *De Christiana Religione* di Marsilio Ficino. Parole Chiave: Religione, Sapienza, Profezia, Vita Civile, Ebrei, Bruniana & Campanelliana 13, 403–428.

Weber, Domizia (2011), Sanare e maleficiare. Guaritrici, streghe e medicina a Modena nel XVI secolo, Rome: Carocci.

Wirth, Jean (2003), «Libertins» et «Épicuriens»: Aspects de l'Irréligion en France au XVIe siècle, in: Jean Wirth (ed.), Sainte Anne Est Une Sorciere Et Autres Essais, Geneva: Droz.

Zanolini, Virgilio (1909), Appunti e documenti per una storia dell'eresia luterana nella diocesi di Trento, VIII Annuario del Ginnasio Pareggiato Principesco Vescovile di Trento, Trent: Tipografia del Comitato Diocesano.

Ziegler, Joseph (1998), Medicine and Religion, c. 1300: The Case of Arnau de Vilanova, New York: Clarendon Press, Oxford University Press.

Simon J.G. Burton

From Minority Discourse to Universal Method

Polish Chapters in the Evolution of Ramism

1. Introduction

In recent years scholars of Reformed thought have shown renewed interest in Ramism. From the start this movement of logical and pedagogical reform won support in the Reformed community, with Ramus himself becoming a Huguenot martyr in the St Bartholomew's day massacre of 1572. In particular, Ramus' desire to restructure Aristotelian and scholastic logic along rhetorical lines, following the traditional pattern of the *loci communes* or commonplaces, proved attractive to a number of prominent Reformed in their own attempts to effect a rhetorical and biblical reform of theology. However, while earlier scholarship, especially that of Perry Miller, tended to assume a deep philosophical and theological affinity between Ramism and Reformed theology, recent scholarship has argued for a more complex and ambiguous relationship between the two.[1] For while Ramism flourished in many of the Reformed *gymnasia* of Central and Eastern Europe, as well as in Scandinavia and the Puritan colleges of Britain and America, it met with considerable opposition in the heartlands of Reformed theology, including Switzerland and the Netherlands, and from prestigious Reformed universities such as Leiden and Heidelberg. Many of the leading humanists from all confessions poured scorn on Ramism and the movement also came under pressure from the scholastic renewal taking place within the Reformed Church. Over the course of the seventeenth century Ramism therefore became, as Howard Hotson has persuasively argued, a phenomenon of the margins (Hotson: 2007, 36–37).[2]

1 For the older scholarship see Miller: 1954; Sprunger: 1966 and McKim: 1987. For an insightful critique see Hotson: 2007, 16–25 and Goudriaan: 2013, 41–43.

2 For an account of the wider reception of Ramism in Europe see the collected essays in Feingold/Freedman/Rother: 2001 and Reid/Wilson: 2011.

Nevertheless, although a minority discourse, it is clear that Ramist methodologies did manage to gain a significant foothold within Reformed thought, and indeed in the Protestant world more widely, for a variety of pragmatic, philosophical and theological reasons. Especially within the Anglo-American Puritan movement and the wider European movement for "universal reformation" Ramism exercised a major influence, and through these helped shape the intellectual and spiritual discourse of both the Old and New Worlds as well as the emerging culture of Enlightenment.[3] Indeed, Ramism was able to survive, and in its own way to flourish, for two principal reasons: its remarkable potential to assimilate, adapt and transform and its impressive ability to tap into deep intellectual and spiritual currents of European reform.

In this chapter I will seek to show how the interplay of these two factors both motivated the adoption of Ramism in minority contexts and fuelled its ongoing transformation. My focus will be on the two central figures of Bartholomäus Keckermann and Jan Amos Comenius. Keckermann's own connection to Ramism has already been discussed in great detail by Howard Hotson, who is also the author of an important article on Comenius' debt to Ramism (Hotson: 2007, 127–168 and Hotson: 2011). While this chapter will cover some of the same territory as Hotson's pioneering studies, it will also seek to go beyond him in pointing to deeper metaphysical and theological factors at work in the transformation of Ramism.

2. The Formation of Keckermann's Methodological Peripateticism

Keckermann was born in Danzig, now Gdańsk, in 1572. Despite the incorporation of Royal Prussia into the Catholic Polish-Lithuanian Commonwealth, Danzig, as a semi-independent city state, was largely Protestant at this time. However, this did not prevent it from being confessionally divided between a Reformed senate and a Lutheran majority. Keckermann's family belonged to the Reformed elite and he was well aware of the tensions between the two sides (Hotson: 2007, 136–137).[4] Indeed, as we shall see, they later played an important role in the formation of his own mature system of thought.

By his own account Keckermann received an education at the Reformed gymnasium in Danzig which was broadly Ramist in character (Hotson: 2007, 137). While the 1568 statutes of Andreas Franckenberger prescribed a strongly

3 The classic study of this remains Miller: 1954. An excellent case-study on the relation between Ramism and Puritanism in Ireland is Boran: 2001.

4 For an account of the Prussian Reformation see Małłek: 2013 and especially Müller: 1997, 77 ff.

Philippist education it seems likely that this would have been flexible enough to incorporate study either of Ramus' own textbooks or the many Ramist-inspired works that flooded the market at this time. Indeed, a tempering of Lutheran Philippism with a more Reformed Ramism may well have been politic at this time. If so, then Keckermann's early education would have clearly marked him out as a mixed Ramist – one combining Ramus' principles with those of Melanchthon.[5] Certainly, Keckermann's later logical works have nothing but praise for Melanchthon "the Phoenix of Europe" and the "great light of every doctrine in Germany" (Keckermann: 1604, 178).

In 1590 Keckermann matriculated at the famous University of Wittenberg. Although a Lutheran university it was at this time still a highly congenial place for Reformed students of a Philippist disposition. It was here, as he later recorded, that he became thoroughly disillusioned with Ramism, becoming an enthusiastic convert to Aristotelianism. Hitherto, Keckermann had most likely known Aristotle only through the veil of Ramist critiques or, perhaps, through those he later disdained as textual peripatetics – scholars who focussed on the minutiae of Aristotelian texts without regard for the unity and coherence of Aristotle's thought as a whole. At Wittenberg and later at Heidelberg, through the teaching of Daniel Claepius, David Paraeus and his own private studies, he encountered a very different Aristotle. This was the Aristotle of the Paduan School, and especially of Jacopo Zabarella, whose works at this time were finding their first enthusiastic readers in German Universities. In these works Aristotelian doctrine was set free from endless scholastic and textual debates and rearranged into an ordered, progressive and methodical system. Keckermann was entranced and the seed that these lectures sowed in him was soon to mature into the philosophy that he called methodical peripateticism. His new zeal for Aristotle enabled a swift progression through the Heidelberg ranks, with Keckermann ascending to the chair of Hebrew by 1600. By 1601 he was poised to succeed as professor of theology at Heidelberg before an urgent missive from his native Danzig changed the course of his life once again.[6]

We shall return below to Keckermann's Danzig phase, but before doing so we must give consideration to the nature of his critique of Ramism and the way this shaped his own influential methodical peripateticism. While he offers a whole series of criticisms of Ramism, his *Praecognita Logica* summarises these in three fundamental objections. The first was that in seeking to "heal the disciplines"

5 For the statutes see Franckenberger: 1568. Bryćko: 2013, 341–344 points to tensions between Lutheran and Reformed elements in the gymnasium during the period of confessionalisation. I am very grateful to Dr Bryćko for sending me a copy of his article and for discussions on the Danzig gymnasium.

6 See Freedman: 1999, 306–309 and Hotson: 2007, 137–142. For more on Keckermann's Aristotelianism see Facca: 2005.

Ramus had only succeeded in mutilating and truncating them further. In particular, Keckermann attacked Ramus for cutting off, or cutting short, three mainstays of Aristotelian logic: the Predicaments, the syllogism and logical sophisms (Keckermann: 1604, 12, 251–257). According to him, in assigning things into their different ontological classes the Predicaments lie at the root of all logical definition and division (Keckermann: 1603, 29–30, 35–36). In abandoning them, Ramist logic therefore severely handicapped itself. While Ramus had thought to replace these with Agricolan logical arguments, Keckermann is swift to point out that such arguments or places (*loci*) are themselves entirely dependent on the Predicaments, which he calls the "little places and repositories of the universe of things" (1603, 30). For the very ability to meditate on simple themes, which for Ramists is the precondition of dialectical invention, derives from the Predicaments. In their application to predication and the syllogism they are also indispensable for dialectical judgement (Keckermann: 1603, 1–5, 30). It is no wonder therefore that Keckermann should claim in the *Praecognita* that in cutting out the doctrine of the Predicaments Ramus makes it impossible to understand anything well (1604, 253). Although mixed Ramists such as Johannes Piscator and Amandus Polanus had sought to reincorporate the Predicaments, Keckermann's own rehabilitation of Aristotelian logic went considerably beyond them (Piscator: 1582, 101; Piscator: 1585, 14–16 and Polanus: 1605, 29–90).[7]

If the Predicaments provided the ground for all definition and division in Aristotelian logic, then the doctrine of the syllogism constituted its central account of proof and demonstration. A vital complement to this was Aristotle's theory of sophisms which, in its analysis of kinds of logical fallacy, allowed errors in syllogistic reasoning to be identified and countered. As is well known, Ramus' dialectic not only simplified dramatically the complex theory of the syllogism but also effectively relegated it to second place behind his own all-encompassing theory of method. Moreover, while Ramus' earliest dialectic had included discussion of logical fallacies, later editions left out all mention of this.[8] Given this, it is scarcely surprising that Keckermann should have found the Ramist account of logical demonstration utterly inadequate. According to him Ramus himself erred by only considering the syllogism in genus and not in species. This led him to leave out proper discussion of necessary and contingent syllogisms and to treat the practical or deliberative syllogism as "monstrous", something for which Polanus had already rebuked him. Even more serious was Ramus' later removal of sophisms, which Keckermann held "miserably mutilated the body of logic and

7 Contrast Piscator's and Polanus' assimilation of Predicaments to Ramist arguments with Keckermann's assimilation of Ramist arguments to Predicaments.

8 This is discussed in Keckermann: 1604, 122–123.

gave occasion to his followers to hack to pieces the minds of its students" (Keckermann: 1604, 150, 254–255).

In compromising Aristotelian accounts of definition and proof it is no surprise that Keckermann should view Ramus as undermining the ability of logic to function as a technical, scientific discipline, reducing it to a mere "poet's logic" (Keckermann: 1604, 148, 217–220). In particular, he found the Ramist reframing of logic in terms of dialectical invention and judgement, itself part of a wider Renaissance "rhetorical turn", deeply problematic. For Ramus, invention was to be understood in general terms as the discovery of arguments, and more specifically of those arguments which could function as the middle term of a syllogism (Ong: 2004, 182–183). According to Keckermann it is here that the problems began. For the Ramist partition of logic into invention and judgement assumes that the one always precedes the other. In fact, he argued, the "principles of nature" demonstrate that the judgement of the conclusion must precede the invention of the mean, the reverse of the Ramist order. In doing the opposite, Ramism transgresses even more than Agricolan invention. For Agricola's notion of intention had at least ordered the means towards the end of reasoning (Keckermann: 1604, 41–44, 220–228).

As Keckermann suggests, lying at the root of this problem is the fact that Renaissance logicians compare invention and judgement as two separate, really distinct, parts of logic. By contrast, he follows the Aristotelian pattern in viewing them as two different aspects of "one and the same most simple operation of the mind". Every act of invention therefore requires reflection of the intellect or judgement. Even sensation, itself the root of intellection, is not nude apprehension but contains within it some kind of judgement. Keckermann conceives this as a kind of two-step process. The intellect first emits a kind of ray to the intelligible object and then these rays are reflected back on themselves allowing it to understand and judge concerning the apprehension. Invention is therefore application of the mind to the thing and judgement the reflection on this application (Keckermann: 1604, 220–226).

While invention and judgement certainly represented important dimensions of reason for Keckermann, he differed from Ramus and other humanist logicians in holding that they did not represent the full scope of logic. Following Aristotle he distinguished logic according to three different acts of the mind. The first of these was the apprehension of simple terms or the forming of simple concepts. The second was the composition or division of the mind leading to the formation of mental propositions. The third was discourse or the syllogistic and methodical connection of different propositions. While Agricola and Ramus had effectively sought to reduce invention to the first act and judgement to the second and third act, Keckermann shifted both of these to discourse, the third act of the mind. In doing so he says that he has "preferred trichotomy to dichotomy". Indeed, he adds that since three is the perfect number, this Aristotelian, threefold division of logic is entirely appropriate. Here we find just a hint, which we shall return to below, of a connection between his trichotomous logic and the Trinity (Keckermann: 1603, 304).[9]

Keckermann's second chief complaint is that Ramus mixes and confuses the disciplines. In fact, from a close reading of the *Praecognita*, it becomes clear that he viewed Ramist logic as a confused jumble of principles taken from grammar, dialectic, rhetoric, physics and metaphysics (1604, 217–220, 252). Keckermann was strongly opposed to the Ramist tendency to swallow up other disciplines, especially metaphysics, in logic. In his *Scholae in Liberales Artes* Ramus had argued that logic, not metaphysics, was the true science of "being as being". This was a claim was not only repeated by pure Ramists like Alexander Richardson and William Ames, but also echoed by mixed Ramists such as Piscator and Polanus, who viewed logic as relating to things and not only to concepts.[10] By contrast, Keckermann's own view of the relation between logic and metaphysics was shaped by scholastics such as Julius Caesar Scaliger, Francisco Suarez and Pedro da Fonseca. Metaphysics, as the transcendental science of being and its affections, he called the first and universal science. Dependent on this is logic which handles being not primarily but only derivatively and materially, as it becomes the subject for logical reasoning. As an art, logic thus concerns not ontology but rather the instruments and modes of human reasoning (Keckermann: 1611, 17–20, 54–56).[11] Indeed, unlike Polanus and Ames, who wished to include them, Keckermann completely excised the transcendentals from logic (Keckermann: 1603, 16; cf. Polanus: 1605, 85 and Ames: 1646, 52–55).

Following a longstanding scholastic tradition, reaffirmed by his close friend Rudolph Goclenius, Keckermann distinguished metaphysics and logic as concerning so-called first and second intentions respectively. In this he opposed many Ramists who sought either to express logic entirely in terms of first intentions, or held that it embraced both first and second intentions (Keckermann: 1611, 54–56; cf. Goclenius: 1599, 14–15).[12] Keckermann's understanding of these first and second intentions was Thomistic, drawing on Aquinas and the fifteenth-century Dominican Girolamo Savonarola. It therefore assumed a sharp dis-

9 His critique of Agricola's and Ramus' assigning of invention to the first part of logic is to be found in Keckermann: 1604, 220–226.

10 See Ramus: 1578, 933–937, 942, 959; Richardson: 1657, 152; Ames: 1646, 52; Piscator: 1585, 89 and Polanus: 1605, 4.

11 Goclenius: 1599, 13–14 handles explicitly this important distinction between material and formal subject but it is at least implicit in Keckermann. Both Goclenius and Keckermann are reliant on Scaliger for their discussion of the relation between logic and metaphysics.

12 Keckermann: 1604, 111, 216–217 attacks those seeking a logic of first intentions or a mixed logic of first and second intentions. A good example of this mixed Ramist logic is found in Polanus: 1605, 7–10, 84–86.

tinction between first intentions, as concepts immediately conceived from the thing itself, and second intentions, as concepts received from the mode of understanding it. According to this view, logical intentions, as the "shadows of things", do not directly represent things themselves, or something inherent in things, but are rather intellectual norms by which we form and order things conceptually (Keckermann: 1604, 257–261). For Keckermann, a good example of second intentions were the Predicaments and Predicables, which concern the logical ordering and disposition of the first intentions of things (1604, 216–217; 1603, 8). Another example was the argument of cause – the mainstay of Ramist logic's metaphysical pretensions – which he distinguishes according to a metaphysical mode of being (a first intention) and a logical instrument of arguing (a second intention) (Keckermann: 1611, 54–56). In all this we may discern an important difference from the Scotistic treatment of intentions offered by Ramists such as Richardson and Piscator, which blurred the distinction between first and second intentions, and thus between logic and metaphysics (Richardson: 1657, 56–59; Piscator: 1585, 14–16).[13]

In bringing a sophisticated treatment of intentions back into logic, Keckermann sought to restore the doctrine of signs and signification to its central place. In seeking to measure up to the complexities of signification, Keckermann, like Polanus before him, therefore reincorporated the important scholastic distinction between categorematic and syncategorematic terms into logic (Keckermann: 1604, 256; Keckermann: 1603, 8–14; cf. Polanus: 1605, 7–10). Indeed, it is clear that for him the Ramist treatment of arguments as simply "things affected for arguing" was too simplistic, failing to distinguish properly between different layers of reality and kinds of signification. Likewise, while Keckermann concurred with the Ramists, that logical method should follow the order of nature, he emphatically rejected their claim that there was a single method for treating all arts and sciences (1603, 149–151). For he held that the variety of disciplines was already signalled in the diversity of their second intentions, something which the Ramists completely missed in their attempt to force them all to fit the same logical mould. Ironically, he therefore accused the Ramists of making disciplines the "measures of things" when it is things themselves that ought to be the measure of our intellect and disciplines (Keckermann: 1603, 135).

Following Scaliger, who had distinguished between the order of nature and the order according to us, and Zabarella, whom he called the "greatest architect of methods", Keckermann distinguished between a twofold order of things handled in disciplines (theoretical and practical) and a twofold mode of understanding things (Keckermann: 1603, 149–151; Keckermann: 1604, 581–584; cf. Scaliger:

13 For discussion of intentions in Aquinas and Scotus see Knudsen: 1982, 480–482, 484–486.

1597, 1–4).[14] According to this complex, fourfold scheme, method could be understood either as synthetic or analytic and could be applied either to the order of cause and effect for theoretical disciplines, or the order of means and end for practical disciplines. A synthetic method proceeded from prior to posterior, or from universals to particulars, and an analytic method from posterior to prior, or from particulars to universals (Hotson: 2007, 144–152).[15] In sweeping aside all these important scholastic distinctions, he argued that Ramism entirely misses the subtlety and complexity of reality, meaning that it cannot ultimately attain to either a true logic or a true metaphysics. In effect, its superficial and premature Realism forecloses a proper engagement with reality.

While these two objections were serious enough, as Hotson suggests, Keckermann's third was even more serious. This was that Ramism was inadequate as a theological method (Hotson: 2007, 142–143). For Keckermann a proper training in logic was essential for a theologian, although not of course for the ordinary Christian. According to him the work of logic is to understand logical order as the "sole mistress of every order". In doing so logic aids the theologian by allowing theology to be expressed as a system of theological rules and precepts derived from divine revelation and the structure of things themselves (Keckermann: 1603, 66–69). While Ramism also sought to reduce theology to a system, he held that it lacked a rich enough notion of method to do justice to the complexities of theology. Moreover, in watering down the doctrines of logical proof and evaluation (syllogisms and sophisms) Keckermann held – and in this his opinion was shared by Paraeus and other Heidelberg Anti-Ramists – that Ramism had rendered logic practically useless for the defence of Reformed doctrine. In order to defeat Catholic Polemicists like Cardinal Bellarmine at their own game Reformed theologians held Aristotelian logic to be indispensable. Ramist logic, which eschewed the precise and technical definition necessary for deconstructing such arguments, was simply inadequate for this purpose (Hotson: 2007, 142–143; cf. Keckermann: 1608, 44–49).

Importantly, Keckermann was also clearly worried about the detrimental effects that Ramism might have on Trinitarian orthodoxy. His own upbringing in Danzig had exposed him to the dangers of the spreading Socinian movement. Indeed, in his unfinished *Systema Sacrosanctae Theologiae*, a work which later aroused the ire of the Polish Socinian Adam Gosławski, Keckermann devoted serious effort to constructing an elaborate rational defence – even proof – of the doctrine of the Trinity (Keckermann: 1610b, 15–54). In his *Gymnasium Logicum* of 1608, written after his return to Danzig, he warned that the Ramists' indiscriminate attack on scholastic metaphysics had the consequence of under-

14 For more on Scaliger's concept of method see Jensen: 1980, 91–101.
15 For Zabarella see Gilbert: 1960, 167–173.

mining those very philosophical categories (essence, person, subsistence etc.) essential for preserving the correct expression of Trinitarian doctrine (Keckermann: 1608, 45–46). Moreover, the Ramist penchant for dichotomising risked reducing the Trinity into a series of dualities (Keckermann: 1603, 135). For Keckermann, Ramism thus risked playing directly into the hands of the Anti-Trinitarians and therefore presented a great danger for the Reformed, and indeed orthodox, cause in confessionally-divided Royal Prussia and Poland.

3. Keckermann's Return to Ramism

Keckermann's persistent and frequent attacks on Ramism must certainly be taken seriously, but they also must not obscure the significant debt that he owed to Ramus himself. As Hotson has suggested this is something that became even more evident after his return to Danzig. For it was here that his methodological peripateticism was pressed into a broader, and much more ambitious, encyclopaedic project. In 1601 the city council of Danzig wrote urgently to Keckermann, in terms he could not refuse, pleading him to come and teach at the ailing Reformed gymnasium, which was increasingly threatened both by Lutheran and Counter-Reformation forces. Seeing how dire the situation was, Keckermann's response was to begin a massive project of rewriting the entire curriculum. He determined to cover the whole of philosophy in just three years, beginning with logic and physics in the first year, proceeding to mathematics and metaphysics in the second year and concluding with the practical disciplines of ethics and politics. The hope was that such a swift education would enable the efficient training of the new army of ministers, lawyers and civil servants necessary to keep the Reformed community in Danzig afloat (Hotson: 2007, 137–157).

In realising such an ambitious curriculum Keckermann necessarily had recourse to Ramist methodology and pedagogy. Each of the textbooks that he and his students produced were scrupulously organised according to a Ramistic pattern of *praecognita* (those general points such as the nature and definition of the discipline), *systemata* (the content of the discipline itself, ordered from general to particular) and *gymnasia* (the use and application of the discipline illustrated through examples) and their essentials were all reducible to Ramist charts. The entire collection could thus be presented, as it was posthumously by his editor Johann Heinrich Alsted, as a "System of Systems", moving from the universal principles of logic and metaphysics, through the theoretical disciplines, to culminate in the practical disciplines of ethics and politics. In this way Keckermann's work represents an important fulfillment of longstanding Ramist encyclopaedic aspirations traceable back to Ramus' own attempt at a philosophical curriculum, the *Scholae in Artes Liberales*. Indeed, as much as Keckermann deplored the simplicity of Ramist methodology, it is clear that he too, like Ramus, sought a universal method adequate for all things. In this sense for all his criticism of Ramus he still remained very much the mixed Ramist of his youth (Freedman: 1999, 307–315; Hotson: 2007, 114–126, 145–151, 157–165).

It would be easy to represent Keckermann's Danzig efforts as purely pragmatic, but this would be to miss their important, underlying reform impulse. For his aim was not just to produce better philosophers but better Christians who could reinvigorate the Danzig Reformed community. Indeed, Hotson has demonstrated that Keckermann linked the notion of the encyclopaedia to the instauration – that is the complete restoration – of the image of God in man (Hotson: 2005, 1–21) – a theme which also had an important resonance for Puritan Ramists (Miller: 1954, 166–180 and Burton: 2012, 54–55). According to Keckermann, before the Fall, man's reason was perfect and contained all the principles of knowledge within itself. As the chief seat of the image of God it was able to deduce conclusions from these general principles almost instantaneously, covering at a stroke the whole field of possible knowledge and in doing so relating every area of knowledge to God as its ground and origin. Since intellect and will were perfectly in harmony this meant that all human actions could be directed towards God with effortless ease (Keckermann: 1604, 57–59; 1610b, 215–233; cf. Hotson: 2000, 66–82).

This perfectly ordered state of affairs, which included within it the subjection of the body and sensitive appetites to the higher reason, was shattered by the Fall. From being a Godlike power of universal scope, reason was reduced to a pale shadow of its former self. No longer able to move with ease from principles to conclusions, and shorn of its innate understanding, reason was forced to limp through the disciplines from one painful syllogism to another (Keckermann: 1604, 57–59; 1603, 2–3). As if this was not bad enough Keckerman held that the devastation of the Fall had been further compounded by the confusion of languages at Babel. For this meant that languages no longer signified naturally, opening up an important gap between language and reality. Indeed, with the exception of Hebrew, which he held, as the "purest, holy and eternal language", to signify through divine imposition, all other languages, which he believed with Conrad Gesner to be derived from Hebrew, now signify solely by human imposition (Keckermann: 1603, 9–13).

For Keckermann philosophy represented an important attempt to mend the damage occasioned by the Fall and Babel. Following the Renaissance tradition of the *prisca philosophia*, he could argue that the earliest philosophers were inspired directly by God. Echoing Ramus, he held that the Prometheus who brought the fire of logic to man was not a thief but a patriarch – perhaps Noah – commissioned directly by God himself. Moreover, in line with an important Augustinian tradition, much rehearsed in Ramist works, Keckermann could insist that the

Holy Spirit is "the first and most principal inventor" of logic as of all the other disciplines and arts.[16] All of this meant that philosophy was particularly suited to the repair of man's fractured knowledge. Indeed, Keckermann even went so far as to correlate each discipline with the restoration of a particular human faculty (cf. Hotson: 2005, 1–21).

In this scheme logic, as the universal, instrumental discipline on which all the rest were dependent, had a particular importance. As he famously said in his *Gymnasium Logicum*, a work written shortly after his return to Danzig:

> It is the greatest glory of logic that it strives to restore that outermost region of the image of God in man, that divine twilight still remaining in us, to a brighter light, to heal the failing of our mind as far as it is possible to do so in this life and to restore to the intellect its rectitude.[17]

Indeed, Keckermann was clear that in following the threefold, Aristotelian order outlined above, logic seeks to correct the error, obscurity and confusion occasioned by the Fall, realising, to the best of its capacity, the original pattern of unfallen human reason. In its analysis of signification and detailed attention to definition and ambiguity it also helps close the chasm which had opened up between language and reality following Babel (Keckermann: 1603, 2–13). In transgressing this scholastic order Ramism thus risked impairing not only the correct functioning of human reason but also the very sanctification of the soul.

Yet while logic, and with it the entire encyclopaedia of disciplines, were vital in Keckermann's understanding for the complete restoration of the image of God, taken alone they were insufficient. For he was clear that all the arts and sciences, and thus the entire range of human cognition and action, were ultimately dependent on the guidance of theology to reach this goal.[18] Indeed, placing Keckermann's account of theology in the broader context of the encyclopaedia helps to understand one of its most puzzling features: his insistence against almost the entirety of the scholastic and Reformed tradition that theology belongs to the genus of prudence and not science or art (Keckermann: 1610b, 1–5).[19] Specifically, he defined theology as a religious prudence leading to salvation. His inspiration for this prudential understanding of theology was clearly Zacharias Ursinus and the Heidelberg Catechism, the latter of which he held to follow the

---

16 Keckermann: 1604, 76–77. For Ramus' own comparison between Prometheus and Noah see Bruyère: 1984, 196, 290–293.

17 Cited from Hotson: 2000, 68.

18 Keckermann: 1612, 6–14 demonstrates the intimate relation of philosophy, theology and prudence. Keckermann: 1610a, 13–24 shows the continuity between ethical and theological virtue.

19 For Keckermann's discussion of the genus of theology in relation to the broader scholastic tradition see Muller: 2006, 1.331–3.

"most correct" Zabarellan method in proceeding from end to means (Keckermann: 1610b, 1–2, 211–215).

For Keckermann the end of theology was union with Christ and participation in the Godhead. For him this not only represented the "one consolation in life and death" of the Heidelberg Catechism, but it also connected to the wider aspiration of philosophy to restore the entire image of God. According to the Bible the means corresponding to this end were twofold. The first, which he called pathological, corresponded to the recognition and sense of the misery caused by sin, the second, which he called therapeutic, corresponded to freedom from this misery. For Keckermann, this unusual division, which he insisted he embraced not by "affection of novelty" but "desire of dexterity and brevity", both included and superseded alternative partitions of theology, such as those into God and his works or into faith and works (both of which were prominent in Ramist systems of theology) (1610b, 211–215).[20] By his own confession it derived from the art of medicine, which he held to have the greatest affinity to theology of any art. Indeed, for him theology was correctly identified as both "spiritual medicine" and prudence, for it dealt with the means of restoring the health of the soul. As the "directrix" of divine virtues it therefore pertained entirely to the regeneration and the sanctification of the affections (Keckermann: 1610b, 1–5, 215).

The harmony of philosophy and theology in Keckermann's thought, famously expressed by his dictum "true philosophy nowhere fights with sacred theology", may therefore be seen to be intimately related to his encyclopaedic aspirations.[21] For Aquinas, it was the role of prudence to coordinate and unify the action of all the virtues (1964–1976, 2a2ae q. 47 art. 5–7). By analogy, as religious prudence, theology governs and directs all the disciplines, including logic, towards the end of eternal life and participation in God (Keckermann: 1610b, 2–5). While Keckermann's view of theology broke with Aquinas, not to mention the wider scholastic tradition, it nevertheless integrated well with his broader Aristotelian and Thomistic view of logic.[22] Where Ramists such as William Ames had tried to remake logic in both the image of theology and the image of the external world, Keckermann steadfastly resisted this temptation (Miller: 1954, 166–180). For him the Ramist approach straitjacketed logic and prevented it from fulfilling its true function. By granting logic its own integrity and freedom he liberated it to become a true "handmaid of theology" (cf. Aquinas: 1964–1976, 1a q. 1 art. 5).

20 For discussion of Ramist systems of theology see Burton: 2012, 51, 63–65.

21 For discussion of this harmony see Muller: 1984, 343–365.

22 Keckermann: 1604, 101–102 praises Aquinas for his "purer theology" and especially his sharp distinction between philosophy and theology.

4. Comenius and Herborn Ramism

Turning from Keckermann to Jan Amos Comenius, the great Czech polymath, it is evident that we are still moving within very much the same intellectual and spiritual milieu. For while Comenius was strictly neither Reformed nor Ramist, but rather a leading member of the Protestant Unity of the Brethren, a movement which traced its lineage directly to the Hussite Reformation, his own thought developed in close dialogue with both traditions. Educated at the celebrated Reformed academy of Herborn, Comenius maintained a lifelong affection and sympathy for the Reformed cause. Indeed, while he has generally been regarded as lying outside the pale of Protestant scholasticism, recent scholarship by Emidio Campi resituates his theology within the broad spectrum of Reformed orthodoxy (2014, 259–284).

Significantly, it was also at Herborn that Comenius came under the influence of the Ramistic methodology which was to shape his own quest for universal method so profoundly. For two of his principal teachers at Herborn, Johannes Piscator and Johann Heinrich Alsted, were at this time central figures in the German Ramist movement. Piscator was a convert from Philippist Aristotelianism who had come to see Ramism as a powerful instrument for Reformed theology and exegesis. From the first he sought to institutionalise this new spiritual and confessionalised Ramism at Herborn. The founding statutes of 1585 for which he had responsibility prescribed the joint study of Ramist and Philippist logic and the Ramist orientation of the academy had been confirmed by new statutes issued in 1609, just a year before Comenius' arrival.[23]

Unlike Keckermann, Piscator's own view was that "logic does not properly concern the symbols and notes of things, that is terms, but the things signified" (1585, 88–89).[24] Indeed, as remarked on above, the evidence suggests that he subscribed to a Realist, most likely Scotistic, mixed logic of first and second intentions. At the same time, in combining Ramism with both Phillipist and Aristotelian thought his logic anticipated important aspects of Keckermann's own discussion. In particular, he sought to integrate Ramism within a broader scholastic context in order to argue that method both reflected the order of nature and the operations of the human mind (Piscator: 1585, 189–90).[25] Elsewhere, Piscator argued that the order of nature itself reflected the order of divine wisdom (1585, 167). Indeed, he paved the way for an important alliance between Ramist method and Scriptural logic, the fruits of which are evident in his massive

23 For Piscator's profound influence on Reformed Ramism see Hotson: 2007, 84–119. His autobiographical account of his conversion to Ramism can be found in Piscator: 1582, "Epistola Dedicatoria".

24 Contrast this with Keckermann: 1603, 10–11.

25 In arguing this he, like Keckermann, drew on Scaliger.

logical commentary on the entire Bible (Hotson: 2007, 118–119). Underlying this was his transformation of the Ramist account of testimony, which Keckermann had strongly criticised (Keckermann: 1604, 227). Ramus himself had downgraded testimony to the lowest form of logical argument, but Piscator elevated divine testimony to the status of self-evident truth. In this his logic provided an important expression, and application, of the developing Reformed doctrine of *autopistia* (Piscator: 1582, 114–130).[26]

At this time, Alsted was a rising star in the Reformed firmament, who had just recently been entrusted with the prestigious task of editing Keckermann's philosophical *opera*. Like Piscator, he was attracted to the Realist and exemplaristic character of Ramism. In contrast to Keckermann, to whom he was greatly indebted, he therefore came to see a metaphysical logic as essential to fulfil their shared encyclopaedic quest. His own route to this was to attempt a kind of fusion of Ramist methodology with the Lullian Art, a combinatorial method grounded on the divine attributes and the Trinity which derived from the thought of the thirteenth-century Majorcan philosopher Ramon Lull.[27] While Keckermann had utterly deplored Lullism, accusing it of both seeking to "transubstantiate logic into metaphysics" and attempting to heal all philosophical and theological ills with a "single panacea",[28] Alsted found the therapeutic approach of Lullist philosophy extremely attractive.

In his 1609 work *Clavis Artis Lullianae* Alsted therefore sought to defend the Realist character of Lullist logic by paralleling the Lullist principles of being, the so-called absolutes and correlatives, with Aristotelian Predicaments and Ramist arguments. While he conceded to Keckermann that all of these were in fact second intentions, he still insisted that logic must be grounded in first intentions (Alsted: 1609, 20–21).[29] Indeed, his more Scotistic account of intentions suggests a definite sympathy for a Realist approach to logic.[30] Just a year later, in his *Panacea Philosophica*, he put forward his vision for an "infinite harmony" of Aristotlelian, Ramist and Lullist philosophy. In this he argues that the universal scope and transcendental character of metaphysics is itself guaranteed by the higher science of Lullism, whose principles are grounded in God's own being (Alsted: 1610, 17–18). Significantly, a similar claim for Ramism had already been

26 See further Muller: 2006, 2.264–267.

27 Alsted's desire to fuse Ramist and Lullist methodologies is clear from Alsted: 1610. For further discussion see Hotson: 2000.

28 Keckermann: 1604, 106–111. For discussion of Lullism as a logic of first intentions see Johnston: 1987, 4, 46–52.

29 Alsted: 1616, 7 argues that logic concerns both first and second intentions. Alsted: 1610, 18 upholds the principle that logic must concern second intentions while affirming that Lullist principles are themselves first intentions and the foundation of all disciplines.

30 Alsted: 1616, 84–85 correlates logical intentions to Scotistic intuitive and abstractive cognition.

made by Friedrich Beuerhaus, an author well-known to Alsted.[31] Following Ramist and Lullist precedent, Alsted therefore clearly understood the universal method of the encyclopaedia as mirroring both the divine order of the universe and the dynamics of the divine being.

Yet while Alsted may be seen as an important defender of Realist logic, his own view of the relation between logic and metaphysics actually takes its lead from Keckermann's earlier discussion. For him metaphysics is the Sun of the philosophical heaven and logic its Moon, while all the other disciplines are its bright stars. As the comparison suggests all the other disciplines are therefore dependent on metaphysics. Using a common Neo-Platonic analogy Alsted therefore compares metaphysics to the centre of the entire circle of disciplines – the Encyclopaedia – in which all of them converge. It is the Sun of metaphysics which proves the principles of all disciplines and constitutes their subject. Logic, which like the Moon is bathed in reflected light, simply influences their order. Like Keckermann, Alsted also recognised a threefold motion of the soul in the cognition of things, but his own discussion of this is quite different. The first motion, from the intellect, is the descent from the most general principles of metaphysics to the particular conclusions of other disciplines. This is followed by an ascent through the senses from singulars to universals. Finally, there is circular motion, the most perfect of all, which is the full conversion of the ascent and descent into the rational discourse of the mind (Alsted: 1616, 4–8). In his dynamic entwining of logic and metaphysics Alsted thus broke away from Keckermann, and in this we see the emergence of a new conception of the encyclopaedia.

That Comenius thoroughly imbibed the Herborn Ramism is evident from the contours of his own later educational programme. As is well known this was centred on the ideal of pansophia – "all wisdom" – which he intended to be a universal Christian philosophy. Pansophia was intended to teach all people, all things, in all ways and was therefore a truly encyclopaedic endeavour. In particular, it sought a plain and easy path to the study of wisdom, scrupulously avoiding "any intricate and thorny difficulties" (Comenius: 1642, 4–5). The Ramist concept of method was central to this pursuit. This was true not only in terms of its general, encyclopaedic aspirations, something which Hotson has explored in depth (2011, 227–252), but also in the manifold details of its implementation. Like Ramus, Comenius taught that method should proceed both from the general to the particular and from the known to the unknown, and should always be oriented to use (1642, 14). Significantly, the detailed structure of his pansophic method also reflected in important ways the encylopaedic methodologies of Keckermann and Alsted. With its roots in what Keckermann had

31 Beuerhaus: 1582, 8–29. See, for example, Alsted: 1610, 20.

called the *praecognita* – the essential pre-requisites of any discipline – it branched out into an elaborate and interwoven system of definitions, ideas, axioms and distributions reminiscent of both Keckermann's and Alsted's own works (Comenius: 1645, 120–121, 133–134; cf. Hotson: 2007, 136–224).

Even more significant, however, than the structural similarities between pansophia and Herborn Ramism are their intellectual and spiritual affinities. Following Keckermann and Alsted, Comenius saw the purpose of pansophia, indeed of all education, as being the restoration of the lost image of God in man (Comenius: 1644, 4–7; cf. Hotson: 2005, 13–21). Central to this was his reform of languages, which attempted to restore language as a pure vehicle of truth. Like Keckermann, Comenius viewed Hebrew as a divine language that was the mother of all languages spoken in the world. In this way Hebrew represented to him an important template for the perfect, universal language. He even held that its root system mirrored the Trinitarian action of God in the world, thus facilitating the dynamic exchange between words, concepts and things that was at the heart of his methodology. Comenius' hope was that once the perfect language had been discovered the effects of Babel and of the Fall would be reversed and the proper relation of humans to the external world, each other and God would be restored (1989, 1–10, 22–29; cf. Keckermann: 1603, 10–12, 17–18).

Going beyond Keckermann, Alsted and the wider Ramist tradition, Comenius saw the purpose of his pansophia as nothing less than deification and the inculcation of the image of divine omniscience. For Comenius it followed that since man has been created in the image of God he must be "naturally capable of acquiring a knowledge of all things". The power of the human mind is therefore effectively "infinite and unbounded". Drawing on the ancient doctrine of the microcosm, but also radically interiorising it, he held that man "inwardly apprehends" the whole universe (Comenius: 1907, 42, 52). In explaining this, Comenius drew implicitly on Nicholas of Cusa's discussion of enfolding and unfolding. Specifically, he claimed that the human mind, imaging the divine mind, contained enfolded within it the forms of all things. This knowledge became actualised and unfolded through the process of sensation. All human knowing could therefore be seen as a kind of dynamic of enfolding and unfolding, a claim echoing not only Cusa but also his own teacher Alsted's account of rational discourse (Comenius: 1907, 42, 52–54; 1645, 155, 157–158).[32]

With its goal of achieving human omniscience pansophic method was clearly intended to reflect the metaphysical structure of the entire creation. Comenius thus described it in evocative terms as the "glasse or mirrour of the universe" (1642, 18; 1644, 31). In reflecting reality he held that method must always be fitted

32 For Cusa's metaphysics of enfolding and unfolding see Miller: 2003, 36–48. For more detailed discussion of a number of points in this section see Burton: 2019.

to reality itself, and in both his linguistic and educational programmes was always concerned to stress the crucial distinction between words and things. Indeed, throughout his life he manifested a profound dislike of the "prickly" logical second intentions so beloved by Keckermann (Comenius: 1642, 15; 1645, 107–109). His preference instead was for a metaphysical logic grounded not only on the order of the universe, but also on the nature of God himself (Comenius: 1645, 107, 112–114).

In this he was undoubtedly inspired by Augustine's desire for a scriptural philosophy, and especially a scriptural logic (Comenius: 1907, 241). Like other Ramists he sought to implement this Augustinian programme in a twofold way. Firstly, following the lead of Piscator, and perhaps also Ames,[33] he sought to place divine testimony at the heart of method. Like Keckermann, Comenius distinguished between sense as a direct ray of the mind and reason as a reflected ray. However, he also added testimony or faith to this picture as a ray of intellectual light proceeding from other humans or directly from God himself (Comenius: 1987, 37–41). Unlike Keckermann, Comenius therefore came to see testimony, and especially self-evident divine testimony (1974b, 51), as fundamental to method. In this way his pansophia sought to harmonise sense, reason and divine testimony directing all things back to their origin in God (Comenius: 1974c, 14–41).

Secondly, following a long tradition of Augustinian Platonism, he held that created beings are patterned after their exemplars or ideas in the mind of God. Following a broader Ramist trend, with roots in the Late Middle Ages, Comenius presented method not only as a scriptural logic but also as a logic grounded on the divine ideas themselves. By binding together God, his creation and human understanding, pansophic method was therefore intended to realise the divine order of reality. Indeed, Comenius' pansophia was ultimately grounded on the parallel between the epistemological enfolding and unfolding of human cognition and method, the divine enfolding of all things in the mind of God and the ontological unfolding of all things in creation (Comenius: 1645, 107, 112–114, 155–158). In this way Comenius' Cusan metaphysics both transformed and deepened his Ramist methodological inheritance.

33 Comenius: 1974a, 154 reveals his knowledge of Ames, although he is critical of his mixing of logic and metaphysics.

5. Comenius' Trinitarian Pansophia

Comenius' pansophia developed out of Herborn Ramism as a Realist and exemplaristic method. Yet, as a number of recent studies have emphasised, his pansophia was also a profoundly Trinitarian method.[34] As Simon Kuchlbauer has reminded us, the development of Comenius' Trinitarian pansophia therefore cannot be separated from his encounter with Anti-Trinitarians during his first Polish exile (2011, 61–89, 197–221). Indeed, while Comenius' first acquaintance with both Nicholas of Cusa and Tommaso Campanella, the major sources for his Trinitarian metaphysics, antecedes this period,[35] it was his debates with Anti-Trinitarians which led him to a new appropriation of their thought.

Evidence for a new engagement with Trinitarian method can be traced to early in his Polish sojourn. It is thus apparent in both his *Great Didactic*, a work which places the instauration of the image of the Triune God at the centre of education, and his *Synopsis Physicae ad Lumen Divinum Reformatum*, in which he develops a scriptural and Trinitarian physics on the basis of Cusan and Campanellan principles.[36] From his later *De Quaestione*, which gives a detailed biographical account of Comenius' relation with the Polish Anti-Trinitarians, we know that Comenius had already come into contact with a number of Socinian philosophers and theologians by this time (Comenius: 1659b, 58–61). However, these early works show no real polemical bent.

This seems to change around the end of the 1630s, when an increasing stream of Socinian visitors made their way to his house in Leszno eager to win him as a convert. For it was around this time that Comenius came into contact with Johannes Ludwig von Wolzogen, an Austrian Socinian from a prominent noble family. While their friendship later soured, it is clear that it had an important influence on Comenius' philosophical development. It was thus at von Wolzogen's instigation that Comenius began to compile his *Ianua Rerum Reserata* (cf. Murphy: 1995, 19). Significantly, it was also von Wolzogen who, during a stay with Comenius in 1641, pressed him on the place of the Trinity in the developing pansophia. Just one year earlier Comenius had been involved in an important theological debate with Jonas Szlychting, whom he calls the "Patriarch of the Socinians". As a result of this discussion Comenius wrote his *De Christianorum*

34 See, for example, Scherbaum: 2008, Raffaelli: 2009 and Kuchlbauer: 2011.

35 Comenius: 1661a, 117–118 allows us to infer that he encountered Nicholas of Cusa's works sometime before 1621. He knew these through Speculum Intellectuale Felicitatis Humanae (Nuremberg, 1510), a Cusan anthology compiled by Ulrich Pinder. Comenius: 1633, "Praefatio" demonstrates that he had gained a detailed knowledge of Campanella's works at least by the beginning of his Polish sojourn.

36 Comenius: 1907, 42, 52; 1633, 1–34. Floss: 1973, 174–178 draws the connection between Comenius' and Cusa's Trinitarian physics.

Uno Deo, a spirited defence of the Trinity on the basis of reason and Scripture. In this work, which draws implicitly on Cusan and Campanellan Trinitarian metaphysics, we find a clear template for his later pansophic writings (Comenius: 1659b, 61–64).[37]

Comenius' Anti-Socinian writings were not published until much later during his Dutch exile. This alerts us to an important second phase in his engagement with Anti-Trinitarianism. Concerned by an intensification of Socinian proselyting activity, which saw the conversion of a close friend of his away from Trinitarian orthodoxy, Comenius published the *De Christianorum Uno Deo* in 1659. This was followed soon afterwards by *De Quaestione*, a response to the Polish Socinian Melchior Scheffer which was also directed at von Wolzogen. In the same year his friend the Danziger Socinian Daniel Zwicker, who was also a fellow exile from Poland, published his *De Irenico Irenicorum*. The work was anonymous but Comenius knew well its author. Zwicker's attempt to promote peace in the Church by dismantling traditional Christological and Trinitarian doctrine stung Comenius to the quick. He not only denounced Zwicker to the Amsterdam Church authorities but swiftly penned a refutation, the *De Irenico Irenicorum* of 1660.[38]

In the ensuing polemical war between Comenius and Zwicker there followed the publication of further treatises. On Comenius' side these included a defence of his *De Irenico Irenicorum*, a point-by-point refutation of the Racovian Catechism, and a new edition, intended as a spiritual panacea for Zwicker, of Ramon de Sebonde's influential *Theologia Naturalis* (cf. Bietenholz: 1997, 84–100). Indeed, it is in these works that we find Comenius drawing not only on the Lullist principles of de Sebonde but also, for the first time explicitly, on Cusa's Neo-Platonic metaphysics.[39] While the main planks of Comenius' pansophic method were already in place by the time of his Amsterdam exile, there is some evidence that Zwicker stimulated an intensification of its Trinitarian character. Comenius' major work of Trinitarian metaphysics, the *Ianua Rerum Reserata*, seems to have been begun in earnest around this time, although its origin goes back to Leszno and his discussions with von Wolzogen.[40] Due to his reading of de Sebonde Comenius began to advocate with great fervour a "mathematical theology", which could prove the doctrine of the Trinity and all the articles of faith (Comenius: 1661b, "*Praefatio*"). At the same time his new appropriation of Cusa took his understanding of the relation of faith and reason onto a new plane, shaping his later pansophic work in a profound manner, the full implications of

---

37 See the close parallels in the discussion of the *vestigia Trinitatis* in Comenius: 1659a, 30–41 and Comenius: 1966b, I.241–246.

38 For discussion of the relation between Comenius and Zwicker see Bietenholz: 1997, 79–103.

39 Comenius: 1660, 72–74; 1661a, 117–119 and 1661b, "Epistola Dedicatoria" and "Praefatio".

40 Schadel: 1989, xlviii and Murphy: 1995, 19.

which are yet to be recognised (Comenius: 1660, 72–74, 197). Indeed, in one of his very last works, the unfinished *Clamores Eliae*, we find Comenius meditating on a new reply to Zwicker and a comprehensive refutation of Socinian philosophy and theology (cf. Bietenholz: 1997, 100–103).

The details of Comenius' Trinitarian pansophia are now becoming increasingly well known. Studies by Patočka, Floss and Kuchlbauer have demonstrated the importance of Cusa and de Sebonde for his thought, while a recent work by Matteo Raffaelli discusses in-depth his appropriation of Campanella.[41] What has been much less discussed, if at all, is the relation of his Trinitarian method to the Herborn Ramism he was educated in. It is to this question that we turn to in conclusion, highlighting three different aspects: trichotomous logic, the metaphysics of the transcendentals and the coincidence of opposites. Ironically, given all of Keckermann's concerns, it will be seen that Comenius developed his Trinitarian method by fusing Ramist and Lullist principles within an overarching Neo-Platonic metaphysics. At the same time, there is important evidence that Keckermann himself played a major role in its evolution.

Comenius' Trinitarian method was founded on the claim that all of reality was patterned metaphysically according to its participation in the Trinity. In arguing this he drew explicitly on Campanella's doctrine of the primalities of being. This held that being itself had a dynamic, Trinitarian structure of Power, Wisdom and Love reflecting the Triune Godhead himself. While there was a long patristic and medieval tradition of appropriating these attributes to the Trinity, Campanella's conception of intrinsic, trinitarian moments of activity within being itself seems to reflect a definite Lullist heritage, one which he moreover shared with Comenius' other sources: de Sebonde, Cusa and of course Alsted himself.[42] Running in parallel to this Campanellan method, which is prominent in all his major works, we find another method, which focusses on the Trinitarian interaction of unity, truth and goodness, the transcendental "affections of being". Indeed, in his *Pansophiae Prodromus* Comenius suggests that it was these transcendentals which first stimulated his interest in Trinitarian method (1644, 92–93).

The importance of both these approaches can be seen from a work like the *De Christianorum Uno Deo*. For here Comenius treats unity, truth and goodness as one of the primary expressions of Campanella's primalities of being. Indeed, drawing implicitly on Cusa's metaphysics, he argues that the whole of space-time reality is unfolded from the transcendentals, with unity, truth and goodness giving rise to what he elsewhere calls the nine Predicaments of place, time, quantity, quality, action, passion, order, use and amiability – his own revision of

41 See further Patočka: 2006a, Patočka: 2006b, Floss: 1973, Kuchlbauer: 2011 and Raffaelli: 2009.

42 For discussion of this broader Lullist tradition and Comenius' place in it see Burton: 2012, 55–63.

Aristotle's Categories – and each of these further unfolding according to their own triune dynamic (Comenius: 1659a, 30–41; 1922, 53).

The transcendentals of being were therefore at the forefront of both Comenius' Trinitarian method and his Trinitarian apologetic. Indeed, it was through the "harvest of ternaries" sown throughout created being that he hoped to convince the Socinians of the rationality of Trinitarian doctrine (Comenius: 1659a, 41). The question remains, however, of their origin in his thought. Jan Patočka has suggested that Comenius' reflection on the transcendentals derives from Cusa (2003, 232–242).[43] However, it seems unlikely that Cusa was the proximate source, even though it is clear that he was an important influence on Comenius' subsequent Trinitarian development of the doctrine of the transcendentals.[44] A more immediate influence was the philosophy of Keckermann and Alsted; a suggestion confirmed by the editors of his early *Primam Philosophiam*, the work in which he first developed a comprehensive transcendental metaphysics.[45] This also fits in well with Matthias Scherbaum's discerning of a Scotistic character to Comenius' doctrine of the transcendentals (Scherbaum: 2008, 154).[46] For, following in Scotus' footsteps, Keckermann and especially Alsted made an important move towards grounding the transcendentals in the dynamics of God's own Triune being.[47] In this sense it was simply left to Comenius to complete the metaphysical movement of their thought.

If Comenius' attempts at a transcendental method are clearly indebted to Keckermann's metaphysics, then there is also good evidence to connect his attempt to develop a Trinitarian method with Keckermann's logic. In his *Pansophiae Prodromus* Comenius gave an important account of his new Trinitarian method. One of the central features of this was a new trichotomous logic which he grounded on the "chiefest divisions of things" – the transcendental attributes of being. Recalling perhaps his *De Christianorum Uno Deo*, Comenius spoke of his experience of wonder in first discovering that the truth of all things should represent itself in "so great an harmony of the sacred Ternary" (Comenius: 1644, 92–93). In a late work, the *Triertium Catholicum* of 1670, he strongly attacked the Ramist attempt to encompass all things within the scope of logical dichotomies. This is something which he viewed as doing violence to the "order of nature", and

43 Patočka: 2003, 232–242. I am very grateful to Petr Pavlas for providing me with a translation of this article.

44 Aertsen: 2012, 554–567 points to Cusa's strong critique of the transcendentals, but this seems to be exaggerated. Nevertheless, Patočka himself is only able to point to Cusa as an inspiration and not a direct source.

45 See the editorial note in Comenius: 1974d, 31.

46 Scherbaum: 2008, 154.

47 Keckermann: 1611, 29–36 and Alsted: 1616, 59–66. Elders: 1993, 59–66 points out that Scotus explicitly connected the transcendentals to the Trinity. By contrast, Aquinas rejected this theological account of the transcendentals.

here he reiterates the importance of following a trichotomous division in treating the Trinitarian structure of reality (Comenius: 1922, 56–59). In this we are clearly reminded of Keckermann's own preferring of trichotomy to dichotomy.

It is in the *Triertium Catholicum* that we find further evidence of Keckermann's influence. In Ramist fashion Comenius defines logic as the "art of reasoning well", suggesting that it concerns both theme, the object of cognition, and argument, that which is thought concerning the theme (1922, 20–21). However, like Keckermann, he insists that invention, disposition (method) and judgement are not three parts of logic but three aspects of a single act of reasoning. Indeed, he insisted that all three were involved at every stage of logic, from the first apprehension of simple concepts, through the formation of propositions and syllogisms to the methodical development of systems of thought (Comenius: 1922, 27 ff). Invention he describes as the "artificial tracking down of the things which are in things", method to the reduction of invented things into their due order and judgement to the constraining of things invented and disposed by logical bonds. Echoing Alsted he held that method had to have the "reason of a circle", unfolding everything which is enfolded in the essence of things themselves. At the same time he was clear that this logical circle of invention, method and judgement itself reflected a Trinitarian pattern, comparing it to Augustine's famous triad of number, measure and weight. For logic always entails a flow from invention into method and from both into judgement, mirroring implicitly the intra-Trinitarian dynamic (Comenius: 1922, 27–32; cf. Alsted: 1616, 4–8).[48] Once again what Keckermann was gesturing towards becomes fulfilled in Comenius.

Invoking Augustine, Comenius therefore held that "thoughts are nothing but the numbering, measuring and weighing of things and logic nothing but the numbering, measuring and weighing of thoughts". In these terms logic is simply "mathesis applied to thoughts" (Comenius: 1922, 27–29; cf. Burton: 2019, 439). We have mentioned above Comenius' quest for a mathematical theology and this was itself but part of a wider quest for what he called a "universal mathesis". However, while the term itself is reminiscent of Descartes, and anticipates Leibniz, it is in fact Alsted whom he cites in support of this "apodictic method" of philosophy. According to Comenius the aim of this is to secure all truth on the basis of self-evident logical and metaphysical axioms, giving all of philosophy and theology the certainty of mathematics. Logic, as a mathesis of thought, is thus derivative of and flows out of metaphysics, as the mathesis of things.[49] This is

48 Comenius: 1659a, 40–41 also links the structure of logic to the Trinity. See Burton: 2019, 439 where this discussion is taken from.

49 Comenius: 1645, 69–71 citing Alsted: 1630, I.55–56. For the relation of logic and metaphysics see Comenius: 1922, 17–19.

another reminder of the potent influence of Keckermann and Alsted, with the idea of a mathematical theology clearly recalling Keckermann's own attempt to prove the Trinity.

Yet while Comenius' attempts at a universal mathesis has important connections with the Herborn encyclopaedism, in one respect it is markedly different. For both Keckermann and Alsted, Aristotle's principle of non-contradiction lay at the foundation of their metaphysics and their logic. Indeed, in founding this principle on the nature of being itself Alsted clearly invoked a divine and transcendent ground for its universal applicability (1616, 16; 1630, III.575). For Comenius, as Kuchlbauer has pointed out, this is no longer true. Rather, following Cusa, he held that God's being transcends the law of non-contradiction in a "coincidence of opposites" (Comenius: 1660, 72–74; 1661a, 117–119). While the coincidence of opposites was an important presence in Comenius' thought long before his encounter with Zwicker (cf. Patočka: 2006a, 245–256), it seems to have been following this that it first became a major methodological theme in his thought. For Comenius the aim of the pansophia was to unite all things in the Triune God. In his later writings the paradigm for this becomes the coincidence of opposites, supremely as this is realised in Christ (Comenius: 1645, 15–16, 80–81, 127–129; 1966a, II.482).

Here once again we see how his (re)discovery of Cusa during his Polish sojourn initiated a deep and lasting transformation of his thought. Yet it is also apparent that this transformation could not have happened without the methodological template of Ramism and the Trinitarian logic and metaphysics of Lullism. Moreover, despite Keckermann's own attacks on both these movements, evidence has emerged which suggests that he himself, together with Alsted, had a shaping influence on Comenius' Trinitarian method. Yet in the case of both Keckermann and Comenius we also see the influence of external factors, challenging and reshaping their own diverse, intellectual inheritances. This leads us to suggest that ultimately Comenius' efforts at Leszno to refute the Polish Socinians may well have been as significant for the evolution of universal method as Keckermann's earlier attempts to revive the flagging Reformed community in Danzig. Once again events on the margin may be seen to have impacted the very heart of European intellectual and theological culture.

Bibliography

AERTSEN, JAN (2012), Medieval Philosophy as Transcendental Thought: From Philip the Chancellor (ca. 1225) to Francisco Suárez, Leiden: Brill.

ALSTED, JOHANN HEINRICH (1609), Clavis Artis Lullianae et Verae Logices Duos in Libellos Tributa, Strasbourg: Lazarus Zetzner.

- (1630), Encyclopaedia Septem Tomis Distincta, Herborn.
- (1616), Metaphysica Tribus Libris Tractata, Herborn.
- (1610), Panacea Philosophica; id est, Facilis, Nova et Accurata Methodus Docendi et Discendi Universam Encyclopaediam, Herborn.

AQUINAS, THOMAS (1964–1976), Summa Theologiae, Blackfriars English Translation, 60 vols., London/New York: McGraw Hill.

AMES, WILLIAM (1646), "Disputatio Theologica adversus Metaphysicam", in: William Ames, Philosophemata, Cambridge: Roger Daniel, 43–58.

BEUERHAUS, FRIEDRICH (1582), De P. Rami Dialecticae Praecipuis Capitibus Disputationes Scholasticae, London: Henry Binneman.

BIETENHOLZ, PETER (1997), Daniel Zwicker, 1612–1678: Peace, Tolerance and God the One and Only, Florence: L.S. Olschki.

BORAN, ELIZABETHANNE (2001), Ramism in Trinity College, Dublin, in the Early Seventeenth Century, in: Mordechai Feingold/Joseph Freedman/Wolfgang Rother (eds.), The Influence of Petrus Ramus: Studies in Sixteenth- and Seventeenth-Century Philosophy and Sciences, Basel: Schwabe, 177–99.

BRUYÈRE, NELLY (1984), Méthode et Dialectique dans l'Oeuvre de la Ramée: Renaissance et Age Classique, Paris: Vrin.

BRYĆKO, DARIUSZ (2013), The Danzig Academic Gymnasium in Seventeenth-Century Poland, in: Jordan Ballor/David Sytsma/Jason Zuidema (eds.), Church and School in Early Modern Protestantism: Studies in Honor of Richard A. Muller on the Maturation of a Theological Tradition, Leiden: Brill, 339–46.

BURTON, SIMON J.G. (2012), The Hallowing of Logic: The Trinitarian Method of Richard Baxter's Methodus Theologiae, Leiden: Brill.

- (2019), "Squaring the Circle": Cusan Metaphysics and the Pansophic Vision of Jan Amos Comenius, in: Simon J. G. Burton/Joshua Hollmann/Eric M. Parker (eds.), Nicholas of Cusa and the Making of the Early Modern World, Leiden: Brill, 417–449.

CAMPI, EMIDIO (2014), Jan Amos Comenius and the Protestant Theology of his Time, in: Emidio Campi, Shifting Patterns of Reformed Tradition, Göttingen: Vandenhoeck & Ruprecht, 259–284.

COMENIUS, JAN AMOS (1659a), De Christianorum Uno Deo, Patre, Filio, Spiritu Sancto, Amsterdam: Johannes Janssonius.

- (1660), De Irenico Irenicorum. Hoc est Conditionibus Pacis a Socini Secta Reliquo Christiano Orbi Oblatis, ad Omnes Christianos Facta Admonitio, Amsterdam: Henricus Betkius.
- (1661a), De Iterato Socinano Irenico Iterata ad Christianos Admonitio. Amsterdam.
- (1659b), De Quaestione Utrum Dominus Jesus Propria Virtute a Mortuis Resurrexit, ad M. Scheffer Responsum, Amsterdam: Johannes Janssonius.

- (1974a), Ianua Rerum Reserata, in: Dílo Jana Amose Komenského: Johannis Amos Comenii Opera Omnia: Vol. 18, ed. Jiří Beneš et al., Prague: Academia.
- (1966a), Lexikon Reale Pansophicon, in: De Rerum Humanarum Emendatione Catholica Consultatio: Editio Princeps: Vol. 2, ed. Otokar Chlup et al., Prague: Academia.
- (1661b), Oculus Fidei. Theologia naturalis, sive Liber Creaturarum, Amsterdam.
- (1987), Panaugia or Universal Light: Being Part Two of his Universal Deliberation on the Reform of Human Affairs, trans. A.M.O. Dobbie, Shipston-on-Stour: Peter Drinkwater.
- (1989), Panglottia or Universal Language: Being Part Five of his Universal Deliberation on the Reform of Human Affairs, trans. A.M.O. Dobbie, Shipston-on-Stour: Peter Drinkwater.
- (1966b), Pansophia, in: De Rerum Humanarum Emendatione Catholica Consultatio: Editio Princeps: Vol. 1, ed. Otokar Chlup et al., Prague: Academia.
- (1974b), Pansophiae Christianae Liber III, in: Dílo Jana Amose Komenského: Johannis Amos Comenii Opera Omnia: Vol. 14, ed. Jiří Beneš et al., Prague: Academia.
- (1645), Pansophiae Diatyposis, Ichnographica et Orthographica Delineatione, Amsterdam: Ludovicus Elzeverius.
- (1644), Pansophiae Prodromus, Leiden: Davidis Lopez de Haro.
- (1974c), Pansophiae Totius Seminarium, in: Dílo Jana Amose Komenského: Johannis Amos Comenii Opera Omnia: Vol. 14, ed. Jiří Beneš et al., Prague: Academia.
- (1633), Physicae ad Lumen Divinum Reformatae Synopsis, Leipzig: Gotofredus Grossi.
- (1974d), Primam Philosphiam, in: Dílo Jana Amose Komenského: Johannis Amos Comenii Opera Omnia: Vol. 18, ed. Jiří Beneš et al., Prague: Academia.
- (1642), Reformation of Schooles, London.
- (1907), The Great Didactic of Jan Amos Comenius, tr. M.W. Keatinge, London: Adam and Charles Black.
- (1922), Triertium Catholicum, ed. George Klima/L. Zelenka Lerando, Prague: Sokol-Packard.

Elders, Leo (1993), The Metaphysics of Being of St. Thomas Aquinas in a Historical Perspective, Leiden: Brill.

Facca, Danilo (2005), Bartłomiej Keckermann i filozofia, Warsaw: PAN.

Feingold, Mordechai/Joseph Freedman/Wolfgang Rother (eds.) (2001), The Influence of Petrus Ramus: Studies in Sixteenth- and Seventeenth-Century Philosophy and Sciences, Basel: Schwabe.

Floss, Pavel (1973), Cusanus und Comenius, Mitteilungen und Forschungsbeiträge der Cusanus-Gesellschaft 10, 172–190.

Franckenberger, Andreas (2008), Constitutio Nova Gymnasii Dantiscani (1568), in: Lech Mokrzecki (ed.), Gdańskie Gimnazjum Akademickie: Tom. II Wybór źródeł z XVI i XVII wieku, Gdańsk: Wydawnictwo Uniwersytetu Gdańskiego, 21–47.

Freedman, Joseph (1999), The Career and Writings of Bartholomew Keckermann (d. 1609), in: Joseph Freedman, Philosophy and the Arts in Central Europe, 1500–1700: Teaching and Texts at Schools and Universities, Aldershot: Ashgate, 306–333.

Gilbert, Neal (1960), Renaissance Concepts of Method, New York: Columbia University Press.

Goclenius, Rudolph (1599), Analyses in Exercitationes Aliquot Julii Caesaris Scaligeri De Subtilitate, Marburg.

GOUDRIAAN, AZA (2013), Theology and Philosophy, in: Herman Selderhuis (ed.), A Companion to Reformed Orthodoxy, Leiden: Brill, 27–64.

HOTSON, HOWARD (2007), Commonplace Learning: Ramism and its German Ramifications, 1543–1630, Oxford: Oxford University Press.

- (2005), The Instauration of the Image of God in Man: Humanist Anthropology, Encyclopaedic Pedagogy, Baconianism and Universal Reform, in: Margaret Pelling/Scott Mandelbrote (eds.), The Practice of Reform in Health, Medicine and Science, 1500–2000: Essays for Charles Webster, Aldershot: Ashgate, 1–21.
- (2000), Johann Heinrich Alsted 1588–1638: Between Renaissance, Reformation and Universal Reform, Oxford: Oxford University Press.
- (2011), The Ramist Roots of Comenian Pansophia, in: Steven Reid/Emma Wilson (eds.), Ramus, Pedagogy and the Liberal Arts: Ramism in Britain and the Wider World, Aldershot: Ashgate, 227–52.

JENSEN, KRISTIAN (1980), Rhetorical Philosophy and Philosophical Grammar: Julius Caesar Scaliger's Theory of Language, Munich: Fink.

JOHNSTON, MARK (1987), The Spiritual Logic of Ramon Llull, Oxford: Oxford University Press.

KECKERMANN, BARTHOLOMÄUS (1608), Gymnasium Logicum; id est, De Usu et Exercitatione Logicae Artis Absolutiori et Pleniori Libri III, Hanover.

- (1604), Praecognita Logica, Hanover.
- (1612), Praecognitorum Philosophicorum Libri Duo, Hanover.
- (1611), Scientiae Metaphysicae Compendiosum Systema, Hanover.
- (1610a), Systema Ethicae, Hanover.
- (1603), Systema Logicae Tribus Libris Adornatum, 2nd edition, Hanover.
- (1610b), Systema S.S. Theologiae Tribus Libris Adornatum, Hanover.

KNUDSEN, CHRISTIAN (1982), Intentions and Impositions, in: Norman Kretzmann/Anthony Kenny/Jan Pinborg (eds.), Cambridge History of Later Medieval Philosophy, Cambridge: Cambridge University Press, 479–495.

KUCHLBAUER, SIMON (2011), Johann Amos Comenius' antisozinianische Schriften: Entwurf eines integrativen Konzepts von Aufklärung, Dresden: Thelem.

MAŁŁEK, JANUSZ (2013), The Reformation in Poland and Prussia in the Sixteenth Century: Similarities and Differences, in: Opera Selecta Vol. II: Poland and Prussia in the Baltic Area from the Sixteenth to the Eighteenth Century, Toruń: Wydawnictwo Naukowe Uniwersytetu Mikołaja Kopernika, 179–190.

MCKIM, DONALD (1987), Ramism in William Perkins' Theology, New York: P. Lang.

MILLER, CLYDE LEE (2003), Reading Cusanus: Metaphor and Dialectic in a Conjectural Universe, Washington, D.C.: Catholic University of America Press.

MILLER, PERRY (1954), The New England Mind: The Seventeenth Century, Cambridge, MA: Harvard University Press.

MULLER, RICHARD (2006), Post-Reformation Reformed Dogmatics: The Rise and Development of Reformed Orthodoxy, ca. 1520 to ca. 1725, 4 vols., 2nd edition, Grand Rapids, MI: Baker Academic.

- (1984), *Vera Philosophia cum sacra Theologia nusquam pugnat:* Keckermann on Philosophy, Theology and the Problem of Double Truth, Sixteenth Century Journal 15, 343–365.

Müller, Michael (1997), Zweite Reformation und städtische Autonomie im Königlichen Preussen: Danzig, Elbing und Thorn in der Epoche der Konfessionalisierung (1557–1660), Berlin: Akademie Verlag.

Murphy, Daniel (1995), Comenius: A Critical Reassessment of his Life and Work, Dublin: Irish Academic Press.

Ong, Walter (2004), Ramus, Method and the Decay of Dialogue: From the Art of Discourse to the Art of Reason, Chicago, IL: University of Chicago Press.

Patočka, Jan (2006a), *Centrum Securitatis* und Cusanus, in: Jan Patočka, Andere Wege in die Moderne: Studien zur europäischen Ideengeschichte von der Renaissance bis zur Romantik, ed. Ludger Hagedorn, Würzburg: Königshausen & Neumann, 245–256.

– (2006b), Comenius und Cusanus, in: Jan Patočka, Andere Wege in die Moderne: Studien zur europäischen Ideengeschichte von der Renaissance bis zur Romantik, ed. Ludger Hagedorn, Würzburg: Königshausen & Neumann, 237–43.

– (2003), Transcendentalia a Kategorie, in: Jan Patočka, Sebrané spisy Jana Patočky: Komeniologicke Studie III, ed. Věra Schifferová, Prague: Oikumene, 232–242.

Piscator, Johannes (1582), Animadversiones Ioan. Piscatoris Arg. in Dialecticam P. Rami, Frankfurt.

– (1585), Exercitationum Logicarum Libri II, Frankfurt.

Polanus, Amandus (1605), Syntagma Logicum Aristotelico-Ramaeum ad Usum Imprimis Theologicum Accommodatum, Basel: Conradus Waldkirch.

Raffaelli, Matteo (2009), Macht, Weisheit, Liebe: Campanella und Comenius als Vordenker einer friedvoll globalisierten Weltgemeinschaft, Frankfurt am Main: Lang.

Ramus, Petrus (1578), Scholae in Liberales Artes, Basel: Eusebius Episcopius.

Reid, Steven/Emma Wilson (eds.) (2011), Ramus, Pedagogy and the Liberal Arts: Ramism in Britain and the Wider World, Aldershot: Ashgate.

Richardson, Alexander (1657), The Logicians School-Master: Or, A Comment upon Ramus Logick, London: Gartrude Dawson.

Scaliger, Julius Caesar (1597), De Causis Linguae Latinae Libri XIII, Geneva: Sanctiandrei.

Schadel, Erwin (1989), Einleitung, in: Jan Amos Comenius, Die Pforte der Dinge: Ianua Rerum, ed. Erwin Schadel, Hamburg: Meiner, i–cvi.

Scherbaum, Matthias (2008), Der Metaphysikbegriff des Johann Amos Comenius: Das Projekt der Pansophie im Spannungsbogen von "Realismus", Heilsgeschichte und Pan-Paideia, Oberhaid: Utopica.

Sprunger, Keith (1966), Ames, Ramus and the Method of Puritan Theology, Harvard Theological Review 59, 133–151.

Ursinus, Zacharias (1570), Catechesis Religionis Christianae quae traditur in Ecclesiis et Scholis Palatinus, Heidelberg.

II. Clandestine Reformation

Christopher Matthews

A Reformed Hiding Place in Sixteenth-Century Seville

The Significance of the Monastery of St. Isidore

1. Introduction

The Monastery of St. Isidore del Campo still stands today in the town of Santiponce in the province of Seville. In the sixteenth-century it served as a hiding place for theological reflection during the brief Spanish Reformation. Its fortified walls protected forbidden Reformation literature and provided a secure location to begin the translation of the Bible into the Spanish language as spoken in the sixteenth century. To understand the role of this monastery as a nucleus for the minority Spanish Reformation is to trace a little-known legacy of truth seekers and to follow the rugged bravery of several Spanish monks under relentless pursuit across sixteenth-century Europe by the kings of Spain.

2. Isidore of Seville, the Namesake

The monastery was named after a native scholar and Archbishop, Isidore of Seville (556–636), who had the reputation for being an early reformer of the Church and society in Spain. He founded schools and published books on theology, science, law and history. Isidore created the first public lending libraries in Europe and composed the first encyclopaedia in history (Viñayo: 2007, 16–20).

When he was thirty years old, Isidore became the new abbot of a monastery in Seville upon the promotion of his brother Leandro to Archbishop. Known for his kindness and his just treatment of others, Isidore preferred to show love rather than force. However, as he wrote later, his rule as abbot included strict adherence to the norms of a monastery, since it had become a matter of prestige in his days to be a monk. While living profligate lifestyles, some roving monks slipped from monastery to monastery and avoided supervision. They grew their hair and beards to appear like prophets, recounted long stories to impress their hearers and began to sell “relics” or supposed bones of saints from history. Isidore saw them as a menace to the monasteries and to society at large and determined to put a stop to them. He initiated a reformation of the monastery, simplifying, deleting and reducing the rule of order to a reasonable size and thus preventing the roving monks from gaining ground under cover of the previous voluminous rules that often contradicted themselves (Pérez de Urbel: 1995, 17–54).

In 601, when around 45 years old, Isidore became the Bishop of Seville upon the death of his brother Leandro. He had by this time written many books on theology, natural science and law, with the purpose of lifting Spain out of ignorance, particularly the clergy. His goal was to improve the culture and morals of his fellow citizens in Seville. Isidore has been considered the creator and founder of seminaries in Seville to train future clergy (Viñayo: 2007, 16–18). When he presided over the Fourth Council of Toledo in 633, Isidore sent orders to all his bishops to create additional seminaries throughout the diocese of southwestern Spain in order to train the leadership in the Scriptures and to teach Greek and Hebrew (Respaldiza: 2002, 170). At the same Council, Isidore established sensible laws, devised useful institutions and set up a unified liturgy of the Church that has lasted until today. He also wrote guidelines for the humane treatment of Jewish people.

Upon his death Isidore received the title of the last Church Father of the West. After the invasion of the Moors from North Africa in 711, Isidore’s remains were discovered four centuries later in 1063 at the site of one of his seminaries to the north of Seville in Campos de Talca where an ancient church building still stood. After negotiations with the Moors in 1089 King Ferdinand I had the casket transferred to his capital city of Leon in northern Spain (Viñayo: 2007, 19–20).

3. The Monastery of St. Isidore in the Middle Ages

3.1 Alfonso Pérez de Guzmán, the Founder

Born in 1256 as the illegitimate son of a nobleman in León during the reign of King Alfonso X the Wise, Alfonso Pérez de Guzmán was twenty years old when he enlisted in the Reconquista of southern Spain from the Moorish sultans as a way to prove his nobility in battle (González: 2002, 33). Having been raised in León, Guzmán was a devoted follower of Isidore, whose bones lay reposing in the basilica nearby, and whose inspiration led northern troops to victory in battles against the Moors in the south.

Guzmán came to own almost half the province of Cádiz and with the protection of his extensive army was able to repopulate the area with Spaniards. Fernando IV, son of Sancho IV, granted him even more land in 1297 including

Sanlúcar de Barrameda (Segura: 2009, 1–21). Guzmán had a home in central Seville, built a palace in Olivares and petitioned both King and Pope for the privilege of founding a monastery. Guzmán wanted his final resting place to be in the countryside town called Campos of Talca (old Seville, as well as the little villa of Santiponce), so he purchased this property from Queen Maria de Molina around 1295. He wished to have his monastery built on the site where Isidore had been buried and where an ancient little seminary had once stood (González: 2002, 36–39). And as a devoted follower of Isidore, Guzmán named the monastery in his honour. The King awarded him patronage for a monastery in October of 1298 and in 1301 the Pope granted him Cistercian monks from San Pedro de Gumiel de Hizán in Burgos to inhabit the future monastery.

3.2 Construction of the Monastery as a Fortress

The original building began in 1297 and was finished in 1301 (Respaldiza: 2002, 169). It consisted of a small chapel, a cloister, and dormitory rooms for forty Cistercian monks of whom twenty were priests (González: 2002, 40). It was constructed in the frontier style of a fortified monastery for protection against raids from the *Banu Marin* Berber dynasty that arose in North Africa after the fall of the Almohad rulers of southern Spain. Originally from Algeria, these Berber warriors conquered Fez in 1248 and declared *jihad* on southern Spain, sailing up the Guadalquivir River in 1285 to the very walls of Seville after burning fields and killing 500 local people who were gathering the harvest. They seized another 150 women and 400 men as slaves for North Africa. Guzmán participated later in the battle to defend Tarifa in 1294, then in the failed siege of Algeciras and finally in the successful conquest of Gibraltar, Estepona and Jimena in early September of 1309. He died later that month after Fernando IV sent him to lay siege to Gauzín in the high mountains near Ronda (Cómez: 2002, 151). The bodies of Guzmán and his wife were buried in the walls of the main chapel and a rule was made that no other relative could be buried closer to the altar than they were. As a condition for living in the monastery, the monks committed to praying ten masses per day (one of them being sung) for the souls of Guzmán and his wife (González: 2002, 29. Segura: 2009, 40).

The Cistercian monks, under Benedictine rule, lived in the building and worked the local fields and olive groves to support themselves for the next ninety years. In 1397, however, the General Chapter of Citeaux silenced Abbot Garcia of the St. Isidore Monastery because he had begun to act in an "uncontrollably reformed" manner. The Guzman heirs began looking for a different order of monks for their monastery (Kinder: 1975, 11).

Founded in 1373, the Spanish chapter of the Hieronymites under the Augustinian rule followed St. Jerome (347 to 420 AD), the original translator of the Bible into Latin. Their abbot instructed them to be above all, humble, hardworking, studious in the classics, and devoted to library research and translation. By 1389, as persecution of Jewish people began in Spain, the Hieronymites received many Jews newly converted to the Roman Catholic faith into their order. Subsequently they became prosperous and enjoyed favour with the Spanish kings. Over time, their emphasis shifted to the emotional rather than intellectual side of monastic living. Consequently, in 1428, Fray Lope de Olmedo instituted a reform to return the various Hieronymite monasteries in southern Spain to the original ideals of their order (in terms of poverty, hard work, abstention from eating meat and wearing cape and cowl). One year later, Count Enrique de Guzmán petitioned Pope Martin V for a change in monastic orders, so the Pope delivered the Monastery of St. Isidore in 1431 to the care of Fray Lope de Olmedo who set up his residence there and made it the head of the seven monasteries of his order (Sánchez: 2002, 52–57). No women were allowed within the walls and no linen could be worn. Nevertheless, the monks were allowed to leave freely and frequently went to Seville as needed (Kinder: 1975, 11).

At the St. Isidore Monastery, the new monks proved to be studious and industrious. Soon the monastery bustled with harvests of olives, oranges and other crops. The Guzmán family built a dairy barn and horse stables to handle the growing livestock. Over time, the Hieronymites opened a herbal pharmacy in the monastery and a private theological study library. Monks joining the order who had less education typically worked in the fields and slept in large common rooms, while the university and seminary educated monks used private cells with small personal libraries. The Guzmán family added a large dormitory cloister in order to hold more monks as the community thrived (Respaldiza: 2002, 180–185).

The monastery had been founded in the tradition of the noted scholar from Seville who effectively reformed the Church and society of his day, and who established new theological seminaries for the study of Greek and Hebrew. It was also built as a strong and secure fortress, able to resist attack. The later recruitment of Hieronymite monks, who were well-known as followers of the Bible translator St. Jerome, put the remaining elements one hundred years before the birth of the sixteenth-century Spanish reformation of the Church in this context of majority/minority dialectics.

4. The Reformation in Seville

As remembered by the monks of St. Isidore, it was around 1540 that a Spanish nobleman, Don Rodrigo de Váler first influenced Juan Gil (also known as Dr. Egidio), a Canon of the Cathedral (and the main preaching priest since 1537) towards a profound knowledge of the Gospel in private discussion, as well as by his bold preaching in the streets of Seville (Kinder: 1975, 6–7). Váler also privately taught influential members of the Cathedral clergy, including Pedro Diaz (who later accused Canon Juan Gil of heresy), leading a Bible study on the epistle of Paul of Tarsus to the Romans, much to the gratitude of these priests (González: 2008, 287). A follower of Dr. Egidio, García Arias Blanco from Baeza, known as Maestro Blanco, served as one of lecturers in the St. Isidore Monastery. Arias was one of the first to teach the St. Isidore monks Reformation doctrine and he encouraged them to pray sincerely and to study the Scriptures (García: 2002, 66–67; Kinder: 1975, 12). The St. Isidore monks engaged in dialogue about these teachings with curious nobility from Seville, such as Juan Ponce de León and the family of María de Bohórques (García: 2002, 68).

By the 1550s, the monks grew aware of theological changes taking place across northern Europe through dialogue with the new Canon of the great Cathedral of Seville, Dr. Constantino de la Fuente (Guillén: 2002, 94). After careful investigation of the works of Luther and other Reformers at some point prior to his arrival in Seville in the early 1540s, Dr. Constantino had become a Reformed believer. In 1543 Dr. Constantino published in Seville his book *Summa de Doctrina Christiana*, which subsequently went through five editions. Along with two other Reformed believers, Dr. Egidio and Dr. Francisco Vargas, Professor of the Holy Scriptures in the University, Dr. Constantino led "the little church", an underground Protestant assembly in Seville during the 1540s with members possibly numbering up to eight hundred citizens (García: 2002, 61–63). Previously, in 1548, the Emperor Charles V had requested Dr. Constantino to accompany his son, Philip, the future King of Spain, to the Netherlands. From 1549 onwards, Dr. Constantino served as the personal chaplain and confessor for Charles V until finally returning to Seville in 1553. He was voted unanimously to succeed Dr. Egidio as Canon and official preacher of the Cathedral in 1557 (Kinder: 1975, 1, 6–8).[1]

One of the leading members of the "little church" in Seville was an attorney and priest of San Vicente parish named Francisco Zafra (M'Crie: 1829, 215–217).

1 All three of these men had studied together along with Juan de Valdés at the University of Alcalá de Henares, which had been founded in 1508 to improve the education of the clergy by Don Francisco Jiménez Cisneros, the same Cardinal who commissioned the Complutensian Polyglot Version of the Bible.

María Gómez, a widow who zealously attended the little church, was lodged in the Zafra home after she fell into a fit of madness one day in 1555. She went to the offices of the Holy Inquisition in the castle of St. George in Triana and betrayed the names of more than 300 members of the little church. Zafra fortunately appeared at the castle of the Inquisition in time to collect the disturbed woman and dissimulate her claims, so the accusation was dismissed (González: 2008, 169–171). The monks of St. Isidore secretly attended meetings of the "little church" in Seville and reflected on the new theology safely behind the walls of their monastery.

4.1 Antonio Del Corro and Theological Reflection

An example of this theological reflection can be seen in a young monk from San Isidore named Antonio Del Corro who used to discuss with Dr. Egidio the book of Romans and the doctrine of justification by faith in Christ alone. Corro had been born in 1527 in Seville and joined the San Isidore convent in 1547. After Dr. Egidio was accused of heresy and faced trial by the Inquisition in 1550, Corro was able to obtain information on the proceedings through his father or uncle who served as an Inquisitor.[2] Soon after Dr. Egidio was released from the Inquisition castle in 1553, Corro interviewed his mentor (Kinder: 1975: 12) and meanwhile obtained forbidden books by Luther, Melanchthon and Bullinger from his relative in the Inquisition to compare with what he had heard.[3] He pored over these books with his good friend Casiodoro de Reina, one of the brightest theologians in the monastery. Both men embraced the Reform before later fleeing from Seville to Geneva in 1557 with ten of their fellow monks.

After his departure, Corro would continue to discuss theology via correspondence from Geneva with the subsequent preacher in the "little church" in Seville, the physician Dr. Cristóbal Losada, who had also been a student of Dr. Egidio (García: 2002, 68–70. Kinder: 1975, 10). Corro moved briefly to Frankfurt to meet Spanish Protestants in a congregation there and attend a book fair to purchase additional Reformation books (where he was spotted by agents of Phillip II). From there he journeyed south to Lausanne for further theological instruction under Theodore de Beza (who later succeeded John Calvin in Geneva). In the spring of 1559, Calvin recommended Corro for a pastoral role in Navarre where he preached and served as rector for various schools in southern France. Upon losing his position as pastor in Bergerac, due to French laws

2 Francisco Ruíz de Pablos, "Introducción" in Del Corro: 2010, 9–11. Corro confirmed this 1554 event of reading these works in a letter to Bullinger from London dated July 7 1574.

3 Francisco Ruíz de Pablos, in Del Corro: 2010, 66–67.

enacted against Protestant churches having foreign pastors, Duchess Renée of Montargis appointed him chaplain for her estate in 1564. Two years later, in 1566, the French Calvinist church in Antwerp called him as their pastor, where he served for a year and left a few months before the invasion by the Duke of Alba in 1567 (M'Crie: 1829, 220). From there Corro crossed to London and attempted to pastor the Spanish-speaking church where his fellow monk Casiodoro de Reina had served from 1560 to 1563. He found the church divided into two factions, one led by the former Prior of San Isidore, Francisco Farias, and worshipping at the Italian Calvinist church; the other attending the French Calvinist church. Corro tried to bring them back together, but suffered attacks for his theological beliefs as he grew less Calvinist and closer to the Church of England in his beliefs. He became a reader at the Inns of Court in London and moved to Oxford to lecture in theology and become a language professor. Corro eventually married, had a daughter and died in London in 1591 (Monjo: 2006, 9–11; Kinder: 1975, 65).

4.2 Early Smuggling of Reformation Literature into the Monastery

With the rise of Phillip II to the throne of Spain in 1556, the new king fully endorsed the growing Counter-Reformation: seeing religious dissenters as political criminals. As an absolutist king, Phillip viewed any sign of division in his kingdom as an invitation to fight to the death. To prevent Spanish university students from exposure to the Reformation in other lands, Phillip cancelled the custom of studying abroad. Despite popular interest among the clergy in having the Bible in the Spanish language, Phillip saw Bible translation as a direct assault on public institutions (Guillén: 2002, 94–95). At that time the Latin Vulgate version alone served as the official text of the medieval Roman Church.

In spite of this danger, a Dominican monk, Domingo de Guzmán, managed to obtain Reformed literature while journeying through Germany and Flanders and may have been one of the first to share them with the Hieronymite monks of St. Isidore (García: 2002, 71). Julian Hernández, a Spanish convert to the Reformation while in Germany, had become a member of the "little church" in Seville and left Spain sometime in the early 1550s and later investigated ways to smuggle in forbidden books in order to speed the Reformation across Spain. The Census of Bibles in Seville, published in 1554, shows a large number of vernacular French Bibles in the city as well as in surrounding municipalities in the province such as Osuna, Jerez de la Frontera and Arcos. Two booksellers and a few monasteries had more than ten French Bibles each, mostly from Lyons (318 copies), Paris (68 copies) and Antwerp (36 copies) where the first translation of the Bible was printed in French in 1528. Julian would later increase this number by smuggling in New Testaments in Spanish printed in Geneva.

4.3 More Reformation Literature for the Monastery

After spending time in Paris and Frankfurt, Julian moved to Geneva where he assisted one of the monks from the St. Isidore monastery, Dr. Juan Pérez de Pineda, in his work of editing key books for printing in Spanish. Born around 1498 or 1500 in Montilla, Cordoba, Pérez appears to have accompanied Charles V in his 1527 sack of Rome as his personal secretary. There he may have met the Valdés twins, Alfonso and Juan (an early Spanish Reformer whose two commentaries Pérez would later edit in Geneva). Upon later joining the St. Isidore Monastery and lecturing in theology in Seville at a parochial school, Pérez fled Spain around 1553 or 1554 to Paris after Dr. Egidio was accused of heresy (Kinder: 1975, 8–9). In 1555, Pérez still lived in Paris but moved to Geneva, where he became a trusted confidant of John Calvin and pastor for the newly formed Spanish Calvinist congregation. In the printing press of Juan Crispin in Geneva, Pérez published his fresh translations from Greek and Hebrew into Spanish of the *New Testament* (1556) and the *Psalms* (1557) – work which he may have begun while a monk at the St. Isidore Monastery near Seville.

With the idea to join Pérez in Geneva, twelve more of the monks fled from St. Isidore Monastery in 1557 and worked their way across northern Spain and southern France to Geneva after a year of travel, though some arrived so late that they found that Pérez had gone to Frankfurt. Antonio Del Corro arrived earliest and found Julian Hernandez with the freshly translated copies of Pérez's *New Testament* and *Psalms* along with the Pérez-sponsored printing of two commentaries of *Romans* and *First Corinthians* written in Spanish by Juan de Valdés. Disguised as a merchant with a mule cart loaded with false-bottomed barrels, Julian completed the long journey from Geneva to Seville in July 1557 and delivered two loads of these books to the Monastery of St. Isidore (García: 2002, 64, 72–74, 76; Kinder: 1975, 13) for safe keeping and subsequent introduction to the city in small quantities (Monjo: 2007, 10–12). Julian also carried a 1557 Spanish translation of the *Imagen del Antechresto* (a pamphlet left behind in Geneva by the Italian Reformer Bernardino Ochino denouncing the Pope as Antichrist) to be delivered to a specific individual in Seville, but Julian erroneously gave it to a cleric with the same name. This man notified the authorities while Julian fled north to the mountains where he was captured near Cazalla on October 7, 1557 (Kinder: 1975, 14). This event caused the Inquisition to inform Phillip II who unleashed a violent storm of pursuit, inquiry and multiple arrests in 1557, including the minority group of monks and the Maestro Blanco of the Monastery of St. Isidore (Kinder: 1975, 9).[4]

4 The Canon, Dr. Constantino, also fell under suspicion in 1558 when the discovery of a secret

5. The Monastery as a Translation Centre

5.1 A Secure Location to Begin the Translation of the Bible into Spanish

As mentioned above, Dr. Juan Pérez de Pineda may have begun his Spanish translation of the New Testament and the Psalms while in Seville, since he published them only a few years after his arrival in Geneva (Nieto: 1997, 441–448). He had spent time in Frankfurt from 1556 to 1558, where he set up a fund in the hands of a merchant, Agustin Legrand, at the French Calvinist church. The idea of the fund was to one day pay for the printing of the entire Bible into Spanish. Pérez returned to Geneva and became a resident in 1558. In Geneva, he published a book warning Phillip II of the dangers of the papacy, along with a translation of Calvin's *Catechism* into Spanish, and he completed the *Epistola Consolatoria* in 1560. This last work was to comfort his fellow monks who along with Julian Hernández lay suffering in the prison of the Inquisition in the Triana section of Seville. Only a year before Calvin died, Pérez moved in 1563 to Blois as a minister in France and along with Antonio del Corro became chaplain to Renée of France in Montargis in early 1565 (Kinder: 1975, 14, 19). Pérez finally returned to Paris where he was in the process of getting his New Testament translation reprinted when he died suddenly in October 1568 (García: 2002, 63, 80; Kinder: 1975, 15).

5.2 Final Translation of the Bible into Spanish

Another of the monks, Casiodoro de Reina, born around 1520 in Montemolín of Seville (now located in the province of Badajoz), began a longer translation. He graduated from the University of Seville, was ordained a priest and took vows as a Hieronymite monk at the Monastery of San Isidore. Reina appears to have been one of the prime catalysts for the "little church" in Seville and especially in the monastery. Under the teachings of García Arias Blanco, Reina persuaded many of the St. Isidore monks to accept Reformed teachings and may have also begun to gather the tools he would need to undertake the translation, particularly a copy of the 1553 *Biblia de Ferrara*, a Jewish translation into Spanish. Feeling threatened by the Spanish Inquisition, Reina fled with eleven other monks to Geneva in the summer of 1557, carrying his parents and sister along with him. Since his fellow monk, Juan Pérez de Pineda was absent in Frankfurt, Reina and his fellow monks from St. Isidore attended the

library disclosed a large number of his documents with affinities to the writings of Luther. He died in prison in Triana two years later.

Italian refugee church in Geneva. He wrote later that while in Geneva he felt more time was spent from the pulpits denouncing the Pope and monks than in showing love, mortification towards sin and edifying the believers (Kinder: 1988, xvii).[5]

Once Pérez finally returned to Geneva in 1558, Reina considered helping him with the Spanish refugee church, but decided instead to move on towards London, shortly after hearing that Elizabeth had become Queen and declared a haven for European Protestants there. Waves of persecuted immigrants made their way to England, as they fled the insecurity of a wandering life on the continent (Kinder: 1988, vii). Pérez flatly disagreed with their leaving, nicknaming Reina the "Moses of the fleeing Spaniards". Reina took his parents and sister, Cipriano de Valera and the former Prior of the St. Isidore Monastery, Francisco Farías along with other monks on the journey to London via Frankfurt, where they probably paid a visit to the French Calvinist church where Pérez had served (Kinder: 1988, viii).[6]

Upon arrival and settling his parents in London, Reina noted that refugee churches for Dutch, French, Italian and Flemish Calvinists had been established in the city before his arrival. These refugee churches reported to the Bishop of London, Edmund Grindal. As the Spanish immigrants had not found a home in any of the refugee churches, although members tended to swap back and forth freely between these foreign churches, in 1559 Reina began thrice weekly conventicles where he preached to the attendees in Spanish. However, without an officially recognised church or legal protection from the Bishop of London, Reina and the Spanish conventicles felt that they were vulnerable to the spies of Philip II in England who might infiltrate a home and accuse them of unofficial teachings. By contrast, if they were located in a public church building, their teaching would be clearly understood as Protestant and accepted. For this reason in 1560 Reina promoted the idea of organising an official Spanish congregation in London, offering himself as pastor. He wrote a Spanish Protestant Confession of Faith, possibly with the assistance of Cipriano de Valera. At first, the foreign pastors opposed the idea and asked to see the Confession of Faith and hear him defend it publicly at a meeting in the French Calvinist church. The *Confessión* did not satisfy the French or the Flemish church leaders for different reasons, although later they appear to have accepted it. Reina then submitted it to the Queen

5 A prominent young noblewoman, Maria de Bohórquez upon examination by the Inquisition mentioned Reina as her mentor in Reformation teachings.

6 Along the way in Strasbourg, officers of the Spanish Inquisition captured his fellow monk Juan de León after discovering his identity. They extradited him to Spain and burned him at the stake in Seville a few years later. To further complicate the journey, agents of Philip II spotted Antonio del Corro at the book fair in Frankfurt but he got away before being arrested (Corro went back to Lausanne, as mentioned above).

for approval through the Bishop of London in 1560. Included was the plea that the new church might not cause any quarrel to take place between the royal houses of England and Spain and even offering to leave England if such might occur (Kinder: 1975, 22).[7]

Royal approval came along with a pension for Reina as pastor of sixty pounds per year. The next year, in 1561, Reina married Anna, daughter of Abraham León of Nivelles (a town located around 88 kilometres south of Antwerp). Upon his marriage to this widow of Dr. Thomas Le Feure, the pension Reina received from the Queen ceased. The Spanish church grew rather quickly due to some membership transfers from the French and Flemish congregations.

The Spanish Ambassador, Don Álvaro de la Quadra, Bishop of Ávila, began to entice the minority Spanish Protestants into the embassy in order to send them swiftly to Spain for prosecution. Mention of this Spanish congregation was passed in notes between the Spanish embassy in London and the court of Philip II. Quadra complained of the protection that the Queen gave to Reina, his parents, and his heretical church members. The Ambassador also intercepted a letter from a Spaniard in Antwerp to Reina in April 1563 which he sent back to the Spanish spymaster in the Netherlands, Alonso del Canto in order to pursue the sender. Reina considered abandoning England after three short years, largely due to being incessantly harassed by spies – Del Canto had even managed to bribe one of Reina's church members, Francisco de Ábrego, to collaborate in doctrinal charges against his pastor. Reina had a reputation as a peaceful man who wished above all to avoid strife in the Church, so rather than provoke a quarrel between church members or governments, Reina chose to leave (Kinder: 1988, xii, xv).

So in September 1563, Reina placed the translation manuscripts in the hands of the Bishop of London and left quickly for Antwerp (Guillén: 2002, 96; Kinder: 1975, 38).[8] His wife, disguised as a sailor, came over later via Flushing and met him in Antwerp (Kinder: 1975, 34). The couple spent some months in hiding with assistance from Marcos Pérez, a prosperous merchant who spoke several languages and was established in many of the financial centres of Europe. Eluding the many spies of the Emperor, the couple finally fled to Frankfurt, arriving around the end of January, 1564.

7 Apparently Spanish Protestants, even in London, could not escape suspicion of holding Anti-Trinitarian doctrine, as had their fellow countryman Miguel Servetus. Reina himself investigated all forms of Protestant thought, from Luther, to Calvin, to Zwingli to Radical writers (in a similar way to Antonio del Corro who had read the many forbidden books provided him by the Inquisition back in Seville). It would appear the St. Isidore monks had inquisitive minds and were unafraid to read from distinct theological perspectives on any point of doctrine.

8 The Spanish King Phillip II soon put a price upon his head in January of 1564 for extradition to Spain.

Reina knew that in Frankfurt, the French Calvinist congregation had been collecting funds to pay for the translation of the entire Bible into Spanish (García: 2002, 77–78).[9] Agents sent from the Bishop of London arrived in Frankfurt shortly after Reina and likely restored the manuscripts to him at this time (Kinder: 1975, 37).[10] From 1564 to 1567, Reina and his wife resided in Frankfurt near her father who had moved there from the Low Countries. Reina kept searching for work as a pastor or as an artisan to allow him some means for completing the translation, but was only allowed to preach on occasion in local German churches due to his Calvinist view of the Eucharist.

Reina received a letter from Antonio del Corro in January of 1564 urging him to complete the translation of the Bible and journeyed to meet with Corro in Bergerac. As mentioned above, in November 1564, when the Duchess Renée of Montargis came through Bergerac, she had chosen to protect Corro by relieving him of his illegal status pastoring a French church as a foreigner and appointing him as her personal chaplain. Renée continued north to Orleans and found Juan Pérez de Pineda also illegally pastoring in Blois and engaged him as chaplain as well. All three former monks reunited as they journeyed north to her castle at Montargis near Fontainebleau. Reina stayed until February of 1565, time enough for the three theologians to discuss the completion of the translation and printing of the entire Bible in Spanish for wide distribution.[11]

Upon returning to Frankfurt, Reina received a call from the French Calvinist church to the south in Strasbourg to become their pastor. While there he concluded the translation of the Bible, but yet needed a year to make corrections and add notes. He received permission to do this work at the University of Strasbourg.

Next, Reina moved in 1567 to Basel, Switzerland, where he entered as a university student and negotiated with authorities to have the Bible printed (this was necessary due to a 1550 city law prohibiting the printing of Bibles in languages other than Latin, Greek, Hebrew and German). In early 1568, the Basel city council finally gave permission to print the Spanish Bible if Reina's notes were omitted. But before the Bibles could be printed, the printer Johan Herbst died. His estate was in debt and so the deposit monies Reina had given him from the

9 Pérez had agents sending large quantities of Bibles, New Testaments and catechisms to Spain (some 30,000 copies of the Institutes by Calvin, translated into Spanish by Cipriano de Valera in 1597). From 1556–1558 Juan Pérez de Pineda had set up a fund for future Bible translation.

10 It is of interest that under the Marian exile, Edmund Grindal had spent several years in Frankfurt and would have likely given Reina the name of a safe house where he could recover his manuscript of the translation.

11 Ruíz de Pablos: 2009, 13; Kinder: 1975, 41. Once again, Reina had as his host Marcos Pérez the merchant who had fled to Basel from Antwerp upon the invasion by the Duke of Alba a year earlier. Reina's wife joined him in Basel and later gave birth to their first son whom they named Marcos.

Frankfurt French refugee church for printing were seized by creditors in the estate settlement procedures.

Fortunately, Thomas Guerin had been subcontracted to complete the work for Reina by Johan Herbst before he died, but Guerin required a guarantee for payment. As new funds came in, the printing was done in sections, taking months at a time to finish. One delay was the proofing of the final section of 2 Corinthians to Revelation, for which Reina needed to review a copy of the New Testament translated by Juan Pérez de Pineda. This text had been in the process of reprinting in Paris in October 1568 when Pérez died suddenly. Pérez left his estate for the publication of the entire Bible into Spanish; however, negotiating the arrival of those funds from Paris proved difficult. Another hold up was the recuperation of the Frankfurt church donations from the estate of Johan Herbst that had been left in deposit for printing. In June of 1569, Reina finally received the proofs for review, but still did not have the funds for printing. A German friend appears to have lent Reina the funds needed to complete the printing. On September 28 1569, Thomas Guerin in Basil printed 2,600 copies of the *Biblia Del Oso* (*the Bible of the Bear*) (Guillén: 2002, 95–99). Guerin had as assistant Samuel Biener who added the frontispiece of a bear trying to rob the bees of their honey as a pun on the name of the city of Bern, which had exiled him, with his own name of Biener (Kinder: 1975, 40–52). The *Biblia Del Oso* translated by Reina over a twelve year period and published in 1569 (with a revision by Cipriano de Valera in 1602) has been the most widely used Bible among Spanish speakers for almost five centuries even to this day.

In 1571, Reina finally celebrated being named a citizen of Frankfurt and two years later published there a commentary on the Greek text of the Gospel of John at the printing press of Nicholas Basse (Reina: 2009, 60). He had at last found an opportunity to publish at least a portion of his notes, which had been previously forbidden by the city council of Basel (Reina: 1988, 368).[12] Reina also republished the *Confessión* in 1577 in order to provide a manual of basic beliefs for the diaspora of Spanish Protestants across Europe.[13] In 1578, Reina traveled to London and presented copies of his commentaries on the Gospel of John with Matthew Chapter 4 and the *Biblia Del Oso* to Edmund Grindal, former Bishop of London and recently appointed Archbishop of Canterbury (Kinder: 1975, 64).[14]

12 Reina dedicated a section of notes included in the Gospel of Matthew chapter 4 in appreciation to Dr. Simon Sultzer and Dr. Ulrich Essich, his theology professors at the University of Basel.

13 Kinder: 1988, xiv. It is interesting that Reina had the foresight to provide a Bible and a Confession of Faith for future ministry to minority Spanish Protestant refugees across the continent.

14 Matthew 4 can be found in the Lambeth Palace Library and in Sidney Sussex College, Cambridge. The Bible dedicated to Grindal is located in Queen's College Library, Oxford.

The rest of Reina's life was dedicated to writing, pastoral work, trading in books and silk, until he died in March 1594 in Frankfurt (Kinder: 1975, 67–80).

6. Final Days of the Spanish Reformation in Seville

Life was hard for the remaining monks who stayed behind in Seville. Three of them from St. Isidore were arrested for heresy in November 1557 and another nine in the *Autos de Fe* Inquisition trials of 1559 and 1560. Twelve more were condemned in 1562, bringing the total of those condemned and burnt in effigy to more than half of the inhabitants of St. Isidore del Campo (Garcia: 2002, 74–75). The minority movement had been effectively halted.

The monastery lay empty for seven years after these events until another group of Hieronymite monks began to serve there quietly from 1567 until 1835, when it was appropriated for government use and turned into a women's prison. In 1881, the historical core was returned to the heirs of the Guzmán family (Rodríguez: 2002, 206) and the rest was purchased by a Scottish malt company to produce beer, most likely due to the abundance of natural springs on the property. From 1956 to 1978 the last of the Hieronymite order of monks returned to serve in the monastery.

Since 1988, most of the monastery has been unused and empty. 430 years ago, in 1558, a mere three months before the defeat of the Spanish armada, Cipriano de Valera, a former monk from St. Isidore Monastery who was living in London wrote: "This day let us expect with patience, if God one day shows mercy to Seville, it will be right that this Monastery of St. Isidore be converted to a university where theology may be chiefly professed. The rents of this monastery, which be great, suffice, with surplus to maintain the said university … Such great and greater things than these has the Lord in our time brought to pass" (Valera: 1588, 256.).[15]

This statement confirms that as the monks laboured on the translation of the Bible into Spanish, penned apologetic works and composed theological commentaries, some of them longed to see the Monastery of St. Isidore del Campo in Santiponce, Seville finally restored once more as a secure place for theological learning, no longer a hiding place for smuggled literature but serving as a gathering place for the minority Spanish reformation once more.

Many factors would have to take place for this longing to be fulfilled, but if it became a reality in these times Spain and all Spanish-speaking people around the world would greatly benefit. Greater things than these have come to pass in our time.

15 Translation by the researcher.

Bibliography

CÓMEZ RAMOS, RAFAEL (2002), La Arquitectura Sevillena en Tiempos de Guzmán el Bueno, in: Actas Simposio San Isidore del Campo 1301–2002, Seville: Junta de Andalucía, Consejería de Cultura, 149–167.

DEL CORRO, ANTONIO (2006), Carta a Felipe II, Obras de los Reformadores Españoles del Siglo XVI, Seville: Editorial MAD.

– (2010), Comentario Dialogado de la Carta a los Romanos, Obras de los Reformadores Españoles del Siglo XVI, Seville: Editorial MAD.

GARCIA PINILLA, IGNACIO (2002), El Foco Reformador de San Isidore del Campo, in: Actas Simposio San Isidore del Campo 1301–2002, Seville: Junta de Andalucía, Consejería de Cultura, 61–91.

GONZÁLEZ JIMÉNEZ, MANUEL (2002), Don Alonso Pérez de Guzmán, Fundador del Monasterio de San Isidore del Campo, en su Tiempo, in: Actas Simposio San Isidore del Campo 1301–2002, Seville: Junta de Andalucía, Consejería de Cultura, 29–42.

GONZÁLEZ MONTES, REINALDO (2008), Artes de la Santa Inquisición Española, Obras de los Reformadores Españoles del Siglo XVI, Seville: Editorial MAD.

GUILLÉN TORRALBA, JUAN (2002), La Biblia del Oso, in: Actas Simposio San Isidore del Campo 1301–2002, Seville: Junta de Andalucía, Consejería de Cultura, 93–106.

KINDER, ARTHUR GORDON (1975), Casiodoro de Reina, Spanish Reformer of the Sixteenth Century, London: Tamesis Books Limited.

– (ed.) (1988), The Spanish Protestant Confession of Faith [London, 1560/1561], Exeter: University of Exeter.

LOZANO SEBASTIÁN, FRANCISCO-JAVIER (1982), San Isidore y la Filosofía Clásica, León: Isidoriana Editorial.

M'CRIE, THOMAS (1829), History of the Progress and Suppression of the Reformation in Spain in the Sixteenth Century, Edinburgh: William Blackwood.

NIETO, JOSÉ C. (1997), El Renacimiento y la otra España, Geneva: Librairie Droz.

PÉREZ DE PINEDA, JUAN (2007), Epístola Consolatoria, Obras de los Reformadores Españoles del Siglo XVI, Alcalá de Guadaira, Seville: Editorial MAD.

PÉREZ DE URBEL, FRAY JUSTO (1995), San Isidore de Seville: Su Vida, Su Obra, y su Tiempo, León: Editorial Labor.

REINA, CASIODORO DE (2009), Comentario al Evangelio de Juan, Obras de los Reformadores Españoles del Siglo XVI, ed. Francisco Ruíz de Pablos, Seville: Editorial MAD.

– (1988), Confessión de Fe Christiana, in: Arthur Gordon Kinder (ed.), The Spanish Protestant Confession of Faith (London, 1560/1561), Exeter: Short Run Press Limited.

RESPALDIZA LAMA, PEDRO JOSÉ (2002), La Conformación del Monasterio de San Isidore del Campo, in: Actas Simposio San Isidore del Campo 1301–2002, Seville: Junta de Andalucía, Consejería de Cultura, 169–188.

RODRIGUEZ HIDALGO, JOSÉ MANUEL (2002), El Monasterio de San Isidore del Campo y las Ruinas de Itálica, in: Actas Simposio San Isidore del Campo 1301–2002, Seville: Junta de Andalucía, Consejería de Cultura, 189–212.

Ruíz de Pablos, Francisco (2009), Introducción, in: Casiodoro de Reina, Comentario al Evangelio de Juan, Obras de los Reformadores Españoles del Siglo XVI, ed. Francisco Ruíz de Pablos, Seville: Editorial MAD.

Sánchez Herrero, José (2002), Los Jerónimos. Desde su Fundación hacía 1366 a la Congregación de la Observancia de la Orden de los Jerónimos "Isidros" Andaluces de Fray Lope de Olmedo, hacía 1428, in: Actas Simposio San Isidore del Campo 1301–2002, Seville: Junta de Andalucía, Consejería de Cultura, 43–59.

Segura González, Wenceslao (2009), Guzmán el Bueno y la Defensa de Tarifa, Tarifa: Asociación Tarifeña de Defensa de Patrimonio Cultural Mellaria.

Valera, Cipriano de (1588), Dos Tratados: Del Papa i de la Misa, London: Arnold Hatfield House.

Viñayo González, Antonio (2007), San Isidore de Seville: De Los Oficios Eclesiásticos, León: Editorial Isidoriana.

José Moreno Berrocal

Sola Scriptura

The Rationale behind the Early Protestant Translations of the Spanish Bible

1. Introduction

One of the main features of the sixteenth-century Protestant Reformation was *Sola Scriptura,* the belief that the Bible is, according to its own testimony, the supreme and final standard of authority for the Church regarding both doctrine and practice. The Renaissance ideal of returning to the original classical sources, *ad fontes,* provided the texture for this vital concept of *Sola Scriptura,* as it insisted on going back to the only true Bible, that is, the original texts of the Old Testament in Hebrew and the New Testament in Greek as the fountain head of all true knowledge of God and His will. The practical outworking of *Sola Scriptura* is a thorough knowledge of the Word of God by all who claim to be Christians. Therefore, the Protestant Reformers – Martin Luther, Pierre Robert Olivétan, Giovanni Diodati and William Tyndale, among others – sought to give the Christian people God's Word as found in the original sources, the extant manuscripts of the Old Testament in Hebrew and the New Testament in Greek, in a language the common people could understand. The translation of the Bible into the vernacular languages of Europe was, therefore, a priority for the Protestant Reformation.

The Spanish Reformers, likewise, maintained that what we hold and do as Christians had to be based on the Word of God. The Spanish translators of the Bible, Juan de Valdés, Francisco de Enzinas, Juan Pérez de Pineda, Casiodoro de Reina, and Cipriano de Valera, and later on men like Adrián Sarabia, who took part in the translation of the King James Bible, shared the same desire present in the heart of other European Reformers. They wanted the entire Bible to be translated from the original languages into Spanish. As with the Reformation in Europe, the Roman Catholic Church chose to suppress the Spanish Reformation. The reasons behind its opposition are varied. But two reasons are apposite to our intent here: First of all, the Church of Rome held teachings based on Church traditions that could not be supported from the Scriptures. Secondly, some of Rome's traditions were based on a translation of the Scriptures into Latin known as the Vulgate. Even staunch Catholics like the Italian humanist Lorenzo Valla found that the Latin translation was inaccurate and unreliable in many places, which, in turn, as the Protestant Reformers postulated, led to many theological errors.[1] In this sense, the Church of Rome did not uphold *Sola Scriptura*, although this position was not stated as such until the Council of Trent.[2]

In Spain, the main instrument in the hands of the Roman Church to suppress the Reformation was the Spanish Inquisition. Many people were burned at the stake or forced into exile in sixteenth-century Spain. But what the Inquisition did not manage to achieve was the destruction of the translation of the Word of God into Spanish. This Spanish Bible, known as *La Biblia del Oso*, or the Reina-Valera Bible, is still, in modern revisions, the main Bible of the Protestant churches in Spain and South America. This paper examines the Prefaces to four sixteenth-century Spanish translations: that of Francisco de Enzinas, printed in 1543; of Juan Pérez de Pineda, printed in 1556; of Casiodoro de Reina, printed in 1569; and of Cipriano de Valera, printed in 1602. In their Prefaces, these men expound the reasons behind the translation of the Scriptures into the Spanish language. They do so taking into account the objections of the Roman hierarchy to their work. These early translations of the Spanish Bible were carried out outside of Spain. Francisco de Enzinas published his *Nuevo Testamento* in Antwerp and Juan Pérez de Pineda published his in Geneva; Casiodoro de Reina undertook the translation of the entire Bible, which he published in Basel, and Cipriano de Valera revised Reina's translation and printed it in Amsterdam.

1 One example was the translation of Luke 1:28 as *ave gratia plena Dominus tecum* in the Vulgate, implying that Mary was possessed of grace and therefore able to convey grace, instead of being a recipient of grace as the Greek word *kejaritomene* suggests. Another was a misunderstanding of the concept of repentance due to the translation of *metanoeite*, in Matthew 4:17, which means a change of mind in Greek as *paenitentiam agite*, literally to "do penance", which the Reformers argued was a concept entirely foreign to the meaning of the text. See in the appropriate places Henry: 1706; Godet: 1872; Vincent: 1888; Stonehouse: 1958; Ladd: 1952; Caird: 1963; Hendriksen: 1973; Ridderbos: 1987.

2 This was enshrined by the Council of Trent when they appoved the following decree: "The Council receives and venerates with the same sense of loyalty and reverence all the books of the Old and New Testament, together with all traditions concerning faith and morality, as coming from the mouth of Christ, or being inspired by the Holy Spirit and preserved in continuous succession in the Catholic Church" (Fourth Session: "Decree on Sacred Books and on Traditions to be Received").

2. The Translators

In order to examine the Prefaces in context, it is necessary for us to first examine briefly the lives of the translators.

2.1 Francisco de Enzinas

The first translator, Francisco de Enzinas, also known as Francis Dryander (from the Greek *drus*, which can be translated *encina* [ever-green oak tree] in Spanish, or Françoys du Chesne, in French), was born in Burgos, Spain, on November 1, 1518. He was the son of a successful wool merchant. Enzinas was sent to the Low Countries around 1536 for commercial training in one of his uncles' firms, but instead of pursuing a promising business career, in 1539, he enrolled at the Collegium Trilingue of Louvain. He may have been encouraged to go to Louvain by his brother Diego, who had been sent to Flanders earlier for commercial training but had enrolled at the Collegium Trilingue the previous year. At Louvain, the two brothers fell under the spell of humanist scholarship. Indeed, it was Erasmus' influence that first turned the two brothers from their family's commercial interests to the world of literature and, ultimately, to the evangelical faith. Taking into account a letter from Francisco Enzinas to John a Lasco, the Polish Protestant Reformer, dated May 1541, it appears that the two brothers came to faith in Christ in Louvain in 1541 (Stoughton: 1883, 84). From Louvain, Diego went to Paris – possibly invited by his uncle Pedro de Lerma, who had just recently become dean of the faculty of theology at the Sorbonne – and Francisco, who showed promise as a scholar, was allowed to continue his studies of Greek under Philipp Melanchthon at Wittenberg. Their uncle Pedro de Lerma (1461–1541) had been professor of divinity and one of the first chancellors of the University of Alcala. He had also represented the pro-Erasmus faction at the conference in Valladolid in 1527, called by Inquisitor General Manrique to investigate Erasmus' writings. Lerma resigned as chancellor at Alcala in 1535 and returned to Burgos. Two years later, in 1537, he was denounced to the Inquisition, suspected of Lutheran opinions and spreading Erasmian views. To avoid further trouble, he moved to Paris later that year, where he became dean of the faculty of theology at the Sorbonne. Pedro de Lerma himself said, "I can no longer remain in Spain. It is impossible for me, a man of learning, to dwell in safety in the midst of so many persecutors" (Stoughton: 1883, 83). In this respect, it is also interesting to notice that,

> Francisco de Enzinas associated the tragedy of Lerma with the cases of Juan de Vergara, Mateo Pascual and the Valdés brothers, and highlights the intransigence and ob-

scurantism of the Spanish friars in comparison with the knowledge and piety of Erasmus and their admirers (Nelson: 2008, 31).

Francisco de Enzinas went on to study in Wittenberg under Philipp Melanchthon. He registered at the University there on October 27, 1541. Francisco's first contribution was a small volume that included a translation into Spanish of John Calvin's 1538 Latin Catechism,[3] and Martin Luther's "Freedom of the Christian Man" to which he added a translation of the penitential Psalms and an epilogue, which he entitled "How the Christian man has to live daily". These were not literal but somewhat free translations, for Enzinas was fully aware of his readers and hence made an attempt to adapt the works to Spanish eyes. With the help of his brother Diego, Francisco published the work in Antwerp in 1542 under the title, *Breve y compendiosa institución de la religion Cristiana.* Diego planned to smuggle copies of the book into Spain, but the Spanish Inquisition learned of his plan and his family sent him to Italy for safety. The Roman Inquisition, which had recently been reinstated, soon arrested him for heresy. He was tried, sentenced, and burned at the stake in Rome in March of 1547 (Luttikhuizen: 2016, 262).

Francisco remained in Wittenberg until 1543 when he went to the Netherlands. His intention was to have his translation of the New Testament from Greek into Spanish printed at Antwerp by Steven Mierdman, despite a new edict from Charles V prohibiting all books printed without imperial permission. Francisco went ahead and printed his New Testament with a dedication to Emperor Charles V, dated October 25, 1543.[4] The title page reads thus: "The New Testament of our Redeemer and Saviour Jesus Christ, translated from the Greek into Castilian. To His Majesty. God spoke thus to Joshua: Keep this Book of the Law always on your lips; meditate on it day and night, so that you may be careful to do everything written in it. Then you will be prosperous and successful" (Josh 1:8).[5] Enzinas had a chance to present the book to the Emperor himself, but due to the Emperor's fear of examining matters of faith, he turned the New Testament and its translator over to his Dominican confessor, Pedro de Soto. The outcome was Enzinas' arrest on December 13, 1543, and imprisonment in Brussels.

Enzinas managed to escape in amazing circumstances on February 1, 1545. In March 1545 he was back in Wittenberg where he wrote an account of his adventures: *De statu Belgico et religione Hispanica* (Report on the situation in

3 For this publication, Enzinas used a pseudonym: Francisco de Elao.

4 Commenting on his style, Menéndez y Pelayo has this to say concerning Enzinas' New Testament: "He kept a middle ground between the rigor of the letter and the freedom of the paraphrase" (Azcárraga: 2001, 58).

5 Francisco de Enzinas, "Dedicatoria del Nuevo Testamento al Emperador Carlos V", accessed 16 July 2017, www.iglesiareformada.com/Enzinas_F_Dedicacion_NT.html. All biblical references are taken from the New International Version.

Flanders and the religion of Spain), better known as his *Mémoires.*[6] In August of 1546, he was in Strasbourg staying with the Reformer Martin Bucer. There he married Margaret d'Elter, a fellow exile from Belgium whom he had met earlier in Basel at the home of the exiled Belgian nobleman, Jacques de Bourgogne, Lord of Falais (Luttikhuizen: 2016, 263). In 1549, the couple went to England where Archbishop Cranmer appointed him professor of Greek at Cambridge. Enzinas was also on a committee with Bishop Cranmer, Martin Bucer, Peter Martyr Vermigli, Pablo Fagius, and Immanuel Tremellius for the reform of the Book of Common Prayer, which evidences both his level of scholarship and the high esteem the other Reformers had for him. He returned to Strasbourg in 1551. The plague that hit the city the following winter first killed Enzinas and a month later his wife Margaret, leaving their two infant daughters orphans. In a letter written to John Calvin, Francisco de Enzinas had aptly summarised his life and aspirations, in words which have come to be true in our days: "I am working, with good conscience, God be my witness. If the people of this time will not thank me, I hope there will come others in the future, of better judgment, to whom our studies will not be useless" (Stoughton: 1883, 89).

2.2 Juan Pérez de Pineda

Juan Pérez de Pineda, also known simply as Juan Pérez, was born around 1500 in Montilla, in the province of Cordoba. He seems to have been in Rome in 1526 in connection with the Spanish embassy. Back in Spain around 1550, he became head of the "College of Doctrine"[7] in Seville. About that time, he became acquainted with the teachings of the Reformers Dr. Egidio and Dr. Constantino Ponce de la Fuente and embraced their teachings. He left Seville when he received notice of the intention of the Inquisitors to arrest him as suspected of Lutheranism. This must have been around 1553 or 1554. He went first to Paris with the pretext of studying there, and then on to Geneva, where he became a trusted friend of John Calvin. In Geneva, he was engrossed in a new translation of the New Testament into Spanish, not just a revision of the work of Francisco de Enzinas. He dedicated this version to the King of Kings, God himself, and published it in Geneva (Pérez de Pineda: 1556). He also made a translation of the Psalms into Spanish. According to Menéndez y Pelayo (1992, 130), his translation

6 Francisco de Enzinas' Mémoires were published posthumously in French (Ste. Marie aux Mines, 1558) through the efforts of his wife's relatives in Strasbourg.

7 The "Colegio de Niños de la Doctrina", also called the "Casa de la Doctrina", took in orphans and abandoned boys between 6 and 20 years of age. The boys were taught the catechism [Doctrina], elementary notions of Latin, geometry, drawing, as well as certain skills, such as tailoring, weaving, carpentry, carding, knitting, etc.

was beautiful: "There is no better translation of the Psalms in Spanish [...] it is written in a pure, correct, clear language, full of freshness and beauty" (Kinder: 1976). This translation was dedicated to the Queen of Hungary, sister of Emperor Charles V. Later on when the flames of the Inquisition in Spain raged against the Protestants, he wrote his most famous work, the *Consolatory Letter to the Faithful of Jesus Christ who Suffer Persecution,* published in Geneva in 1560. Pérez de Pineda was also involved in the republication of the works of Juan de Valdés, particularly his commentaries to the Epistle of Paul to the Romans and to the Corinthians. While in Paris in 1555, he was given these commentaries by a Spaniard called Juan de Morillo who had been a dependent of Reginald Pole, the English cardinal who had been to the Council of Trent and who was a friend of Familio and Friuli (Pastore: 2010, 310). Concerning Valdés, Pérez wrote: "he piously and wisely considered that true nobility consisted, not in holding himself to be of 'blue blood', or purer blood than others, but in being an imitator of Christ, and in obeying the laws of Christian Chivalry" (Stoughton: 1883, 286). Pineda was deeply concerned about how to evangelise his native Spain. Through people like the courageous *colporteur* Julián Hernández, he managed to send books and tracts to the Spanish Protestants, particularly in Seville (Luttikhuizen: 2016, 210–212). Juan Pérez de Pineda was a prolific writer and editor. Between 1556 and 1560 he published a half dozen works.[8] Pérez's stay in Geneva also coincided with that of the English Marian exiles – 1555–1560 – which would also explain how two of works were so soon translated into English.[9] Shortly after 1560, Perez de Pineda left Geneva. After stopping off at Frankfurt and Paris, he received a call as preacher in Blois, France, where he also became chaplain to the godly Duchess of Ferrara, Renée, in her castle of Montargis. Juan Pérez de Pineda died in Paris in 1567. In his testament, he left all his goods for the purpose of printing the Bible into Spanish.

8 Commentario a los Romanos de Juan Valdesio (Geneva, 1556); Catechismo (Geneva, 1556); El Testamento Nuevo (Geneva, 1556); Comentario a los Corintios, de Juan Valdesio (Geneva, 1557); Carta a Don Philippe, Rey de España (Geneva, 1557); Los Psalmos de David Traducidos por el Doctor Juan Pérez (Geneva, 1557); Breve Tratado de la Doctrina (Geneva, 1560); Epístola Consolatoria (Geneva, 1560).

9 Jehovah a Free Pardon, first written in the Spanish tounge, and now translated into the mother English tounge, by Iohn Danyel, London: Thomas East, 1576; An Excelent Comfort to all Christians, compiled by Iohn Perez, a Spaniard (in Spanish) and now translated into English by Iohn Daniel (London: Thomas East, 1576).

2.3 Casiodoro de Reina

Casiodoro de Reina is perhaps the most famous of the Spanish Reformers, no doubt because he was responsible for the translation of the entire Bible into Spanish from the original languages. There had been some translations of the Bible into Spanish before Reina, but they were partial translations and, as far as the New Testament was concerned, were done from the Vulgate, not from the Greek. Reina was born in 1520 in Montemolín, in what would be today the province of Badajoz. Some considered him to have been of *morisco* ancestry, i. e. descending from Christian converts of a Muslim background. Reina entered the Hieronymite order in the monastery of San Isidoro del Campo in Santiponce, outside Seville. The order, following the example of their founder St. Jerome, was particularly concerned with the translation of Bible. Reina became acquainted with evangelical doctrines within the walls of the monastery through the study of the Bible. At that time there were several sources of biblical influence in Seville. A good number of brilliant men had had an enormous thirst for the gospel. Among them were Rodrigo de Valer, Francisco de Vargas, Dr. Egidio (Juan Gil), and Dr. Constantino Ponce de la Fuente.[10] There were others who were zealous to disseminate the Gospel in the San Isidoro Monastery, among them, the prior of the monastery, Master García-Arias, known as Maestro Blanco. There were also books coming to Seville from Geneva and from Germany, containing the evangelical message that was shaking the Continent: *Sola Scriptura, Sola Gratia, Sola Fide.* Such was the influence of evangelical teachings in the San Isidoro Monastery that the impact of Reformation doctrines in Seville could no longer be hidden with safety. Aware of the danger, just before they were discovered by the Inquisition, Casiodoro fled from Seville to Geneva in 1557 in the company of eleven other monks. The Inquisition kept trying to capture them and they had to spend their lives moving from one place to the other. Casiodoro lived in London, where he married the daughter of Abraham Leon of Nivelles, and in 1559 was serving as pastor to the Spanish Protestant refugees there. He also lived in Frankfurt, Heidelberg, Antwerp, Orleans, Bergerac, Montargis, Cologne, Hesse-Cassel and Basel. It was in Basel where, in 1569, Casiodoro de Reina published his translation of the Bible. Regarding this translation, Reina's main modern biographer, Arthur Gordon Kinder (1975, 54), states:

> Although Reina's debt to other Spanish translations is undoubted, in the best humanist tradition he went back to the original Hebrew and Greek texts [...] His achievement is all

10 Juan de Valdés' Dialógo de Doctrina Cristiana (Alcalá de Henares, 1529) was one of the main influences. This was particularly true in the cases of Vargas, Egidio and Constantino. All three had coincided with Valdés at Alcalá. Vargas had been one of Valdés' teachers and Constantino a fellow student.

> the more remarkable when one realizes that it has remained to the present day as basically the translation that is still in daily use by Spanish-speaking Protestants throughout the world, although it has been through several revisions since 1569.

Casiodoro was a pastor and, as such, published a Spanish Confession of Faith in 1561 for the Spanish-speaking congregation in London (Kinder: 1988). This *Confessio Hispánica* constituted the basis of faith of the Spanish church in London. He also wrote a commentary to the Gospel of John in Latin, which has recently been translated into Spanish, and an exposition of Matthew chapter four on the Temptations of Christ. Both of these works were published in 1573.[11] Several of his letters have also been preserved. He attended the famous Colloquy of Poissy, a meeting of Catholics and Protestants in August 1561. He died in Frankfurt in 1594, a city that had granted him citizenship.

Casiodoro de Reina's Bible is known as the *Biblia del Oso* because of the printer's device on the title-page, which represents a bear reaching for honey from a bee's nest in a tree. On the ground, an open Bible displays the four Hebrew letters of God's sacred name. The image has been identified as the printing device of Samuel Biener, or Apiarius ("the Bee-keeper"), a Swiss printer active in Basel. The bear refers to the heraldic animal of Biener's native city, Bern, and the bees refer to his name. A deeper meaning of the image is revealed by a quote from Psalm 119:103: "How sweet are your words onto my taste, sweeter than honey to my mouth" – an allegorical depiction of the thirst for God's word (Bible: 1569). For this undertaking, Casiodoro used the oldest and most reliable texts at hand. For the Old Testament he used the *Biblia de Ferrara*,[12] Pagninus' Hebrew-Latin Bible,[13] and the Septuagint; for the New Testament he used the 1551 edition of Robert Estienne's Greek New Testament,[14] and the Syriac (Peshitta) New Testa-

11 Evangelium Ioannis: hoc est, iusta ac vetus apologia pro aeterna Christi divinitate; & Expositio primae partis capitis quarti Matthaei; Exposición de la Primera Parte del Capítulo Cuarto de San Mateo sobre las Tentaciones de Cristo (Frankfurt: Nicolas Bascus, 1573).

12 The Biblia de Ferrara was for the exiled Spanish Jews expelled from the Iberian Peninsula what the Septuagint had been for the Jews at Alexandria and the Babylonian Talmud had been for the Jews in Mesopotamia. The Biblia de Ferrara is called a "ladinada" version – that is, written in Spanish but with Hebrew syntax. It was printed in Ferrara in 1553 by Abraham Usque (Duarte Pinel), a Portuguese Jew originally from Huesca, Spain, and financed by another Spanish Jew, Yom-Tob ben Levi Athias (Jeronimo de Vargas). It enjoyed several reprints: Salonica (1568) and Amsterdam (1611, 1630, 1646, 1661, 1695, etc.).

13 Pagninus' Hebrew-Latin Bible gave an interlinear and word-for-word translation of the Hebrew with the Hebrew vowel points and with the Latin translation appearing above the Hebrew text. This Bible was long considered the most convenient Hebrew Bible for those beginning to learn Hebrew.

14 He may also have copied Estienne's "numbered verses" división within each chapter, which was introduced for the first time in Estienne's 1551 Geneva edition (Fernández Campos: 2012, 209).

ment printed in Vienna in 1555.[15] In the "*Amonestación al lector*", Reina regrets the fact that it was too late for him to consult Immanuel Tremellius' edition of the Peshitta, which appeared in Geneva the same year as Reina's *Biblia del Oso*. Of course, it goes without saying that Reina also consulted both Francisco de Enzinas' and Juan Perez de Pineda's Spanish New Testaments. Casiodoro's translation came off the press in 1569, forty years before the King James version appeared in England. The text was slightly revised thirty-three years later by Cipriano de Valera and reprinted in Amsterdam in 1602.[16] About that same year, Giovanni Diodati published his translation of the Bible into Italian. In a letter to the Synod of Alencon, France, dated May 1, 1637, Diodati had this to say regarding the Valera revision:

> The new Spanish translation of Cyprian de Valera hath produced incredible effects in Spain; no less than three thousand copies having penetrated, by secret ways and conveyances, into the very bowels of that kingdom. Let others publish the fruit of my Italian version, both in Italy and elsewhere (M'Crie: 1829, 374).

2.4 Cipriano de Valera

Cipriano de Valera can be considered the most thoroughgoing Calvinist of our translators. Known as the "Spanish heretic" by the Inquisition, he was hated above all the other Reformers. He was born in 1532, in Frejenal de la Sierra in the province of Badajoz.[17] Like Casiodoro de Reina, Valera entered the Hieronymite Order in the monastery of San Isidoro del Campo in Santiponce, outside Seville. He was also among the monks who fled from the Inquisition to Geneva in 1557, "seeking a land of freedom in order to talk and deal with the things of God" (Colón Calderon: 2010, xix). Later, he moved to England, first to London where he married. He and his wife had three children: Isaac, John and Judith. Then he moved to Cambridge where he taught theology at Magdalene College between 1559 and 1567. In 1599, we find him in Amsterdam where he had gone to have his revision of the Reina version of the Bible printed (Valera: 1602). To this day, this Bible, known as the Reina-Valera Bible, is still the most popular version of the

15 For a history of of how Syriac came to occupy a prominent place among biblical languages, see Luttikhuizen: 2006.

16 Later revisions were made in 1862, 1909 and 1960.

17 Frejenal de la Sierra was also the birthplace of Benito Arias Montano, the supervisor of the 8-volume Biblia Regia, commissioned by Philip II and printed in Antwerp in 1572. Frejenal de la Sierra has preserved the memory of Arias Montano with a plaque on his house, a street that carries his name, and a commemorative bust that adorns a park. By contrast, it has totally ignored Cipriano de Valera.

Bible in Protestant churches in Spain and in Spanish-speaking countries in America.

Valera also translated other books. For instance, in 1597 he translated Calvin's *Institutes* into Spanish with a preface of his own that, to this day, still accompanies the translation of the *Institutes.* In his lengthy preface he outlined what can be properly called an incipient Christian philosophy of history (Moreno Berrocal: 2012). By that time he had already published his two treatises, one on the papacy and another on the mass (Valera: 1588). The treatise on the papacy is basically a history of the popes. It includes a study of key Bible passages seeking to demonstrate that the pope was the antichrist. The idea that the papal office was the fulfilment of biblical prophecies concerning the antichrist was a doctrine shared by many Protestants in Valera's day. The treatise also contains interesting accounts of the evangelical preaching carried out in Seville and Valladolid at that time. The second treatise is an exposition of Question 80 of the Heidelberg Catechism:

> What difference is there between the Lord's supper and the popish mass? The Lord's supper testifies to us, that we have a full pardon of all sin by the only sacrifice of Jesus Christ, which he himself has once accomplished on the cross; and, that we by the Holy Ghost are engrafted into Christ, who, according to his human nature is now not on earth, but in heaven, at the right hand of God his Father, and will there be worshipped by us. But the mass teaches, that the living and dead have not the pardon of sins through the sufferings of Christ, unless Christ is also daily offered for them by the priests; and further, that Christ is bodily under the form of bread and wine, and therefore is to be worshipped in them; so that the mass, at bottom, is nothing else than a denial of the one sacrifice and sufferings of Jesus Christ, and an accursed idolatry (Van Lennep: 1984, 232f).

Several times in his treatise Cipriano de Valera makes a moving appeal to his own countrymen, using expressions such as "Open your eyes, Spain, or rather may God open them, so that you may contemplate in what esteem the Pope has the sacrament that he himself sells you for your money, saying it is your God" (Colón Calderon: 2010: 34). This shows both his vehement nature and his concern for his own people. Prior to this, in 1594, Valera had published *Tratado para confirmar en la fe cristiana a los cautivos de Berbería* (A Treatise to confirm the faith of those captive in Berbería in the catholic and old Christian faith and religion, and to comfort with the Word of God in the afflictions that they suffer for the sake of the Gospel of Jesus Christ).[18] Valera must have died shortly after 1602. It is also worth noting that, under the pseudonym Guillermo Massan, Cipriano de Valera published his translation of William Perkins' *Reformed Catholic* (Colón Cal-

18 For details regarding these captives and Valera's concern for them, see Luttikhuizen: 2016, 224–226.

derón: 2010, xxxiv). Perkins is considered to be one of the founders of Puritanism. Perkin's work, published in 1597, sought to demonstrate that Protestants were the real Catholic Christians. This provides an interesting link between Valera and the early Puritans. Incidentally, Cipriano de Valera is also the origin of a common saying in the Spain of his day: "he is such a learned man that he is in danger of being a Lutheran". The former Spanish King, Juan Carlos I even mentioned Valera in a speech he made at Oxford on April 24, 1986, in which he said, that "in moments of political and religious instability, Oxford offered hospitality to eminent Spanish students like Cipriano de Valera, author of the precious Castilian Bible that, modernized, is still being published" (Fernández Campos: 2000, 313).

3. The Prefaces and the Word of God

The prefaces to these translations are a fascinating testimony of the immense value the early Spanish Reformers gave to the Word of God. In them, we find some of the reasons that led the Spanish translators to render the Bible – the Word of God – into Spanish. This was clearly done in the context of the opposition found in the Roman Catholic hierarchy of Spain towards the translation of the Word of God into the Spanish language. Despite this hostility, the Spanish Reformers were convinced of the imperative need for the Bible in the Spanish language. They shared the same concerns that ruled supreme in the hearts of other European Protestant Reformers: that is, the need to give the Word of God back to the people in a language they could understand. This was their overwhelming logic: "only what we understand can do us good". The Spanish Reformers also shared the humanist ideal that appeared in Erasmus' preface to his Greek New Testament:

> I would to God that the ploughman would sing a text of the Scripture at his plough; and that the weaver at his loom with this would drive away the tediousness of time. I would the way-faring man, with this pastime, would expel the weariness of his journey. And in short, I would that all the communication of the Christians should be of the Scripture; for in a manner, such are we ourselves, as our daily tales are.[19]

We must remember that the Bible was originally written in the language of the people who were to receive it, that is, Hebrew for the people of Israel, or Greek Koine, in New Testament times, the *lingua franca* of that era. Regarding this, Juan Pérez de Pineda (1556) says:

19 Quote taken from 1529 English edition of Erasmus' *Paraclesis* (1516) modernised and edited by Bernard Aubert and Paul Wells. Cited from Erasmus: 2016, 19.

> What use is there in the death of the Lord Jesus Christ, and its benefits, if those for whom he died do not know, or understand? Failure to understand this means, then, not esteeming this benefit, or worse, despising it. On the other hand, it means to give vices free hand, and to remain in them at will. To read and know the words of God is the sovereign remedy to destroy, and banish vices, to convert the vicious to Him, and subject them to His fear, and the true knowledge of Himself. Is there any other explanation for the fact that today vices and sins reign everywhere, but that men do not know, and do not cherish these benefits?[20]

It was for the sake of the souls of the Spaniards and the honour of the Spanish nation that this translation of the Scriptures in the sixteenth century was undertaken. The aim was that all Spaniards from the King to the humblest citizen of the kingdom could come to appreciate in their hearts the feeling of the Psalmist when he said: "Oh how I love your law! I meditate on it all day long" (Ps 119:97). Perez de Pineda tells us that,

> This doctrine was not given to one nation, or to a certain people, nor to be written just in one or two languages only. It was a common good given to all the nations of the earth, to be put into their tongues and understood by them. Doctrine is necessary for young and old, for rich and poor, for bond and free, for ignorant and wise men, high and low, sinners and righteous. Everyone has a part in it.[21]

The translators sought the protection of the authorities to this great end of the translation and spreading of the Scriptures in a romance language. Writing from Antwerp on October 1, 1543, Francisco de Enzinas, in his prologue to Emperor Charles V, emphasises this aspect of his New Testament:

> These reasons, sacred Majesty, have induced me to undertake this work. Not to say that it is a most just and holy cause, it is certainly worthy of your Majesty's royal dignity, worthy of your knowledge, worthy of your judgment, worthy of your approbation and worthy of your protection. And since I am well assured, with Solomon, that the hearts of good princes are governed by God, I trust in Heaven that your Majesty, will take this my work in good part, that you will encourage and defend it by your authority; and that you will employ all means to procure it a favourable reception by others. This ought to be done the more on this account, that the good which may be expected to result from it throughout the kingdom, is neither wealth, nor honour, nor worldly advantages, but spiritual blessings, and the glory of Christ Jesus. May he prosper His Majesty on the journey and enterprise you have undertaken, and in all others of a like nature; and after you have reigned long upon earth, may he receive you to reign with himself in heaven. Amen (M'Crie: 1998, 257).

This ardent desire for delivering the Word of God to the people greatly stands out in contrast with the attitude of those who refused to give the Bible to the people.

---

20 Pérez de Pineda: 1556, "Prefacio" cited from Stockwell: 1939, 63. The translation of these excerpts of the Prefaces are mine unless indicated.

21 Pérez de Pineda: 1556, "Prefacio" cited from Stockwell: 1939, 60.

The Index of Forbidden Books compiled during the eighteenth session of the Council of Trent and published in 1564 by Pope Pius IV, banned the reading of the Bible in Spanish or any other vernacular language. An excerpt from Rule IV reads:

> Insomuch as it is manifest from experience that if the holy Bible, translated into the vulgar tongue indiscriminately allowed to everyone, the temerity of men will cause more evil than good to arise from it, it is, on this point, referred to the judgement of the bishops or inquisitors, who may by the advice of the priest or confessor permit the reading of the Bible, translated into the vulgar tongue by Catholic authors, to those persons whose faith and piety, they apprehend, will be augmented, and not injured by it; and this permission they must have in writing. But if anyone shall have the presumption to read or possess it without such written permission, he shall not receive absolution until he have first delivered up such Bible to the ordinary. Booksellers, however, who shall sell or otherwise dispose of Bibles in the vulgar tongue, to any person not having such permission, shall forfeit the value of the books, to be applied by the bishop to some pious use; and be subjected to such other penalties as the bishop shall judge proper, according to the quality of the offense. But regulars shall neither read nor purchase such Bibles without a special licence from their superiors.[22]

The Spanish theologian Melchor Cano, who was a delegate at the sessions said that: "Even though women want with insatiable appetite to eat of this fruit (Scripture) it is necessary for us to prevent the people from having it … for experience has taught that the lesson from such books, especially the freedom to read the Sacred Scripture, all or a great part of it and translate it into the vulgar tongue, has done much harm to women and common people" (Moreno Berrocal: 2012, 44). This contrasts strongly with Casiodoro de Reina (1569), who in the "Admonition to the Reader" that precedes his translation, states:

> The source of this divine light (Scriptures) is God Himself […] the mysteries of true religion want to be seen and understood by all, because they are light and truth; and because being ordained for the salvation of all, the first thing is that they may be understood.[23]

It is also important to highlight that there was a clear contrast between the attitude towards the Word of God at the beginning of the sixteenth century in Spain,[24] and the one held from 1530 onwards – an attitude that was to find its

22 Rule IV of Pope Pius IV's Index of Forbidden Books cited from Townley: 1856, 161–162.

23 Reina: 1569, "Amonestación del interprete de los sacros libros al lector" cited from Stockwell: 1939, 84, 86.

24 From the early sixteenth century limited portions of the Bible were available in Spanish through Ambrosio Montesino's rendering of the lithurgical passages read in Latin every Sunday at mass, known as the Epístolas y evangelios por todo el año, con sus doctrinas y sermones. Likewise, the publication of the Polyglot Bible by Cardinal Cisneros as well as the founding of the University of Alcalá evidence he was also very keen to promote biblical

decisive statement at the Council of Trent. The change in Spain was most clearly felt after the Conference of Valladolid in 1527 in which a number of leading Spanish theologians took a stand against Erasmus and his teaching. The Spanish Reformers, as the dates of their prefaces clearly show,[25] were responding to this growing antagonism towards the Word of God in the vernacular.

4. Reasons for Translation

In the Prefaces, the Reformers state several reasons why the Scripture should be in the hands of all the people, without exception. We can highlight two: 1) only through Scripture can we discern truth from error; 2) only through Scripture do we come in direct contact with God and attain a saving knowledge of Jesus. Elaborating on their rationale, it should be noted in the first place that for these Spanish translators Scripture is the supreme and final authority in all matters regarding Christian faith and practice. However, in order for Scripture to be such an authority, it needs to be read by people in their own mother tongues. Therefore, Cipriano de Valera (1602) tells us that:

> The reason why our enemies forbid the Scriptures and persecute with fire and blood those who read them is that they understand, for the great experience they have, that Sacred Scripture is the only means that God, in His great mercy, has left in the world to differentiate between true and false religion.[26]

This stands in antithesis with the statements made by the Catholic authorities at that time. They held that people can misunderstand what they read and fall into heresy. They claimed that only the clergy can handle the text properly. Therefore the translation of the Scriptures into the vernacular could only do harm. This was the position taken at the Council of Trent by the Spanish Cardinal Pedro Pacheco's Franciscan theologian-jurist, Alfonso de Castro. He held that: "all theological error is traceable to vernacular Scripture, the mother and origin of all heresies" (McNally: 1966, 213).[27] This fear of Scriptures in the hands of the common people became Catholic dogma at the Council of Trent:

---

knowledge among the clergy. He also encouraged the translation of many of the early mystics into Spanish. See Nieto: 1979. On this issue of vernacular Bible translations in the rest of Europe before and at the time of the Reformation see McGrath: 2004; Lamberigts/Den Hollander: 2006; François/Den Hollander: 2009 and Gordon/McLean: 2012.

25 Francisco de Enzinas, 1543; Juan Pérez, 1556; Casiodoro de Reina, 1569 and Cipriano de Valera, 1602.

26 Valera: 1602 cited from Stockwell: 1939, 162.

27 "Alfonso de Castro adds, 'In a word, Scripture is a dangerous source of religious error for the faithful, for the simple laity and the ill-instructed. It is not, therefore, to be read by them. Rather, in learning the mysteries of salvation they should depend on the preaching and

> We have learned by experience that if the sacred books, translated into the vernacular, are indiscriminately circulated, there follows because of the weakness of man more harm than good. In this matter the judgment of the bishop or the inquisitor must be sought, who on the advice of the pastor or the confessor may permit the reading of a Bible translated into the vernacular by Catholic authors. This may be done with the understanding that from this reading no harm, but an increase of faith and piety, results. The permission must be in writing. But he who dares to read or possess Scripture without this permission cannot receive absolution from his sins until he has returned the Bible to the ordinary… (McNally: 1966, 226–227).

Against this common objection, Juan Pérez de Pineda (1556) writes:

> Bread and wine are necessary foods to sustain human life. The fact that many get drunk or gorged themselves, as often happens, does not mean we must refrain from all common use of it. It would be a strange way to correct the vices of some who are to be blamed, by starving others who are without guilt.[28]

Likewise, Cipriano de Valera (1602), attacking the idea that only the Roman Catholic hierarchy can handle properly Scripture, reminds the people that we are all required to read the Scriptures no matter who we are.

> As God in so many places, both in the Old and the New Testament commands us not only that we read the sacred books, but that we meditate and ruminate on them, and this He commands to every faithful Christian, to everyone who desires to be saved: be that person man or woman, young or old, rich or poor, king or subject, clergyman or a layman (as they call them) it is reasonable, and it would be our duty to do so as well, unless we are rebels, that we obey that which our God, Father and Lord commands us, being assured that He will not command but what is holy and good, convenient for His glory and for our good and benefit.[29]

Furthermore, convinced that it is the ignorance of Scripture that brings a much greater evil to the Church, Cipriano de Valera continues:

> Those who have banned the reading of Sacred Scripture to the faithful have undoubtedly caused the many heresies that have arisen in the Church. Because ignoring the Scriptures causes heresies as Chrysostom witnesses … And before him, Irenaeus had said the same. Irenaeus says of the Valentinian heretics speaking in Book 4, Chapter 12 and 13: Ignoring the Scriptures has made them fall into heresy. And to say everything in one word; The Lord, speaking to the Sadducees, in Matthew 22:29 says, you do err, because ye know not the Scriptures.[30]

---

teaching of the clergy'. This narrow concept of the role of the Bible in Catholic life was not peculiar to Trent nor was it formed under the impact of the Reformation. It expresses rather a medieval pattern of thought whose roots go back to (and even beyond) the days of Innocent III (d. 1216)" (McNally: 1966, 209).

28 Pérez de Pineda: 1556, "Prefacio" cited from Stockwell: 1939, 72.

29 Valera: 1602 cited from Stockwell: 1939, 168–169.

30 Valera: 1602 cited from Stockwell: 1939, 160.

Indeed, nothing good can come from banning the Scriptures in the vernacular as Casiodoro de Reina tells us in the conclusion of his preface: "At least this is beyond dispute, that God had given his Word to men, wishing to be understood by all, no good end can come then by forbidding the translation into any language".[31]

Secondly, it is necessary to affirm that only through Scripture do we come in direct contact with God through him who inspired the Holy Scriptures, namely, the Holy Spirit of God. In fact, it is impossible to fully appreciate the Protestant Reformation without highlighting not only the primacy of Scripture but also its connection with the Holy Spirit. This is particularly true with regard to John Calvin, who has correctly been called the "Theologian of the Holy Spirit". This relationship between Scripture and the Holy Spirit answers the theological formulation: "the Spirit through the Word (*per verbum*) and by the Word (*cum verbo*), but not apart from or without the Word (*sine verbo*)". In this regard, Cipriano de Valera (1602) elaborates on the importance and essential dependence on the Holy Spirit as one studies the written word:

> But it (the study of God's Word) has to be undertaken with a spirit of humility not trusting in one's own understanding to understand the things of God ... In that state, he is to call upon the Lord to give him His Spirit to open his understanding (as it opened the understanding of the Apostles. Luke 24:45) to understand the Scripture ... Only the spiritual man, who is governed by the Spirit of God understands, believes and esteems the Scriptures as the highest wisdom. May His Majesty give us grace to understand, and that, understanding them, we may live according to them, serving our good God in spirit and in truth so that we may not be children of darkness but of light.[32]

One of the most fascinating teachings of the Spanish Reformers has to do with what Scripture really achieves through the Spirit. That is, that Christ is with us now through His Word as He was with his disciples while He was on earth in His body. In the words of Perez de Pineda (1556):

> But this sacred history of living works and events that still speaks, and teaches us to know and please God, comes together with the spirit and power of the Lord that wrought them. So that we may know and believe truly that just as then Christ himself was, by the power of his virtue, with those that went to Him and received Him, so today, he still does the same with all who read, hear, and receive his word. And although He is absent from us as to His bodily presence, nevertheless He does not cease in his Gospel (as promised) to be present with his power, truth, mercy, justice, virtue, and Spirit that saves, delivers, enlightens, and transforms those who receive Him and believe as He commands. And since He is already ascended into heaven where He is seated at the right hand of the Father, and we do not see or hear the way they that were living when He preached in this

31 Reina: 1569, "Amonestación del interprete de los sacros libros al lector" cited from Stockwell: 1939, 91.

32 Valera: 1602 cited from Stockwell: 1939, 165.

> world saw Him and heard Him, it is necessary (if we want to be saved) that, as if in a living mirror, we might see Him in his Testament, where, with much fruit, and healthy relief for our consciences, we can hear Him preach to all, forgive their sins, comfort the afflicted, free the possessed, heal lepers and the ill, fill the hungry, raise the dead, and give sight to the blind. Hearing it and seeing it this way, we will have free entrance to Him and, unembarrassed to ask confidently for everything in any needs and anxieties we may experience because He is always the same and has never changed his natural condition, or changed the love He has for those He has redeemed. And together with this most wonderful gift, He has also left us with His Spirit and virtue, that He may work no less effectively in his listeners and readers today than He did then with his preaching in those who heard Him with humility.[33]

Our translators longed to translate the Bible into Spanish because it is only through the Scriptures that we can attain a saving knowledge of Jesus. The Bible reveals the only way of salvation: the person of the Lord Jesus. In fact, it was Jesus Christ who said: "You study the Scriptures diligently because you think that in them you have eternal life. These are the very Scriptures that testify about me" (John 5:39). This is essential. The knowledge of the Scriptures has an eternal value because our eternal salvation or damnation depends on them, for only the Scriptures bring the only and true Christ to us. So Cipriano de Valera (1602), in his exhortation to the reader, in the preface to his translation, tells us:

> My intent has been to serve my God and do good to my nation. What greater good can I do to them than to introduce the means God has ordained to win souls, which is the lesson of the Holy Scripture? Here is given good news to the poor, here are given medicines to heal the broken hearted; to the captives freedom is proclaimed and to the blind sight; here is published the year of the Lord; here the sad are comforted … May it please His Majesty to bless this His work so that His holy name, who is announced in it, shall be sanctified in Spain, as it is in other nations.[34]

Writing to the Romans, the Apostle Paul tells us that whoever calls on the name of the Lord shall be saved. But then the Apostle has a series of questions: "How, then, can they call on the one they have not believed in? And how can they believe in the one of whom they have not heard?" The Apostle himself gives the answers: "Consequently, faith comes from hearing the message, and the message is heard through the Word" (Rom 10:14; 10:17). Cipriano de Valera restates the Apostle's reasoning when he says:

> Our great God and Father, who so much seeks our salvation and that none of us should be lost through ignorance, but that we all come to the knowledge of the truth and so be saved, commands us very explicitly, and not in one place but in many that we read the Sacred Scriptures.[35]

---

33 Pérez de Pineda: 1556, "Prefacio" cited from Stockwell: 1939, 58–59.
34 Valera: 1602 cited from Stockwell: 1939, 189–190.
35 Valera: 1602 cited from Stockwell: 1939, 144.

The great value of the Scriptures is to reveal the glory of the Son of God as our only Lord and Saviour. Significantly, the recovery of the Bible during the Reformation in the sixteenth century had always, as a natural consequence, the placing of the person and work of Jesus Christ at the very centre of the Christian life. As Valera states,

> If, as St. Paul says, Christ is the power of God and the wisdom of God, and those who ignore Scripture, ignore the power and wisdom of God, then it follows of necessity that those who ignore the Scriptures, ignore Christ. Experience shows that the more superstitious people are, so much the more ignorant they are. Thus the duty of the Christian is not to be ignorant, but wise in the knowledge of God as revealed in Holy Scripture: and so should he read, scrutinize, ruminate, discuss and meditate on it day and night.[36]

Over against this way of interpreting the function of Scripture, there stands the Tridentine understanding that it is only through the Church and its sacraments that we can be in direct contact with God and receive blessing from Christ. According to Roman Catholic dogma, ceremonies, whether understood or not, put the people in contact with God through the *ex opere operato* working of the sacraments. Scriptural knowledge of Christ that leads to personal faith in Him, is not essential to be a Christian according to the teaching formulated at Trent:

> Moreover, the Church alone has the legitimate worship of sacrifice, and the salutary use of the Sacraments, which are the efficacious instruments of divine grace, used by God to produce true holiness. Hence, to possess true holiness, we must belong to this Church. The Church therefore it is clear, is holy, and holy because she is the body of Christ, by whom she is sanctified, and in whose blood she is washed.[37]

As expressed by Friedrich G.E. Schleiermacher (1963, 103): "For Protestants the individual's relationship to the Church depends upon a relationship to Jesus Christ, whereas in Catholicism the reverse is true".

5. Conclusion

The Prefaces of the Holy Scriptures in Spanish by Francisco de Enzinas, Juan Perez de Pineda, Casiodoro de Reina, and Cipriano de Valera are a powerful testimony to their desire to bring God's revelation of himself, the Bible, to his people. Their translations from the original languages – Greek and Hebrew – had to do with the fact that these Spanish Reformers were aware that the Vulgate was clearly full of errors and could no longer be thought to be a reliable source for

36 Valera: 1602 cited from Stockwell: 1939, 165.

37 Council of Trent, Article IX ("I believe in the Holy Catholic Church, the Communion of Saints").

theological reflection and dogma. Therefore, there was an urgent need to go back to the original sources, the oldest Hebrew and Greek manuscripts in order to find accurate and responsible theology. Following the decrees of the Council of Trent, the Roman Catholic authorities in Spain clung to the Vulgate in spite of the errors it contained:

> Moreover, this sacred and holy Synod, - considering that no small utility may accrue to the Church of God, if it be made known which out of all the Latin editions, now in circulation, of the sacred books, is to be held as authentic, - ordains and declares, that the said old and Vulgate edition, which, by the lengthened usage of so many years, has been approved of in the Church, be, in public lectures, disputations, sermons and expositions, held as authentic; and that no one is to dare, or presume to reject it under any pretext whatever (Canons and Decrees of the Council of Trent, The Fourth Session, 1546).

Translation into the vernacular had to do with the aspiration of the Spanish Reformers that all people may have access to the Word of God in their mother tongue. This had been done earlier, to a small degree, with translations of the Old Testament by the Jews, and works encouraged by Cardinal Cisneros. The attitude of the Catholic authorities in Spain became increasingly one of intolerance towards vernacular translations, as well as Latin versions printed outside of Spain as is evidenced by the confiscation of over 300 Latin Bibles in Seville in 1552 (Luttikhuizen: 2016, 96–97).

The translation project, as a whole, was also closely linked with the desire that people might see for themselves, through reading the Scripture, that Rome had departed from the simplicity of the Gospel in both doctrine and practice. Like Paul, the translators encouraged their readers to strive to "Let the message of Christ dwell among you richly as you teach and admonish one another with all wisdom" (Col 3:16). And this for the sole purpose of finding the One in whom are hidden all the treasures of wisdom and knowledge, namely, the person of Jesus. (Col 2:3). In other words, that the Christian's main maxim be *Sola Scriptura.*

Bibliography

Azcárraga, Mª Josefa (2001), Versiones Españolas de la Biblia. Reseña Bíblica 31, 53–62.

Caird, G.B. (1963), Saint Luke: Pelican New Testament Commentary, Harmondsworth: Penguin Books.

Colón Calderón, Isabel (ed.) (2010), Cipriano de Valera, Tratado del Papa, Sevilla: Fundación José Manuel Lara.

Enzinas, Francisco De (1543), El Nuevo Testamento de Nuestro Redemptor y Salvador Iesu Christo. Traduzido de Griega en Lengua Castellana, por Francisco de Enzinas, Dedicado a la Cesarea Magestad, Enueres [Antwerp]: En casa de Esteuan Mierdmanno.

Erasmus, Desiderius (2016), An Exhortation to the Diligent Study of Scripture, Unio Cum Christo 2:2, 13–28.

Fernández Campos, Gabino (2000–2001), Apuntes para una Bio-bibliografía de Cipriano de Valera, Boletín de la Real Academia de Extremadura, 305–338.

– (2012), La Biblia en la Literature del Siglo de Oro, in: Manuel Garcia Lafuente (ed.), Huellas del Cristianismo en el Arte, La Literatura, Madrid: Consejo Evangélico de Madrid, 161–221.

François, W./A. A. Den Hollander (eds.) (2009), Infant Milk or Hardy Nourishment? Leuven: Peeters Publishers.

Godet, Frédéric (1872), Commentaire sur l'Evangile de Saint Luc, Paris: Sandoz.

Gordon, Bruce/Matthew McLean (eds.) (2012), Shaping the Bible in the Reformation, Leiden/Boston: Brill.

Hendriksen, William (1979), New Testament Commentary: Exposition of the Gospel According to Matthew, Grand Rapids, MI: Baker Book House.

Henry, Matthew (1706), Commentary on the Whole Bible, London.

Kinder, Arthur Gordon (1975), Casiodoro de Reina, London: Tamesis Books.

– (1976), Juan Pérez de Pineda (Pierius): A Spanish Calvinist Minister of the Gospel in Sixteenth-Century Geneva, Bulletin of Hispanic Studies 53, 4, 283–300.

– (ed.) (1988), The Spanish Protestant Confession of Faith [London, 1560/1561], Exeter: University of Exeter.

Ladd, George Eldon (1952), Crucial Questions about the Kingdom of God, Grand Rapids: MI, Eerdmans.

Lamberigts, M./A.D. den Hollander (eds.) (2006), Lay Bibles in Europe 1450–1800, Leuven: Peeters Publishers.

Luttikhuizen, Frances (2006), El Siríaco en la Transmisión de Documentos Bíblicos, Tu Reino 13, 9–37.

– (2016), Underground Protestantism in Sixteenth-Century Spain. A New Look at a Much Ignored Side of Spanish History, Göttingen: Vandenhoeck & Ruprecht.

McGrath, Alister E. (2004), The Intellectual Origins of the European Reformation, Oxford/Cambridge, MA: Wiley-Blackwell.

Mcnally, Robert E. (1966), The Council of Trent and Vernacular Bibles, Theological Studies 27, 204–227.

M'Crie, Thomas (1829), History of the Progress and Suppression of the Reformation in Spain in the Sixteenth Century, Edinburgh: W. Blackwood.

– (1998), The Reformation in Spain, Rapidan, VA: Hartland Publications.

Menéndez y Pelayo, Marcelino (1992), Historia de los Heterodoxos Españoles, Madrid: CSIC.

Moreno Berrocal, José (2012), La Primera Reforma en España/La Segunda Reforma en España, in: José Moreno Berrocal/Bernard Coster/José de Segovia, La Reforma Ayer y Hoy, Barcelona: Andamio, 12–55.

Nelson, Jonathan L. (ed.) (2008), Francisco de Enzinas, Breve y compendiosa institución de la religión cristiana [1542], Cuenca: Ediciones de la Universidad de Castilla La Mancha.

Nieto, José C. (1979), Juan de Valdés y los origenes de la Reforma en España e Italia, Mexico/Madrid/Buenos Aires: Fondo de Cultura Económica.

Pastore, Stefania (2010), Una Herejía Española, Madrid: Marcial Pons.

Pérez De Pineda, Juan (1556), El Testamento Nuevo de Nuestro Señor y Salvador Jesu Christo, Venecia: Juan Philadelpho [Geneva: Jean Crespin].

Reina, Casiodoro De (1569), La Biblia, que es, los Sacros Libros del Viejo y Nuevo Testamento. Trasladada en Español, Basilea: Thomas Guarin.

Riderbos, H.N. (1987), Matthew, Grand Rapids, MI: Zondervan.

Roldan-Figueroa, Rady (2004), Casiodoro de Reina as Biblical Exegete: Studies on the 1569 Spanish Translation of the Bible, ThD Dissertation, Boston University School of Theology.

Schleiermacher, Friedrich G.E. (1963), The Christian Faith. New York: Harper Torchbooks.

Stockwell, Bowman Forster (1939), Prefacios a Las Biblias Castellanas del Siglo XVI. Buenos Aires: Librería La Aurora.

Stonehouse, Ned Bernard (1958), The Witness of Matthew and Mark to Christ, Grand Rapids, MI: Eerdmans.

Stoughton, John (1883), The Spanish Reformers. Their Memories and Dwelling-Places, London: Religious Tract Society.

Townley, James (1856), Illustrations of Biblical Literature, New York: Carlton and Porter.

Valera, Cipriano de (1588), Dos tratados: El Primero es del Papa y de su Autoridad; El Segundo es de la Missa, London: Arnoldo Hatfildo.

– (1602), Exhortacion al Cristiano Lector à Leer la Sagrada Escritura, Amsterdam: L. Jacobi.

Van Lennep, M.F. (1984), La Historia de la Reforma en España, Grand Rapids, MI: TELL.

Vincent, Marvin R. (1888), Word Studies of the New Testament, New York.

Frances Luttikhuizen

Clandestine Protestant Literature Reaches Spain

As the fifteenth century came to a close, Spain was ready – if not anxious – for reforms. Francisco Jimenez de Cisneros, better remembered as Cardinal Cisneros, must be given credit for this.[1] Once installed in his new position as Archbishop of Toledo in 1495, Cisneros set about reforming the Franciscan order, which at that time was experiencing a bitter conflict between the "conventuals", who had diverged considerably from the austere regulations of St. Francis, becoming feudal lords and indulging in worldly pleasures, and the strict "observants". Cisneros' rigid reforms did not leave the monks indifferent. Several hundred fled to North Africa but those that remained became very observant. The frenzy created by Cisneros' reform also had an impact on society and developed into a more profound, inner spirituality among Humanistic-minded individuals. To make their experience meaningful, Cisneros began commissioning Spanish translations of medieval mystical texts that would raise the cultural and spiritual level of both the clergy and the common people. He especially encouraged the reading of Jean Gerson, St. Augustine, St. Jerome, St. Bonaventure, John Climacus, Angela of Foligno, Santa Catalina of Sienna, Girolamo Savonarola, and a new vernacular rendering of the *Epistles and Gospels for the Liturgical Year.*[2] These passages of Scripture, read in Latin in the churches each Sunday, were interspersed with commentaries and sermons by Hugo de Prato, Johann Herolt of Basel, Walafrid Strabo, Anselm of Laon, Nicholas of Lyra, and others (Bustos Táuler: 2010).

As scholasticism gave way to Christian Humanism and Christian Humanism to greater inner spirituality and the belief that individual freedom is compatible with Christian doctrine and practice, people – throughout Europe, as well as in

1 See Luttikhuizen: 2017.

2 Epistles and Gospels can be considered the first printed edition of large portions of the Scriptures in the Spanish language available for the common people. It enjoyed many reprints until it was put on the Index of Prohibited Books in 1559 as a result of the decree that prohibited the printing of Scripture in the vulgar tongue. After 1586 the work was again reprinted but with corrections (nuevamente visto y corregido).

Spain – began to question the education they had received and the way they worshiped God. Christian Humanism had not only planted the seed of inquiry but also argued for a new focus on education. As more Spaniards travelled to Italy in the fifteenth century to complete their education, they returned with a new worldview. In Italy Lorenzo Valla had opened the way to textual criticism. Antonio Nebrija – sometimes called the Erasmus of Spain – wanted to do the same, but the times were yet not ripe.

Cisneros had taken a giant step in matters of education. Besides offering Thomism at his newly founded university, he also created chairs of Scotism and Nominalism. Likewise, biblical studies benefitted from the study of ancient languages and patristic literature. His second great project was the publication – and financing – of the first complete polyglot bible, the *Biblia Sacra Polyglota*, known today as the Ximenez Polyglot or the Complutensian Polyglot. Initially, Nebrija was part of Cisneros' team, but soon the two men clashed. Nebrija tried to persuade Cisneros that the Latin text of the Vulgate should be revised, but Cisneros would not give in. He was willing to collate – and correct – the Greek, Hebrew or Aramaic text, but he would make no changes in Jerome's Latin text, which he, like many others in his day, considered inspired (Luttikhuizen: 2016a, 88). As a result, Nebrija resigned from the project. By the time Erasmus' Greek-Latin New Testament reached Alcala in 1516 several years had passed and Cisneros may have had second thoughts on the matter. His chief editor, Diego Lopez de Zuñiga, known also by his Latin name Jacobus Stunica, wanted to publicly denounce Erasmus for certain errors he found in his translation. Cisneros discouraged him from publishing his findings and suggested he communicate them privately to Erasmus. As soon as Cisneros died, however, which was the following year, Zuñiga gave vent to his anger and published his criticisms in *Annotationes contra Erasmum Roterodamum* (Annotations against Erasmus). Zuñiga was averse to innovation and became involved in controversies in defence of the Vulgate against both Lefévre d'Etaples and Erasmus that went on for years (Preston/Jenkins: 2007, 59–65; cf. Bedouelle: 2008, 129). Despite these early misgivings regarding Erasmus, the die had been cast and Cisneros' focus on biblical studies had issued in a new era for Humanism in Spain.

Christian Humanism was soon having a heyday at Alcala.[3] Indeed, the enthusiasm shown among the faculty and students for Erasmus and his writings made the University of Alcala an important focal point for Erasmian studies in Europe. Among the laity, Erasmus also had many enthusiastic followers for his

3 His most enthusiastic followers were among the most prestigious humanists of the day: Francisco and Juan de Vergara, Bernardino Tovar, Mateo Pascual, Pedro de Lerma, Miguel Carrasco, Hernan Vazquez, the printer Miguel de Eguia, educators such as Bernabe del Busto, Lucio Marineo Siculo, Francisco de Bobadilla, Diego Gracian de Alderete, Bernardo Perez de Chinchon, etc.

attacks on clerical abuse. In those early years, both Martin Luther and Desiderius Erasmus had taken up pen and pulpit to denounce the corruptions of the Church. Their attacks on clerical abuse had found echo in earlier northern writers such as Sebastian Brant, but it is unsure whether Brant's *Ship of Fools* reached Spain. Although some of the works of Luther were circulated in Spain, until the 1530s, enthusiasm for Erasmus' works – especially *Tractado de las querellas de la paz* (Seville, 1520) and *Enchiridion: O manual del cavallero cristiano* (Alcalá de Henares, 1524) – outweighed general interest in the German Reformer. In fact, in a letter to Erasmus, Alfonso Fernandez, the translator, stated, "At court, in the cities, in the churches, in the monasteries, even in the inns and the byways, there is hardly a soul who does not have a copy of *Enchiridion* in Spanish" (Coroleu/Taylor: 2010, 3).

That said, already in 1519, even before Luther had been excommunicated, and before he appeared before the Emperor at the Diet of Worms, his books were being sent to Spain. This is evidenced from a letter dated February 14, 1519, written from Basel by Johannes Froben to Luther in which he informed him that:

> Blasius Salmonius, a bookseller of Leipzig, presented me with certain treatises composed by you that he bought at the last Frankfort fair, which being approved by learned men, I immediately put to press, and sent six hundred copies to France and Spain. My friends assure me, that they are sold at Paris, and read and approved of even by the Sorbonists. Several learned men there have said, that they have long wished to see divine things treated with such becoming freedom. [Francesco] Calvus, a bookseller of Pavia, himself a scholar and addicted to the muses, has carried a great part of the impression into Italy (Luther: 1913, 125).[4]

Another letter to Luther, written only four days later by Wolfgang Capito, dated Basel, February 18, 1519, confirms the former:

> We have printed your collected works, as you will learn from Froben's gift, and within six weeks after the Frankfurt Fair sent them to Italy, France, Spain and England, in this consulting the public welfare, which, we think, is advanced by having the truth spread as widely as possible. Nature by means of truth allures even an enemy to love her (Dau: 1919, 221, 222).

According to M'Crie (1829, 124), in the course of the 1520s, in Antwerp, Luther's commentary on Galatians was translated into Spanish, followed by his treatise on Christian Liberty and his reply to Erasmus on free-will. At that time these works

4 The first to distribute the works of Luther and Melanchthon in Italy was a bookseller of Pavia, Francesco Calvi, a friend of Erasmus; this was as early as 1519 and done purely in the way of business, with no intention of promoting religious propaganda. The commercial centres of Pavia, Venice, Bologna and Milan, and the University of Padua acted as distributors. In 1531 Lutheran doctrine seems to have been fashionable among the students of the University of Padua (Elton: 1990, Vol. 2, 292–93).

were not yet considered heretical, though printing them without a licence did break the existing laws regulating printing established in the *Recopilacion* (Laws of the Kingdom), decreed by the Catholic monarchs in Toledo in 1502, which established that books – either in Latin or in Spanish – could not be printed or imported without the consent and licence of a member of their *Consejo* (Council) or some other civil authority.[5] This was the first restriction on printing. Earlier, in 1480, the monarchs had issued a decree whereby they encouraged the entry and sale within their kingdom of imported books to the point that they were allowed to enter "duty free".[6] This would gradually change. In 1554, Charles V limited the granting of licenses to members of the *Consejo* only; his daughter Princess Juana issued even stricter laws, requiring that all books printed after 1558 carry a licence signed by the King and endorsed by the *Consejo*. All books were to be presented to the *Consejo* both before printing and again afterwards to make sure nothing had been changed or added, and that records should be kept of the year, the place, the author, and the printer of all licenses granted.[7]

Besides these legal restrictions established by the Spanish state, the Spanish Inquisition also stepped in with its relentless "heresy hunting" activities. In March of 1521, only three months after Luther had been excommunicated,[8] Pope Leo X addressed a brief to the Spanish governors warning them against the introduction of Luther's books via the Spanish Netherlands. One month later, on April 7, 1521, even before the Diet of Worms had concluded, Adrian Florensz, now Inquisitor General of Spain, sent the Inquisitors in Aragon the following directive against the writings of Martin Luther:

> We have been informed that some persons, with evil intent and in order to sow cockles in the Church of God and to rend the seamless tunic of Christ our Redeemer, have extended their efforts to bring into Spain the works recently written by Martin Luther, of the order of Saint Augustine, which works are said to be printed in Spanish for publication and sale in this kingdom. It is eminently proper for the honour and service of God and the exalting of our holy Catholic faith that such works not be published or sold, nor appear anywhere in this kingdom, because they contain heretical errors and many other suspect things about the faith. We therefore direct you to order, under pain of grave censures, as well as civil and criminal punishment, that nobody dare to own, sell, or permit to be sold in public or in private, any such books or any parts of them, and that within three days of the publication of your order such books, in both Latin and Spanish, be brought and presented before you. When this is done you will then burn them all in public, directing the notary of your Holy Office to record the names of all

5 Novísima recopilación de las leyes de España. Madrid: Sancha, 1805, Tomo IV, 122–125.

6 Novísima recopilación, 121.

7 In 1610, Filipe III issued a decree prohibiting Spaniards to print their works abroad even after having obtain a licence from the Consejo. Novísima recopilación, 126.

8 On January 3, 1521, Pope Leo X issued the papal bull Decet Romanum Pontificem, which excommunicated Martin Luther from the Catholic Church.

persons who possess, sell, publish and bring before you such books, and the records of their burning, including the number of books burned.[9]

The following month - May 1521 - the Supreme Council of the Inquisition - known better as the *Suprema*[10] - issued instructions, in the name of Charles V, that "no person should sell nor have nor read nor preach about the books of this heretic [Martin Luther] nor speak of his errors and heresies either in public or in secret" (Longhurst: 1969, 15). It is evident that these instructions were not strictly heeded because two years later, on May 7, 1523, the *Suprema* sent a letter to the inquisitors in Navarre denouncing the distribution of Lutheran books. Moreover, it appears that even more books were also being translated into Spanish because the edict stated that, under pain of excommunication and other heavy civil punishments, any doctor, licentiate, *bachiller*, cleric or other person, of whatsoever estate, grade or condition he be, who has in his possession any such book - in either Latin or Spanish - must turn them in within fifteen days. Six months later, in November 1523, the Council sent out another note:

> We are informed that in the province of Guipuzcoa there are some of the said [Lutheran] books [in circulation], from which it appears that you did not take the proper action to carry out our directive [of May 7] or to do what we charged you to do. We are very surprised at this.[11]

Dispatches sent out two years later by the next Inquisitor General, Alonso Manrique, continued in the same vain. He issued an edict on April 15, 1525, in which he complained that,

> Some persons, showing little fear of God and of the Inquisition, have brought into Spain and have in their possession many books of the accursed heretic Luther and his followers. All persons were ordered to bring to the Inquisition whatsoever books and writings of any and all works written by the said perverse heretic and his followers, and to denounce any persons whom they knew or suspected of having such accursed books of that perverse heretic.[12]

These were the days when enthusiasm for Erasmus and his works - printed and reprinted throughout Spain - was still widespread, though there were some who opposed him and accused him of heresy (Coroleu: 2008, 73–92). In order to settle the matter, in the summer of 1527, Inquisitor General Alonso Manrique summoned scholars from Salamanca, Alcala, and Valladolid to Valladolid in order to pass judgement on certain suspicious passages (Homza: 1997, 82–83). All the

9 AHN, Inquisicion, Libro 317, fols. 182r–v.
10 The Supreme Council of the Inquisition (or Suprema) was a combination of civil and ecclesiastical powers, established by the Catholic Monarchs to which all the local tribunals were subject.
11 AHN, Inquisicion, Libro 319, fol. 13v; fol. 14r–v.
12 AHN, Inquisicion de Toledo, Proceso contra Juan de Vergara, Legajo 223, no. 42, fols. 15r–v.

delegates from Salamanca and Valladolid except Alonso Enriquez, Abbot of Valladolid, pronounced themselves anti-Erasmian. In contrast, all those from Alcala, with the exception of Pedro Sanchez Ciruelo, were pro-Erasmian. It basically boiled down to a debate between scholastics and biblical humanists. No agreement was reached, and Manrique dissolved the conference, leaving things as they were.

By the 1530s, heresy hunting was becoming a national sport in Spain. A great public burning of Lutheran books was staged in Toledo; a similar event took place in Salamanca.[13] The *Suprema* kept a vigilant eye on incoming literature and on March 28, 1534, sent out another circular letter to the various courts of the Inquisition regarding Lutheran books:

> As you know, some time ago we wrote to you telling you to find a way that those that have books or writings or treaties of that evil heretic Marin Luther or of any of his followers or adherents should hand them over to you; and those that know of others who have them should tell to you. We believe this measure has been very successful. But because we know that many people from this country have gone to Germany in service of the Emperor, our Lord, where those evil heresies, for our sins, are very widespread and observed, it could have happened that they brought back some book, or books, containing that perverse doctrine and errors, it would be a good thing to publish the edicts anew and to add to the list more books and other authors that contain new errors and doctrines contrary to our holy Catholic faith and against the Holy Apostolic See.[14]

Several of the leading Erasmians were brought to trial (Longhurst: 1969, 230). Others left the country. One leading personality who fell under suspicion but left was the chancellor of the University of Alcala, Pedro de Lerma. In 1537, he was called upon to abjure eleven Erasmian propositions. To avoid further trouble, he left for Paris later that year, where he became Dean of the Faculty of Theology at the Sorbonne. In short, by the early 1540s, Erasmianism was no longer an articulate force in Spanish intellectual life and soon his works would also have to be brought into the country clandestinely.

As the sixteenth century moved on, many of those that had earlier declared themselves Erasmians turned to the German Reformers, especially those who had travelled abroad as part of the Emperor's entourage or had taken part in the discussions at Trent. Likewise, students – and even book dealers trading at the northern fairs – returned with broader outlooks and more eclectic mind-sets that gave way to inquiring minds in search of more satisfying spirituality. Three individuals that deserve mention in this respect are Constantino Ponce de la Fuente, Carlo Sesso, and Julian Hernandez.

13 AHN, Inquisición de Toledo, Proceso contra fray Bernardo, leg. 190, no. 4.
14 AHN, Inquisición, lib. 573, f. 14.

In the summer of 1548, Constantino Ponce de la Fuente, a famous preacher at Seville, was appointed Crown Prince Philip's preacher during his European tour. This took him to Genoa, Milan, Mantua, Trent, Innsbruck, Munich, Augsburg, Heidelberg, Ghent, Leuven, etc., and finally Brussels. The tour ended in the summer of 1551, which is when Constantino returned to Seville, though he would later leave again to accompany Prince Philip to England for his marriage with Mary Tudor. Towards the end of 1555 Constantino seems to have returned to Spain for good. He had been absent for seven years. On the return trip the Prince stopped again at Augsburg, which coincided with another session of the diet that his father the Emperor had convened in 1547. The particular session Prince Philip and his entourage attended was an opening session held on July 8, 1550. There were delegates – both Catholic and Protestant – from Mainz, Trier, Cologne and the Palatinate. Though Constantino may not have had time to make acquaintance with all the delegates, he would have found time to visit some of the bookshops and to meet with the "undercover Protestant" diplomat Caspar von Nidbruck, who may have oriented him regarding Protestant authors. Their meeting would not have been looked on with suspicion because Nidbruck was there negotiating for the Catholic party (Kess: 2008, 136–137). Nidbruck was well-connected. His position at the court of Maximilian would have allowed him to pursue contacts with Catholics and Protestants alike, especially bearing in mind Maximilian's rather tolerant attitude towards Protestantism (Kess: 2008, 133). Curiously enough, in the list of confiscated books inventoried around 1563 (Luttikhuizen: 2016b, Appendix A), there are three works published in Augsburg, which could have been purchased by Constantino that day and later formed part of his secret library discovered by the inquisitors in 1561.[15] The three books were: Arsatius Schofer, *Enarrationes Evangeliorum Dominicalium ad dialecticam Methodum, & Rhetoricam dispositionem accommodatae* (Augsburg: H. Steiner, 1539, 1541, 1544); Bernardino Ochino, *Expositio Epistolæ diui Pauli ad Romanos* (Augsburg: P. Ulhardus, 1550); Johannes Pistorius the Elder [Johannes Pessellius], *Omnium operum Divi Avrelii Avgvstini, episcopi hipponensis, Epitome* (Augsburg: H. Steiner, 1537), which was a collection of St. Augustine's works.

Bernardino Ochino's commentary on Romans could have belonged to the collection of books Carlo de Sesso brought back to Spain from Italy in 1550, where he had gone to collect an inheritance. Before leaving for Italy, an inquisitor at Calahorra (near Zaragoza) had given him a list of books to bring back. The list included Calvin's *Institutes*, Wolfgang Musculus' Commentaries on Matthew and John, Joannes Brenz on John and Luke, Calvin on several Epistles by St. Paul, and Luther's commentary on Psalm 130, traditionally called "*De profundis*". Besides copies of the above-mentioned volumes, Sesso also brought back several others

15 See Luttikhuizen: 2018.

that had just come off the press, namely, sermons in Italian by "el Capuchino" (Ochino: 1550), and several copies of Valdés' *110 Considerations* in Italian (Valdés: 1550). Sesso, who had married into a well-connected family and may have enjoyed diplomatic immunity, which would have exempted him – at least still in 1550 – from being searched for clandestine literature, shared his books later with members of the evangelical circle at Valladolid.

The arrival, in 1550, of a large trunk of "Lutheran" books sent from Brussels by Gaspar Zapata, smuggled in the belongings of a nobleman returning to Seville, put the inquisitors on their guard. The books were seized and a dispatch was immediately sent from the *Suprema* to Emperor Charles V in Brussels stating:

> Instructions for His Majesty's court: First, let Gaspar Zapata, servant of Fadrique Enriquez, brother of the Marquis of Tarifa, who lives in His Majesty's court, be examined under oath and tell and declare if he knows where the priest Diego de la Cruz, who lived some years in Seville and is now in Flanders... Gaspar Zapata should also be asked if he delivered a trunk of Lutheran books to Antonio de Guzman, a knight from Seville, when he left Brussels. These books have been seized by the Inquisitors at Seville. Have him declare who the books were for and if he sent them in his own name or in the name of another, and who wrote to him asking him to send them and who bought them and anything else related to this business, such as what he did with them before he embarked, etc., that is, anything else that might shed light on the case. This information should then be carefully and secretly sent to the Inquisitor General or to the Supreme Council of this kingdom of Spain in a sealed envelope.[16]

Another courier was Julian Hernandez, known as "Julianillo". Julian Hernandez made several journeys from Geneva to Spain between 1553 and 1556 with loads of Protestant literature (Luttikhuizen: 2016, 210–212). In the fall of 1556 he set off again for Spain with literature and letters for friends and acquaintances in Seville from Juan Perez de Pineda, a Spaniard who had fled the Inquisition in 1550 and was living in Geneva. Julianillo's arrival in Seville in the summer of 1557 with a new load of books alerted the authorities.[17] The capture of Julian Hernandez and his load of clandestine literature led to the discovery of the "little underground church" and the imprisonment of all its members, or, as the inquisitors acknowledged, the capture of Julian Hernandez was "the thread that led them to a great ball of wool".[18] The *Suprema* immediately dispatched the following warning to all the tribunals throughout Spain:

> The Inquisitors at Seville have written to us saying that a Spaniard coming from Flanders and from Germany has brought into the city certain books. We charge you to

16 AHN, Inquisición, lib. 574, f. 216r.
17 Julianillo was imprisoned and sent to the stake on December 22, 1560.
18 BNE, ms. 6176, f. 48v.

> visit all the bookshops and to publish edicts throughout the area and to bring these books to the Holy Office.[19]

The following year, the *Suprema* was obliged to clarify certain information sent out earlier that year:

> We sent you some days ago edicts to be published in your district, prohibiting anyone to read or have in his possession books on Christian Doctrine or theology printed outside Spain from the year 1550 to the present. Because there seems to be some confusion whether this prohibition refers to books in Latin or in Spanish, or both, may it be known that the edict refers to books written in Spanish, not those written in Latin.[20]

Inquisitor General Fernando de Valdés lost no time in informing the Pope Paul IV that everything possible was being done to stop the selling and the entrance into Spain of prohibited books, which "is the main cause of this disaster, nevertheless, heretics in Germany and other places, who have correspondence with persons here, keep finding new ways to introduce them".[21] In January of 1562, the Inquisitors at Seville gathered all the books they had confiscated, and classified them. Of all the heretical authors they saved one copy of each "in case they might need them in the future" and burned the rest, "which were many".[22] They saved several Bibles and New Testaments, and deposited the rest in the Hospital del Cardenal. It occurred to them that since these Bibles no longer had owners it would be more useful if, instead of burning them, they were "censured" – that is, if the printer's name were inked out – and sold at public auction for the expenses of the Holy Office. Many other books that still required examination and censuring were taken to the Hospital del Cardenal for Dr. Gonzalo Millan, chaplain of Cardinal Cervantes and administrator of the hospital, to inspect.

Despite the edicts and confiscations, prohibited literature continued to arrive. Bales of books were confiscated at several northern ports. In 1560, ten bales sent from Lyons for the book dealer Adrian Gemart in Valladolid were confiscated at Bilbao: at Laredo seventy bales for Carlos Pernot at Medina del Campo were seized. Likewise, in 1563 and again in 1564 numerous bales coming from Lyons were intercepted at the French border (Thomas: 2001, 242). On December 12, 1563, the Inquisitors received information from Andrea Pejioni, a Florentine book dealer, that from Lyons (France) books were shipped to La Rochelle,[23] where one Peregrino del Baño, "a great Lutheran heretic", shipped them along

---

19 AHN, Inquisición, lib. 575, f. 53 y ss.

20 AHN, Inquisición, lib. 575, f. LXXXI r.

21 AHN, Inquisición, lib. 245, f. 230r.

22 AHN, Inquisición, leg. 2942, doc. 96.

23 La Rochelle was an important Huguenot stronghold on the Atlantic coast. With its impregnable walls and its own powerful navies, Rochelle was the Venice of France. It was also the Geneva of France, the city of refuge to which Protestants from all parts of the country fled.

with other merchandise to his brother Andrea del Baño, who had a shop in Seville.[24]

On October 9, 1566, the *Suprema* sent a note to the inquisitors at Seville in which they urged them to appoint a sheriff to search the ships, as well as the personnel aboard, and to visit all the bookshops, especially those in Cadiz. Three weeks later, the inquisitors at Seville informed the *Suprema* that,

> The visits to the bookshops and the book dealers began yesterday, the 25th. At 9 o'clock in the morning all the shops in Seville were simultaneously occupied by *familiares* of the Holy House so that it was impossible for one to warn another, or to hide or remove a single book. Later, we – licenciado Carpio and licenciado Quintanilla –, the archbishop's deputy, and the ecclesiastical judge ordered that each one of the shops be secured with new locks. We will visit them one by one.[25]

After 1566 the ecclesiastical authorities became much more vigilant in Cadiz, where many large foreign ships docked that could not sail up the Guadalquivir to Seville. Diego Diaz de Esquivel was sent as commissioner to search both incoming and outgoing ships for banned literature. Esquivel complained to the inquisitors that foreigners would leave the ships before there was time to "visit" them and would meet with other foreigners living in the city. And, likewise, Spaniards also entered the ships before the ships could be visited, giving them the opportunity to warn those on board.[26] As a result, the commissioners at Cadiz, San Lucar de Barrameda, Puerto de Santa Maria, Ayamonte, Palos, and Moguer – all the important Atlantic port cities in southern Spain – were ordered to take note of all persons that visited the ships.[27]

One would suppose that after the severe repression and *autos-de-fe* carried out between 1558 and 1563, there would have been no potential buyers/readers of Protestant literature left in Spain. Even Pope Pius V seemed to have thought that reading prohibited books was not enough of an offence to send people to the stake. Indeed, one of his first measures, in 1566, was to issue a jubilee that absolved all those who had – or had read – prohibited literature. The notification perplexed the members of the *Suprema*, who immediately alerted all the tribunals throughout Spain not to make the document public until they had consulted with Philip II, who in turn was to confer first with the Pope.[28] Ten years later, in the summer of 1576, the *Suprema* was alarmed again by information regarding clandestine literature coming into Seville. They had learned from "a Lutheran, who *en tierra de moros* (in the land of the Moors) had renounced his faith", that

---

24 AHN, Inquisición, leg. 2943, doc. 124.
25 AHN, Inquisición, leg. 2944, doc. 29–2.
26 AHN, Inquisición, leg 2944, doc. 37–1.
27 AHN, Inquisición, leg. 2944, doc. 29–2.
28 AHN, Inquisición, lib. 497, f. 96v.

more than twelve thousand Lutheran books had arrived in the city and four thousand had already been distributed. This may have been a vast exaggeration, however, the letter continues:

> Because this can cause great harm to the Catholic faith, especially here, where the Lutherans with such diabolic diligence and endless manners endeavour to sow the seed of their sect, a remedy must be found. [...] With all caution, you must find out in whose hands these books are, who brought them here, in what port they arrived, how they entered, who distributed them and to whom, where they were deposited once in the city, and just what books they are.[29]

Ships docked in Spanish ports continued to be searched and if heretical literature was found, even for personal use, the entire crew was arrested and all the books seized, as was also the case of "The Angel Gabriel", seized in San Lucar de Barrameda in 1580.[30] As late as 1583, the inquisitors at Seville were still wondering if the less restrictive measures towards Englishmen, issued in 1575, were still in effect.[31] That agreement, on the other hand, did not stop them from sending other foreigners to row in the galleys. In 1583 alone, thirty-nine offenders, mainly Polish, German, and Dutch sailors, were sent to the galleys (Thomas: 2001, 283). Another group under special scrutiny for fear of their bringing into the country prohibited books printed in Germany and sent to Spain via Brussels or Antwerp were Spaniards with connections in Flanders. The inquisitors at Seville warned the *Suprema* that,

> Based on the testimonies arriving daily in this Holy Office, and the confessions of Flemish citizens we have sent to the stake and others that are at present prisoners in this Holy Office, we have learned that much harm is being caused in Flanders by this damned Lutheran sect, which is increasing daily.[32]

All sorts of measures were taken to stop the "Protestant menace" and the flow of heretical literature into Spain. Processions were organised; false distribution networks were set up as bait in order to trap contacts into disclosing their identity (Thomas: 2001, 245; Reguera: 1984). New groups were discovered in Valencia, Teruel, Galicia, Malaga, Cuenca, and Zaragoza and their leaders brought to trial. A few were sentenced to the stake but the majority were sent to row in the King's galleys. In 1561, the inquisitors at Zaragoza informed the *Suprema* of an *auto-da-fe* celebrated a few days earlier, and added,

29 AHN, Inquisición, lib. 579, f. 4v.
30 AHN, Inquisición, leg. 2947.
31 AHN, Inquisición, leg. 2947.
32 AHN, Inquisición, leg. 2942, 97.

> It is paramount that the punishment, both of Lutherans and of *conversos*, be exemplary because we are in a part of the country where there are many Bearnese and Frenchmen and other foreigners that profess Luther's heresies, hence we send them to the galleys.[33]

That same day they wrote to Philip II, saying,

> We have taken very strong actions against the Lutherans, as strong as the law permits, in order to make them aware of, and fear, the sort of punishment they will receive if they come into your majesty's kingdom.[34]

Six years later, these same inquisitors sent Philip II another letter in which they informed him that,

> Fifty-six offenders were brought out in the last *auto-da-fe*, nearly all of them Lutherans. They were all foreigners, from France, Gascuña and Bearn, and were all condemned to serve in your majesty's galleys because that is the punishment we feel that most terrifies them and keeps them from entering your kingdom.[35]

Able bodies to supply the King's galleys were welcome, but they posed another problem: did the King want his ships filled with heretics? After the Battle of Lepanto in 1571, in which Spain participated with 14 ships, which necessarily carried many Lutheran rowers, Philip II came up with a plan to

> Create an Inquisition for heretics who might be found on ships. As the authority of the Inquisitor General did not extend beyond the dominions of the King of Spain, it was considered necessary to apply to the Pope, who in 1571 granted the brief, which was demanded, authorizing the Inquisitor General to create the new tribunal, and appoint judges and officers. It was first known by the name of the "Inquisition of the Galleys", but it was afterwards called the "Inquisition of the Fleets and Armies"; it existed but for a short period, as it was found to impede the progress of navigation (Llorente: 1843, 190–191).

With all the confiscations the "Protestant" problem had not been solved. Enlarging the Index of Prohibited Books did not solve the problem either. Among the 200 books inventoried in 1583 by Dr. Heredia,[36] there was a copy of Calvin's *Commentary on Isaiah* (Geneva, 1551), Wolfgang Musculus' *Commentary on Romans* (Basel, 1555), Savonarola's *Exposicion del psalmo In te domine speraui*, a book by Sebastian Munster, another by Justus Jonas, several by Petrus Ramus, Bartolome de Carranza's *Catechism* (Antwerp, 1558), Juan Perez de Pineda's *Letter to Philip II* (Geneva, 1557), a half dozen books by Erasmus, including his New Testament, and a rare copy of Ambrosio Montesino's *Epistles and Gospels for the Year* (Seville, 1537). Justus Jonas, who today might be considered one of

33 AHN, Inquisición, Lib. 988, f. 84.
34 AHN, Inquisición, Lib. 988, f. 87.
35 AHN, Inquisición, Lib. 988, f. 134.
36 AHN, Inquisición, leg. 4426, doc. 31.

the forgotten reformers, was one of the most popular Protestant authors in Spain in the 1540s. In the list of confiscated books published by the Inquisition in 1563, a total of 28 of Jonas' works appear.

A document, written up some time after 1610, lists the books confiscated – and prohibited – by the Inquisition at Seville between 1583 and 1609. Among other publications, mainly by Catholic authors, there were Bibles in Spanish "sent from La Rochelle" that contained "*ciertas cosas del Calepino*" (certain things by Calepinus). This was actually the Bible translated by Casiodoro de Reina and printed in Basel in 1569, known as the *Biblia del Oso* (Bible of the Bear).[37] To facilitate entry into Spain, in Antwerp the title page of these Bibles was substituted for that of Ambrosio Calepinus' famous Latin Dictionary, which explains the phrase "*con ciertas cosas del Calepino*". This policy of inserting false title pages went back to the early 1530s when tactics for introducing Reformed literature had changed. On June 13, 1530, the *Suprema* wrote, "there is reason to suspect that the writings of such heretics are being brought to Spain and sold as approved works". All tribunals were urged to obtain from booksellers a list of all the books in their shops so that the books by authors whose names were unfamiliar might be examined for theological errors. Two months later the *Suprema* sent out another circular letter:

> A few days ago we were informed that Martin Luther and others among the followers and adherents of his false opinions, and inventors of other new errors, realising that they are unable to spread their books and poisonous doctrine in these lands as freely as they would like, have introduced many of their harmful opinions under the names of Catholic authors, giving false titles to their books, and in other instances inserting glosses and additions of false expositions and errors to well-known books of approved and good doctrine. All bookstores are to be diligently searched, and because such books might already be in the hands of private parties, the inquisitors are to include in future edicts against Lutheran books a provision requiring the faithful to come forward and inform them of any Lutheran literature in such Catholic disguise.[38]

Other books confiscated between 1583 and 1609 were Calvin's *Institutes* "printed in England in Spanish" and two catechisms by Calvin, "printed by Ricardo del Campo, one in 1596 and the other in 1600" (Calvin: 1596). Cipriano de Valera, one of the exiled monks from Seville living in England, was responsible for the translation of the *Institutes.* For the *Catechism* he used Juan Perez de Pineda's 1559 rendering to which he added a prologue. There also appeared a New Testament and Catechism "in Spanish", attributed to Theodor Beza. This is an

37 In 1581, the Bishop of Basel, Blarer von Wartensee, informed Cardinal Charles Borromeo, Archbishop of Milan, that 1,600 copies of a Bible in Spanish had been printed in Basel and that 1,400 copies had been sent from Frankfurt to Antwerp.

38 AHN, Inquisicion, lib. 320, fols. 321v–322r and 343r–v.

evident error because Beza's works were not translated into Spanish, and suggests that whereas the Bibles carried the false title page of Calepinus' Dictionary, the New Testaments carried a false title page attributing them to Theodor Beza. The publication actually refers to Casiodoro de Reina's *Testamento Nuevo,* revised by Cipriano de Valera and printed in London by Richard Field. Another work by Cipriano de Valera printed by Richard Field that appeared on this list was his *Treatise on the Pope and the Mass* (1599). Parts of the work are mentioned separately, such as the *False Miracles of María de la Visitación, Prioress the Convent of Anunciada in Lisboa.* Still another work translated by Cipriano de Valera and printed by Richard Field was William Perkins' *A Reformed Catholike* (1597). Besides the abovementioned books, the Index of 1612 included all of Erasmus' works, those of the Bishop of Granada Hernando de Talavera, *Dialogo de Mercurio y Caron* by Alfonso de Valdés, *El Lazarillo de Tormes*, etc.

The last comprehensive Index of Prohibited Books published in Spain appeared in 1790. It included books of all types: religious works, vernacular translations of the Bible, scientific works, and even some of the great works of Spanish literature. Some books were banned straightaway; others were subtly expurgated. One example is Calvete de Estrella's account of Crown Prince Philip's tour throughout Europe. Among the preachers that accompanied the Crown Prince on his journey, Calvete tells us that,

> There was also Dr. Constantino, a great philosopher and profound theologian, and one of the most well-known and eloquent men in the pulpit [...] Easter of 1550 was spent in Brussels, where the three great preachers of the court preached: Doctor Constantino, Fray Bernardo de Fresneda, and Doctor Augustine de Cazalla, an excellent theologian, a man of sound doctrine and eloquence (Calvete: 1552, fol. 7v).

Calvete published his account of the tour in 1552. Ten years later, after the autos-da-fe in Seville and Valladolid that condemned both Constantino and Cazalla for their Protestant views, Calvete's text was expurgated and all mention of these two preachers was erased. Instructions stated:

> Calvete de Estella (Juan Christov.). In his book, *Journey of the Prince*, Book 1, section entitled "Embarkation", fol. 5, page 2, and fol. 7, page 2, remove all that is in praise of Constantino de la Fuente; in Book 4, fol. 325, remove all that is in praise of Constantino and Agustin de Cazalla (Indice: 1790. Translation mine).

A century later, another historian, who narrated the important events that took place in Seville from 1246 to 1671, reluctantly restored their names, but with the following reservations:

> The Prince set sail from Rosas on November 2, accompanied by many grandees, noblemen and knights [...] in whose company also went Doctor Constantino de la Fuente, applauded then for being a great theologian and preacher, condemned later for being a perverse heretic, whose pride and presumption were a restraint on him, but being so far

from being suspected, he preached for the Prince in Barcelona on All Saints' Day (Ortiz de Zuniga: 1677, vol. III, 402).

Unfortunately most of the books banned prior to 1570 were burned (Kamen: 2011; Perez: 2012). The person responsible for introducing a policy of expurgation was Benito Arias Montano, Philip II's chaplain and librarian. In 1569, he began work on an Expurgatory Index, which was published in 1571. This compromise solution in which trustworthy officials blotted out words, lines or whole passages of otherwise acceptable texts, allowed expurgated editions to circulate. Criteria varied over the years (Bujanda: 1988; 2002). *La Celestina,* for example, was not included in the Indexes of the sixteenth century, but was expurgated in 1632 and prohibited in its entirety in 1790. A French rendering of Daniel Defoe's Robinson Crusoe, *La vie et les avantures de Robinson Crusoe* (Amsterdam, 1720), appeared in the Index of 1747 and remained there. By the mid-eighteenth century, Liberalism had become the Spanish Inquisition's main target. In an attempt to stop it, all books, pamphlets, and newspapers relating to the revolution were seized. Likewise, under the pretext that novels had scanty moral and artistic value, the Council of Castile decreed that no licence be granted for the publication of works of fiction written or translated from French.

In the Index of 1640, the following sentence was expurgated from Don Quixote: "works of charity done in a lukewarm and half-hearted way are without merit and of no avail" (DQ II.36). Although Miguel de Cervantes' *Exemplary Novels* (1613) were never included in the list, nevertheless, a 1624 edition printed in Seville by Francisco de Lyra reveals one of the most subtle examples of "non-official" expurgation. One example suffices. One of the main characters in the story of "La Señora Cornelia" is Alfonso II d'Este (1533–1597), the fifth and last Duke of Ferrara. In the fictionalised version of Alfonso's adventures, he postpones his marriage to Cornelia until his mother, who is at the point of dying, passes away. Though Cervantes never mentions the mother by name, any discerning reader knew that the mother of Alfonso II d'Este was none other than Renee de Valois (1510–1575), known for her Huguenot sympathies. Lyra, as a prosperous entrepreneuring printer, was not about to incur the disfavour of the Inquisition and have the edition confiscated once it was printed, so wherever the word *madre* (mother) appears, he simply substituted it for *padre* (father). At first sight this may look like a typographical error, but Lyra did not want to leave the reader in doubt and further along introduces the phrase "*el duque viejo*" (the old Duke). Lyra's manipulated text became the standard version of Cervantes' *Exemplary Novels* until the end of the eighteenth century, when a printer in Valencia caught the error (Luttikhuizen: 1997). Today poetic distortions of history are seen as charming literary devices, but for the seventeenth- century reader they held specific socio-political meaning.

Until the Inquisition was definitively abolished in 1834, there was no freedom of press in Spain. Even after that, due to constant political changes and agreements established in the Concordats signed with the Vatican, Protestantism and Protestant literature remained proscribed. The efforts of the Hebrew scholar and philanthropist Luis de Usoz y Rio is a good case in point. Usoz had to publish clandestinely his twenty-volume set of *Reformistas Antiguos Españoles* (1847–1865).[39] It took great stamina for him to build a library of thousands of prohibited books and to edit and reprint the writings of compatriots condemned by the Inquisition at a time when freedom of press was still more theoretical than real (Vilar: 1994), or as the eminent Hispanist, William Knapp (1899, I, 328) put it, at a time "when liberty of conscience in Spain still meant ruin to those who embraced it, unless they be too poor to have social bonds or too lowly to attract official persecution". Full freedom of press would have to wait another 100 years!

Bibliography

Archival Sources

Archivo Historico Nacional (AHN). Unless indicated, notes, brackets and translation mine.

Biblioteca Nacional De Espana (BNE). Unless indicated, notes, brackets and translation mine.

Primary and Secondary Sources

Arias Montano, Benito (1571), Indice Expurgatorio, Antwerp: Plantini.

Bataillon, Marcel (1966), Erasmo y España: estudios sobre la historia espiritual del siglo XVI, Mexico: Fondo de Cultura Económica.

Bedouelle, Guy (2008), Attacks on the Biblical Humanism of Jacques Lefèvre d'Etaples, in: Erika Rummel (ed.), Biblical Humanism and Scholasticism in the Age of Erasmus, Leiden: Brill, 117–142.

Brown, Rawdon (1864–1886), Calendar of State Papers Relating to English Affairs in the Archives of Venice, 38 vols. British History Online. www.british-history.ac.uk/source.aspx?pubid=999&page=1.

Bujanda, J.M. de (1988), Index d'Anvers, 1569, 1570, 1571, Sherbrooke/Geneva: Droz.

– (2002), Index Librorum Prohibitorum. 1600–1966, Montreal/Geneva: Droz.

39 The writings of the sixteenth-century Spanish Protestant Reformers: Juan de Valdés, Constantino Ponce de la Fuente, Francisco de Enzinas, Pérez de Pineda, Antonio del Corro, Cipriano de Valera, and others. See Luttikhuizen: 2016b, 333–342.

BUSTOS TÁULER, ALVARO (2010), Ambrosio Montesino y el "Exercicio de la continua predicación": poesía, mecenazgo y sermón en su Cancionero (Toledo, 1508), Revista de poética medieval 24, 93–126.

CALVETE DE ESTRELLA, JUAN CRISTOVAL (1552), El felicissimo Viaje del muy alto y muy poderoso principe Don Phelippe, hijo del emperador Don Carlos Quinto maximo, desde España á sus tierras de la baxa Alemaña, con la descripcion de todos los estados de Brabante y Flandes. Antwerp: M. Nucio.

CALVIN, JOHN (1596), Institucion de la Religion Christiana: compuesta en quatro libros, y dividida en capitulos. Y ahora Nuevamente traduzida en Romance Castellano (London: Ricardo del Campo, 1597)

– (1596), Catecismo, que significa forma de instruccion: que contiene los principios de la religion de Dios, util y necessario para todo fiel Christiano. Compuesta en manera de dialogo, donde pregunta el maestro y respuesta el discipulo. London: Ricardo del Campo.

COROLEU, ALEJANDRO (2008), Anti-Erasmianism in Spain, in: Erika Rummel (ed.), Biblical Humanism and Scholasticism in the Age of Erasmus, Leiden: Brill, 73–92.

COROLEU, ALEJANDRO/BARRY TAYLOR (eds.) (2010), Humanism and Christian Letters in Early Modern Iberia (1480–1630), Newcastle: Cambridge Scholars.

DAU, W.H.T. (1919), The Great Renunciation: Leaves from the Story of Luther's Life, St. Louis, MO: Concordia Publishing House.

HOMZA, LU ANN (1997), Erasmus as Hero, or Heretic? Spanish Humanism and the Valladolid Assembly of 1527, Renaissance Quarterly 50, 78–118.

Indice ultimo de los libros prohibidos y mandados expurgar para todos los rey de las Españas, Carlos IV: Contiene en resumen todos los libros puestos en el Indice Expurgatorio del ano 1747, y en los Edictos posteriores, hasta fin de Diciembre de 1789, (1790), Madrid: Antonio de Sancha.

KESS, ALEXANDRA (2008), Johann Sleidan and the Protestant Vision of History, Aldershot: Ashgate.

KNAPP, WILLIAM I. (1899), Life, Writings and Correspondence of George Borrow, 2 vols., New York: G.P. Putnam's Sons/London: John Murray.

LLORENTE, JUAN ANTONIO (1843), A Critical History of the Inquisition of Spain: From the Period of Its Establishment by Ferdinand V to the Reign of Ferdinand VII, Philadelphia: James M. Campbell.

LONGHURST, JOHN E. (1969), Luther's Ghost in Spain 1517–1546, Lawrence, KS: Coronado Press.

LUTHER, MARTIN (1913), Luther's Correspondence and other Contemporary Letters Translated and Edited by Preserved Smith, Ph.D. Fellow of Amherst College, Philadelphia, PA: The Lutheran Publication Society.

LUTTIKHUIZEN, FRANCES (1997), ¿Fueron censuradas las Novelas ejemplares?, Cervantes 20, 165–174.

– (2016a), The Ximenez Polyglot, Unio cum Christo 2, 1, 83–98.

– (2016b), Underground Protestantism in Sixteenth-Century Spain. A New Look at a Much Ignored Side of Spanish History, Göttingen: Vandenhoeck & Ruprecht.

– (2017a), Cisneros, precursor del movimiento evangélico en España", Aletheia 50/2, 101–124.

- (2018), Constantino de la Fuente (1502–1560), de predicador aclamado a hereje olvidado, Hispania Sacra 70, 29–38.

M'Crie, Thomas (1829), History of the Progress and Suppression of the Reformation in Spain in the Sixteenth Century, Edinburgh: W. Blackwood.

Martínez Millán, Jose (2000), La corte de Carlos V, Madrid: Sociedad Estatal para la Conmemoración de los Centenarios de Felipe II y Carlos V. Novísima recopilación de las leyes de España, (1805), Madrid: Sancha.

Ochino, Bernadino (1550), La quarta parte de le prediche en toscano. Geneva.

Ortiz De Zuñiga, Diego (1677), Annales ecclesiasticos y seculares de la Ciudad de Sevilla, 3 vols., Madrid: Garcia Infançon.

Preston, Patrick/Allan Jenkins (2007), Biblical Scholarship and the Church: A Sixteenth-Century Crisis of Authority. Aldershot: Ashgate.

Reguera, Iñaki (1984), La Inquisición española en el País Vasco: el tribunal de Calahorra 1513–1570, San Sebastián: Txertoa.

Rummel, Erika (ed.) (2008), Biblical Humanism and Scholasticism in the Age of Erasmus, Leiden: Brill.

Tellechea Idígoras, José Ignacio (1962), Biblias publicadas fuera de España secuestradas por la Inquisición de Sevilla, Bulletin Hispanique 64, 236–247.

Thomas, Werner (2001), La represión del protestantismo en España 1517–1648, Leuven University Press.

Valdés, Juan de (1550), Le cento et dieci divine considerationi del S. Giovanni Valdesso. Basel: J. Oporinus,

Vilar, Juan Bautista (1994), La formación de una biblioteca de libros prohibidos en la España isabelina: Luis Usoz y Río, importador clandestino de libros protestantes (1841–1850), Bulletin Hispanique 96, 2, 397–416.

III. Refugee Reformation

Barbara A. Kaminska

A Religious Minority between Triumph and Persecution

Frans Hogenberg's *Hedge-preaching outside Antwerp* and the Flemish Community in Cologne

1. Introduction

On June 25, 1566, the Deputies to the Estates General in Brussels received an alarming letter from their colleagues, the members of the Antwerp Magistracy. These city officials wanted to let the government know immediately about a gathering, which had happened a day before just outside the city, in the Berchem neighbourhood. From one until five in the afternoon, a Reformed minister preached in French, while a few local citizens translated his words into Dutch. The Magistrates continued their report:

> And from what we could understand, the listeners were mostly Walloon [i.e. members of the clandestine Walloon congregation], and many among them French, so that together with people from Berchem and from elsewhere, who were drawn by novelty [of the gathering], there were between four and five thousand people, both men and women; although the majority were men, there were also women who were caring for small children. And some were so eager, that they stood on elevations, others climbed on bushes that were thick enough, so that they did much damage in the forest and in the field (Prims: 1940, 18).

Over the next few months, until April 1567, similar letters would flood authorities in Brussels, and the quoted numbers of listeners would only increase. Sermons like the one described here became known as *haagpreken* (hedge-preaching) or *veltpredicatie* (field-preaching), and constituted one of the most remarkable and glorious – albeit short-lived – episodes in the history of the Reformed movement on the eve of the Dutch Revolt, during the so-called Wonder Year.[1] An important

1 The word haagpreken refers to hedges, which demarcated city limits, and indicated that these open-air Protestant sermons took place outside of the cities' jurisdiction. The term "Wonder Year", sometimes spelled as "Wonderyear" (Dutch: Wonderjaar; Latin: annus mirabilis), designates the period in Dutch history between Spring 1566 and Spring 1567 that was marked

factor in shaping the collective memory and confessional identity of Dutch society, these open-air gatherings became a subject of late sixteenth- and seventeenth-century drawings and prints, which were at once images of triumph and of the defeat that followed just a few months after the preaching began.

This essay focuses on an early graphic depiction of the hedge-preaching, included by Flemish printmaker Frans Hogenberg in his series *Scenes of the Religious and Civil Wars from the History of the Netherlands, France and England from 1559* (Fig. 1). Many features of Hogenberg's image conform to the description of the sermon provided by the disquieted magistrates: large crowds are gathered outside Antwerp, whose emblematic cityscape is depicted in the far background; these curious men and women are attentively listening to preachers, and some of them are looking for shelter under the trees, with little concern for doing "damage in the forest and in the field".[2] Their safety is guaranteed by armed men on horseback, mentioned by the officials later in their letter (Prims: 1940, 18–19). But other elements of the engraving set it apart from contemporary reports of the *veltpredicatie*, particularly of its early phase. Hogenberg depicts three sermons taking place simultaneously, in contrast to the letter of the Deputies, which mentions only one Walloon priest, whose French sermon was translated into Dutch to all of the gathered listeners. Furthermore, Hogenberg's three sermons – Walloon, Calvinist and Lutheran – remain conspicuously separated in the image. Finally, we know from the letter that the minister and his escort chose for the place of the gathering Berchem, which is now one of Antwerp's districts, and was in the mid-sixteenth century a small recreational neighbourhood just south of the city walls (Prims: 1940, 18–19). While the print acknowledges the suburban residential character of the setting by the inclusion

---

by a considerable weakening of the central government, which in turn allowed for the strengthening of Protestant congregations and the influence of the local nobility. See, for example, Marnef: 1999, 193.

2 I would like to make a case that Hogenberg's print in fact intends to depict the sermon on June 24, as described in the quoted letter. While the inscription at the bottom of the image gives the date "Anno Domini M.D. LXVI in Junio XIIII", "Junio" has been corrected from "Julio", as the outline of letter "l" is still visible. However, the date June 14 would be too early. Although Protestant ministers occasionally preached outside of the city walls earlier that spring, it is the sermon on June 24 that marks the beginning of haagpreken, after the consistory of the Walloon Church decided it was time to act publicly. It is therefore my conclusion that "Junio XIIII" was intended as "Junio XXIIII". German verses above the date, which I discuss later in this essay, further support the idea that the print is meant to show the moment when the hedge-preaching has already become a semi-legal, open manifestation of the Protestants' discontent with the corruption of the Catholic Church (the verses do not mention opposition against the Habsburgs' harsh persecution of the religious dissidents in the Low Countries). In addition, in correlation with the switch from "Julio" to "Junio", the text suggests that Hogenberg wanted to commemorate the beginning of the hedge-preaching as the climactic moment of the so-called Wonder Year.

of villas, the distance between the sermon and the city is oddly expanded. This sense of alienation of the gathered citizens is strengthened by the detail of the gallows exactly on the axis between the preaching and Antwerp's cathedral.

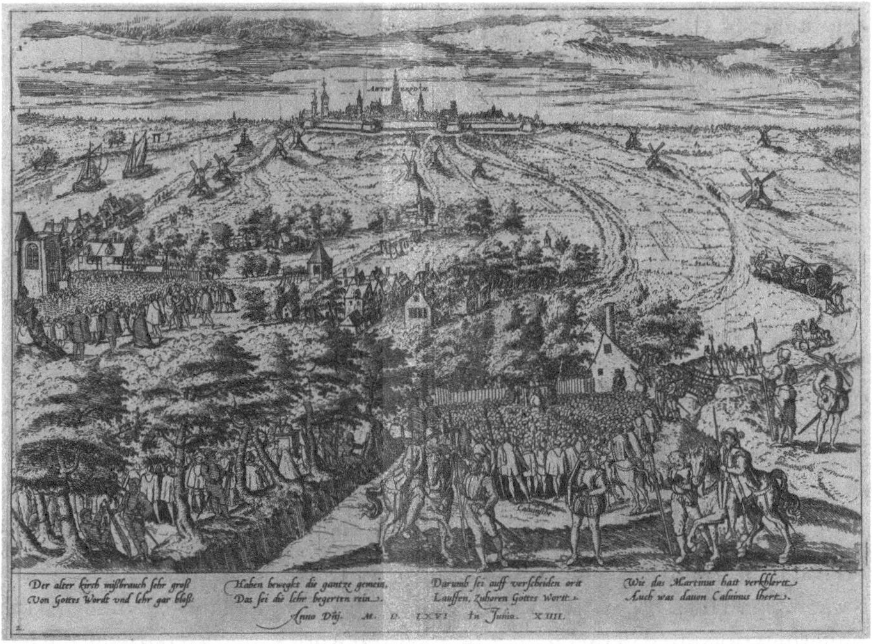

Fig. 1: Frans Hogenberg, *Hedge-preaching outside Antwerp*, after 1570, engraving, 210 × 288 mm, Rijksmuseum Amsterdam.

Hogenberg designed and first published this engraving in Cologne in the 1580s, where he settled as one of many Flemish refugees after the Habsburgs, who relied mainly on the cruel methods of Fernando Alvarez de Toledo, the Third Duke of Alba, restored their authority in the Low Countries. In what follows, I will make a case that fundamental to the understanding of the print's specific iconography and the socio-political argument it advanced was its design for both the exiles and the native inhabitants of Cologne. As I shall demonstrate, the image was conceived as an active instrument of confessional reconciliation among the Flemish community in Cologne, and aimed at securing this community's space among the Germans. It was intended to gain the latter's sympathy, and refute allegations that the exiles were trouble-makers who rebelled against the divine rule of their sovereign.[3] My analysis will reveal that Hogenberg's careful selection of episodes

3 As I argue elsewhere, a similar, albeit more historically and legally complex agenda was advanced by Dirck Volkertsz. Coornhert and Adriaan de Weert in their series "The Moral Decline of the Clergy, or the Root of the Dutch Revolt and the Iconoclastic Fury", also designed

from the history of the *haagpreken* and, more specifically, the alterations he introduced in its portrayal that veer away from the written accounts, were essential for meeting these two objectives. I will begin my discussion of Hogenberg's visual argument with a brief historic overview of the hedge-preaching, and continue with a discussion of the situation of the Flemish community in Cologne, including Hogenberg's artistic activity during the period of exile. Two aspects of refugee life are of particular importance for this study: their confessional identities and the relationship with the native local population. This socio-historical background is necessary for recognizing the print's independent agenda within the contemporary discourse of the Wonder Year, on which I shall focus next in my essay. My comparative analysis of the verbal accounts of the hedge-preaching versus its depiction by Hogenberg will, in turn, contribute to our understanding of images as agents in shaping the religious and political beliefs and behaviours of early modern viewers.

2. *In zyne Huysen oft buyten inde Bosschen:* Hedge-Preaching in the Low Countries

Protestant sermons outside Antwerp and other Netherlandish cities quickly became immensely popular among the country's population. Some of the gatherings organised between June 24, 1566 and April 9, 1567 (reportedly the last day of the hedge-preaching) were attended by as many as 20,000 listeners, even though neither the Brabant nor the Spanish authorities had ever officially given their consent to the open-air sermons. But in 1566, the authority of Margaret of Parma, the Governess of the Netherlands, was too weak and the influence of the local nobles, who were discontented with the Habsburgs' harsh religious policies, too strong to effectively exercise the prohibition of such preaching.[4] However, it should be noted that only a tiny fraction within those crowds openly broke with the Catholic Church and supported one of the Protestant congregations. The majority of the audience was drawn by curiosity, their interest piqued by the

---

and first published in the early 1570s in Cologne. The plea for religious tolerance, addressed to Protestants rather than Catholics only, thus constitutes a part of a broader political discourse, advanced both in written and visual polemics in Cologne. See Kaminska: 2013, 83–126.

4 The phrase in zyne huysen oft buyten inde bosschen – "in their houses or outside [the city] in the woods" – appears in the following prohibition of religious gatherings: Ordonnancie ende Statuyt ghemaect by mijnen Heere[n] Schouteth, Borghemeesteren, Schepenen ende Raede der Stadt va[n] Antwerpen, Aengaende secrete co[n]venticulen ende vergaderingen. Met meer andere puncten ende articulen daer toe dienende. Gheboden ende wtgheroepen op den sesten dach Octobris. M.D.LXV (Antwerp: Willem Silvius, 1565). The date should be 1566, according to the Julian calendar.

allure of a novel form and content of religious instruction, as well as by their entertainment value. In a letter from late June 1566, magistrates commented that a recent sermon attracted so many people driven by curiosity that it was *alsof men een comedie speelde* ("as if there were a farce performed") (Prims: 1940, 22). This comparison is indeed telling if we keep in mind that theatrical performances counted among the most popular entertainments of Netherlandish society. Godevaert van Haecht, a contemporary chronicler with Lutheran sympathies, did not remain oblivious to the relaxed atmosphere of hedge-preaching either, reporting that *ontrent de predicatie vondt men oock bier en ander dinghen te copen* ("at the sermon one could also find beer and other things for sale") (Van Haecht: 1929–1930, 72).

Overall, hedge-sermons did not resemble the tightly structured Catholic liturgy, recently further codified by the Council of Trent and performed in Latin, which was incomprehensible to many. Repetitive and alienating rituals, the length of which Erasmus criticised in *Modus orandi Deum* as engendering boredom rather than inspiring piety, contrasted sharply with the lively and engaging hedge-sermons of charismatic and often well-educated ministers, which were organised in a leisurely setting of *groen kercke* and embellished with the singing of psalms in the vernacular (Erasmus: 1998, 217).[5]

Authorities soon recognised curiosity and novelty – *nieuwsgierigheid* and *nieuwigheid* – as major factors behind mass attendance of the sermons, and insisted they were not acceptable justification for joining those meetings. Still, the novelty and entertainment value of *veltpredicatie* were at that time rather harmless. Yet, over the course of a few summer weeks, hedge-preaching shifted in a much more alarming direction. A growing number of participants came to the meetings carrying weapons, and sermons were occasionally disrupted by cries such as "*vive les gueux*" from anti-government and pro-dissent attendees. As both eyewitnesses and scholars have pointed out, the presence of the armed Calvinists and their supporters, combined with the helplessness and weakness of a government unable to find a viable solution to the religious crisis, shifted the significance of hedge-preaching from its central focus on religiosity to the manifestation of the power of the Reformed movement (Van Haecht: 1929–1930, *passim*; Van Vaernewijck: 1872–1881, vol. 1, *passim*; Burgon: 1839, vol. II, esp. 131–136; Marnef: 1999, 198–199). This aspect of hedge-preaching was particularly prominent in cases where ministers and participants walked back together to the city in a quasi-processional order. Possibly the most disquieting among such incidents, prior to the Iconoclastic Fury of August 1566, occurred at

5 The term groen kercke, green church, is mentioned several times in Godevaert van Haecht's chronicle as commonly used since summer 1566 among the crowds attending hedge-preaching.

a sermon outside Ypres, where a crowd of 25,000 people was escorted by 150 armed men, who accompanied the psalm-singing listeners and ministers back into the town (Marnef: 1999, 39). As we shall see shortly, despite the presence of armed guards at the sermons, Hogenberg cleverly mitigated the militant aspect of the Reformed preaching in his print, redirecting viewers' attention toward the attendees' religious zeal.

Despite the official restrictions of the Spaniards, Protestants did win considerable privileges in the summer and fall of 1566. While a provisional religious peace introduced in September 1566 clearly privileged the Catholic Church, it granted Protestants places for open worship, and, most fundamentally, acknowledged the existence of these clandestine groups and their struggle for religious freedom (Marnef: 1999, 202, 209). But that triumph of confessional minorities was short-lived, and came at a very high price. In the winter and spring, the Habsburgs restored their power, and hedge-preaching ended on April 9, 1567. Five months later, the newly arrived Duke of Alva established the so-called Council of Troubles, soon to be nicknamed the Council of Blood, to persecute – and execute – religious and political dissenters involved in the hedge-preaching and the Iconoclastic Fury which swept through the Low Countries in the summer of 1566. In doing so he was partially inspired by the anti-Catholic agenda of Calvinist preachers. The radically changed socio-political circumstances forced many citizens of Brabant and Flemish cities, and most notably of the previously thriving metropolis of Antwerp, into exile. Clandestine Lutherans, Calvinists, and supporters of other local "sects" fled to cities in the Northern Provinces, England, and Germany. Many Catholics also chose emigration, as the unstable political and economic situation was not conducive to business. Hundreds of the refugees, including Frans Hogenberg, chose Cologne as their destination, and it is their situation in this newly adopted homeland to which I shall now turn.

3. Frans Hogenberg and Flemish Refugees in Cologne

Cologne, with a rich middle and upper class increasingly interested in visual arts, who had often had a broad humanistic education, was a perfect destination for emigrating Netherlandish artists, whose livelihood after the sudden economic decline in the Low Countries became threatened (Veldman: 1993, 34–58). In 1570, in hopes of finding new patrons and clients, the city was chosen by the Mechelen printmaker Frans Hogenberg, who in the 1560s had collaborated with Abraham Ortelius on *Theatrum Orbis Terrarum*, first printed in Antwerp in 1570.[6]

6 Hogenberg first fled from the Low Countries to England, but he stayed there only two years.

Hogenberg spent twenty years in Cologne, making brief trips to Hamburg in 1585 and Cologne in 1588 to make sketches for his works. He remained active as an artist and as a member of a local Lutheran congregation until his death in 1590. In conjunction with his sectarian identity in exile, Ilja Veldman has analysed some of Hogenberg's earlier engravings and convincingly argues that in the Low Countries, Hogenberg had most likely joined the Reformed movement. However, since the attitude of the local German population, i.e. his potential clients, was much more tolerant towards Lutherans than Calvinists, Hogenberg decided to adopt the Augsburg Confession (Veldman: 1993, 43–44). In Cologne, he continued to produce city views and maps for projects such as *Civitates Orbis Terrarum* published with Georg Braun (begun 1572), Michael Baron Aitsinger's *Terra Promissionis Topographice* (1582) and *De Leone Belgico* (1583), and, finally, in 1587, *Itinerarium Belgicum.* While he also designed portraits and mythological prints, it was his historical series of the *Scenes of the Religious and Civil Wars from the History of the Netherlands, France and England from 1559*, including the *Hedge-preaching outside Antwerp* and the well-known *Iconoclastic Riot of August 20, 1566* (Fig. 2) that really brought him fame among local and foreign collectors. Hogenberg cleverly marketed his engravings to diverse audiences by including inscriptions in different languages, which we can see, for example, in *Hedge-preaching outside Antwerp*, since it is accompanied by rhymed verses in German. Navigating the local market was not always as simple as the purchasing power of potential clients would suggest. Cologne was a Catholic city, with a strong Jesuit presence, and from 1574 it was the seat of an Apostolic nuncio representing the Pope in the entire German kingdom of the Holy Roman Empire. The arrival of Protestant rebels was thus accepted reluctantly, if not met with plain hostility. Calvinists in particular had the reputation of being iconoclasts and troublemakers, prompting the city council to initially object to the settlement of the refugees. Their opposition, however, was weakened by financial motivation: the presence of Netherlandish craftsmen and merchants was quite correctly recognised as beneficial for the local economy (Veldman: 1993, 35). But political and dynastic liaisons between the Low Countries and Germany were also not to be dismissed either, including, most importantly, the marriage of William of Orange to the Princess Anna of Saxony. Eventually, it was agreed that foreigners were to be tolerated, as long as they did not cause troubles, and did not manifest their dissident religious views in public (Veldman: 1993, 35–36).[7] Therefore, the actual challenge for the city was to shelter the native population from the dan-

7 Cologne's policies towards Netherlandish immigrants fluctuated over time, depending on the political and religious situation in the Low Countries. In the early 1570s, under the direct pressure of the Duke of Alva, Cologne followed the example of Antwerp and required a certificate of Catholic orthodoxy from all newcomers. Nonetheless, Lutherans continued to enjoy the rather tolerant attitude of the city council.

Fig. 2: Frans Hogenberg, *Iconoclastic Riot of August 20, 1566*, after 1570, engraving, 186 × 276 mm, Rijksmuseum Amsterdam.

gerous influences of confessionally-dubious new residents. The exiles, on the other hand, needed to secure their place within the city by presenting themselves as a peaceful and trustworthy new addition to the community, actively refuting their seditious reputation by reshaping the local discourse of historical events in the Low Countries. What they needed was a narrative that would present them as victims rather than rebels, and as persecuted, freedom-seeking citizens who had no choice but to protest against political and religious circumstances in the Low Countries.

One way of achieving this goal was disseminating among Cologne burghers the constitutional document, which guaranteed the rights and privileges of Netherlandish citizens, and defined their and their sovereign's mutual obligations. It was upon this document, the *Blijde Inkomst van Brabant* (Joyous Entry of Brabant), that every Duke of Brabant from 1356 took an oath in order to become a legitimate ruler; Charles V took his in 1515, and Philip in 1549. The document limited the power of the central government in favour of the Estates of Brabant and decisions made at the local level of provinces and towns, aiming at achieving the "ideal of self-governing independence" (Van Gelderen: 1993, xiv). The *Blijde Inkomst* was regarded as a regulation securing the ancient political order and freedom, both of which were fundamental to the peace and prosperity of the

Netherlands and the well-being of its citizens. The Joyous Entry included a clause – the famous 58th article, called a *verzetsartikel* – which allowed citizens to disobey their ruler in cases where he abused the negotiated contract, and to "refuse him their services until he mended his ways" (Van Gelderen: 1992, 115). With the outbreak of the rebellion against the Spaniards, this clause was used in justification.[8] The text of the *Blijde Inkomst* was published in Cologne in 1565 and 1566 by Godfried Hertshorn (Cervicornus), a printer with close ties to Antwerp and a friend of Philips van Wesenbeke, brother of Jacob, the city secretary (De La Fontaine Verwey: 1975, 119).[9] Eventually, the *Blijde Inkomst* began to be interpreted as a document which protected the universal order. This was an important shift since it followed from it that the violation of the oath taken by the sovereign equalled trespassing against the natural law. It was jurists in Cologne who were chiefly responsible for advancing this new interpretation of the "ancient" document.

Frans Hogenberg began publishing his *Scenes of the Religious and Civil Wars* simultaneously with this legal discourse. While the engravings with the events in the Low Countries depict the most dramatic episodes of the early years of the Eighty Years War, the images and the accompanying verses focus on the damage caused in the cities and the countryside during particular battles rather than expressing openly anti-Spanish sentiments. Hogenberg did not spare the Dutch either in prints such as the *Iconoclasm in Antwerp, August 20, 1566.* Overall, his images and inscriptions appear to pursue a primarily documentary, and not a polemical or propagandistic, agenda. This is not to say, however, that they did not actively shape their audience's views and knowledge of the depicted events, and the *Hedge-preaching outside Antwerp* print provides a perfect illustration of this precise phenomenon. Let us see now how the specific iconography of this print secured the immigrants' place in Cologne, and motivated attempts to promote harmony among the exiles themselves.

4. Historical Account as a Socio-Religious Argument: The Visual Rhetoric of Hogenberg's *Hedge-preaching outside Antwerp*

Frans Hogenberg depicts three sermons taking place at the same time, all of which he identifies with inscriptions. To the left, at the shore of the Scheldt, are the gathered followers of the Augsburg Confession. At the bottom, we have a

8 For the use of the Blijde Inkomste in apologies for the Dutch Revolt see Vrankrijker: 1936, 101–137; Geurts: 1958, 3–15; De la Fontaine Verwey: 1975, 113–132; Kaminska: 2013, 109–111.

9 The Blijde Inkomst was published for the first time in the Dutch Provinces in 1574 in Delft, the seat of the States of Holland.

smaller group of members of a clandestine Walloon, that is, a French-speaking Reformed congregation in Antwerp; the group mentioned in the letter quoted at the beginning of this essay. To their right are those attending the sermon of a Dutch Calvinist community. Interestingly, in contrast to the testimony of the Antwerp officials, the smallest group in Hogenberg's print is that attending the Walloon sermon, whereas the crowds gathered to listen to a Lutheran and a Calvinist preacher are of roughly the same, and a considerably larger, size. We shall see shortly that this seemingly minor quantitative difference has major consequences for the print's interpretation. Furthermore, the three sermons are clearly distinct and separated from one other. There is a dike between the French- and the Dutch-speaking Reformed communities, while the Lutherans are gathered on a square beyond the forest and bushes farther from the Walloon congregation. What are the implications of this choice to depict three completely independent and isolated gatherings? First, I wish to argue that Hogenberg constructs here a visual argument concerning divisions between the Protestant and Protestantizing populations of the Low Countries, and appears to suggest that differences between them are not possible to overcome.

Hogenberg's argument is congruent with the mainstream political discourse of the period. Throughout the Dutch Revolt, its leader William of Orange affirmed that the rebellion was a struggle for the independence of the entire nation, and not a religious crusade of a selected confessional minority. William recognised the danger of sectarian disputes and divisions as potentially leading to the distrust of, and even hostility, toward German princes, whose support was essential for the success of the armed resistance against the Habsburgs. Although in the early 1570s the conflict was far from being resolved, for the Flemish exiles, William's fears had already materialised. It was, among other factors, the internal religious conflict within the Netherlandish society that made the success of the Wonder Year so short-lived.

To be sure, some citizens embodied the ideal of overcoming sectarian boundaries. For instance, Gillis Hooftman, a Calvinist merchant, hosted learned dinner parties (*convivia*), at which he enjoyed the company of his Lutheran, Catholic, and spiritualist friends, most of whom belonged to the financial, administrative, and intellectual elite of Antwerp. As I demonstrate elsewhere, conversations among those guests were stimulated by a series of paintings with the episodes from the apostolic mission of Saint Paul, created by Martin de Vos in collaboration with Abraham Ortelius and Johannes Radermacher, Hooftman's apprentice who had broad humanistic and antiquarian interests.[10] The iconog-

10 On this series and the preaching of Antonio del Corro in Antwerp see my forthcoming article, "'That There Be No Schisms among You': Saint Paul as a Figure of Confessional Reconciliation in a Series of Paintings by Martin de Vos".

raphy of the paintings, in turn, can be associated with the irenic preaching of a former monk Antonio del Corro, who spent a few months during the Wonder Year in Antwerp. His activities in the metropolis provide an excellent illustration of the local sectarian divisions, and are therefore worth discussing here at some length.

Antonio del Corro (1527–91) came to Antwerp from Lausanne, where he had spent nine years studying Protestant theology after leaving the monastery of Saint Isidoro in Seville in 1557, the place at which he was first exposed to the variety of dissident texts. Such a long and extensive study of diverse doctrines, from orthodox Catholicism and illuminism, to Erasmus, the early Swiss Reformation of Heinrich Bullinger, the teaching of John Calvin and the French Huguenots, rendered del Corro extremely well versed in different theological traditions and contemporary confessional teachings. However, no less important for his formation was the conflict he witnessed between different factions within the nascent Reformed Church in Switzerland. Eager to embrace diverse doctrines, del Corro considered it more important for Christians – particularly those belonging to Protestant sects – to unite in brotherly love than to engage in highly abstract theological speculations that created further division within the Church of Christ. It was this irenic spirit that prompted del Corro to come to Antwerp at the invitation of the consistory of the Walloon church, which was in need of a pastor. Even though he was not granted a licence to preach and the consistory pledged not to allow him to teach in public unless he obtained one, he did so nonetheless.

If del Corro came to Antwerp to offer spiritual and pastoral reinforcement to the Walloon church, the competing Lutheran congregation welcomed their own preachers. Among four new ministers who arrived in the fall of 1566 from Germany was Matthias Flacius, known as Illyricus. Illyricus shared del Corro's erudition but not his irenic attitude, and he was certainly not sent by his congregation in Mansfeld to seek reconciliation with Antwerp Calvinists and members of other local sects. Indeed, quite the contrary appears to have been the case. From the early years of the Reformation movement, Antwerp had been a major centre of Lutheranism outside Germany. However, over time it ceded much of its appeal to Anabaptism and Calvinism.[11] What is more, this shift towards the Reformed confession in the Low Countries overlapped with Lutheranism's increasing popularity among German princes. According to ministers in Germany, they needed to regain their Dutch followers in order to prevent further dissemination of Calvinism across Europe (Vermaseren: 1990, 213).

11 On the shifting popularity of specific confessions in Antwerp see, for example, Andriessen: 1975, 203–32; Marnef: 1996, 48–87.

Therefore, their intention behind sending ministers to the metropolis was anything but peacemaking with other sects.

In two pamphlets published almost immediately after his arrival in Antwerp – *Incitement to penitence and prayer* and *Confession of faith of the Antwerp ministers* – Illyricus exalted Martin Luther, and completely dismissed John Calvin, Heinrich Bullinger, and Theodor Beza (Vermasaren: 1990, 215). Despite the absolute rejection of Reformed teachings by Flacius, del Corro engaged in an exchange of letters with him. The main point of contention between the two theologians – and between Antwerp Protestants – was the understanding of the Lord's Supper. This matter had been the cause of divisions ever since the beginning of the process of codification of Christian dogma and liturgy. Del Corro witnessed first-hand this theological "splitting of hairs" during his stay in Switzerland, and thus wanted to alleviate the same conflict in the Low Countries. However, while for del Corro the matter was precisely a dogmatic "splitting of the hair", confusing and dangerous for "the common folk" (Vermasaren: 1990, 220), to Illyricus, the Real Presence was beyond dispute. Del Corro entered the debate with the hope that it would lead to signing a confession of faith accepted by both Lutherans and Calvinists, but any such hopes were soon to be crushed.

One may conclude that the Spaniard ultimately gained nothing from the exchange, since Illyricus did not modify his position and Calvinists began to resent him for his attempts to negotiate with Lutherans.[12] The zealots' grievance only intensified after del Corro published the first of his two pamphlets prepared in Antwerp: *Epistre aux pasteurs de l'Eglise Flamengue d'Anvers de la Confession d'Augsburg* (1567; English translation: 1569). This open letter presents del Corro's theological position on the question of the Last Supper and offers practical solutions to the conflict in the Low Countries by advocating that Christ instituted this sacrament first and foremost for the unity of all his followers, whereas a "chosen sign of recognition for His disciples is mutual love" (Vermasaren: 1990, 221). The pamphlet complements del Corro's irenic doctrine as found in, among other works, his letter to Cassiodore de Reina sent on Christmas 1563 from Théobon; the second Antwerp pamphlet (*Lettre envoyée a la maiesté du roy des*

12 The confrontation between del Corro and Illyricus, in particular the former's willingness to forego theological differences and the latter's uncompromising position, offers an interesting perspective on the interaction between Calvinists and Lutherans in Antwerp in the 1550s and 1560s, as well as on both sects' attitudes towards the authorities. Contemporary sources, e.g. Godevaert van Haecht's chronicle, Thomas Gresham's letters, and the correspondence of Antwerp local officials usually portray "Martinists" as more moderate and docile, and contrast them sharply with militant Calvinists who seemed to have interrupted meetings and sermons of the Lutherans. While such rhetoric is understandable in the case of Van Haecht, who was secretly a member of the Lutheran community, in other cases the explanation is not that simple. The Illyricus – del Corro dispute certainly nuances this somewhat black and white picture of amicable Lutherans and antagonistic Calvinists.

Espaignes, 1567; English translation: 1577); and finally *Dialogus Theologicus* (London, 1574).

Del Corro attempted to restore, or rather introduce, unity among Christians in Antwerp partially through a strategy of fashioning himself as Saint Paul. Rady Roldan-Figueroa persuasively analyses how in the London *Dialogus Theologicus* del Corro employed paratextual, autobiographical, and eisegetical methods to model his identity on the Apostle's in order to advance his irenic agenda (Roldan-Figueroa: 2009, *passim*) However, much of the same strategy – particularly the paratextual allusions – can already be discerned in the Antwerp *Epistre aux pasteurs de l'Eglise*. The letter opens with del Corro's regretful complaint about the discord among Christians in Antwerp. As the Spaniard notes, while the Gospel has been broadly disseminated in the city, quarrels between denominations destroy this godly work or, rather, lets Satan destroy it. This deplorable lack of unity and confusion created an impression that all Protestantizing Christians are merely "purveyors of human opinions, such as those of Luther, Calvin, [Melanchthon], Osiander, Brentius, etc." (Vermasaren: 1990, 219). Del Corro's language immediately brings to mind the first chapter of Paul's First Letter to the Corinthians:

> Now I beseech you, brethren, by the name of our Lord Jesus Christ, that you all speak the same thing, and that there be no schisms among you; but that you be perfect in the same mind, and in the same judgment. For it hath been signified unto me, my brethren, of you, by them that are of the house of Chloe, that there are contentions among you. Now this I say, that every one of you saith: I indeed am of Paul; and I am of Apollo; and I am of Cephas; and I of Christ. Is Christ divided? (1 Cor. 1:10–13).

Later passages of del Corro's pamphlet warn against the consequences of a "schism" within the Antwerp communities. According to del Corro, their members already face the hostility of Catholic fellow citizens and the danger of religious persecution, and are threatened by the Inquisition and the civic government. Discord among them only contributes to their reputation as troublemakers who are not to be trusted, discredits claims about the peaceful nature of their meetings, and undermines calls for religious tolerance. His pamphlet notes that in current circumstances, they should give up *subtiele speculaties en quaesties* ("subtle speculations and disputes") for the sake of Christian peace (Sepp: 1875, vol. 3, 114). This call to unity in the brotherly love and peace of Christ is a recurring theme of Paul's letters to communities that he visited during his apostolic mission. Not only the Corinthians, but also the Galatians seem to have been divided. What is more, they also apparently faced the danger of following false teachings:

> As we said before, so now I say again: If any one preach to you a gospel, besides that which you have received, let him be anathema. For do I now persuade men, or God? Or

> do I seek to please men? If I yet pleased men, I should not be the servant of Christ. For I give you to understand, brethren, that the gospel which was preached by me is not according to man. For neither did I receive it of man: nor did I learn it but by the revelation of Jesus Christ (Gal. 1:9–12).

Del Corro seemed to have found much of the same situation in Antwerp when he commented, "For their confessions, catechisms, and interpretations become a fifth Gospel, and it is quite lost sight of that they are all derived from men, be they never so full of edification" (Vermasaren: 1990, 219). This condescending attitude towards the plethora of sectarian writings in the metropolis, which too many began to regard as *vijfde evangelie*, characterises the entire *Epistre aux pasteurs de l'Eglise.* In addition to being directly reminiscent of the first chapter of the Letter to the Galatians, it also alludes to several passages elsewhere in the Epistles, in which Paul admonishes his Christian disciples to be wary of false teachers and those who teach the "tradition of men" instead of Christ's Gospel.[13]

Contrary to what del Corro had hoped for, attempts to bring together members of Protestant congregations in Antwerp remained isolated and unsuccessful. Thus, the conspicuous separation of the three sermons in Hogenberg's print not only comments on the divisions among Protestants in Antwerp, but more specifically criticises the shortsighted confessional zeal of the followers of the new doctrines in the Low Countries. Their refusal to forgo theological hair-splitting for the sake of the nation's sovereignty eventually forced many citizens – including Antwerp Protestants themselves – into exile. The future fate of their homeland depended on their ability to unify and to establish themselves as a peaceful, harmonious community abroad, whose good reputation could gain them the sympathy and support of the local population.

In addition to these religious and political meanings, the simultaneous depiction of three sermons stands as a proxy for the history of hedge-preaching in the Low Countries. All of the surviving accounts of the first sermon on June 24, 1566 state that there was just one sermon preached that day, organised by the Walloon congregation. While this sermon was attended mostly by the congregation's own members, many other people from the neighbourhood and beyond were drawn by curiosity. Hogenberg's print thus reinterprets the history of the Wonder Year in two ways. First, it includes all three major clandestine churches in Antwerp as actively involved in hedge-preaching from its very beginning, even though it was actually in the next weeks that the Calvinist and Lutheran congregations joined the movement. Second, it depicts the French sermon as the least numerously attended, and gives priority to the Dutch communities, both the followers of the Augsburg Confession and the Reformed. The first change can be understood as a part of Hogenberg's agenda as a visual

13 See, for example, Paul's Letter to the Colossians: Col. 2: 8.

chronicler of the Revolt, following from his objective to provide the Revolt's apology and explanation of the events to non-Netherlandish viewers. The entire series of the Scenes of the Religious and Civil Wars aims at offering a comprehensive synopsis of up-to-date events of the Eighty Years War, but not by day-by-day printed reportage. Thus, Hogenberg creates an inclusive image of the phenomenon of hedge-preaching rather than depicting its first instance.

The second deviation from the written report that Hogenberg makes in the print – one that diminishes the importance of the Walloon in favour of the Dutch congregation – is arguably even more curious. Most contemporary eyewitnesses emphasise the role of exiled Huguenots in the dissemination of Calvinism in its militant incarnation, thereby supporting anti-Habsburg sentiments among the locals. According to those accounts, these were supposedly French immigrants, and not native citizens, who showed up at open-air sermons with weapons and raised anti-government cries. As is often the case during turbulent times, there was thus an attempt to blame foreigners and strangers for a tension within the society in order to claim that the society itself was perfectly content with its government. By privileging the Dutch-speaking communities, Hogenberg opposes this interpretation of the Wonder Year. His print makes a case that it was indeed the Dutch society itself that was dissatisfied with the corruption of the Catholic Church and its most fervent defenders: the orthodox Spanish Habsburgs.

The hostility and disjunction between the central government and the local population is visually communicated in the print by a significantly expanded spatial distance between Antwerp and the open-air sermons. In reality, the hedge-preaching was organised just outside the walls of the city to the south. This dramatic separation of the city and the gatherings is yet another transformation introduced by Hogenberg to communicate the rupture in the country. It is only strengthened by the conspicuous addition of gallows, with bodies still hanging on them, exactly on the axis between the sermons and the Antwerp cathedral, which at the time had become the seat of an Inquisitor.[14] Therefore, the engraving is sending a clear message to German viewers in Cologne about their Netherlandish neighbours: it is not us who chose to break with the authorities; it is the government and the Church who alienated and persecuted us.

Any analysis of Hogenberg's print needs to take into account the German inscription accompanying the image: *Der alter kirch mißbrauch sehr groß / Von Gottes Wordt und lehr gar bloß: // Haben bewegkt die gantze gemein, / Das sei die lehr begerten rein. // Darumb sei auff vescheiden ortt / Lauffen, zuhoren Gottes Wortt. // Wie das Martinus hatt verkhlertt / Auch was davon Calvinus lhert.* The

14 On the territorial reform of the Catholic Church in the Low Countries, which gave the Habsburgs an official excuse to introduce Inquisition, see, for example, Carroll: 2008, 84.

verses can be translated as follows: "The old church's abuse of God's Word and teaching moved the whole community, who longed for uncorrupted doctrine. For that reason they wandered to different places to listen to God's Word as it was explained by Martin [Luther], and taught by Calvin". This inscription, addressed primarily to the native audience in Cologne, thus underlines the audience's dissatisfaction with the Catholic Church and identifies their desire to listen to the Gospel as the exclusive reason to attend Protestant sermons. It does not mention, in fact does not even allude to, the political climate of the period, nor the Habsburgs' persecution of clandestine congregations. It is the Church alone that is blamed here for the corruption of the doctrine, which is a source of deep disappointment for its members. Hence, Hogenberg portrays former listeners of open-air sermons, many of whom are now refugees in Cologne, as zealous and pious Christians, with no intention to rebel against the king.

The inscription below the image further strengthens the non-confessional agenda of the print, which I discussed above. By stating that the entire community rushed to sermons because it was dissatisfied with the Catholic Church and its corrupted doctrine, and was eager to listen to the Word of God as honestly explained by Martin Luther and taught by John Calvin, it virtually designates the Augsburg and the Reformed confessions as equally valid alternatives to the corrupted Roman Church. This, in turn, supports Veldman's suggestion that Frans Hogenberg might have possibly been a member of a clandestine Calvinist congregation back in the Low Countries and had only adopted the Lutheran confession in Cologne. His conversion would have been motivated economically, as native authorities and citizens displayed a more tolerant attitude towards Lutherans than Calvinists. If this was indeed the case, then the artist himself embodied the ideal of confessional reconciliation and the ability to overcome minor theological differences. Nonetheless, more important than this possible personal implication of the print's iconography and the accompanying inscription, is their participation in a contemporary discourse of religious tolerance as advanced by, most notably, Franciscus Junius in the mid-1560s. In a short polemical text addressed to Philip II, the humanist argued that the King should grant freedom of worship to Lutherans and Calvinists because by attending their services, they became honest and God-fearing people, respectful of civic authorities, and thus helped to create a law-abiding, pious Christian society. According to Junius, it is only the Anabaptists and other sects that should be persecuted, as they posed a threat to public order (Marnef: 1999, 195).

Hogenberg further accentuates the attendees' interest in religious reform over political sedition by conspicuously moving to the foreground of the image, to the right of the central axis, two armed men who are deeply immersed in the reading of what can only be interpreted as religious booklets. Standing at the edge of the crowd and facing us rather than the preacher, they were entrusted with the task of safeguarding the sermon; and yet, they do not want to miss the religious lesson provided by the preacher.

The portrayal of these two men guides us toward the affinities between the textual and the visual reports of the hedge-preaching. Written accounts of *haagpreken* often underlined that it was not only through oral/aural communication that the Protestant ministers taught their message about Christ to the gathered listeners. They also approached these mass gatherings as an opportunity to disseminate pamphlets, images, poems, and excerpts from vernacular translations of the Bible. Printed texts reinforced the spoken word, whereas excerpts from the Bible legitimised teachings of Protestant priests as truly based on "the teaching of the first apostles" (Marnef: 1999, 198). Some of the texts and images were sold or distributed to be used during the sermon itself, and later to be taken home by participants, despite repeated prohibitions against keeping any unorthodox images and books, and severe penalties for trespassing against these laws.[15]

Overall, Hogenberg's focus on listeners' sincere interest in the Word of God as a path to their spiritual growth conforms to contemporary reports of *veltpredicatie*. In two extensive eye-witness accounts of the phenomenon, the aforementioned Godevaert van Haecht and Marcus van Vaernewijck consistently emphasise Protestant ministers' preoccupation with the text of the Bible. The former author was Lutheran and the latter Catholic, and yet, in passages dedicated to the content of open-air sermons, both of them describe how preachers thoroughly explained the Old and New Testament to their listeners. Their profound exegesis impressed not only *veel ghemeen volck, ende die niet zeer bewandelt waren in de helighe scriftuere ende in die oude doctueren* ("many common folk, who were not well-versed in the scriptures and [the writings] of the Church Fathers"), but also good, devout, and learned Catholics who had never experienced comparably beautiful and moving theological instruction (Van Vaernewijck: 1872–1881, vol. 1, 13–15, 81). Despite his own orthodoxy, Van Vaernewijck did not hesitate to quote the opinion of some "good Catholics", who went to a hedge-preaching and underlined that their emotional response was truly stimulated by the very words of the Scripture, hence, the Word of God:

> The Holy Scripture, they said, that they heard there so thoroughly explained, made their hearts leap up with joy, and they were thoroughly moved, and in tears, caused by great devotion and piety towards God, [tears] running from their eyes, but really from their hearts (Van Vaernewijck: 1872–1881, vol. 1, 81).

15 See, for example, an order from May 11, 1566: Copye van de principaelste articulene, die van weghen der governante den staten van Vlaenderen voorgeleet werden, om te onderhouden op de den 11 Meye. Quoted in: Van Haecht: 1929–1930, 44.

This emphasis on *het woerdt Godts* occasionally took a comic turn in the popular discourse of the period. In the entry from July 24, 1566, Van Haecht recounts that, in an attempt to regain their congregations who had eagerly wandered outside the city to listen to Protestants, Catholic priests placed announcements on church doors across the city that in the Borchtkerk, the "Word of God" would be preached. The popular reaction to this announcement was quite different from the anticipated one, as those who saw it commented: *Sullen sy nou Godts woerdt preeken eerst? Wat hebben sy sulange jaeren geleert?* ("Shall they only begin now to preach the Word of God? What have they been teaching so far all these years?") (Van Haecht: 1929–1930, 73–74). In the context of Hogenberg's print, however, the focus on the attendees' desire to learn the "uncorrupted doctrine" cleverly redirects the historical narrative from political sedition to religious piety. By matching eye-witness reports, it becomes part of a broadly disseminated and accepted vision of the *haagpreken*. This, in turn, proves that the print oscillates between truthfulness and manipulation by constructing a believable image of the hedge-preaching, which simultaneously allows the author to proceed with his own socio-political agenda.

5. *Noch Calvinist, noch mertinist...?* A New Approach to Confessional Identities among Flemish Exiles in Cologne

I began this essay with a quote from a letter describing the first public Protestant sermon outside of Antwerp's city walls – the most immediate response to this new phenomenon – and continued with a comparison of the magistrates' report to the depiction of the gathering in Hogenberg's engraving. In other words, I introduced the print as providing us chiefly with information on the history of *haagpreken* in the Low Countries.

Having carefully examined the iconography and circumstances of the print's design, I wish to offer now a somewhat different conclusion. Although *Hedge-preaching outside Antwerp* was part of a series, *Scenes of the Religious and Civil Wars*, its value as a historical and socio-political document lies primarily not in the depiction of an open-air sermon, but in the commentary it offers on the aftermath of the *annus mirabilis*, and the role it assumes in shaping the national and confessional identities of the Flemish refugees in Cologne. While the image claims to represent the same meeting as the one described by the magistrates, it offers in fact a synthetic vision of the development of *haagpreken* between June 1566 and April 1567. Most importantly, it anachronistically privileges certain later characteristics of the hedge-preaching – and not necessarily those which were given the most attention in the textual accounts. First, by focussing on the simultaneous depiction of three sermons, which are then radically separated, Hogenberg acknowledges the calamitous divisions among Antwerp Protestants and, consequently, advocates the reconciliation of the nation as a necessary precondition of achieving independence. Second, he mitigates the militant aspect of Calvinist preaching by moving to the foreground two standing men armed at once with weapons and religious booklets. This interpretation of hedge-preaching as aiming at religious rather than political reform continues in the German verses beneath the print. Third, the relative prominence of Dutch-speaking communities in comparison to the Walloon one emphasises their role in initiating the resistance against contemporary circumstances in the Low Countries. This resistance, however, as we have seen, is motivated by religious zeal rather than seditious political ideology aimed at overthrowing the monarch, whose power comes from God. Still, the implications of the print do take a political turn: the engraving effectively presents Netherlandish subjects of Philip II as having no other choice than to rebel against their sovereign if they sought the Church's renewal. By underlining the listeners' piety – even the men carrying weapons are mainly focussed on studying the scriptures – the print offers a very effective apology for the Revolt addressed to Cologne citizens. The widespread image of the exiles as trouble-makers with no respect for the royal authority is replaced by that of good Christians.

Nonetheless, these "good Christians" failed to learn an important lesson – one that Antonio del Corro tried to teach them. The same lesson was also preached in Antwerp three months after the first public sermon, on August 24, when one of the ministers declared: *Ick en ben noch Calvinist, noch mertinist; men hoeft de doctoren niet te gelooven, maer d'woerdt Godts, dat ick U leere*" ("I am neither a Calvinist nor a Lutheran; man should not believe [in] doctors, but [in] the Word of God, which I teach you") (Van Haecht: 1929–1930, 101). It was this failure to acknowledge the precedence of brotherly love over doctrinal disputes that soon turned the triumph of Netherlandish Protestant communities into their defeat, and led to persecution that was harsher than ever before. Members of those communities seem to have embraced a less dogmatic and a more inclusive attitude only in Cologne. Biographies of artists such as Adriaan de Weert and Frans Hogenberg, who most likely converted from Calvinism to Lutheranism during their exile, testifies to this important change in defining the confessional identities of Netherlandish citizens. It is, however, these artists' oeuvre that presents this choice of religious tolerance within the Protestant movement as an exemplary and a necessary one. As a religious minority in the Low Countries, Protestants lost everything to the Catholic majority in the late 1560s. In Cologne meanwhile, Protestants were offered a second chance to find a compromise with that majority without giving up their own sectarian identity. Hogenberg's print encourages Protestants to reexamine their past to craft their presence and future, and thus becomes an active instrument of shaping political and religious discourse.

Bibliography

Andriessen, Jos (1975), Het geestelijke en godsdienstige klimaat, in: Genootschap voor Antwerpsche Geschiedenis (ed.), Antwerpen in de XVIde eeuw, Antwerp: Mercurius, 203–232.

Burgon, John William (1839), The Life and Times of Sir Thomas Gresham, London: R. Jennings.

Carroll, Margaret D. (2008), The Conceits of Empire: Bruegel's Ice-Skating Outside St. George's Gate in Antwerp and Tower of Babel, in: Margaret D. Carroll (ed.), Painting and Politics in Northern Europe: Van Eyck, Bruegel, Rubens and Their Contemporaries, University Park, PA: Pennsylvania University Press, 64–87.

De la Fontaine Verwey, H. (1975), De Blijde Inkomst en de opstand tegen Philips II, in: H. De la Fontaine Verwey (ed.), Uit de wereld van het boek. Humanisten, dwepers en rebellen in de zestiende eeuw, Amsterdam, 113–132.

Erasmus, Desiderius (1998), On Praying to God (Modus orandi Deum), in: John W. O'Malley (ed.), Collected Works of Erasmus, vol. 70 (Spiritualia and Pastoralia), Toronto and Buffalo, NY: University of Toronto Press, 141–230.

Geurts, P.A.M. (1958), Het beroep op de Blijde Inkomste in de pamfletten uit de Tachtigjarige Oorlog, Standen en Landen 16, 3–15.

Kaminska, Barbara A. (2013), Looking beyond Confessional Boundaries: Discourse of Religious Tolerance in Prints by Dirck Volkertsz. Coornhert and Adriaan de Weert, Renaissance and Reformation/Renaissance et Réforme 36, 83–126.

Marnef, Guido (1996), Antwerp in the Age of Reformation: Underground Protestantism in a Commercial Metropolis 1550–1577, Baltimore and London: Johns Hopkins University Press.

Marnef, Guido (1999), Dynamics of Reformed Militancy in the Low Countries: The Wonderyear, in: N. Scott Amos/Andrew Pettegree/Henk van Nierop (eds.), The Education of a Christian Society. Humanism and the Reformation. Papers delivered to the Thirteenth Anglo-Dutch Historical Conference, 1997, Aldershot: Ashgate, 193–210.

Ordonnancie ende Statuyt ghemaect by mijnen Heere[n] Schouteth, Borghemeesteren, Schepenen ende Raede der Stadt va[n] Antwerpen, Aengaende secrete co[n]venticulen ende vergaderingen. Met meer andere puncten ende articulen daer toe dienende. Gheboden ende wtgheroepen op den sesten dach Octobris. M.D.LXV (1565), Antwerp: Willem Silvius.

Prims, Floris (1940), De briefwisseling tusschen Magistraat van Antwerpen en Gedeputeerden, Bijdragen tot de Geschiedenis 31, 1–94; 99–184.

Roldan-Figueroa, Rady (2009), Antonio del Corro and Paul as the Apostle of the Gospel of Universal Redemption, in: R. Ward Holder (ed.), A Companion to Paul in the Reformation, Leiden and Boston: Brill, 387–426.

Sepp, Christiaan (1875), Geschiedkundige Nasporingen. 3 vols. Leiden: De Breuk & Smits.

Van Gelderen, Martin (1992), The Political Thought of the Dutch Revolt, 1555–1590, Cambridge/New York: Cambridge University Press,
– (1993), The Dutch Revolt, Cambridge; New York: Cambridge University Press.
Van Haecht, Godevaert (1929–1930), De kroniek van Godevaert van Haecht over de troebelen van 1565 tot 1574 te Antwerpen en elders, ed. Rob van Roosbroeck, Antwerp: De Sikkel.
Van Vaernewijck, Marcus (1872–1881), Van die beroerlicke tijden in die Nederlanden en voornamelick in Ghendt, 1566–1568, ed. Ferdinand vander Haeghen, Ghent: Annoot-Braeckman.
Veldman, Ilja M. (1993), Keulen als toevluchtsoord voor Nederlandse kunstenaars (1567–1612), Oud Holland 107, 34–58.
Vermaseren, B.A. (1990), The Life of Antonio del Corro (1527–1591) Before his Stay in England. Vol. II. Minister in Antwerp, Archives et Bibliotheques de Belgiques 61, 175–275.
Vrankrijker, A.C.J. (1936), Het beroep op de Blyde Incomste en andere privileges in Brabant tegen de inquisitie en de nieuwe bisdommen in de XVIe eeuw, Historisch Tijdschrift 16, 101–37.

Leon van den Broeke

Acceptance and Organisation of the French Protestants in the Northern Netherlands

A Reformed Minority within the Reformed Majority

1. Walloon Congregations

A few years ago the foundation of the Walloon church in Flushing was discovered.[1] In 1809 the church building had been damaged due to an attack by English soldiers (Wagenmakers: 2015). Sixteen years later the church building was destroyed. The foundation serves as a memory of a long forgotten French-speaking Reformed congregation in the Northern Netherlands. The local historian Cees Sleutel deems it important to preserve this piece of history and dedicated a book to the history of this specific congregation and its members (Sleutel: 2015). However, today many Dutch people, including members of the Protestant Church in the Netherlands, are not aware of the history and presence of this specific congregation, or indeed of any of the Walloon congregations.[2] This is despite the fact that the Protestant Church in the Netherlands as of 2015 still included thirteen historic Walloon congregations:[3]

Congregation	French Name	Year of Foundation
Amsterdam		1578
Arnhem		1684
Breda	Bréda	1590
Delft		1586
Dordrecht		1586
Groningen	Groningue	1619
Haarlem	Harlem	1586
Leiden	Leyde	1581
Maastricht	Maestricht	1633

1 I would like to express my gratitude to Samira Talhaoui MA for her great help in editing this paper.

2 The Dutch name is Protestantse Kerk in Nederland (PKN).

3 Waalse Kerken, accessed 5 March 2015, http://www.waalsekerken.nl/nl_home.html.

(Continued)

Congregation	French Name	Year of Foundation
Middelburg	Middelbourg	1574
Rotterdam		1590
Utrecht		1583
Zwolle		1686

Number of Walloons in the Netherlands according to the census

Year	1849	1859	1869	1879	1889	1899	1909	1920	1930	1947	1960	1971
Number	8435	9689	10258	9529	8953	9857	9660	8962	6358	4067	3058	1505

The Protestant Church in the Netherlands is the result of the 2004 merger of the Netherlands Reformed Church, the Reformed Churches in the Netherlands, and the Evangelical-Lutheran Church in the Kingdom of the Netherlands. This Church order includes the Walloon congregations, which have been part of the Reformed Church for more than four centuries. The number of Walloon congregations has fluctuated through the ages. There were two main periods of influx: the first, starting in the 1560s, was a result of the flight of French Protestants from their own war-torn country. The second was related to the revocation of the Edict of Nantes in 1685.

From 1 March 1562 (the massacre at Wassy-sur-Blaise) onwards, French Protestants were persecuted and murdered as a result of the Wars of Religion. On the night of 23–24 August 1572, the war culminated in the St. Bartholomew's Day Massacre in Paris. Large numbers of French Protestants left France. After the installment of the *Conseil des Troubles* (Council of Blood) by the Duke of Alba in 1567, many of these Walloons had already fled to other places, such as the German territories, the French Islands in the West Indies, British North America, and the Northern Netherlands. Many sought refuge in the Northern Netherlands because of the Union of Utrecht of 1579, the thirteenth article of which granted freedom of conscience. It was not until the Edict of Nantes of 1598 that French Protestants were protected by French law. However, this itself only lasted until 18 October 1685 when King Louis XIV (1638–1715) revoked this by issuing the Edict of Fontainebleau. This edict led to a new Protestant exodus and exile: that of the Huguenots. The Huguenots who fled to the Northern Netherlands found a French Reformed infrastructure that had already been established about a century earlier.

The first Walloon congregation in the Northern Netherlands was established in Middelburg in 1574. After the revocation of the Edict of Nantes in 1685, as a result of the influx of the second wave of Walloon refugees, the Huguenots, the congregation rapidly grew. Eventually 82 congregations were established. These French Protestants were not scattered over the rural areas of the Northern

Netherlands, but were located in the cities. The Walloon Church in the Northern Netherlands was, and still is, an urban Church. Because the Walloons integrated (well) into Dutch society and the Dutch Church, the number of Walloon congregations decreased. As of 2015, the Northern Netherlands had only thirteen Walloon congregations left.

Taking into account this contemporary, less well-known, ecclesiastical organisation, the current debate on minorities, and the theme of this volume related to minorities and (in)tolerance, the aim of my contribution is to analyse the acceptance of this Walloon minority by Dutch society and the Dutch Church, and to examine the ecclesiastical organisation of this minority within the Reformed majority in the Northern Netherlands (Dutch Reformed Church). I will argue that the Walloon Church has been more than just a minority. Moreover, because it was a Reformed minority, it became a privileged minority. In 1578 the Synod of Dordrecht decided that Dutch and Walloon churches were allowed to gather in separate Church councils, classis assemblies, and particular synods on account of their language difference. The acceptance and the organisation of the Walloons was thus not only related to shared Calvinistic doctrine, but also to their specific social and economic context. Acceptance and organisation go hand in hand, and express the level of tolerance, the freedom of religion, and, in addition, the level of freedom of ecclesiastical organization on account of language. A large part of the identity of the Walloon and Huguenot Reformed Church was rooted in the French language. In short, the first section deals with the reasons the Dutch had for accepting the Walloons and the Huguenots. Thereafter I will shed light on the ecclesiastical organisation as a dimension of this acceptance. Finally, the last section will conclude the discussion.

2. Acceptance

2.1 Solidarity and Tolerance

The Northern Netherlands was a tolerant nation. The historian Jules Michelet (1798–1874) called Holland "*l'arche dans le déluge*" (the refuge in the flood) (Michelet: 1898, 414–415). The French theologian and philosopher Pierre Bayle (1647–1706) wrote that the Holland of 1697 was "*la grande arche des fugitifs*" (the great refuge of the refugees) (Bayle: [1974]). The Dutch were shocked by the cruelties that the French Catholics had committed against the Walloons and French Protestants. The Reformed believers shared with the French Protestant refugees the same Calvinistic doctrine. The *Confessio Belgica* of 1561 that was written two years after the *Confessio Gallicana* of 1559 by the Walloon Calvinist Guido (Guy) de Brès (1522–1567), was adopted by the Dutch Reformed Church.

The pastor of the Walloon congregation of Utrecht Frank le Cornu stated: "*La Confession de foi des Eglises wallonnes ... est devenue le drapeau de l'Eglise réformée néerlandaise des deux langues*" (Le Cornu, s.a., 33). The Reformed believers who had to flee the Southern Netherlands or France were not considered primarily as Walloon or Huguenot refugees, but as Calvinist brothers. Even so, it must be said that among the refugees there were also Mennonites, Lutherans, and even Catholics. Furthermore, there is the question of whether the refugees fled their homeland because of their faith or whether the specific economic and political privileges granted to French refugees played a role. The refugees sought to find a place to live, earn a living, and celebrate the Gospel in their own French-speaking congregations in the Netherlands.

Concerning this ecclesiastical aspect: the Dutch church historians A. Ypey and I.J. Dermout have correctly observed that the Walloon congregations were not (only) included in the Dutch Reformed Church, but it was also the other way around (Ypey/Dermout: 1819, 305). The Dutch Reformed Church and the French Reformed Church mutually influenced each other, or as Le Cornu stated: "*Les Eglises wallonnes sont donc la mère de l'Eglise réformée néerlandaise générale qui a reçu d'elles son organization, sa confession de foi et sa discipline*" (Le Cornu, s.a., 38). From this point of view he continued saying: "*C'est donc une grande erreur d'appeler les Eglises wallonnes des Eglises étrangères. Pour les coeurs nobles et reconnaissants, une mère n'est pas un étrangère*" (Le Cornu: s.a., 39).

As an expression of Calvinistic fellowship the Dutch raised funds for the benefit of the Huguenots. However, by the end of the seventeenth century the willingness of the Dutch to raise money diminished and so they organised lotteries instead, for instance in Amsterdam in 1695. The Walloon synod requested the States-General to organise a collection of money. This was sustained due to sympathy with the persecuted and oppressed co-believers, and out of disgust with the cruelties the Huguenots had met. In addition, the Dutch East Indies Company frequently offered a considerable amount of money (cf. Bots: 1986, 72/73).

The Dutch invested a considerable amount in order to attract French Protestants to relocate to the Northern Netherlands. They even advertised in French journals. Also, merchants were asked to persuade their French colleagues to come and live in the Northern Netherlands where there was a benign economic environment (cf. Bots: 1986, 69). The French Protestants were granted many privileges: tax reduction, civil right(s) (*burgerrecht*), exemption from participation in the city guard (*burgerwacht*), grants for starting their own companies, free membership of the guilds and financial aid for the deaconry of the Walloon Church (Memorie Amsterdam 1681; cf. Bots: 1986, 69). These privileges, called the "Memorie Amsterdam", were also advertised in France. Bots concludes that from 1681 onwards every Dutch city offered such privileges to the Huguenots (Bots: 1986, 70). On 15 February 1686 the States of Groningen and Ommelanden, in the North-East part of the Netherlands, decided to extend privileges to the French refugees. However, while this was obviously intended to aid integration, given the fact that every Dutch city or province could make its own arrangements for the refugees, it could actually be an obstacle. For sometimes refugees went from city to city in order to benefit from more and even better privileges.

Apart from economic, financial, political, educational, and institutional impulses for accepting the French refugees in the Northern Netherlands, there was also a military aspect. A number of these refugees had been soldiers and officers and joined the army of the stadholder Willem III (1650–1702). With a view to the war with England he included around 300 Walloon officers in his States Army.

The Walloon Church also shared in the preferential treatment of the privileged Dutch Reformed Church. They were often given church buildings and the salary of Walloon ministers was paid by the civil authorities, as happened, for example, in Leiden (cf. Van Meeteren: 2006, 149).

Even the institution of a Walloon College, for the education of future pastors, was supported. The Walloon synod had written a request to the States of Holland in September 1604 concerning this (cf. Posthumus Meyjes/Bots: 2005, 20). On 31 May 1606 this college was opened at the Groenhazengracht, close to the Rapenburg. The graduates were first sent out to the Walloons "under the cross" – the persecuted French congregations, before they could return to serve a congregation in the Northern Netherlands (cf. Posthumus Meyjes: 1975, 24; Scheltus: 1735, 138). The regulations for the college were approved by the (Walloon) Synod of Zierikzee on 16 April 1606 (Posthumus Meyjes/Bots: 2005, 31–32). The ceremony was an exact copy of the institution of the Staten College, the college instituted for training future pastors of the Dutch Reformed Church.

While the Walloon Church shared in many of the privileges of the Dutch Reformed Church, there were differences. Although both the Walloon and the Staten College (at the Cellebroersgracht, currently Kaiserstraat) received funding, the amount given to the Walloon College was eight times less than for the Dutch College (1,000 versus 8,000 guilders). Furthermore, only eight stipendiary staff were allowed, rather than the thirty of the Staten College. The connection between the Walloon College and the university was more informal and at times became non-existent. By contrast, the Staten College had strong ties with the university, the mayor and the senate. This college was a real college of the civil authorities, whereas the Walloon College was rather a seminary of the Walloon Church (cf. Posthumus Meyjes: 1975, 2). The Staten College operated for more than two centuries, between 1592 and 1801. However, the Walloon College only existed between 1606 and 1699, and in the last three decades without any Walloons. Nevertheless, when the Walloon College was first founded the authorities, the university and the Church had all been present, and had all shared the joy of their French-speaking brethren.

2.2 Self-Serving and Intolerance

From the 1680s the above-mentioned privileges raised questions among the Dutch. Due to envy, the willingness to fund and accept the French refugees diminished. Moreover, the expected economic growth, especially of the textile and cloth industry, was not attained. Indeed, in this the Dutch proved themselves once again to be merchants and ministers at the same time. Although they had welcomed both the Walloons and the Huguenots warmly for social and religious reasons, the economic reason had never been forgotten.

A fine demonstration of this may be seen in the decision of the Staten van Vriesland of 4 August 1683 concerning agricultural land. Their first motive to sell land was economic but their second was to increase Protestant solidarity. Another economic benefit to the Dutch was from the increase on the capital market. Some refugees were wealthy and brought with them a great deal of money, so much so that the Amsterdam bank felt the necessity to decrease the interest rate from 3% to 2% from 1684 onwards (cf. Bots: 1986, 74). In 1690 the City of Amsterdam decided to grant privileges only under particular circumstances to Huguenots (cf. Bots: 1986, 117 and 118). On 21 October 1715 the States General decided to make the French refugees equal to native Dutch citizens (cf. Bots: 1986, 119). This was, in a number of respects, a step backwards. French Protestants could no longer benefit from economic, financial and political privileges.

Unlike their Dutch Reformed brethren, the Huguenots also had no access to official positions in Dutch society. Consequently they focussed on commerce and industry, with many becoming excellent merchants and businessmen. Yet, despite their initial warm welcome (cf. Koenen: 1846, 262–263), the promised financial benefits for Dutch society never materialised – ironically, this was probably due to the burden that their special privileges placed on them and on Dutch society.

Overall, therefore, the relationship between the two groups continued to be complex. On the one hand, the Dutch had difficulties with refugees who were not able to find work, but continued to express their French lifestyle. On the other hand, the Dutch upper classes were attracted by this lifestyle, and integrated it into their own lives. At the same time while some refugees were highly regarded because they were successful in their work, especially trade, industry (mainly fashion and textile) and the book market, others struggled economically and culturally (cf. Israel: 1996, 697–700; Van der Linden: 2015).

3. Ecclesiastical Organisation

A close-reading of the acts of the sixteenth- and seventeenth-century provincial synods, does not indicate that the Walloons experienced difficulties with the Dutch Reformed, as, for example, the Lutherans, Anabaptists, and Roman-Catholics had done (cf. Van den Broeke: 2015). The Walloons had their own ecclesiastical organisation within the Dutch Reformed Church, except at the general synod level. At the particular synod of Hoorn of 4 June 1602 it was asked whether it would be recommended for a minister to serve both a Dutch- and French-speaking congregation. (Reitsma/Van Veen: 1892, 323). The synod was of the opinion that each congregation needed its own minister. However, if the situation required it, due to necessity, then the synod would not oppose such a situation.

In addition, the fact that the National Synod of Dordrecht of 1578 gave Walloon congregations the permission to organise themselves as "separate" French-speaking classes and particular synods is a fine demonstration of acceptance. This took place after the Walloon congregations were brought together on June 21 1577 (Rutgers: 1980, 184). The Dutch felt strong fellowship with the Walloon Church since they considered it as belonging to the same confession. It also had the same (Reformed) system of Church polity. This made it possible within the same framework to separate Walloon ecclesiastical organisation on the local and supra-local level. This type or organisation was not strange to the refugees. Moreover, the Edict of Nantes had enabled the French Protestants to organise their Reformed Church into consistories at the local level, and *colloques* or classes, provincial synods and national synods on the supra-local level (cf. Koenen: 1846, 319).

As mentioned above, the Acts of the Synod of Dordrecht of 1578 were the first acts, after those of the Synods of Emden 1571, and Dordrecht 1574, which included the permission to establish a separate Walloon ecclesiastical organisation. This synod decided that the German and Walloon churches were allowed to convene in separate Church councils, classes and synods on account of the language difference (art. 44, and 46). The Walloon particular synod was granted the opportunity to send two preachers and two elders as delegates to the general synod. Moreover, the Synod of Dordrecht of 1578 also offered a place for a peculiar Walloon general synod to gather. However, this synod firmly stated that such a Walloon general synod was not supposed to execute changes in the confession and the Church order (art. 46).

Nonetheless, the Synod of Middelburg 1581 was of the opinion that it would not accept a separate Walloon general synod (art. 36). It did allow Walloons to gather in separate Church councils, classes and a particular synod, but not in a general synod. The Synod of Gravenhage 1586 continued this policy (art. 45). It explicitly stated that a Church council that was assigned to convene the next general synod should gather the provincial synods, and also the provincial synod of “another language”, i. e. the Walloon provincial synod (art. 44). This implied that the particular synod of the German and Walloon speaking congregations had the possibility of sending four representatives.

Although the Walloon congregations were granted ecclesiastical liberty to meet in separate assemblies, the Synod of The Hague, 1586, stated that in the cities where Walloon congregations existed, individual preachers and elders of both the German and the Walloon churches, should meet together and offer each other help and advice (art. 46). As legitimated by the Acts of the Synod of The Hague, 1586, the Walloons had requested permission to do just this. The Synod of Dordrecht 1618/1619 affirmed the decisions and the policies made by these sixteenth-century synods.

Despite its peculiar place within it, the Walloons were still part of the privileged (Dutch) Reformed Church. This also became apparent in their sending of representatives to the meetings of the general synods. This practice dates back officially to 1578. Although unofficially, Walloon ministers Jean Taffin, ministers at Antwerp; and Carolus or Charles Nielles, minister at Wezel, had attended the Synod of Emden in 1571. Johannes Polyander, a minister at Emden, also attended this meeting. In fact, he was the clerk of this synod. He took along two of his elders, Carolus de Noude and Christophorus Becanus. While no Walloon ministers or elders attended the Synod of Dordrecht in 1574, which had a provincial rather than a national character, the Walloon congregations sent two representatives to the Synod of Dordrecht in 1578: Guillaume Feugere, a professor at the University of Leiden and Jean Taffin, minister at Antwerp. Three years later the number of representatives was doubled. The Synod of Middleburg of 1581 was attended by Jean Taffin, minister at Antwerp; Loluis d’ Outreleau, minister at Middelburg; Petrus Marimont, elder, and Michiel de la Houe, elder. So not only had the number of representatives doubled, but also the number of ministers and elders was equal. However, this was not the case at the Synod of Gravenhage in 1586. No elder was delegated, and only two ministers attended: Johannes de la Vigne from Amsterdam, and Pierre Moreau from Delft and Rotterdam. At the famous Synod of Dordrecht in 1618/1619 four ministers and two elders represented the Walloon congregations: Daniel Colonius, minister at Leiden; Joannes Crucius, minister at Haarlem; Joannes Doucher, minister at Vlissingen; Jeremias de Pours, minister at Middelburg; Evenrardus Beckius, elder at Middelburg; and Petrus Pontanus, elder at Amsterdam.

According to W. Bachiene (1770) there were attempts to establish correspondence between the Walloon synod and the provincial synods of the Dutch Reformed Church, since after the general synod of Dordrecht in 1618/1619 the civil authorities did not sustain a new general synod. However, these attempts were not successful.

The Walloon synod gathered twice a year: at the end of April/the beginning of May, and at the end of August/the beginning of September. Usually about fifty members attended the gatherings of the Walloon synod (Bachiene: 1770, 216). Despite the general resemblance with the particular synods of the Dutch Reformed Church there were also some differences. The Walloon synod did not implement an adsessor besides the *secretaire* (stated clerk) and the *moderateur* (president). Also, no representative of the civil authorities attended the meetings of the Walloon synod, as was the case at the Dutch synods (Bachiene: 1770, 221). Another difference was the absence of regular deputies, except in the case of extraordinary circumstances. If this happened the deputies who were appointed were called "extraordinary deputies" (Bachiene: 1770, 221).

When these deputies convened they were called "*la classe*". This was quite different from the nomenclature in the Dutch Reformed system of Church polity. Therein, the classis is the name of the Reformed bishopric, and the classis assembly the name of the Reformed bishop (cf. Van den Broeke: 2005, 49–50). However, the Walloon Church in the Northern Netherlands used the word "*classe*" for the extraordinary deputies. The Dutch borrowed the word "*classis*" from the Church in Waadtland/Vaud (Van den Broeke: 2005, 54–56). In 1536/1537 the synod of Lausanne had decided to divide the Church in this region into six classes. The gathering of ministers, sometimes also together with elders, in a certain region was quite common in the European Reformed denominations. However, these had several names and different emphases with view to their duties and position. In 1571 the Synod of Emden decided to divide the Reformed Church in the Netherlands into classes. A year later, it was the Synod of Nimes which did the same concerning the Reformed Church in France.

The extraordinary deputies, *la classe*, of the Walloon Church in the Northern Netherlands convened in between sessions of the synod when there were urgent matters, such as approbation of a call or examination of a candidate or a pastor. The so-called synodical congregation had the right to convene the deputies, i.e, the classis. This synodical congregation had to write a circular letter with a request for permission for calling such a gathering. The classis could only make decisions regarding the items that were listed in this letter. Everything which the classis determined had to be approved by the next synod.

Apart from the assembly of synodical deputies which was called "*la classe*", the assembly of delegates of the Walloon congregations in the Province of Zeeland was also called "classe", e.g. *la Classe de Zélande* (Posthumus Meyjes: 2005, X). The same was true for the Walloon congregations in Limburg, e.g. *la Classe de Limbourg [et du pays d'Outre-Meuse]*. The fact that classes were not considered as necessary at first, had to do with the fact that the Walloon congregations were present in cities and not (so much) in rural areas.

Thus, in the Walloon ecclesiastical understanding "*la classe*" could mean the gathering of synodical deputies who convened in between two sessions of synodical meetings, as well as a regional ecclesiastical body.

3.1 Walloon Church 1816–2004

The Walloon ecclesiastical organization changed over the centuries. In 1816 the situation for the Walloon Church changed. In fact, the ecclesiastical situation had already changed before 1816. Due to the process of assimilation the number of Walloon congregations diminished. But, there was also an opposite process: Dutch Reformed believers became members of Walloon congregations because of the French language, which gave them cultural cachet at a time of the "Frenchification" of Dutch culture due to Huguenot influence. However, in 1816 it was established, according to Section 13 of the General Regulations (*Algemeen Reglement van 1816*), that the Walloon congregations, along with the the Presbyterian English and Scottish congregations, would now be more officially integrated into the Reformed Netherlands. These regulations were imposed by King Willem I. He considered himself as *summus episcopus* and felt the need to centralise the Dutch Reformed Church. Section 14 allowed the Walloon congregations to make its own internal rules. The same went for the Dutch, Presbyterian English and Scottish congregations of the Dutch Reformed Church. However, these rules were not supposed to be in conflict with the general regulations. Additional general regulations were provided by the General Regulations of 1816 in sections 68–77. Walloon congregations were given freedom to maintain relationships among themselves as required by financial and/or linguistic matters, without losing sight of the well-being of the entire Dutch Reformed Church (art. 68.) A special Committee for the internal affairs of the Walloon Congregations in the Netherlands was instituted (art. 69). It consisted of six members: five pastors and one elder.

This Committee was assigned to delegate a pastor to the general synod (section 17 and 73). Separate Walloon synods were no longer permitted. It was the King who appointed the members of this committee (section 70). The Church order attributed to the committee the assignment of supervising the financial affairs of the Walloon congregations, and the examination of candidates for the Walloon ministry. Moreover, this committee also functioned as the classis board and the provincial church board. The Walloon congregations were allowed to convene annually as a classis assembly (section 74), but this does not seem to have been a frequent occurrence. The last Wednesday in June was assigned as the annual meeting date of all the classis assemblies in the Dutch Reformed Church (section 65). According to the Royal Decree of August 19 1817 the Northern Netherlands counted 21 Walloon congregations and 28 pastors:

Amsterdam	Four pastors
's Gravenhage	Three pastors
Rotterdam	Three pastors
Leiden	One pastor
Utrecht	One pastor
Haarlem	One pastor
Middelburg	One pastor
Groningen	One pastor
Dordrecht	One pastor
Leeuwarden	One pastor
Delft	One pastor
Nijmegen	One pastor
Arnhem	One pastor
's Hertogenbosch	One pastor
Breda	One pastor
Zierikzee	One pastor
Vlissingen	One pastor
Zwolle	One pastor
Schiedam	One pastor
Deventer	One pastor
Zutphen	One pastor

The Walloon congregation of Voorburg, near The Hague, was given permission to call a pastor. This means that the number of Walloon congregations was not 21, but 22. This also implies that the number of Walloon pastors increased from 28 to 29.

King Willem's General Regulations of 1816 were valid for 135 years. In 1951 the regulations were replaced by a confessional Church order: the Netherlands Reformed Church Order of 1951. The very first section stated that the Dutch Reformed Church also included the Walloon congregations. They together formed a Walloon classis – the Walloon Reunion (section 14). It had the same position in Church order as other classis assemblies and the provincial church board of the Dutch Reformed Church. Concerning the classis structure this situation remained the same in the Protestant Church in the Netherlands and in its Protestant Church Order of 2004. As this Church and Church order did not include provincial structures anymore there is now no Walloon provincial synod. However, the Walloon classis assembly does function as a provincial synod for Walloon affairs.

Today the Walloon churches still retain a particular place in the Protestant Church of the Netherlands. This is not something that only belongs to an ecclesiastical past. In the Protestant Church of the Netherlands, the Walloon congregations meet in the *Réunion Wallone*, the Walloon circuit (*ring*). This circuit, elects one member of the classis (Ord. 4–20); recently the church order has changed. Its executive committee is called the *Commission Wallone.* The *Réunion Wallone* has the power to oversee matters of worship. This concerns Bible translation, the reforming of psalter and hymnbook, and overseeing the order of the liturgy.

4. Final Remarks

The French historian Bertrand Van Ruymbeke included in his chapter on minority survival, a paragraph on the Huguenot Diaspora in the Atlantic World entitled "An Invisible Minority" (Van Ruymbeke: 2003, 11). On the one hand, the Walloon Church can now also be called an invisible minority. When they arrived French Protestants were welcomed and accepted by the Dutch Reformed. This was more than just being tolerant. This acceptance also included ecclesiastical organisation within the denomination, not only on the local, but also on the regional and provincial level. As it was not possible for the general synod of the Dutch Reformed Church to convene for two centuries, the representatives of the Walloon Church could not officially meet the delegates of the Dutch-speaking Church as they did at the general synods of 1578, 1581, 1586 and 1618/1619. Likewise, attempts to have the Walloon synod and the provincial synods of the Dutch-speaking churches in correspondence with each other were not successful, while no general synod was organised for two centuries. Also, the use of a different language, French, constituted an obstacle for many Dutch to join the French congregations. Only a few members of the Dutch Church were attracted to the French-speaking Walloon Church. For these few, attracted as they already were to the "Frenchification" of Dutch culture, it allowed them to upgrade their social position. By contrast to the Dutch the Walloons left their French-speaking Church in great numbers and assimilated into the Dutch churches. Today many members of the Protestant Church in the Netherlands are not familiar with, and hardly aware of this specific Walloon ecclesiastical organisation.

On the other hand, the Walloon Church was far from being an invisible minority. The Dutch in general, and the Dutch Reformed Church especially, showed solidarity with the victims (the Walloon and the Huguenot Protestants) of French religious persecutions. King Louis XIV replaced the Edict of Nantes by the Edict of Fontainbleau which implied that the rights of the French Protestants were taken away. The Northern Netherlands thus became a refuge for the French-speaking Reformed refugees. They were offered economic, financial and political privileges. The Dutch, and the Dutch Reformed Church, demonstrated their famous tolerant attitude. Apparently, however, tolerance also had its price. The Dutch as a nation of ministers and merchants were not only generous, but also considered their own (economic) position and situation, and hoped that the arrival of the French Protestants would help advance the Dutch economy, especially commerce and industry, the financial market, the book market, and intellectual and cultural life. Not all of the refugees sought refuge from religious prosecution in their homeland. Not all of them were heroes of faith. Those who fled did this for a combination of reasons, not only religious, but also financial, economic, and/or political. Whatever the reasons were, the French refugees were accepted by the Dutch Reformed Church. For the Dutch and French Protestants shared the same Reformed heritage, the *Confessio Belgica* of 1561, and the same system of Church polity.

In short, the acceptance of the French Protestants by the Dutch Reformed Church also included the privilege of a "separate" ecclesiastical organisation at first under the umbrella of the Dutch Reformed Church, and today under that of the Protestant Church in the Netherlands. The Walloon congregations formed a Reformed minority, but very much a privileged Reformed minority.

Bibliography

ARNAL, J. (1929), De l'Influence des Réfugies Francais aux Pays-Bas: Discours Prononce au Nom du Consistoire de l'Eglise Wallonne d'Amsterdam par son Président Mr. le Pasteur J. Arnal à l'Occasion du 350me Anniversaire de la Fondation de l'Eglise Wallonne d'Amsterdam, [Delft: s.n.].

BACHIENE, WILLEM ALBERT (1770), Kerkelyke geographie der Vereenigde Nederlanden 3, Amsterdam: Dirk onder de Linden en zoon.

BAYLE, PIERRE (1974), Dictionnaire Historique et Critique, ed. Alain Niderst, Paris: Éditions sociales.

BENOIST, ELIE (1696), Historie der gereformeerde Kerken van Vrankrijk: Vervattende het Begin en den Voortgang der Reformatie..., Amsterdam: Jan ten Hoorn, 1696.

BOTS, H. (1985), Vlucht naar de vrijheid: De Hugenoten en de Nederlanden, Amsterdam/Dieren: De Bataafsche Leeuw.

BOTS, J.A.H./G.H.M. POSTHUMUS MEYJES (eds.) (1986), La Révocation de l'Édit de Nantes et les Provinces-Unies 1685/The Revocation of the Edict of Nantes and the Dutch Republic: Colloque International du Tricentenaire Avril 1–3/International Congress of the Tricentennial 1–3 April 1985, Amsterdam/Maarssen: APA-Holland University Press.

BOURLIER, É. (ed.) (1896), Livre synodal contenant les articles résolus dans les synodes des Églises Wallones des Pays-Bas, le Commission de l'Histoire des Églises Wallones, La Haye: Nijhoff.

CORNU, FRANK LE (s.a.), Origine des Eglises réformées wallonnes des Pays-Bas, 2nd edition, Utrecht: J. van Boekhoven.

DAAMS, F.H.C.M. (1991), Quatrième Centenaire de l'Église Wallonne de La Haye: Kroniek van de laatste 100 Jaar, Amstelveen: IMPROCEP.

DUKE, ALASTAIR/GILLIAN LEWIS/ANDREW PETTEGREE (eds.) (1992), Calvinism in Europe 1540–1610: A Collection of Documents, Manchester/New York: Manchester University Press.

DRESSELHUIS, J. AB UTRECHT (1848), De Waalsche gemeenten in Zeeland, voor en na de herroeping van het Edict van Nantes: Een bijdrage tot de geschiedenis van de Hervormde Kerk in de Nederlanden, Bergen op Zoom: J.C. Verkouteren.

FRIJHOFF, WILLEM (2003), Uncertain Brotherhood: The Huguenots in the Dutch Republic, in: Bertrand Van Ruymbeke/Randy J. Sparks (eds.), Memory and Identity: The Huguenots in France and the Atlantic Diaspora, Columbia/South Carolina: University of South Carolina Press.

GELDERBLOEM, OSCAR (2000), Zuid-Nederlandse kooplieden en de opkomst van de Amsterdamse stapelmarkt (1578–1630), Hilversum: Verloren.

GIBS, G.C. (1975), Some Intellectual and Political Influences of the Huguenot Emigres in the United Provinces, c. 1680–1730, in: Bijdragen en Mededelingen Betreffende de Geschiedenis der Nederlanden 90, vol. 1, 255–287.

ISRAEL, JONATHAN I. (1966), De Republiek 1477–1806, Franeker: Van Wijnen.

JOSPIN, MARC (1963), Les Eglises Wallonnes des Pays-Bas, Amsterdam: Édition de l'Écho des Églises Wallones.

KNETSCH, F.R.J. (1967), Pierre Jurieu: Theoloog en Politkus der Refuge, Kampen: Kok.

KNUTTEL, W.P.C. (ed.) (1908–1916), Acta der Particuliere Synoden van Zuid-Holland 1621–1700, 6 vols., 's Gravenhage: Nijhoff.

KOENEN, H.J. (1846), Geschiedenis van de vestiging en den invloed der Fransche vluchtelingen in Nederland, Leiden: Luchtmans.

KUIJPERS, ERIKA (2005), Migrantenstad: Immigratie en sociale verhoudingen in 17e-eeuws Amsterdam, Hilversum: Verloren.

MEETEREN, ARIES VAN (2006): Op hoop van akkoord: Instrumenteel forumgebruik bij geschilbeslechting in Leiden in de zeventiende eeuw, Hilversum: Van Meeteren/Verloren.

MICHELET, JULES (1898), Histoire de France au sixième siècle, tome X, La Réforme, Paris: Callman Levy.

NUSTELING, H.P.H. (1986), The Netherlands and the Huguenots Émigrés, in: J.A.H. Bots/G.H.M. Posthumus Meyjes (eds.) (1986), La Révocation de l'Édit de Nantes et les Provinces Unies: Colloque International du Tricentenaire/The Revocation of the Edict of Nantes and the Dutch Republic International Congress of The Tricentennial, Avril 1–3/1–3 April 1985..., Amsterdam/Maarssen: APA-Holland University Press.

POSTHUMUS MEYJES, G.H.M. (1975), Geschiedenis van het Waalse College te Leiden 1606–1699, Leiden: Universitaire Pers.

POSTHUMUS MEYJES, G.H.M./J.A.H. BOTS (eds.) (2005), Livre des Actes des Eglises Wallones aux Pays-Bas 1601–1697, The Hague: Instituut voor Nederlandse Geschiedenis.

POUJOL, D.F. (1902), Histoire et Influence des Églises Wallonnes dans les Pays-Bas, Paris: Librairie Fischbacher.

REITSMA, J./S.D. VAN VEEN (eds.) (1892–1899), Acta der provinciale en particuliere synoden, gehouden in de Noordelijke Nederlanden gedurende de jaren 1572–1620, 8 vols., Groningen: Wolters.

RUTGERS, F.L. (ed.) (1980), Acta van de Nederlandsche Synoden der Zestiende Eeuw, 2nd edition, Dordrecht: J.P. van den Tol.

Scheltus, P. (1735), Kerkelyk Placaatboek II, The Hague.

Selderhuis, H.J. (ed.) (2006), Nederlandse kerkgeschiedenis, Kampen: Kok.

Sleutel, Cees (2015), De Waalse Kerk van Vlissingen of l'Eglise Wallonne de Flessingue van 1572 tot 1825, Vlissingen: Cees Sleutel.

Van Den Broeke, Leon (2015), Baptism, Marriage and Funeral: Reformed Exclusivity or Religious Intolerance? in: Herman J. Selderhuis and J. Marius J. Lange van Ravenswaay (eds.), Reformed Majorities in Early Modern Europe, Göttingen/Bristol USA: Vandenhoeck & Ruprecht, 213–225.

– (2005), Een geschiedenis van de Classis: Classicale Typen tussen Idee en Werkelijkheid 1571–2004, Kampen: Kok.

Van der Linden, Daniel (2015), Experiencing Exile: Huguenot Refugees in the Dutch Republic, 1680–1700, Farnham Surrey: Ashgate.

Van Eijnatten, Joris/Fred van Lieburg (2005), Nederlandse religiegeschiedenis, Hilversum: Verloren.

Van Ruymbeke, Bertrand (2003), Minority Surival: The Huguenot Paradigm in France and the Diaspora, in: Bertrand Van Ruymbeke and Randy J. Sparks (eds.), Memory and Identity: The Huguenots in France and the Atlantic Diaspora, Columbia/South Carolina: University of South Carolina Press, 1–25.

Van Ruymbeke, Bertrand/Randy J. Sparks (eds.) (2003), Memory and Identity: The Huguenots in France and the Atlantic Diaspora, Columbia: University of South Carolina Press.

Verheul Dzn., J. (1941), De Waalsche Gemeente te Rotterdam en haar kerkgebouwen voorheen en thans, 's Gravenhage: 't Verguld Blazoen.

Wagenmakers, Wendy (2015), De Waalse Kerk van Vlissingen, Zeeland geboekt, accessed 15 July 2017, http://zeelandboeken.pzc.nl/?p=13218.

Ypey, A./I.J. Dermout (1819), Geschiedenis der Nederlandsche Hervormde Kerk 1, Breda: W. van Bergen & Co.

IV. Marginal Reformation

Felicita Tramontana

An Unusual Setting

Interactions between Protestants and Catholics in the Ottoman Empire

1. The Implementation of Tridentine Catholicism and the Ottoman Empire

In 1615 the Bishop of Chios, a Greek island conquered by the Ottomans in 1566, reported to the Sacred Congregation for the Propagation of Faith (*De Propaganda Fide*) that heresy was spreading among the local Catholics because of the presence of Protestants on the island. He claimed that Catholics had their daily meals with Lutherans, eating meat on Fridays and during fasts. He also added that such behaviour was supported by the Ottoman rule, under which it was impossible for the clergy to punish the sinners.[1]

Since the 1950s, historical research has profusely described how both the Catholic and Protestant Churches tried to reform late medieval Christianity, eradicate well-established religious practices, enhance social discipline and encourage the development of strong confessional identities.[2] Using the "confessionalisation paradigm",[3] moreover, scholars have described how the developing states in the sixteenth and seventeenth centuries cooperated with the established Churches to enhance conformity and social discipline among pop-

---

1 ACDF (Archive of the Congregation of the doctrine of faith, Rome) St. St. (Stanza Storica), Q.3-b, *folio* 397. This research has been funded by the EURIAS- fellowship program (2014).

2 See for example, Dixon/Freist/Greengrass: 2009; Bossy: 1970, 51–70; Janelle: 1949; Daniel-Rops: 1962; Searle: 1974. For an overview of major trends in Reformation historiography, see Holt: 2003, 133–144; Hillerbrand: 2003, 525–552. See also Tracy: 2006.

3 The "confessionalisation paradigm", as Heinz Schilling called it, was worked out by Schilling himself and Wolfgang Reinhard on the concept of Konfessionsbildung (confessional formation) as developed in the late 1950s by Ernst Walter Zeeden. See Reinhard, 1989; Schilling: 1992.

ulations through different methods, for example by implementing clear norms of religious practice, using propaganda, or fostering education.[4]

With specific regard to the implementation of the Catholic Reformation (or Counter-Reformation),[5] studies of individual dioceses show that newly trained priests fought against well-established religious practices and imposed reforms on their flocks. Also, in places where Catholics and Protestants lived side by side, they endeavoured to create a divide between Catholics and Protestants and strengthen confessional identities (Hoffman: 1984; Luria: 1991; Fehleisen: 2010; De Boer: 2004). No less important was the role that missionaries and religious orders played in this process. In some parts of France, for example, only after the arrival of the Jesuits was a divide between Huguenots and Catholics created, with the two religious communities being buried in separate cemeteries (Luria: 1996, 25–38).[6] More recently, analysis of the documentation kept by the Roman Congregations has shed light on the constant negotiation between the central authorities of the Church, local clergy and their flocks, which accompanied the implementation of canon law in lands ruled by Protestants.[7]

In spite of the many different approaches, most research about the implementation of Tridentine Catholicism and confessional orthodoxy has only taken into account the territories under either Catholic or Protestant rule,[8] consequently examining related issues through the prism of majority-minority dynamics. What happened, however, when both Catholics and members of the Reformed Churches were minorities (or foreigners) living under a hostile political ruler? Did the Catholic clergy try and eventually manage to establish clear boundaries between the Catholics and the Protestants? What were the problems that Catholic missionaries and clergymen faced in imposing Tridentine orthodoxy and what attitudes did the Roman congregations display in response to this?

My paper seeks to answer such questions focussing on the example of the Ottoman Empire. Whereas the relationships between Catholics and the Eastern Churches have been amply described, there have been few comprehensive works

4 Over the years, scholars have criticised many aspects of the confessionalisation paradigm – such as the original link between confessionalisation and modernisation, the alleged emphasis on the similarities of the confessional Churches, and the statist focus. On the subject, see for example Ehrenpreis/Lotz-Heumann: 2002. Recently, scholars have argued that even the link between state building and confessionalisation should be re-shaped with more flexibility than in the original formulation

5 Jedin: 1999, 21–45. The two words are used mostly interchangeably. On the Catholic Reformation see, for example, Mullet: 1999; Birley: 1999.

6 On France and Italy see also Fragnito/Tallon: 2015.

7 Dompnier: 2009. On Catholic practices in Protestant lands see also: McClain: 2004; Parker: 2008; Questier: 2006; Kaplan/Moore/Van Nierop/Pollmann: 2008.

8 But see Windler: 2010.

on the interactions between Protestants and Catholics in the Sultan's realm.[9] However, research dealing with miscellaneous topics like diplomacy, travellers and trade shows clearly that daily interactions and forms of collaboration were by no means rare. In Europe, as in the Ottoman Empire, these interactions raised the concerns of the clergy, which struggled to keep the two confessions separated and, safeguard Catholic confessional identity.

Works on the implementation of Tridentine orthodoxy have remarked that this process varied from one place to another and was influenced by different factors. Firstly, one should mention the distinction between a "Tridentine space" – with an established Church hierarchy and parish system – and places with a negligible Catholic presence and difficulties practicing the faith (Pizzorusso: 2009, 48). No less important were political circumstances. These considerations, as the paper will show, hold true also with regard to the Ottoman Empire. Here the features of the process for enforcing canon law varied consistently with the presence or lack of a parish system. Local circumstances also played their part. First of all, in the Sultan's realm, Islam was the rulers' religion, with Christians – whether Catholics, Protestants or members of the Eastern Churches – and Jews being "protected minorities". This meant that, in accordance with the prescription of Islamic law, they were allowed to practice their religions and were granted protection over their lives and properties, as long as they paid a tax called the poll tax, and recognised the superiority of Islam. Even more important for the scope of this research is the fact that in most parts of the seventeenth- and eighteenth-century Ottoman Empire, the process that would lead to the establishment of Catholic communities and the formation of a local Catholic identity was only just beginning.

Indeed, the Catholic Church decided to expand its influence in the East only in the sixteenth century, as a result of the spread of the Reformation and the loss of territory in Northern Europe. During the sixteenth century initiatives toward the Eastern Churches grew steadily and Pope Gregory XII (1572–1585) encouraged their adhesion to the Council of Trent. The arrival of the missionaries and the spread of Catholicism in the Ottoman Empire was also facilitated by the nascent dominance of French trade in the area. In fact the legal pretext under which Latin clergymen entered the Ottoman territories was provided by the capitulations signed between France and the Porte, which allowed religious orders to enter the Ottoman realms in order to take care of the Christian merchants.[10] In 1583 five

9 On Protestants in the Ottoman Empire see Friedrich/Schunka: 2012; on French Huguenots in Tunisia see Windler: 2002, 116–117; 2001, 251–252. On Protestants in Jerusalem see Tramontana: 2014; 2013.

10 At a yet earlier date, however, missionaries had arrived in the Ottoman territories, often enjoying the protection of Western diplomats. In 1561, for example, the Jesuits Gian Battista

Jesuits were sent to Galata and in the second decade of the seventeenth century Capuchins and Jesuits arrived in the Syro-Palestinian region (Frazee: 2006, 73). Prior to the second decade of the century the only religious order that was permanently settled in *Bilād al-Shām* were the Franciscan Friars Minor of the Custody of the Holy Land whose presence in Jerusalem dates back to the Middle Ages (Frazee: 2006, 59–60; Pieraccini: 2000, 266–270).

Because Islamic law prohibited proselytising among Muslims, the missionaries' work was mostly directed toward Eastern Christians. After a difficult beginning, the number of "reconcilations" with the Church of Rome grew, especially during the eighteenth century. Nonetheless the development of Catholic communities separated from the Eastern Churches was a long and difficult process, which required many efforts. The Catholic clergy's attempts to control the behaviour of the flocks were jeopardised by the features of Oriental Christianity, the porousness of the boundaries between Christian denominations, and the attraction exerted by the rulers' religion, with the clergy fearing that an intransigent attitude might encourage migration by Catholics to another Church or conversion to Islam. Through the seventeenth century boundaries between Catholics and other Christian denominations remained extremely porous and Catholicism a private matter. Neophytes only changed their names, still attending the same churches and taking part in the same ceremonies with their former co-religionists (Masters: 2001, 88). In spite of the protests of *Propaganda Fide*, mixed marriages and *communicatio in sacris* between Catholics and members of the Eastern Churches were common occurrences. During the eighteenth century, and with the number of Catholics growing, the attitude toward these practices became more intransigent. The first period of missionary activity, in which compromises had to be accepted in order to spread the faith, was now over. With the number of converts growing, it became necessary to develop a Catholic identity among the newly established Catholic communities. This change is exemplified by the crackdown on *communicatio in sacris* with Oriental Christians. In fact, after long maintaining an ambiguous position toward the issue, in 1729 Rome issued a general prohibition against it (Santus: 2014).[11] In spite of missionary efforts and Rome's firmness, however, the eradication of well-established practices would not be easy, and well into the 18th century, the difficulty of disciplining the conduct of the converts is amply attested by missionary sources.

Eliano and Cristobald Rodriguez were sent by the Pope into Egypt in order to negotiate the unification of the Coptic community with Rome.

11 In 1704 the Congregation De Propaganda Fide issued a decree which prevented the new converts from joining the ceremonies of the "heretics", Heyberger: 1994, 386. See also Hamilton: 2006, 89.

Departing from these premises, the article investigates how the Church faced the challenges raised by interactions between Protestants and Catholics in the Ottoman territory, in an age characterised by the confessionalisation and implementation of Tridentine orthodoxy in Europe, as well as the diffusion of Catholicism and consolidation of Catholic communities in the Ottoman Empire. More specifically, I will investigate what challenges the coexistence of Protestant and Catholic communities created for clergymen living in Ottoman territories, what problems they faced in maintaining confessional borders and managing the behaviour of their flocks, in a place where both Catholics and Protestants were minorities. Secondly, I will consider the solutions suggested by the central government of the Church and evaluate how they were affected by local circumstances.

The article argues that the presence of Protestants in the Ottoman Empire gave rise to challenges similar to those that the Catholic clergy faced in places that were under Protestant rule. In the Ottoman realm, as in Europe and other missionary territories, missionaries, clergymen and the Roman congregations negotiated with each other and with their flocks to build and maintain boundaries between the two communities. However in the Ottoman Empire the struggle to develop a Catholic identity also influenced the attitude of the Holy Office toward interactions between Protestants and Catholics, and more specifically with regard to mixed marriages.

As for the sources, my research relies mostly on documents from the archives of the Roman Inquisition, first of all the *dubia circa sacramenta.* Here, the word *dubia* is an archival denomination referring to questions and doubts that arose during the implementation of canon law in a specific context. These started to be submitted by the missionaries spread all over the world to the central government of the Church in the sixteenth century. The *dubia circa sacramenta* regard particular doubts concerning the administration of sacraments (Pizzorusso: 2009, 39–61; Broggio/Castelnau-L'Estoile/Piszzorusso: 2009, 5–22).

In addition to this, the clergy in missionary territories sent to Rome their requests for spiritual powers (*facultates*) – such as the faculty to reconcile from heresy. Since the Middle Ages, the Papacy had accorded such special faculties to missionaries in order to facilitate the fulfilment of their tasks and the dissemination of Catholicism. In the sixteenth century, decisions about the faculties to be granted to the missionaries were taken by the Congregation of the Holy Office, i. e. the Roman Inquisition, founded in 1542. This arrangement did not change until after 1622, when the Congregation *De Propaganda Fide* was created to supervise missionary activities (Metzer: 1971; Pizzorusso: 2000). Soon, the Congregation *De Propaganda* became a vital mediator between the Inquisition and the missionaries, as the latters' patents were issued by its offices. The newly created Congregation also tried to absorb the important task of answering the missionaries' doubts, which had been carried out until then by the Holy Office (Pizzorusso: 2009, 40). The Congregation *De Propaganda*'s attempts, however, were not successful, and in 1658 Pope Innocent X decided that the new Congregation would forward the doubts submitted by the missionaries and all the related information to the Holy Office (Pizzorusso: 2009, 46: Id: 2011, 393–423). It would then forward its decision to the Congregation *De Propaganda* which, after having it recorded in its own archives, had to inform the missionaries. Evidence of the exchanges between the two congregations can be found in the documentation kept in their archives where dossiers were stored for future reference, with the decisions filed by topic. The doubts concerning the application of canon law in the Ottoman Empire were often recorded together with similar questions – and corresponding answers – arriving from other places where Catholics and Protestants lived side by side. This is consistent with the Holy Office's methodology of answering doubts submitted by missionaries worldwide. Indeed, without disregarding the single issues, problems were connected to a well-known case-in-point in order to establish a general framework of jurisprudence (Dompnier: 2009, 29).

Recently, interest in this documentation has been growing. Historians have increasingly used the letters that the missionaries forwarded to the Inquisition and the related answers in order to analyse the implementation of canon law and the way that sacraments were administered in different locations around the world (Pizzorusso: 2011; Broggio/Castelnau-L'Estoile/Pizzorusso: 2009, 5–22. Dompnier: 2009, 23–38). With regard to Ottoman territory, the material kept in the archives of the Roman congregations has been almost exclusively used for research on the *communicatio in sacris* with Eastern Christians (Santus: 2014). Nonetheless it is also a valuable source on the relationship between Protestants and Catholics in the Ottoman Empire.

The article is organised as follows, I will firstly describe the interactions between Catholics and Protestants in the Ottoman context; I will then focus on the missionaries' letters, first of all on the requests for *facultates* and afterwards on the *dubia circa sacramenta* and on the answers given by the Holy Office. I will pay special attention to the doubts concerning the sacrament of marriage (*dubia circa matrimonium*).

2. Interactions between Protestants and Catholics and the Concerns of the Clergy: General Concerns and Local Circumstances

Up to the sixteenth century, the concerns of Catholic clergy and missionaries settled in the Ottoman realm resulted from the difficulties of administering the sacraments in a foreign context and from Catholics' interaction with Eastern Christians and Muslims. However, the diffusion of the Reformation and subsequent arrival of Protestant merchants, diplomats and travellers in the Ottoman Empire occasioned new worries for the Catholic clergy and for the members of religious orders. In fact, in the Sultan's realm, interactions between Catholics and Protestants were extremely common, as testified by diplomatic sources, travellers' reports, correspondence etc. Protestant and Catholic diplomats, for example, frequently attended each other's celebrations and even religious ceremonies. Moreover in the Ottoman land it was by no means rare for Catholic consuls to help Protestants in need and, conversely, Catholic missionaries would not refrain from seeking the help of the consuls and ambassadors of Protestant countries. Additionally, as far as diplomats were concerned, Catholics would occasionally act as representatives of Protestant countries and vice-versa. Indeed, as a general rule, the protection of a government's commercial interests could be entrusted to the representatives of another government. This was common especially for those countries whose volume of trade was small and which therefore decided to seek the protection of foreign diplomats. Patronage over foreigners increased the diplomats' prestige and incomes and, in any case, religious matters were not at issue here.[12] Encounters between travellers were common, and Catholics and Protestants would also share the condition of captives and slaves and find themselves in the same *bagno*.[13] Besides contacts between foreigners, in some parts of the Ottoman Empire Protestants also had daily contact with local Catholics. The establishment of business partnerships was common and Catholics were often hired by Protestant merchants or diplomats (Masters: 2001).

Such a multifaceted picture is also displayed in the documentation filed in the archive of the Roman congregations. From the clergy's letters we can see that such relations frequently proved to be a constant source of worry or at least uneasiness. This is hardly surprising considering that during the sixteenth and

12 Problems, however, might occasionally arise. The Philibert brothers, French Huguenots under Dutch protection, reported persecution by the French consul – a Catholic in charge of the protection of Dutch tradesmen of the city. See Schutte, *Repertorium der Nederlandse vertegenwoordigers*, cited by Van der Boogert: 2000, 195. On the interaction between Protestants and Catholic missionaries in the Safavid Empire see Windler: 2010.

13 The *bagno* was the place where slaves were kept at night and where captives were imprisoned while waiting to be sold as slaves or to be ransomed.

the seventeenth centuries the main concern of the Catholic Church was to avoid the dissemination of Protestant theories, promote Tridentine orthodoxy in Europe and create a divide between the two confessions.

In the Ottoman territories these same concerns were heightened by the fact that Muslim rule jeopardised the control that Catholic clergymen were able to exercise over their flocks. The tools available to the European Catholic Church to educate the worshippers – catechisms, confession, punishments and excommunication – could also be adopted in Ottoman lands. But while in many parts of Europe these methods were implemented with the support and even the aid of the secular élite, this was not the case in the Sultans' realm. As the Bishop of Chios pointed out, in the Ottoman Empire Catholic clergymen and the members of religious orders could only count on their moral authority, which was not always enough.[14] Even the diplomats of Catholic countries, to whom Catholic missionaries would appeal in case of need (Heyberger: 1994, 249; Masters: 2001, 82), in most case were of no help. In 1635 Andrea d'Arco, then Prefect of the Franciscans in Cairo, reported to *De Propaganda Fide* that in Cairo there were two Lutherans, one of whom had learned Arabic in order to go to Ethiopia and "disseminate his pestiferous poison" there. When asked by the Prefect and other religious men to stop him, not only did the French consul fail to comply; he even granted the Lutheran his letters of recommendation.[15]

Beside these generic considerations, the interaction between Catholics and Protestants and, consequently, the issues that the Catholic missionaries had to face, varied from one place to another within the Ottoman territory; indeed, they were shaped by local factors. One of these were the characteristics of the Catholic presence, that is, whether the Catholics were local or foreign, and the size and presence or lack of a parish system. Indeed, in the Sultan's realm the features of the Catholic presence greatly varied from one place to another. Whereas in some parts of the Ottoman Empire such as in the Maghreb, Catholics were almost exclusively foreigners well into the eighteenth century, in the same period some Greek islands hosted large Catholic communities with established Church hierarchies. In the Middle East, to give another example, Catholic communities were developing in the main cities, such as Aleppo. Istanbul hosted a substantial Catholic population, made up of both foreigners and locals. Elsewhere Catholics were still mostly foreigners.

This variety also shaped the challenges that missionaries faced. Thus the letters forwarded to the Holy Office from the Greek Islands mirrored the local clergy's concern to preserve Catholic orthodoxy among their flocks. The clergy lamented the dissemination of Protestant ideas and the "contamination" of

14 A.C.D.F., St. St., Q.3-b, *folio* 397.

15 A.D.P.F, S.O.C.G. (Scritture originali riferite ai congressi generali), vol. VI, 59, *folio* 168.

religious practices. The aforementioned Bishop of Chios reported not only that Catholics worked with Protestants but that they also had meals together. He mentioned the case of a Catholic man in the island of Andros who, after living in the house of a Flemish merchant, died without confession and without taking the last sacrament. Moreover, according to the Bishop, a growing number of Catholics expressed Protestant ideas and died without confession.[16]

The same worries regarding the risk of the "contamination" of local Catholic practices are also reflected in letters arriving from the Middle East. In some cities, such as Aleppo, as early as the 1620s there was a local Catholic community whose members were often hired as dragomans by Protestant diplomats. In addition to this, clergymen and missionaries settled in the area were also often suspicious about the familiarity between merchants of the two confessions who lived side by side in the merchant communities (Heyberger: 1994, 277–278). Similar concerns are also mirrored in the letters that were sent from the Maghreb.

The concerns of missionaries and clergymen were also influenced by the presence – or the lack – of Protestant pastors. This varied from one place to another. During the seventeenth and the eighteenth centuries they usually lived in merchant colonies established by Protestant countries, where they provided spiritual assistance to merchants and diplomats. Reformed clergy also resided in those cities in which Protestants were numerous, such as Aleppo and Istanbul. In many other parts of the Ottoman Empire, however, because of the lack of pastors, Protestant merchants had to ask Catholic priests to administer the sacraments, raising concerns related to the *communicatio in sacris.* Tunis, for example, did not host any reformed minister until the nineteenth century, which implies that Protestants received the sacraments from either Greek or Catholic priests. Indeed this was also the case in the French *échelles* in Lebanon and Palestine where a Catholic majority lived together with Reformed merchants – French Huguenots[17] and merchants from countries where the Reformation had been implemented, who conducted business under the French flag[18] – who had to rely on the spiritual assistance of Catholic priests.

16 A.C.D.F., St. St., Q3-b. The diocese of the island was established in 1204 and depended upon the Archbishop of Rhodes (in 1642 it was put under the Archbishop of Naxos). In the seventeenth century the Catholic community numbered more than 6000 followers.

17 As far as French Protestants are concerned, after the revocation of the edict of Nantes (1685) the *Chambre de Commerce* of Marseille prevented Protestants from travelling to Ottoman territories. In reality, however, many Huguenots managed to reach Tunis, where they lived under the protection of either the Bey or the British consul. Conversions to Catholicism in order to enjoy the benefits of French protection were also frequent. On French Protestants in Tunis see Windler: 2002, 116–117. See also Id.: 2001, 251–252.

18 This was a common practice for merchants whose country of origin had not been granted a capitulation by the Sultan.

In places where Protestant ministers lived, the worries of missionaries and clergy were of a different nature. Firstly they were occupied with preventing Catholics from receiving the sacraments from them. If that did not succeed they often raised doubts on the validity of sacraments administered by the Protestants.[19]

3. *Facultates*

The nature of the Catholic presence, or more precisely the presence of an established Church hierarchy, not only influenced the concerns of the clergy and the missionaries but also the very identity of those who wrote to the Congregation *De Propaganda*, requesting faculties or expressing *dubia*. In fact, if there was a diocese, as in the Greek islands, its bishop would be in charge of writing to the Roman congregations, otherwise the letters would be prepared by the apostolic vicar, if there was one. After the foundation of the vicariate of Constantinople in Istanbul (1652), for example, the vicar in office was the author of most of the correspondence addressed to the Congregation *De Propaganda*. The existence of vicars and bishops, however, did not prevent missionaries or members of religious orders from writing their own letters to the Roman congregations, in order to express doubts or request faculties. Despite the presence of an apostolic vicariate in Algiers, for example, in 1731 a Trinitarian who lived in the city wrote to ask about the validity of a marriage celebrated by a non-Catholic minister.[20]

As for the Syro-Palestinian region, letters to the Congregation *De Propaganda* from this area were mainly written by the Guardian of the Holy Land – who acted locally as the apostolic vicar – and by members of religious orders. As for the latter, in the seventeenth century those who forwarded the information to the Congregation *De Propaganda* were mostly missionaries, while in the following century this task was undertaken by the local superiors of the orders, as Heyberger has pointed out (Heyberger: 1997, 548). Ordinary members of religious orders would maintain correspondence with the Congregation *De Propaganda* in areas where there were neither bishops nor an apostolic vicariate, such as in most of the Maghreb before the foundation of the apostolic vicariate of Algiers.

The expression of missionaries' concerns was often followed by a request for faculties. Since the Middle Ages, because of the exceptionality of the situations in which missionaries served, the Papacy had granted to them some special prerogatives. The concession of faculties was legitimised by the idea that in missionary territories the missionaries acted as representatives of the Pope himself.

19 See for example, A.C.P.F., DV. DV (1570–1668), folder 10. See below.
20 A.C.D.F., St. St., M3-i, folder 21.

From the thirteenth century, the concession of faculties to the mendicant orders became a well-established custom, and between the Middle Ages and the early modern period members of religious orders enjoyed wide powers. During the second half of the sixteenth century, however, the privileges of the missionaries began to appear excessive and caused conflicts with the newly established bishops, as happened, for example, in India. The need to frame the prerogatives granted to the missionaries in a consistent scenario prompted Pope Urban VIII to establish a commission, *Super Facultatibus Missionarum*, the *Congregazione Urbaniana* (1633) (Pizzorusso: 2009, 41).

According to the works of the commission, the missionary territory was divided by specific parameters, such as the ratio of Catholics to the total population or the freedom to practice the Catholic faith. No less important was the existence of a Church hierarchy. Wherever there were bishops, missionaries who worked within the borders of the dioceses would receive their faculties from them. This was the case with France, where bishops were the recipients of the faculties granted by the Pope and could decide to transmit them to missionaries and clergymen. On the contrary, in the Protestant countries of Northern Europe, it was the Apostolic Nuncio who would grant faculties to Catholic missionaries (Dompnier: 2009, 28; cf. Sanfilippo and Pizzorusso: 2001). The commission also decided that, in accordance with the logic of the Tridentine norms, missionaries would need the permission of the parish priest in order to administer the sacraments in territories hosting an established parish system.[21] Despite these efforts, it was not easy to promote respect for the new norms, because the religious orders tried to keep hold of the powers they had enjoyed since the Middle Ages. This resulted in an endless stream of requests for faculties.

In those places where Catholics and Protestants lived side by side, the extension of the clergy's and missionaries' prerogatives was aimed at facilitating conversions to Catholicism and at integrating the neophytes into the Catholic communities (Dompnier: 2009, 25). In France missionaries who had to fight against "the heresy", for example, were often granted the power to resolve cases of simony – which would usually fall under the competence of higher ecclesiastical officers – to read Protestant books and to absolve "heretics" (Luria: 2005, 69). Letters from Protestant countries also contained requests for the faculty to grant dispensation from disparity of cult and from consanguinity.[22]

---

21 See on the point Dompnier: 2009, 26 and in particular n. 11.

22 During the seventeenth and eighteenth centuries the issue of consanguinity appears regularly in the correspondence between the Roman Congregation and the missionaries and inspires the latter's doubts or requests for faculties. In fact, due to the Protestants' rejection of the impedimentum consanguinitatis, those who converted to Catholicism might have found themselves in an illicit situation. In order to amend these situations, missionaries requested the faculty to grant dispensations to converts.

Some of the requests that arrived from the Ottoman territory were clearly linked to the Protestants' presence. This is the case, for example, with the letter of a priest from Ragusa (Dubrovnik), Don Vincenzo di Augustino, who asked to be sent to Ottoman Hungary in order to take care of his Catholic countrymen who had settled there for business. Some of the faculties that he believed a missionary should enjoy in that land were strictly connected with the presence of Protestants. In order to substantiate his request the clergyman reported that the merchants' faith was threatened by an excessive familiarity with Lutherans. Catholics worked and ate with them, mixed marriages were common and Catholics hired Protestants as servants. According to the priest they even sent their children to Lutheran schools, claiming that it was only to "teach them to read and write".[23] The clergyman ended his description stating that in those places the chaplain should have the faculties to reconcile, absolve and marry.

Generally spoken the requests for faculties that arrived from the Ottoman Empire were not very different from those forwarded from places where Catholics were a minority or that were ruled by Protestants.[24] This was the case, for example, with the faculty to read Protestant, and therefore forbidden, books. The spread of Protestant ideas and books in the region began to raise Catholic missionaries' concerns as early as the sixteenth century. In 1560, for example, the Bishop of Chios denounced the circulation of prohibited books among local Catholics.[25] At the beginning of the eighteenth century the Guardian of Jerusalem reported to the Congregation *De Propaganda* that in order to prevent the circulation of some Protestant books that were shipped into the area, he had to buy all the copies with the money of the Custody of the Holy Land[26] and burn them in person (Heyberger: 1994, 476). Not less feared was the diffusion of the Reformation among the oriental Christians. Therefore in 1668, the Vicar of Istanbul reported the circulation in the city of books printed in Holland highlighting the similarities between Calvinism and Greek Orthodox beliefs.[27]

Another faculty that was commonly requested by missionaries and clergymen who worked in Protestant territories was the faculty to reconcile "heretics". Similar requests were also put forward by those missionaries who lived in the Ottoman Empire, where circumstances might require that this faculty be given to the chaplain of a *bagno*. In 1642 Innocenzio Marziale, commissioner of the Dominicans in Istanbul, asked that the faculty to reconcile heretics be given to the Latin chaplain of the *bagno*, Don Antonio Sivigliano, who was the only one with

23 The letter dates back to 1559. A.C.D.F., St. St., Q3-b, *folio* 336.
24 On this topic see Tramontana: 2017, 201–13.
25 A.C.P.F., St. St, Q3-b, *folio* 417.
26 This is the name that the province of the Holy land, funded by the Franciscan order in the Middle Ages took over the centuries.
27 A.C.D.F., St. St., Q3-c, letter of the 28th September 1668.

permission to enter that place.[28] As the author of the letter said, in the *bagno* there were in fact numerous Protestants who wanted to be reconciled with the Church of Rome. Others, too, could ask to be reconciled, "inspired by God and by the beautiful ceremonies" that the Catholics performed.

With regard to the answers to the missionaries' requests and the way faculties were granted, the Holy Office showed the same concerns for the rights of the hierarchy and desire to limit the powers of the missionaries as may be observed in the contemporary bestowal of faculties in Europe. Therefore, for example, consistent with the policy that the faculty to read prohibited books was generally granted only to the higher clergy, when the Vicar of Algiers asked permission to pass the same faculty to other clergymen, he received a negative response (1741).[29]

4. Missionaries' Letters and the *dubia circa sacramenta*

In general, missionaries' *dubia* were linked to the implementation of canon law in foreign contexts; more specifically, they arose when the actual situations that the missionaries had to face were particularly complex and the instructions of the Church were insufficiently accurate for the clergy to apply on the spot. Furthermore, those who submitted the doubts generally also suggested, in a more or less explicit way, what was, in their opinion, the most suitable solution (Broggio/Castelnau-L'Estoile/Pizzorusso: 2009; Pizzorusso: 2009). Sometimes doubts were not expressed by the missionaries themselves. It was rather their letters and reports to the Congregation *De Propaganda* that raised doubts in the mind of the Congregation concerning the legitimacy of some practices. In 1763, for example, a report sent by Filippo Montevarchi, prefect of the Franciscans in Tripoli, to the Congregation *De Propaganda*, raised doubts concerning whether the participation of Protestant consuls in Catholic funerals and baptisms was admissible.[30]

Even though the doubts forwarded from the Ottoman Empire often originated from habits common among the *nazioni*, such as the above-mentioned case (Heyberger: 1994, 258; Masters: 2001, 82), in general the issues at stake were similar to those faced by the representative of the Church in Protestant countries or countries of mixed confession. The main concerns of the clergy were linked to the *communicatio in sacris* and to the administration of sacraments. The latter, in missionary territory, was a constant source of doubts (Broggio/Castelnau-L'Es-

28 A.C.D.F., St. St, Q3-c.
29 A.C.P.F., St. St, OO5-a, folder 46.
30 A.C.D.F., DB – *Dubia circa Baptismus* –, vol. 5 (1760–1766). The dossier has been analysed by Dompnier: 2009, 37–38.

toile/Pizzorusso: 2009). The most common ones concerned the validity of the sacraments administered by non-Catholics. Missionaries, for example, would often ask whether a baptism administered by a Protestant minister was valid and whether converts had to be baptised again. The same concerns about the validity of the sacraments were raised by mixed marriages (Dompnier: 2009).[31] Doubts were also expressed over participation in each other's religious ceremonies and daily interactions.

With regard to the answers of the Holy Office, it has been suggested that they were a mixture of intransigence on the one hand, and recommendations to conciliate and encourage conversion on the other (Dompnier: 2009, 38). In the answers given to missionaries in the Ottoman Empire, the appreciation of local circumstances varied greatly according to the issue at stake. Recognition of the situation on the ground is clearly reflected, for example, by the answers given to the Vicar of Algiers on the admissibility of the behaviour of Catholic servants who were hired by Protestant consuls and merchants. Consistently with the answers given to similar questions that arrived from countries with a mixed population,[32] the Inquisition stated that in the servants' case, behaviour such as cooking meat on fasting days and not celebrating the feasts was not to be considered sinful.[33]

On issues related to religious ceremonies, however, the Holy Office was more intransigent. When the Vicar of Smyrna asked whether Catholics could listen to Protestant preaching, the Inquisition requested more details on the circumstances and then answered that, even though hearing Protestant sermons was not *per se* a form of "*communicatio in sacris cum Hereticis*", nonetheless Catholics were not allowed to do so because of the danger of corruption.[34] A similar answer was given to another doubt submitted by the same clergyman who asked whether Catholics were allowed to attend Protestant marriages and baptisms. In this case, while answering in the negative, the Holy Office clarified that even when such behaviour was not to be considered a *communicatio in sacris*, Catholics' participation in Protestant ceremonies might "cause scandal" and was therefore prohibited.[35]

Sacramental sharing was always rejected in territories ruled by Protestants,[36] and the documents concerning the Ottoman Empire show that, as already suggested by Dompnier, *communicatio in sacris* was absolutely rejected, even when

31 Dompnier: 2009. On the *Dubia circa matrimonium*, see Scaramella: 2009. On the doubts that were submitted from missionary territory, see Castelnau-L'Estoile: 2009

32 A.C.D.F., St. St., M3-c, folder 1.

33 A.C.D.F., St. St., M3-b, folder 6.

34 A.C.D.F., St. St., M3-c, folder 1.

35 A.C.D.F., St. St., M3-c, folder 1. The dossier from Smyrna dates back to 1770.

36 With regard to the *communicatio in sacris* with Protestants see Dompnier: 2009.

resulting from a shared condition as foreigners. It is not surprising therefore that, answering to the aforementioned doubt occasioned by the report of the Franciscans of Tripoli, the Holy Office affirmed that baptising Protestants' children was not permissible (Dompnier: 2009, 37–38).[37] When, in 1780, the Vicar of Istanbul asked the permission to administer the Eucharist to an eighteen-year-old boy born to a Catholic mother but forced by his father to attend Lutheran services, he obtained the same cautious answer. Even the Vicar's assertions that the boy was not participating in the communion rites of the Protestant Church failed to soften the Inquisition's position.[38]

5. *Dubia circa Matrimonium*

A large percentage of the doubts that were forwarded to the Inquisition concerned the sacrament of marriage. The Catholic Church, like all Christian Churches at that time, prohibited and tried to prevent marriage between spouses of different confessions. However, once celebrated, such unions were considered valid. In Catholic countries, the Church succeeded in preventing this occurrence by forbidding the parish priests' presence at this kind of wedding.[39] However, in places where the Tridentine canons had not been published,[40] spouses could ask a non-Catholic minister to celebrate the marriage, and indeed even missionaries and priests often agreed to celebrate them, providing that the offspring would be raised in the Catholic faith.[41] Missionaries and clergymen's letters to Rome often solicited a more forbearing attitude. Missionaries who lived in the English and Portuguese colonies,[42] for example, argued that if they could not celebrate mixed marriages, the couple would ask the clergy of other Churches to bless the wedding (Dompnier: 2009, 33–34). The Nuncio of Cologne wrote that, as from 1668 marriages between Protestants and Catholics were permitted in the area, if Catholics did not receive dispensation, they would get married before Lutheran pastors and many souls would be lost.[43]

---

37 Dompnier: 2009, 37–38.

38 A.C.D.F., St. St., M3-c, folder 5.

39 According to the *Tametsi* decree, the presence of the parish priest of one of the spouses was a necessary condition for the celebration to be valid.

40 The canons of the Council of Trent applied only in those lands in which they had been published.

41 It was also possible to ask a dispensation *mixtae religionis* which was to be granted by the Holy Office. Where Protestant countries are concerned, these dispensations were not considered necessary by theologians on the ground that in these places mixed marriages were permitted *ex tacita tolerantia.* This opinion, however, was not shared by the Holy Office.

42 A.C.D.F. St. St., UU 25, folder 1.

43 A.C.D.F. St. St., UU 25, folder 1.

As far as the Ottoman Empire is concerned, the *dubia circa matrimonium* were very diverse. Catholic clergymen complained that the spouses-to-be did not want to be instructed by a priest.[44] Other concerns were linked to the habit of Catholic men of keeping concubines. Such a problem was also voiced by the Bishop of Istanbul, who claimed that it was impossible to punish such behaviour because "the Turks" would defend the sinners.[45] Marriages between Catholics and Eastern Christians were another of the main concerns, despite the prohibitions frequently issued by the religious authorities on both sides. Furthermore, letters mailed from the Ottoman territories often expressed concerns over the validity of marriages celebrated by an Islamic judge or Oriental priest (Caffiero: 2013, 253–270). As in other missionary territories, Catholics resorted to such solutions either because it was difficult to obtain a dispensation of consanguinity or because there were no Catholic priests.[46] On this matter, it is worthwhile to mention a discussion – recently analysed by Marina Caffiero – which took place within the Holy Office in 1758. It originated in requests for clarification submitted by the Bishop of Sofia and focussed on marriages celebrated before an Ottoman judge (Caffiero: 2013, 259–262). Contradicting Pope Benedict XIV's encyclical, *Inter omnigenas* (1744) – according to which weddings celebrated before the Turkish authorities were to not be considered valid (Caffiero: 2011) – on this occasion the Holy Office affirmed the validity of marriages celebrated before a Greek priest or a Muslim judge. By doing so, the Congregation and the new Pope showed more forbearance, justifying their decision on the ground that in Bulgaria the decrees of the Council of Trent, including the encyclical *Inter omnigenas*, had not been published (Caffiero: 2013).[47]

Letters that arrived from the Ottoman Empire also expressed doubts regarding marriages between Catholics and Protestants.[48] In 1559 the Guardian of Aleppo asked whether a wedding celebrated before a Calvinist minister was valid and if the Catholic priest could bless it.[49] In 1765 the Vicar of Constantinople asked about the validity of a marriage between a Dutch Catholic merchant and a local "heretic" woman before an Anglican minister and a Dutch magistrate. A few years later, in 1768, the Vicar of Constantinople submitted a similar case. This time he asked permission to re-validate the marriage of a Catholic woman and a

44 A.C.D.F., St. St., I7-a, folder 13). The letter is sent from Bulgaria.

45 A.C.D.F., DD e DV, (1570–1668), folder 10.

46 Cfr. A.C.D.F., DD e DV, – *Dubia Varia* – (1731–1753). A letter from the Ottoman Balkans (1752) reports that in the absence of a Catholic priest, marriages were often celebrated before the Ottoman judge, and afterward, if possible, were validated by a missionary. On Catholic marriages celebrated by Greek clergy in Dalmatia see Minchella: 2014.

47 On mixed marriages and on in general on the *dubia ciarca matrimonium*, see also Scaramella: 2009.

48 A.C.D.F. St. St., UU 25, folder 1.

49 A.C.D.F., DD e DV (1570–1668), folder 22.

Protestant English merchant that had already been celebrated by a non-Catholic minister.

Following the general principle according to which marriages celebrated in the Ottoman Empire without following the prescription of the *Tametsi* decree were valid, the answer to the aforementioned doubt, submitted by the Vicar of Constantinople, was positive. The same position was repeatedly affirmed by the Inquisition and the priest's or missionary's desire to revalidate a marriage that had already been celebrated by a non-Catholic minister was always rejected. This was the case, for example, with the Vicar of Constantinople's request (1768) to revalidate a marriage already celebrated by Protestant clergy.[50] The same position was expressed by the answer given to the doubt submitted in 1730 by a Trinitarian of Algiers who asked whether he was allowed to revalidate a marriage, celebrated by an English minister, between the Catholic Elisabeth Wisten and an English Protestant.[51] The same approach shaped the Congregation's answer to a case presented in 1769 by the apostolic Vicar of Smyrna, who invalidated a wedding contracted by a Catholic woman with a Protestant before a Capuchin. In this instance, according to the clergymen, the *disparitas cultus* was not the only reason why the marriage was not valid. In fact, in contrast with the *Tametsi* Decree,[52] the officiating minister was not the parish priest of either of the prospective spouses.[53] In this case, too, the Congregation affirmed that the marriage was not licit, nonetheless it was valid. The same position is mirrored also in the answer to a doubt forwarded from Hungary, concerning a Catholic man who had married a Calvinist woman, thus committing apostasy. In this case as well, the Holy Office reaffirmed the validity of the marriage and therefore rejected the man's request to leave his wife and remarry.[54]

Without questioning their validity, the Holy Office, however, always emphasised that mixed marriages were prohibited and that those who contracted them had to be warned about their illicit situation and given a penance. Consequently, when asked by the Vicar of Algiers whether the already mentioned Elisabeth Wisten could be admitted to confession, the answer was affirmative.[55] Nonetheless, when asked whether a Catholic spouse who had contracted the

50 "Non indigere rivalidatione sed habemus ipse validum", see A.C.D.F., St. St., UU 25, folder 1.
51 A.C.D.F., St. St., M3- i, folder 21.
52 This was a ruling of the Council of Trent on matrimonial law (1563). Among other things, it stipulated that any marriage that took place outside the presence of a parish priest would be void.
53 A.C.D.F., St. St., UU 25, folder 1.
54 A.C.D.F., St. St., UU 25, folder 1.
55 A.C.D.F., St. St., M3- i, folder 1.

illegal marriage was allowed to receive the Eucharist, the Holy Office answered that this was possible only after penance had been inflicted.[56]

Despite the similar attitude displayed by the Inquisition toward doubts regarding marriage, there is an important difference between the Ottoman Empire and Protestant Europe. In Northern Europe, the Inquisition's forbearance (Dompnier: 2009, 33–36, 38) culminated in the issue, by Pope Benedict XIV, of the *Declaratio Benedictina* for Holland and Germany (1741). Exempting Protestant spouses from complying with the Tridentine norms, it made *de facto* mixed marriages easier to celebrate. Yet the *Declaratio* was not extended to Istanbul. The issue was considered by a commission established by Pope Clement XIII. However the commission decided not to implement the papal pronouncement in Istanbul on the grounds that its application in a place where many different Christian denominations coexisted side by side might raise unwanted consequences in terms of the volume of mixed marriages.[57]

This explanation clearly reflects the fear that the implementation of a decree that in practice facilitated mixed marriages would jeopardise the Church's fight against nuptials between members of different denominations in the Ottoman Empire and, more generally, its efforts to establish clear borders between Catholic communities and the Eastern Churches. Indeed marriages between members of different denominations were extremely common among Eastern Christians and widespread among Catholics as well. Religious authorities of both sides repeatedly prohibited them. To give just a few examples, in 1637 the Guardian of the Holy Land, Andrea d'Arco, banned marriages between Catholics and "Greeks, Armenians, and other persons heretical and schismatic" (Serino: 1939, 19). In Egypt the sermons of Coptic clergymen condemned the separation of husbands and wives who prayed in different Churches (Armanios: 2011). Such prohibitions, however, had little impact, and marriages between Christians of different denominations remained common throughout the eighteenth century.

In her work on Venice, Cristellon has suggested a connection between the Church's concerns for the Catholic flock's familiarity with Orthodox Greeks and a stricter attitude toward marriages with Protestants. According to her, the strictness with which the Roman Inquisition regarded such nuptials in the city was a consequence of the presence of a well-established Greek community that enjoyed a lot of autonomy and of the large number of unions between Greeks and Catholics (Cristellon: 2013b).

The similarities between the two cases suggest that, where mixed marriages with Protestants are concerned, the Holy Office's attitude was stricter in places

56 A.C.D.F., St. St., UU 25, folder 1. This is the answer to the aforementioned doubt expressed by the Vicar of Istanbul in 1768.

57 A.C.D.F., St. St., UU 25, folder 1. I have analyzed the issue also in Tramontana: 2017, 201–13.

where the Church was already struggling to maintain borders between Catholics and other denominations. This resulted from the fear that forbearance with regard to the Reformed Churches could be considered receptiveness toward nuptials with Orthodox Greeks and members of other denominations.

6. Conclusions

The presence of Protestant merchants and diplomats in the Ottoman Empire raised the concerns of the Catholic Church. Doubts and requests for faculties that arrived from the area show the wish to maintain a separation between the two communities and safeguard the orthodoxy of Catholic religious practices. Moreover, Catholic clergymen expressed fear of the dissemination of Protestant ideas among Catholics and Eastern Christians. The correspondence also sheds light on a constant negotiation between Rome, the missionaries and clergymen who worked in the field, and the laity. This process was influenced by local circumstances, and especially the lack of political support. Furthermore, in the Ottoman Empire clergymen and missionaries also had to deal with the presence of other Christian denominations and the porousness of boundaries between them. Indeed, in the period under consideration, the Catholic Church was still struggling to spread Catholicism in many parts of the Ottoman territory and establish local communities with a well-defined religious identity.

The answers given by the Inquisition reflect its wavering between the acknowledgment of local circumstances and the wish to discipline the practice of faith. As research on the implementation of canon law in Protestant countries has already observed, such hesitations resulted in a certain indulgence with regard to marriages and daily contact. Even the impossibility of celebrating holy days for those who were hired as servants by Protestants was tolerated. The attitude of the Holy Office, however, changed when the orthodoxy of religious practice was at stake. Any form of *comunicatio in sacris* was then rejected.

Departing from this consideration, Dompnier (2009) has argued that the intransigence of the Inquisition was not softened by the fact that in the Ottoman Empire, Protestants and Catholics were both foreigners. My analysis confirms this argument. The debate on the extension to Istanbul of the *Declaratio Benedictina*, moreover, suggests that in the Ottoman lands, the attitude of the Inquisition toward interactions with Protestants may have been even stricter than in other missionary territories as a consequence of the ongoing struggle to create a divide between newly established Catholic communities and other Christian denominations. Certainly this was the case with mixed marriages, as suggested by the very fact that the *Declaratio Benedictina* was not extended to Istanbul. Indeed, these two facts reveal Rome's worries that implementation of a decree that practically facilitated mixed marriages would jeopardise the Church's fight against marriages between Catholics and members of other denominations and, more generally, its efforts to shape a well-defined oriental Catholic identity by maintaining the divide between the newly established Catholic communities and other Christian ones.

Bibliography

Archival Sources

Archive of the congregation of the doctrine of faith (Rome)
Dubia circa Baptismus: DB vol. 5 (1760–1766).
Dubia Varia: DV. D.V. (1570–1668); D.V. D.V. (1731–1753).
Stanza Storica: Uv 50; Q3-b; I7-a; M3-i; M3-b; M3-c; OO5-a.
Archive of the Holy Congregation for the Propagation of Faith (Rome)
SOCG (Scritture originali riferite ai congressi generali), Levante, 59 (1635).

Secondary Sources

Armanios, Febe (2011), Coptic Christianity in Ottoman Egypt, Oxford: Oxford University Press.

Bireley, Robert (1999), The Refashioning of Catholicism, 1450–1700: A Reassessment of the Counter Reformation, Washington, D.C.: Catholic University of America Press.

Boer, Wietse de (2004), La conquista dell'anima. Fede, disciplina e ordine pubblico nella Milano della Controriforma, Turin: Einaudi.

Bossy, John (1970), The Counter-Reformation and the People of Catholic Europe, Past and Present 47, 51–70.

Boudens, Robrecht (1971), Aspects de la vie ecclésiastique dans les Provinces-Unies des Pays-Bas, in: Joseph Metzler (ed.), Sacrae Congregationis de Propaganda Fide Memoria Rerum. 1622–1972, Rome/Fribourg/Wien: Herder, II, 630–646.

Broggio, Paolo/Charlotte de Castelnau-L'Estoile/Giovanni Pizzorusso (2009), Le temps des doutes: Les sacrements et l'Église romaine aux dimensions su monde, Mélanges de l'École française de Rome – Italie et Méditerranée modernes et contemporaines 121, 5–22.

Caffiero, Marina (2009), L'Inquisizione romana e i musulmani: le questioni dei matrimoni misti, Cromohs 14, 1–10.

– (2011), Per una storia comparativa: l'Inquisizione romana nei confronti di ebrei e musulmani in età moderna, in: A dieci anni dall'apertura dell'archivio della Congregazione per la Dottrina della Fede: storia e archivi dell'Inquisizione (atti del colloquio, Roma, 21–23 febbraio 2008), Roma: Accademia dei Lincei, 497–518.

– (2013), Lorenzo Ganganelli consultore del Sant'Uffizio. I pareri sui battesimi di infedeli e sui matrimoni dei cattolici in terra ottomana, in: Giuliana Ancona/Dario Visintin (eds.), L'Inquisizione e l'eresia in Italia: Medioevo ed età moderna, Montereale Valcellina: Sanna, 253–270.

CASTELNAU-L'ESTOILE CHARLOTTE DE (2009), Le mariage des infidèles au XVIe siècle: doutes missionnaires et autorité pontificale, Mélanges de l'École française de Rome – Italie et Méditerranée modernes et contemporaines 121, 95–121.

CRISTELLON, CECILIA (2013a), L'inquisizione, il duca di Neoburgo e i matriomoni misti in Germania in età moderna, Rivista Storica Italiana 125, 76–108.

– (2013b), Sposare (o non sposare) "l'eretico". Matrimoni misti e politica del Santo Uffizio: Venezia nel contesto europeo, in: Michael Matheus/Uwe Israel (eds.): Protestanten zwischen Venedig und Rom in der Frühen Neuzeit, Berlin: Akademie Verlag, 159–178.

DANIEL-ROPS, HENRI (1962), The Catholic Reformation, trans. J. Warrington, London: J.M. Dent & Sons Ltd.

DIXON, C. SCOTT/DAGMAR FREIST/MARK GREENGRASS (eds.) (2009), Living with Religious Diversity in Early Modern Europe, Aldershot: Ashgate Publishing.

DOMPNIER, BERNARD (2009), L'administration des sacrements en terre protestante à la lumière des *facultaes* et des *dubia* des missionaires (XVIIe–XVIIIe siècle), Mélanges de l'ecole française de Rome 121:1, 32–38.

EHRENPREIS, STEFAN/UTE LOTZ-HEUMANN (eds.) (2002), Reformation und konfessionelles Zeitalter, Darmstadt: Wissenschaftliche Buchgesellschaft.

FEHLEISEN, JILL (2010), Boundaries of Faith: Catholics and Protestants in the Diocese of Geneva, Kirksville, MO: Truman State University Press.

FRAGNITO, GIGLIOLA/ALAIN TALLON (2015), Hétérodoxie croisées: Catholicismes pluriels entre France et Italie, XVI–XVII siècles, Rome: École française de Rome.

FRAZEE, CHARLES A. (2006), Catholics and Sultans: The Church and the Ottoman Empire 1453–1923, Cambridge: Cambridge University Press.

FRIEDRICH, MARKUS/ALEXANDER SCHUNKA (2012), Orientbegegnungen deutscher Protestanten, Frankfurt am Main: Vittorio Klostermann Preis.

HAMILTON, ALASTAIR (2006), The Copts and the West, 1439–1822: The European Discovery of the Egyptian Church, Oxford: Oxford University Press.

HEYBERGER, BERNARD (1994), Les Chrétiens du Proche-Orient au temps de la Réforme catholique (Syrie, Liban, Palestine XVI–XVII s.), Rome: Ecole Française de Rome.

– (1997), "Pro nunc, nihil respondendum". Recherche d'informations et prise de décision à la Propagande: l'exemple du Levant (XVIII' siècle), Mélanges de l'École française de Rome – Italie et Méditerranée modernes et contemporaines 109, 539–554.

HILLERBRAND, HANS J. (2003), Was There a Reformation in the Sixteenth Century?, Church History 72, 525–552.

HOFFMAN, PHILIP T. (1984), Church and Community in the Diocese of Lyon, 1500–1789, New Haven, CT: Yale University Press.

HOLT, MACK P. (2003), The Social History of the Reformation: Recent Trends and Future Agendas, Journal of Social History 37, 1, 133–144.

JANELLE, PIERRE (1949), The Catholic Reformation, Milwaukee: Bruce Publishing.

JEDIN, HUBERT (1999), Catholic Reformation or Counter-Reformation? in: David Luebke (ed.), The Counter-Reformation: The Essential Readings, Oxford: Blackwell, 19–45.

KAPLAN, BENJAMIN J./BOB MOORE/HANK VAN NIEROP/JUDITH POLLMANN (eds.) (2009), Catholic Communities in Protestant States: Britain and the Netherlands c. 1570–1720, Manchester: Manchester University Press.

Luria, Keith P. (1991), Territories of Grace: Cultural Change in the Seventeenth-Century Diocese of Grenoble, Berkeley, CA: University of California Press.
- (1996), The Politics of Protestant Conversion to Catholicism in Seventeenth-Century France, in: Peter van der Veer (ed.), Conversion to Modernity: The Globalization of Christianity, New York: Routledge, 23–46.
- (2005), Sacred Boundaries: Religious Coexistence and Conflict in Early-Modern France, Washington, D.C.: The Catholic University of America Press.

Masters, Bruce (2001), Christians and Jews in the Ottoman Arab World: The Roots of Sectarianism, Cambridge: Cambridge University Press.

McClain, Lisa (2004), Lest We Be Damned: Practical Innovation and Lived Experience among Catholics in Protestant England, 1559–1642, New York: Routledge.

Metzler, Joseph (ed.) (1971), Sacrae Congregationis de Propaganda Fide Memoria Rerum. 1622–1972, Rome/Fribourg/Wien: Herder.

Minchella, Giuseppina (2011), La frontiera veneto-ottomana nel XVII secolo: aspetti di una coesistenza singolare 7, 1–18 (www.giornaledistoria.net)
- (2014), Musulmani, ebrei e cristiani nella Repubblica di Venezia (XVII secolo), Roma: Viella.

Mullett, Michael A. (1999), The Catholic Reformation, London: Routledge.

Parker, Charles H. (2008), Faith on the Margins: Catholics and Catholicism in the Dutch Golden Age. Cambridge, MA: Harvard University Press.

Pieraccini, Paolo (2000), Il Cenacolo e i frati minori (origine della Custodia di Terra Santa), in: Michele Piccirillo (ed.), Dalla Crociata alla Custodia dei Luoghi Santi, Milan: Skira.

Pizzorusso, Giovanni (2009), Agli antipodi di Babele. Propaganda Fide tra immagine cosmopolita e orizzonti romani (XVII–XIX secolo), in: Luca Fiorani/Adriano Prosperi, Storia d'Italia Einaudi Annali 16: Roma la città del papa. Vita civile e religiosa dal Giubileo di Bonifacio VIII al Giubileo di Papa Wojtyla, Torino: Einaudi, 476–518.
- (2009), I dubbi sui sacramenti dalle missioni "ad infideles": percorsi nelle burocrazie di curia, Mélanges de l'École française de Rome – Italie et Méditerranée modernes et contemporaines 121, 39–61.
- (2011), Le fonti del Sant'Uffizio per la storia delle missioni e dei rapporti co Propaganda Fide, in: A dieci anni dall'apertura dell'archivio della Congregazione per la Dottrina della Fede: storia e archivi dell'Inquisizione, Roma: Accademia dei Lincei, 393–423.

Pizzorusso, Giovanni/Matteo Sanfilippo (2001), Gli archivi della Santa Sede come fonte per la storia moderna e contemporanea, Viterbo: Sette Città.

Questier, Michael (2006), Catholicism and Community in Early Modern England: Politics, Aristocratic Patronage and Religion, c. 1550–1640, Cambridge: Cambridge University Press.

Reinhard, Wolfgang (1989), Reformation, Counter-Reformation, and the Early Modern State: A Reassessment, The Catholic Historical Review 75, 383–404.

Santus, Cesare (2014), La communicatio in sacris con gli scismatici orientali (XVII–XVIII sec.), Mélanges de l'École française de Rome – Italie et Méditerranée modernes et contemporaines 126, 2, online, http://mefrim.revues.org/1790.

Serino, Francesco da (1939), Croniche... continuate dal padre Francesco da Serino... (ed. by T. Cavallon), in: Golubovich Girolamo (ed.), Biblioteca bio-bibliografica di Terra Santa e dell'Oriente francescano/Nuova serie: documenti, vol. XI, Florence: Quaracchi.

SEARLE, GRAHAM WILLIAM (1974), The Counter Reformation, London: University of London Press.

SCHILLING, HEINZ (1992), Religion, Political Culture and the Emergence of Early Modem Society: Essays in German and Dutch History, Leiden: Brill.

SCARRAMELLA, PAOLO (2009), I dubbi sul sacramento del matrimonio e la questione dei matrimoni misti nella casistica delle congregazioni romane (secc. XVI–XVIII), Mélanges de l'École française de Rome - Italie et Méditerranée modernes et contemporaines 121, 75–94.

TRACY, JAMES D. (2006), Europe's Reformations, 1450-1650: Doctrine, Politics, and Community, Lanham, MD: Rowman & Littlefield Publishers.

TRAMONTANA, FELICITA (2014), Protestants' conversion to Catholicism in the Syro-Palestinian region (17th century), Zeitschrift für historische forschung 41, 3, 401–422.

– (2014), "Getting by the Resort of the Pilgrims": The Franciscan Friars of Jerusalem and their Anglican Guests (1600–1612), Giornale di Storia 13.

– (2017), 'Né si potevano castigare per la libertà del loco e il dominio che vi è': cattolici e protestanti nell'Impero ottomano attraverso i *dubia* e le *facultates*, in Mélanges de l'École française de Rome, 129/1

VAN DEN BOOGERT, MAURITS H. (2000), European Patronage in the Ottoman Empire: Anglo-Dutch Conflicts of Interest in Aleppo (1703-1755), in: Alastair Hamilton/ Alexander Hendrik de Groot/Maurits H. van den Boogert (eds.), Friends and Rivals in the East: Studies in Anglo-Dutch Relations in the Levant from the 17th to the Early 19th century, Leiden: Brill, 187–222.

WINDLER, CHRISTIAN (2001), Representing a State in a Segmentary Society: French Consuls in Tunis from the Ancien Régime to the Restoration, Journal of Modern History 73, 233–274.

– (2002), La diplomatie comme expérience de l'Autre. Consuls français au Maghreb (1700–1840), Geneva: Droz.

– (2010), Katholische Mission und Diasporareligiosität. Christen europäischer Herkunft im Safavidenreich, in: Henning P. Jürgens/Thomas Weller (eds.), Religion und Mobilität, Göttingen: Vandenhoeck & Ruprecht.

Mihály Balázs

Aus der Mehrheit in die Minderheit

Der Weg des siebenbürgischen Antitrinitarismus im 16.–17. Jahrhundert

Es wirkt - wie ich hoffe - nicht als Stilbruch, wenn ich den im Titel angesprochenen siebenbürgischen Prozess vor dem polnischen Hintergrund darstelle. Damit befinde ich mich sogar in der Tradition, denn auch wenn Sprachbarrieren die vergleichenden Untersuchungen gehindert hatten, gab es trotzdem einige, die sich dabei auf das lateinische Quellenmaterial gestützt haben. In den vergangenen Jahrzehnten verfassten namhafte Experten des Themas wie Antal Pirnát (1961), Lech Szczucki (1982) oder George Huntston Williams (1990) einschlägige Studien. Mein Anliegen ist, in Anlehnung an neueste ungarische Studien[1] Gedanken zu formulieren, die eine Erwägung wert sind.

Wie bekannt ist, schöpfte der siebenbürgische Antitrinitarismus, der sich ein knappes Jahrzehnt nach dem polnischen entfaltet hatte, aus fast den gleichen Quellen wie dieser, und man weiß ebenfalls, dass der Initiator Giorgio Biandrata war. Ausführlich dokumentierte Studien belegen, dass neben Miguel Servets Werken die ins Exil gezwungene italienische Heterodoxie sowie der auf Erasmus basierende Baseler Humanismus die größte Wirkung auf die geistige Werkstatt am Fürstenhof in Alba Julia ausübten. Zwar gibt es weiterhin viele Streitfragen unter den Experten, jedoch steht außer Zweifel, dass die Errichtung eines Beziehungsnetzes mit lebhaften Auswirkungen mit Giorgio Biandratas Namen zu verbinden ist, der durch seine intensiven Kontakte zu Landsleuten, die nach Polen oder nach Siebenbürgen kamen, aktuelle Informationen über die Situation in Europa besaß.

Neueste Untersuchungen beweisen ferner, dass Biandratas siebenbürgischer Kollege Ferenc Dávid sich nicht durch seine neuen und originellen Ansichten unter seinen Zeitgenossen hervortat, sondern durch seine außerordentliche Fähigkeit zur Synthese und dadurch, dass er die entdeckte Wahrheit auch in einem größeren Kreise effektiv verbreiten konnte (Balázs: 2008).

Ihm ist zu verdanken, dass der hiesige Unitarismus sehr früh - von dem der Polen abweichende - eigenartige Züge annahm. So versuchte er z. B. auf dem

1 Der neueste bibliographische Überblick: Balázs/Keserű: 2013, 11–36.

Gebiet der Trinitätslehre im engeren Sinn, die Konzeptionen von Servet und der großen italienischen Religionserneuerer Lelio und Fausto Sozzini zu synthetisieren. Unter diesem Zeichen verwendete er Servets dogmenkritische Ansichten bzgl. der Trinitätslehre, harmonisierte diese aber mit der wichtigsten neuen Lehre der Italiener.

In Siebenbürgen stand diese Christologie im Mittelpunkt der Auseinandersetzungen, wie es zuerst von George Huntston Williams erkannt wurde; gemildert meldeten sich folgende theologische Begleiterscheinungen, die in Polen fast so bedeutsam waren wie die Antitrinität selbst. Die wichtigste war die vielfältige Gedankenwelt des Anabaptismus. Diese anabaptistische Denkweise zog in Polen sogar viele Angehörige des Kleinadels an, aus Siebenbürgen kennen wir keine ähnlichen Tendenzen. Ferenc Dávid war zwar davon überzeugt, dass die Kindertaufe nicht biblisch ist (er verfasste darüber lateinische wie ungarische Schriften), diese Lehre trennte er aber strikt von den anabaptistisch gesinnten sozialethischen Ansichten. Nicht weniger wichtig ist, dass er auch jenen spiritualistischen Tendenzen keinen Raum gewährte, deren Vertreter, die Buchstaben der Heiligen Schrift unbeachtet, ausgesprochen oder eben unausgesprochen die Notwendigkeit jedweder Kirchenorganisation in Frage stellend, mit Berufung auf die ihnen erteilten göttlichen Offenbarungen von der Notwendigkeit grundsätzlicher Erneuerung predigten. Es ist vielleicht wichtig, an dieser Stelle daran zu erinnern, dass diese Tendenzen ausschlaggebend bei der Gründung von Raków waren. Dávids Vorhaben wird jedoch insbesondere dadurch außerordentlich spannend, dass er die spiritualistisch-anabaptistischen Bestrebungen nicht einfach ablehnte, sondern fähig war, deren sanftere Variante in seine Theologie einzubauen und dadurch lange die gemeinsame Sprache mit seinen polnischen Glaubensgenossen zu bewahren (Balázs: 1996; 2005, 147–161).

Dadurch wird verständlich, dass seine Lehren Anfang der 1570er Jahre nicht nur in Städten akzeptiert wurden, in denen es eine bedeutsame ungarische Population gab, sondern sich ihm auch etwa die Hälfte des Adels anschloss. Wie bekannt, wurden diese Lehren selbst von Fürst Johann Sigismund akzeptiert. Vieles spricht dafür, dass sich Johann Sigismund als jemand darstellen wollte, in dessen Reich die verschiedenen protestantischen Konfessionen Gottes Wort frei verkünden durften und der für die in ganz Europa zu errichtende Einheit der Protestanten kämpfte. Das Schlüsselmoment dieser Bestrebung wäre nach der Ansicht der antitrinitarischen Theologen natürlich die Abschaffung der Trinitätslehre gewesen, und sie waren der Meinung, dass das Fürstentum Siebenbürgen, dieses neu entstandene politische Gebilde, dazu berufen sei, das historische Ziel der Reformation zu vollenden. Sie verkündeten mit Überzeugung, dass hier die wahren Nachfolger und Vollbringer des Werkes von Luther lebten. Der spannendste Beleg dafür ist, dass sie ihre wichtigste Veröffentlichung, das Werk *De falsa et vera unius Dei… cognitione*, mit einer eigenen Widmung an Königin Elisabeth verschickten. Darin erinnern sie die Herrscherin Englands, die entschlossenste Hüterin des Glaubens, dass für die Protestanten in Siebenbürgen die Zeit gekommen sei, in der Gott sich der Leiden des „Sion" erbarme. Gott erleuchtete nämlich Johann Sigismunds Geist, der ein würdiger Mitstreiter Edwards VI., des Bruders der Königin und ehemaligen Herrschers Britanniens war, der ihm ähnelte wie ein Ei dem anderen, da unter seiner Obhut in zahlreichen Kirchen die wahre Gotteskenntnis aufleuchte. So nimmt es auch nicht wunder, dass es in Gallien, Helvetien und Germanien viele gab, die in Fesseln und in schlimmerer Gefangenschaft als der babylonischen sehnsüchtig nach Siebenbürgen blickten und gelegentlich auch mit ihren gelehrten Schriften die Siebenbürger ermutigten, an der leidenschaftlichen Suche nach der Wahrheit festzuhalten und standhaft gegen den Papst, den Antichrist anzukämpfen (Balázs: 2003, 53–64).

Auch die tolerante Religionspolitik des idealisierten siebenbürgischen Fürsten wurde von den antitrinitarischen Predigern als Beweis der universalen Verpflichtung dem Protestantismus gegenüber gewürdigt. In dem fast vollständig protestantisch gewordenen Land wurde die alte Kirchenstruktur so vererbt, dass im Unterschied zu den evangelischen Sachsen, deren Zentrum in Hermannstadt war, auf den von Ungarn bewohnten Gebieten bis Anfang der 1570er Jahre keine eigenständigen Kirchenorganisationen für Lutheraner, Reformierte und Unitarier entstanden sind, sondern alle Gemeinden unter die Hoheit eines einzigen Bischofs kamen. So sprechen die Religionsgesetze der Epoche – in einer einmaligen Weise in Europa – mit theologischer, genauer gesagt mit universeller protestantischer Begründung (fides ex auditu) darüber, dass die Prediger das Evangelium auf jene Weise verkünden mögen, die ihnen als richtig erscheint. Im Gegensatz zur allgemeinen Auffassung kam es erst viel später, im Jahre 1595 dazu, dass es in Siebenbürgen vier legitime Religionen – *receptae religiones* – geben konnte, was wiederum nicht heißen musste, dass die nach dem Triumphzug des Protestantismus in den 1570er Jahren noch erhalten gebliebenen katholischen Inseln hätten aufgelöst werden sollen. Über die Rechte dieser verfügte man von Fall zu Fall auf den Landtagen (Balázs: 2013, 85–108). Daraus geht klar hervor, dass eine sich gegenüber den Habsburgern als protestantisches Land definierende Formation nach ihrer Legitimation und Berufung suchte, deren Fürst sich des öfteren für die Aufhebung der innerhalb des Protestantismus bestehenden Gegensätze einsetzte.

Als diese langfristigen politischen Vorstellungen formuliert wurden, standen die Antitrinitarier auf dem Höhepunkt ihrer Erfolge. Anhand der Quellen ist dies auf die Zeit 1570–1571 zu datieren, ferner konnte auch festgestellt werden, dass mehr als 90 % der ungarischen Bevölkerung Siebenbürgens protestantisch war. Die Mehrheit dieser protestantischen Gemeinden hatte einen antitrinitarischen Pfarrer. Es spricht für sich, dass es im obersten Machtorgan des Fürstentums, in dem aus 21 Mitgliedern bestehenden Fürstenrat, im Jahre 1570 insgesamt 3

Katholiken gab und unter den Protestanten nachweislich mindestens 10 Trinitätsleugner waren.[2]

Im scharfen Kontrast dazu gehörte Mitte des 17. Jahrhunderts höchstens noch ein Fünftel der ungarischen Bevölkerung dieser Gemeinde an und aus den Staatsorganen verschwanden die Trinitätsleugner fast vollständig. Da es hier nicht möglich ist, alle wichtigten Stationen dieses Vorgangs anzusprechen, scheint es mir sinnvoll, doch zumindest einige der Gründe bzw. Erklärungen anzusprechen.

Der verbreiteste Ansatz ist jener, die Erklärung in der eigenartigen Dogmatik des siebenbürgischen Antitrinitarismus zu suchen. Ohne ausführlich darauf einzugehen, soll jedoch so viel gesagt werden, dass außer Zweifel steht, dass in der bereits selbständig gewordenen Kirche ab der Mitte der 1570er Jahre bis 1638 jene radikale, nonadorantistische Variante des Antitrinitarismus die Hauptrolle gespielt hatte, die auf der Basis der Werke von Jacobus Palaeologus[3] und Johann Sommer stand. Mit der Zeit ist die Position dieser Richtung schwächer geworden, nach der Verurteilung des Ferenc Dávid ist sie sogar in den Untergrund geraten. Laut neuester Erkenntnisse erstarkte sie aber im letzten Jahrzehnt des 16. Jahrhunderts wieder deutlich und blieb bis zum Landtag 1638, der sie schließlich verboten hat, markant (Keserű: 2005, 163–188).

Schon die im 18. Jahrhundert entstandenen ersten historischen Reflexionen sahen die Hauptursache in dieser kühnen Christologie und in den damit einhergehenden endlosen inneren dogmatischen Diskussionen. Viele vertraten die Ansicht, dafür sei Ferenc Dávid verantwortlich gewesen, der in der Dogmenkritik zu weit gegangen sei (Kénosi Tőzsér and Uzoni Fosztó: 2002). Zwar berufen sich die einzelnen Autoren auf unterschiedliche Momente, der Hauptargumentationsstrang bleibt aber wie auch in der modernen Fachliteratur derselbe. So ist mit Antal Pirnát (1982, 157–190) bspw. einer der bedeutendsten modernen Vertreter der Ansicht, dass Biandrata vor dem im Umfeld des Ferenc Dávid erscheinenden Nonadorantismus und den sich daraus entfaltenden sabbatarischen oder judaisierenden Tendenzen (die er vielleicht sogar selber verbreitete) zurückschrak und sich deshalb aktiv an der Verurteilung des kirchenstiftenden Bischofs beteiligte. Von Lech Szczucki werden wiederum zwar Argumente aufgeführt, die in vielerlei Hinsicht in eine andere Richtung weisen, trotzdem stehen seine Feststellungen aber mit denen von Pirnát im Einklang. Szczucki meint, die eine kühne Christologie ausarbeitenden, nonadorantistischen Theologen und die in deren Umfeld positionierten Denker hätten sich gerade wegen dieser Kühnheit nicht bewähren (Szczucki:

2 Eine ausführliche, auf Archivmaterialien basierende Analyse: Horn: 2009.

3 Nach wie vor grundsätzlich zu seiner Person: Szczucki: 1972b. Neuere, auf Archivmaterialien basierende Erkenntnisse: Rothkegel: 2013, 91–134.

1972a, 171) und im Unterschied zu Fausto Sozzini und dessen Anhängern keine bedeutsamen, lebensfähigen Gemeinden ins Leben rufen können. Gleichfalls konnten sie weder auf ihre Zeitgenossen noch auf die sich später entwickelnden europäischen Geistesbewegungen wirken. Im Folgenden soll versucht werden, Argumente gegen diese Thesen anzuführen.

An allererster Stelle muss festgehalten werden, dass es keineswegs gesetzmäßig war, dass die Nonadorantisten auch Mitglieder der Sabbatarier-Gemeinden wurden, die die alttestamentarischen Riten teilweise neubelebt haben. Diese Tatsache hätte für einen Adeligen die aktive Teilnahme am öffentlichen Leben in der Tat fast unmöglich gemacht. Die siebenbürgische Sabbatarier-Gemeinde, die die Speisegebote und andere rituelle Regeln rigoros einhielt, bildete letztendlich eine schwindend kleine Minderheit, während für die Strömungen und die Persönlichkeiten, die den Nonadorantismus um individuelle Züge bereicherten, gerade nicht die Selbstisolation, sondern vielmehr die Offenheit typisch war.

Das beste Beispiel dafür in Ostmitteleuropa ist der aus Litauen stammende Bibelgelehrte Szymon Budny (Pietrzyk: 1991, 8–94; Kamieniecki: 2002; Feischmann: 2006), dessen Tätigkeit uns bei der Auslegung der siebenbürgischen Erscheinungen behilflich sein kann. Bemerkenswert ist schon die Tatsache, dass er die siebenbürgischen Entwicklungen aufmerksam verfolgte, als noch wichtiger ist aber zu erachten, dass Budny diese in seine breit angelegten geschichtsphilosophischen Ansichten integrierte. Dies illustrieren die folgenden Beispiele eindrucksvoll:

Mehrere antitrinitarische Theologen der Region diskutierten darüber, warum diese Konfession gerade in jenem Land Fuß fasste, in dem sie gewirkt haben. Marcin Czechowic (Czechowic: 1979, 5) sprach zum Beispiel äußerst impulsiv über jene besondere göttliche Gnade, auf Grund derer gerade den Polen vor anderen respektierten Nationen diese Jahrhunderte lang verborgene Wahrheit verkündet worden sei. In der Fachliteratur ist ferner folgende Antwort Fausto Sozzinis auf die Frage eines seiner Anhänger (vielleicht war es Hieronymus Moskorzowski) bekannt: Sozzini beruhigte seinen Gesprächspartner zunächst, Polen sei keineswegs ein verstecktes Nest, wenn man bedenke, welch wichtige Persönlichkeiten des Glaubens in früheren Jahrhunderten hier gelebt hätten. Ferner sei Polen zu dieser Zeit dem ehemaligen Judäa vergleichbar, das bei den heidnischen Völkern verhasst war, weil Gott hier zum ersten Mal das Christentum verkündet habe. Polen sei nun Gegenstand des Hasses, weil hier zum ersten Mal die wahre Lehre über die Natur des Gottvaters und des Sohnes verkündet wurde (Szczucki: 2005, 127). Auch in Anlehnung daran konnten in der *Historia reformationis Poliniae* von Stanisław Lubieniecki weitere Parallelen zwischen der Geburt Christi und der Verbreitung der wahren Lehre gezogen werden: Wie Jesus Christus während der Herrschaft von Kaiser Augustus geboren wurde, so wurde die wahre Lehre während der Herrschaft eines Augustus wiedergeboren, nämlich während der Sigismund Augustus (Sigmund August), in einem Land, das hinsichtlich der Heilsgeschichte für diese wichtige Rolle vorgesehen war (Lubieniecki: 1971, 14; Williams: 1995, 90).

Wie bereits erwähnt, wurden ähnliche Gedanken in Bezug auf die Rolle dieses Landes schon recht früh von Autoren, die in Siebenbürgen tätig waren, formuliert. Jacobus Palaeologus verfasste in seinen in den 1570er Jahren entstandenen Werken immer wieder Elogen auf Johann Sigismund. In der Widmung zur *Cathechesis christiana* vergleicht er Johann Sigismund mit Friedrich dem Weisen und sagt, die Sonne der Wahrheit hätte nicht aufleuchten können, wäre in dem viel zu jung verstorbenen Herrscher der Geist des für den Tod von Johann Hus veratwortlichen Kaiser Sigismund und nicht der Geit des weisen Friedrich erwacht (Růžena: 1971, 17). Es geht hier aber nicht nur um die Verherrlichung des Herrschers, sondern auch um die beispiellose historische Rolle von Land und Leuten. So ist in der Widmung zur *Catechesis* zu lesen, dass aus England, Hispanien, Gallien, und Germanien sowie aus Helvetein, Italien und Griechenland Briefe und Gesandte nach Siebenbürgen und Ungarn gekommen waren, um zu erfahren, wie denn diese Lehre beschaffen sei, die sich aus Gottes Gnade so verbreitet hatte. Diese Fremden flehten die Hiesigen regelrecht an, aus ihren Lehren für die andere Konfessionen eine Art Katechismus zusammenzustellen. Die *Cathecesis christiana* ist demnach nichts anderes als die Erfüllung dieses Wunsches. Besonders hervorzuheben ist, dass die Gemeinschaft der Ungarn so charakterisiert ist, dass es als einziges unter den heidnischen Völkern am längsten eine Art archaische und wahre Gotteskenntnis bewahren konnte. Des öfteren spricht im letzten Drittel des 16. Jahrhunderts der bedeutenste Theologe dieser Periode, György Enyedi von der besonderen historischen Mission Siebenbürgens: Es sei Gottes außerordentlicher Gnade zu verdanken, dass dem kleinen siebenbürgischen Fürstentum die historische Rolle zukam, die Wahrheit hier zu erkennen und zu pflegen. Als typologische Parallele dient bei ihm das Moment „klein": Viele sehen in Siebenbürgen bzw. in dessen geistigem Zentrum einen ebenso kleinen und unbeachteten Ort wie Betlehem, der Geburtsort Jesu Christi, einer gewesen ist (Kanyaró: 1905, 161–166).

Es geht aus dem bisher Gesagten klar hervor, dass die Verfasser dieser Aussagen in jedem Fall von einer einzigen Region oder einem Volk sprachen. Umso bemerkenswerter ist vor diesem Hintergrund, was Budny in einem Brief, der auch in *O urzędzie miecza używającem* Eingang gefunden hat, beschreibt. Darin antwortet er seinem Briefpartner, der die Gnade, die Polen erleben durfte, erörtert, wie folgt: „Ich verstehe auch nicht, mein Bruder, warum du diese Gnade nur auf Polen beziehst, wenn du behauptest, sie sei keinem anderen Land zuteil geworden. Man sieht doch, dass auch die Ungarn und die Deutschen im Besitz von dieser Wahrheit sind und leiden auch deswegen viel. Denke nur an Sylvanus, der in Heidelberg sein Leben opferte, oder auch an andere".[4] Die Randbemerkung „Nicht nur die Polen sind im Besitz von der Wahrheit"[5] verleiht den Zeilen, die des 1570 in Heidelberg hingerichteten Jakob Sylvanus' gedenken, noch mehr Gewicht.

Diese breit angelegte Ansicht wird in den nachfolgenden Teilen des zitierten Werkes theologisch untermauert. Wie bekannt ist, steht im Mittelpunkt der Argumentation, dass dem Christen nicht verboten werden könne, staatliche Dienste zu übernehmen, wie dies unter den polnischen Antitrinitariern unter dem Einfluss der anabaptistischen Ideen oft der Fall war. Die Widerlegung dieser Thesen wird ferner auch um eine Begründung bereichert, die mit der radikalen Christologie im Einklang steht: Über Christus, den man weder anbeten noch anrufen dürfe, sei logisch zu behaupten, dass seine Aufgabe nicht die Aufhebung der Gebote des Alten Testaments war, sondern lediglich gegen deren Entzerrung und Missbrauch aufzutreten. Gleichzeitig muss eingeräumt werden, dass die aktuelle Forschung noch nicht soweit ist, diese Argumentation in einem nonadorantistischen Kontext zu untersuchen, und dazu kann es auch in diesem Aufsatz nicht kommen. Zu erwähnen ist allerdings die individuell anmutende Eigentümlichkeit, dass Budny klar unter den Geboten von Moses und Noah unterscheidet. Im Falle der mosaischen Gebote bleibt er in gewisser Hinsicht im traditionellen Rahmen und trennt moralische Vorschriften von den zeremoniellen. Er zweifelt nicht darüber, dass die moralischen von ewiger Gültigkeit sind, und führt als Bestätigung jene Bibelstellen auf, in denen Jesus sagt, er sei nicht gekommen, um das Gesetz zu tilgen, sondern um es zu verwirklichen. Im Zusammenhang mit den zeremoniellen Vorschriften (Speisegebote, Sabbat, Beschneidung) akzeptiert er aber, dass diese für die Christen nicht mehr gültig seien, und betrachtet sie als Zeichen und Vorbilder für höhergestellte seelische Bezüge. Es ist äußerst spannend, dass er bei der Erörterung der Gebote Noahs keine ähnliche Unterscheidung vornimmt. Er führt die Bibelstellen Gen. 9, 1–15 sorgfältig auf und stellt fest, diese seien unverändert gültig. Überraschenderweise hält er nach wie vor das Gebot für gültig, dass das Blut der geschlachteten Tiere nicht verzehrt werden darf. Um dies zu veranschaulichen, soll hier die ganze Textpassage zitiert werden: „Das vierte Gebot bezieht sich auf das Blut der getöteten Tiere und Vögel, dass man es nicht essen soll. Zwar wird dies von manchen Christen angegriffen, sie handeln jedoch nicht recht. Denn die heiligen Apostel behielten dies in der Gemeinde in Jerusalem bei und schrieben es den Christen vor, die aus den Reihen der Heiden, und nicht der der Juden kamen,

4 Budny: 1930, 222: „K temu nie wiem jako to bracie sobie albo Polsce tylko śmiesz przypisować. Nie uczynil tak żadnemu narodowi: gdyź widzimy, że i Węgrzy i Niemcy tę prawdę mają i dla niej wiele cierpią. Jako Sylvanus dal gardlo Heldeberdze i ini".

5 „Znajomość nie sami Polacy mają".

damit sie sich vor dem Blut und den erwürgten Tieren hüten sollen. Dieses Gebot wurde von den Griechen, unseren russischen Brüdern, den Serben, den Moskoviten und anderen Slaven bis in die jüngste Vergangenheit eingehalten, es begann erst vor etwa 30 Jahren, dass man es unbeachtet ließ (nach dem Beispiel der Papisten und der Lutheraner) und Heide wurde. Laut den heiligen Aposteln ist also dieses Gebot Gottes, das er den Söhnen Noahs gegeben hatten, gültig bis ans Ende der Welt".[6]

Lassen wir fürs Erste die Frage außer Acht, ob es stimmt, dass die slawische Bevölkerung erst seit dreißig Jahren an der strengen Einhaltung des Gesetzes festhielt. Bemerkenswerter ist, dass in dieser ausgeklügelten Lösung das Festhalten am Speisegebot nicht zur Herausbildung einer isolierten Sekte geführt hat. Im Gegenteil, das Resultat war ein Universalismus, der dem des Palaeologus' nahekam. Alle, die sich dazu bekannten, befanden sich auf der Seite der Griechen, der russischen Brüder, der Serben und Moskoviter, das heißt der Ostkirche. Es handelt sich dabei um eine außerordentlich spannende Vorstellung, die das östliche und westliche Chriastentum umfasst und deren Schöpfer an der Grenze dieser zwei Kulturkreise lebte und imstande war, seine Aufmerksamkeit auch nach Osten zu richten. Das Zusammengehörigkeitsbewusstsein der Slawen, das auch unter Polen immer wieder zum Vorschein kam, geht hier mit einer eigentümlichen Dogmatisierung einher.

Nicht minder interessant ist, dass in der Theologie des litauischen Antitrinitariers das Gesetz Noahs dem sehr nahe steht, was auf natürliche Weise ins menschliche Herz geschrieben worden und daher ewig ist. Er verwendet zwar den Ausdruck *religio naturalis* nicht, bei der genauen Erklärung seiner Syllogismen im Kapitel *Przedniejsze z pisma świętego* legt er aber dar, dass es eine Zeit in der Menschheitsgeschichte gegeben habe, in der Gott noch keine Gebote verkündet habe, weder schriftlich noch mündlich. Das menschliche Leben sei demnach durch die ins Menschenherz geschriebenen moralischen Gesetze geregelt worden, und dies sei nicht nur damit zu belegen, dass es für Kain klar war, dass er Abels Tötung mit seinem Leben büßen müsse, sondern auch damit, dass derartige grundsätzlichen moralischen Gesetze auch bei anderen Völkern nachzuweisen seien, deren Gesetzgeber (Drakon, Lykurg, Solon) sie später verschrift-

6 Budny: 1930, 128: „Czwarta rzecz jest zakaz Boży o krwi źwirzècej i ptaszej, aby jej nie jedzionono. To zakazanie, acz niektórzy krześcianie gwalcą, ale nie dobre to czynią. Gdyź je święci apostolowie przy mocy na onem świętem Jerozolimskiem zborze zachowali, i do onych Chrystyan, krórzy nie z Izraelitów, ale z pogan nawróceni byli, źrzetelnie napisali, aby sie nie jedno od rzezi balwańskiej, ale i od jedzenia krwie i od dawionych rzeczy hamowali. Którego zakazania Grekowie, in naszy bracia Rusacy, Serbowie, Moskwiczy i inni Slowianie aż do naszego niniejszego wieku pilno strzegli, dopiro od lat trzydziestu poczęli pattrząc na Papieżniki i Ewangieliki) to zakazanie mijać i takim sie pogaństwem mazać. A tak wedle świętych Apostolów wyroku i ten Boży zakaz do Noacha i synów jego, i do nas ich nasienia od samego Boga wyrzeczony ptzy swej mocy i do skończenia świata trwać ma".

licht hätten. Budny sieht also in Noahs Geboten die erste mündliche Verkündigung Gottes und betont deren universalen Charakter, indem er diese auch unter den Heiden belegt. Er führt nämlich die Geschichte des Deukolon aus der griechischen Mythologie an, den er mit Noah identifiziert. Es sei offensichtlich, dass die Geschichte von letzterem handle, nur hätten die Griechen den ursprünglichen Namen vergessen.

Es ist ersichtlich, dass Budny bei der Verifizierung der These, die Tötung müsse durch die Todesstrafe gesühnt werden, eine überaus wichtige theologische Konzeption formuliert, bei der er auch auf die Gültigkeit des Speisegebotes bei Noah zu sprechen kommt. Es wäre jedoch ein großer Fehler, diese Auffassung mit der der zeitgleich wirkenden siebenbürgischen Sabbatarier in Beziehung zu setzen, die die Speisegebote bei Moses in ihrer Vollständigkeit übernehmen wollten (Dán: 1982; 1987). Es geht nämlich nicht nur um das eben Erörterte (Aktualisierung eines Speisegebotes, um die Gemeinschaft von Protestanten und der Ostkirche zu deklarieren), sondern auch darum, dass die gerade zu dieser Zeit entstehenden sabbatarischen Abhandlungen[7] jedwede Orientierung in Richtung einer natürlichen, ohne Verkündigung zu erlangenden Gotteserkenntnis aufs Entschiedenste abgelehnt haben. Mit leidenschaftlich kondemnierenden Worten wurde dargelegt, dass diejenigen, die sich auf die Gesetze der Natur berufen, Philosophen seien, die aus Liebe zur weltlichen Wissenschaft aus der „Ethik der Lateiner" ihre Kenntnisse über die Gesetzmäßigkeiten des menschlichen Lebens zusammenstellen und ihre Umgebung glauben lassen würden, sie hätten auch über das ewige Heil was zu sagen. Dem sei aber nicht so, Gott habe das Heil immer an die Verkündigung gebunden, was auch daraus zu ersehen sei, dass angefangen mit Adam über Noah und Abraham bis hin zu Moses immer Gebote verkündigt worden seien, die im Gegensatz zu den Naturgesetzen gestanden hätten. Denn sei es nicht gerade wider die Natur, dass jemand nicht von der Frucht eines Baumes essen oder kein Fleisch zu sich nehmen oder gar seinen einzigen Sohn töten soll? Die Botschaft Gottes sei also, dass man durch die strenge Einhaltung seiner verkündigten Gebote das Heil erreiche. Die besagte Abhandlung zählt die vier Zeitalter auf, für die die Gebote gegolten haben, und die einzuhalten die Bedingung des Heils war. Die *leges Adamitae*, die *leges Noamitae*, die *leges Abrahamitae* und die *leges Mosaycae* bedingten sich wechselseitig und waren Heilsbedingung. Im Falle der *leges Mosaycae* ist in den Abhandlungen von der Zeit der aktuellen Gegenwart die Rede, denn – auch ihrer Ansicht nach hatte Christus keine neuen Gebote verkündet – die Gebote Moses seien auch für die Zeit nach Christus gültig.

Hier kann nicht auf jeden Zusammenhang der Theologie des frühen Sabbatariertums eingegangen werden und wir müssen auch von der Schilderung

7 Ausgabe ungarischsprachiger Abhandlungen: Varjas: 1970, 483–518.

dessen absehen, was in diesen Texten hinter der starken Rhetorik kaum erörtert wird, nämlich wie diese Gesetze überliefert und allgemein bekannt geworden sind, und dass die Autoren der Abhandlungen stets vorgeben, es handele sich in jedem einzelnen Fall um verschriftlichte Gesetze. Es muss jedoch unbedingt betont werden, dass in den facettenreichen nonadorantistischen Gemeinden in Ungarn und Siebenbürgen dies nicht die vorherrschende theologische Position war. Ich möchte mich in erster Linie auf die vielfältige antitrinitarische Gemeinde bei Pécs/Fünfkirchen auf dem von den Osmanen besetzten Gebiet berufen, deren wichtigste schriftliche Quelle der *Pécser Disput* von György Válaszúti ist. Dieser umfangreiche Text enthält nicht nur eine mit Reformierten geführte Glaubensdiskussion, sondern er tradiert auch viele Momente der Geschichte des hiesigen Antitrinitarismus. Aus dem Text geht klar hervor, dass diese antitrinitarischen Gemeinden auf jene Weise eindeutig nonadorantistisch waren, dass sie weder den Synkretismus des Palaeologus', der den Glauben der Christen, der Muslime und der Juden in Einklang bringen wollte, noch die rigorose Strenge der Sabbatarier, die die Gebote Moses befürworteten, teilten. Ein bekenntnisartiger Teil stellt fest – und erinnert dabei stark an Budny – die Meinung derer sei nicht akzeptabel, die ununterbrochen verkünden würden, dass seit der Schöpfung der Welt niemand das Heil gefunden habe, der nicht an Christus glaubte. Der Glaube an Christus sei als Heilsbedingung nämlich erst möglich, seit Maria ihn geboren hatte. Es soll hier darauf verwiesen werden, dass sich diese Feststellung nicht nur gegen die Reformierten richtete, die an die ewige Macht Jesu Christi glaubten, sondern auch gegen den antitrinitarischen Standpunkt, der im Neuen Testament eine radikal neue Soteriologie sah. Das heißt, sie trat gegen den Standpunkt auf, den die polnischen und siebenbürgischen Trinitätsleugner in ihrem oben erwähnten Werk *De falsa et vera unius Dei...cognitione* noch gemeinsam in Worte fassten, und auf den sich später auch Fausto Sozzini bei der Weiterentwicklung und Verteidigung seiner Theologie stützen wird. Die radikale Wende im Neuen Testament bestreitend behauptet der *Pécser Disput* demnach, dass es seit der Schöpfung der Welt „immer eine heilige Kirche und Gemeinde Gottes gab, in der er gekannt und gepriesen wurde" (Válaszúti: 1981, 742–743). Anschließend ist wie bei Budny davon die Rede, dass diese Gotteskenntnis nach der Sintflut umfassender geworden sei, und es wird ferner erörtert, dass nach Abrahams Berufung Gott dem Judentum Gesetze gegeben habe. Daraufhin habe Gott dann durch Jesus Christus seine Gnade auf alle Völker ausbreitet. Auch bei Válaszúti wird keine soteriologische Wende mit Christi Person in Verbindung gebracht, er sieht in ihm nicht den Urheber des neuen Gesetzes, sondern „lediglich" den, der die göttliche Gnade auf andere Völker ausdehnte. Ohne detaillierte und aktualisierte Ausführungen zu Noahs Geboten zu liefern, wird hier eine Konzeption formuliert, die der von Budny nahe kommt, von dieser natürlich aber auch in manchen Punkten abweicht, da den ungarischen Antitrinitarier, der unter osmanischer Herrschaft gelebt hat, die Frage, ob ein Christ öffentliche Ämter bekleiden darf, naturgemäß nicht beschäftigte. Seine christologischen und soteriologischen Lösungen fanden aber nicht nur in der Gegend um Pécs/Fünfkirchen Nachfolger. Dafür sprechen die in Siebenbürgen erhalten gebliebene Auszüge aus dem Pécser Disput.

Da uns das Schrifttum der Wende vom 16. zum 17. Jahrhundert und der ersten Jahrzehnte des 17. Jahrhunderts deutlich umfangreicher überliefert ist als das ältere (Keserű: 2000, 73–84), kann auch ohne eine ausführliche Darstellung desselben behauptet werden, dass sich nur die Sabbatarier in die ritualisierte Welt der mosaischen Gebote zurückzogen. In den erhalten gebliebenen nonadorantistischen handschriftlichen Traktaten und Predigten begegnet man zwar vielfältigen Lösungen, aber Vorstellungen, die das „Judaisieren" verwirklichen wollten, sucht man vergeblich. Die Sektiererei, vor der Biandrata so große Angst hatte und die ihn dazu bewog, bei der Verurteilung des Ferenc Dávid eine Rolle zu spielen, und vor der auch Sozzini in seinen Schriften gegen den Nonadorantismus ständig warnt, trat nicht ein. Sehr stark sind demgegenüber die Ideen aus den Predigten des György Enyedi vertreten, die vielfach in handschriftlichen Kopien verbreitet wurden, und die Válaszúti für jeden Christen als maßgeblich erscheinen lassen wollte.[8]

Das wollte er einerseits mit der Betonung der moralischen Gebote erreichen. Es ist dementsprechend in einer seiner Predigten zu lesen: „Der Wille Gottes ist in vielen Sachen klar. Die Anhänger aller christlichen Konfessionen, sowohl die Katholiken als auch die Lutheraner, die Kalvinisten, die Anabaptisten verkünden es mit denselben Worten: du sollst nicht streiten, du sollst niemand verleumend und keine Unzucht treiben..." Jene aber, die sich nicht in der Vielfalt der Religionen auskennen, würden diese Gebote nicht befolgen. Es sei also keineswegs verwunderlich, daß sie nicht zur Wahrheit gelangen würden. Andererseits versuchte Enyedi auf einer dogmatischen Grundlage die Eintracht unter den verschiedenen Konfessionen zustandezubringen. Darüber schrieb er in einer Predigt am ausführlichsten, die gegen seinen ehemaligen Schüler, János Szilvási verfaßt wurde, der vom Antitrinitarismus zum kalvinistischen Glauben, und später zum Katholizismus konvertierte. Hier spricht Enyedi über die Vereinigung der Christen und beschreibt mit dem verbreiteten Gleichnis des *corpus christianorum*, wie die hilfreiche und schützende Zusammenarbeit der verschiedenen Kirchen als die der einzelnen Körperteile verwirklicht werden kann. Der Ausgangspunkt ist bei ihm – ähnlich wie bei mehreren Denkern der frühen Neuzeit – die Minimalisierung der dogmatischen Gegensätze. Diese Konzeption der *fundamentalia fidei* bekommt aber bei ihm nicht nur einen antitrinitarischen, sondern auch eine bemerkenswert persönliche Tendenz. Zuerst betont er die

8 Siehe dazu samt ausführlicher Quellenangabe: Balázs: 2000, 15–22.

gemeinsame Hoffnung aller Christen auf die Auferstehung und das ewige Leben, dann spricht er – unverkennbar nach der Theologie des Palaeologus – darüber, daß alle Christen Christus zu ihrem Herrn anerkennen müssten. Er macht klar: Es ist dabei zweitrangig, wie eine Konfession die Herrschaft Jesu auffaßt. Die Argumentation, die auf der vielfältigen Anwendung des lateinischen Ausdrucks *dominus* und seiner griechischen und hebräischen Gegenstücke aufbaut, versucht so den Antitrinitariern in der christlichen Universalität einen Platz zu schaffen, damit sie nicht auf den Standpunkt verzichten müssen, daß Christus kein Gott und dem Vater nicht identisch war. Andererseits sollten sie auch tolerieren, daß die anderen an den dogmatikbedingten Ergänzungen der Grundthese als *adiaphoron* festhalten. Mit ähnlicher Argumentation stellt er fest, daß alle Christen durch den gemeinsamen Glauben miteinander verbunden seinen; Jesus sei der Christus, der Gottessohn, und sie sollten in ihrem Leben seiner Lehre folgen. Auf ähnliche Weise grenzt er von diesem Glauben die verschiedenen Erscheinungsformen des Glaubens und Vertrauens im Alten und Neuen Testamen ab. Er führt das vielbenutzte biblische Beispiel der Unabdingbarkeit der Toleranz an und plädiert mit dem Gleichnis des Sämannes (Matthäus 13. 24–30) dafür, daß die weitere – besonders die gewaltsame – Vereinigung keine biblischen Grundlagen habe. Die nächste Garantie der christlichen Einheit sei die Gemeinsamkeit der Taufe, deren Grunsatz – ganz abgesehen von den verschiedenen Formeln und Sitten des Aktes – derselbe sei; nämlich nichts anderes als die seelische Taufe. Enyedi spricht zwar nicht ausdrücklich darüber, es ist aber ganz naheliegend, daß von der Höhe dieses Standpunktes aus gesehen der Streit über die Form der Taufe nebensächlich wird. Gleichzeitig werden selbst die Streitigkeiten über die Dreifaltigkeitsfrage sinnlos im Lichte des Schlußsatzes, der die Einheit des Christentums beweisen soll und besagt, dass es nur einen einzigen Gott gebe, den Vater des Universums. Es steht außer Zweifel, daß der Autor in diesem letzten Fall all dem gegenüber weniger tolerant eingestellt ist, was seine „Gegner" als das christliche Minimum zur Rechtfertigung der Trinität anführen. An diesem Punkte kommt also seine Voreingenommenheit zum Vorschein, aber seine Bemühungen um die christliche Vereinigung bleiben nichtsdestotrotz außerordentlich bemerkenswert.

Enyedis Vorstellungen fanden natürlich auch bei den siebenbürgischen protestantischen Konfessionen keinen Anklang, es kann höchstens davon die Rede sein, dass unter den hiesigen Protestanten Ende der 1580er und Anfang der 1590er Jahre eine gewisse politische Kooperation zustande kam. Der Misserfolg ist aber keineswegs auf den sonderbaren christologischen Radikalismus der nonadorantistischen Unitarier zurückzuführen. Es sei hier daran erinnert, dass sich Ähnliches, wenn auch unter anderen Bedingungen, auch in Polen abspielte. Vergeblich verkündeten die polnischen Sozinianer in Synodalbeschlüssen und im Katechismus von Raków, dass sie die Nonadorantisten für keine Christen hielten. Diese klare Trennung machte sie in den Augen der Pastoren der großen protestantischen Konfessionen jedoch nicht attraktiver. Sie mussten eine Ablehnung erleben, als sie in den 1610er Jahren den Versuch unternahmen, sich den protestantischen Konfessionen zu nähern. Das Gleiche passierte ihnen auch auf dem *Colloquium charitativum*, das 1645 in Toruń stattfand.

Ferner stellte sich in den ersten Jahrzehnten des 17. Jahrhunderts auch endgültig heraus, dass für die führenden Strömungen des europäischen Protestantismus keine akzeptable Variante des Antitrinitarismus existierte. Bekannterweise scheiterte jeder Versuch der Sozinianer, bei den irenischen Bestrebungen unterzukommen, die eine protestantische Einheit ins Leben rufen wollten, unabhängig davon, ob ihre Mitglieder Lutheraner, Reformierte oder eben böhmische Brüder waren.

Angesichts dieser Überlegungen sind die Gründe und Ursachen für den beispiellosen Positionsverlust also nicht in dem spezifischen dogmatischen Radikalismus zu suchen. Es muss vielmehr vom eigentümlichen Zusammentreffen der sich allgemein verschlechternden europäischen Bedingungen und der siebenbürgischen gesellschaftlich-politischen Verhältnisse gesprochen werden. Bei Ersterem geht es natürlich darum, dass es die heterodoxen Gruppierungen durch die sich verbreitende Konfessionalisierung immer schwerer hatten. Was Letzteres betrifft, so muss das sich grundsätzlich geänderte Umfeld erwähnt werden, in dem sich in den 1560er Jahren der Unitarismus entfaltet hat.

Die erste wichtige Änderung trat ein, als 1571 Johann Sigismund starb, dem der katholische István Báthory auf den Thron folgte. Die Inthronisation des katholischen Fürsten dürfte nach dem oben Gesagten verwundern, das Land war aber eindeutig protestantisch, sodass man dies als nicht riskant einschätzte. Für Báthory sprachen nämlich seine riesigen Grundbesitze und sein politisches Ansehen, das er dadurch erwarb, dass er trotz seiner katholischen Gesinnung als beständiger Vertreter der anti-habsburgischen politischen Linie tätig war. Der eifrige katholische Fürst respektierte das protestantische Land, sein Hofprediger wurde ein evangelischer Geistlicher und er betrachtete sich wie sein Vorgänger als Patron aller Untertanen. Gleichzeitig machte er aber auch ständig Unterschiede zwischen ihnen und auch keinen Hehl daraus, dass er von ihnen eigentlich nur die Lutheraner bzw. den Augsburgischen Glauben für einigermaßen akzeptabel hielt (Binder: 1976, 153–156). Seine Maßnahmen trafen zweifelsohne in erster Linie die Unitarier, deren Präsenz, vor allem aber deren ununterbrochene Streitsucht in der Dogmenkritik er für politisch schädlich hielt, da sie das ganze Fürstentum in eine Isolation treibe.

Neueste Untersuchungen ergaben, dass die Maßnahmen, die die Isolation verhindern sollten, den Anfang für die radikale Änderung der bisherigen außenpolitischen Richtlinien bedeuteten. Unter Johannes Sigismund hatte noch als Grundprinzip gegolten, dass das Hauptziel des siebenbürgischen Fürstentums –

zumal mit der Existenz des osmanischen Reiches auf unbestimmte Zeit zu rechnen sei – nur Folgendes sein kann: Bei zwangsläufiger Anerkennung der osmanischen Oberhoheit bewahrt es seine Selbständigkeit und akzeptiert, dass die Wiederherstellung des mittelalterlichen ungarischen Königreiches nicht auf der Tagesordnung steht. Der 1576 zum polnischen König gewählte István Báthory hielt dies für ungenügend. Sein Ziel war es, die Einheit wiederherzustellen, wofür er im Vatikanstaat, der in den letzten Jahrzehnten des 16. Jahrhunderts immer neue Pläne geschmiedet hatte, um die Türken aus Europa zu vertreiben, Unterstützung fand. Dieser Umstand prägte Báthorys Religionspolitik, in deren Mittelpunkt von nun an die Zurückdrängung der radikalsten Variante des Protestantismus stand (Kruppa: 2013, 11–36). Während seiner Herrschaft ging dies noch mit friedlichen Mitteln von statten, als jedoch sein Nachfolger Sigismund Báthory an die Macht kam, kam es zu bewaffneten Auseinandersetzungen zwischen dem Fürsten und den Vertretern der Beamtenaristokratie, die auf die herkömmliche Politik bestand. Während dieser Konflikte wurde die Beamtenaristokratie, in deren Reihen es sehr viele unitarische Hochadelige gab, auch physisch vernichtet. Durch die Hinrichtung dieser auch „Philosophen" oder „Türkenherren" geschimpften Aristokraten[9] wurde es Siebenbürgen möglich, in der katholischen Welt nach Verbündeten zu suchen. Als spektakuläre Konsequenz trat das Fürstentum in den sog. langen Türkenkrieg ein, man schloss sich also dem vom Papst initiierten Feldzug gegen die Osmanen an.[10]

Zu Beginn des 17. Jahrhunderts verlor also die unitarische Kirche den Großteil ihrer aristokratischen und adeligen Förderer und ab dieser Zeit galt es als eine Ausnahme, wenn ein unitarischer Hochadeliger eine führende Rolle in der Politik des Landes spielte. Zu ähnlichen Entwicklungen kam es in den größeren unitarischen Städten, so auch in Klausenburg. Wenn auch unter anderen Bedingungen, setzten sich diese Tendenzen auch unter den reformierten Fürsten im 17. Jahrhundert fort. Sie glaubten zwar nicht mehr an die schnelle Wiederherstellung des mittelalterlichen Ungarns und suchten nach natürlichen Verbündeten unter den führenden Staaten und Herrschern des protestantischen Europas. Dieser wesentliche Unterschied änderte jedoch nichts an den Lebensbedingungen der Unitarier, zumal während des Dreißigjährigen Krieges die Existenz der Trinitätsleugner für die protestantischen Länder genauso inakzeptabel waren wie für die Katholiken.

Die Ereignisse in einem breiteren Zusammenhang sehend, kann behauptet werden, dass in den 1620er Jahren klar wurde: Im konfessionalisierten Europa kann es selbst im entferntesten Winkel im Osten keinen Staat geben, in dessen Regierung die Unitarier eine noch so kleine Rolle spielen. Für die Lebenstaug-

9 Über die hervorragende geisteshistorische Bedeutung dieser Gruppe: Pirnát: 1971, 363–392.
10 Darüber anhand neuer Quellen: Kruppa: 2014.

lichkeit ihrer siebenbürgischen Gemeinden spricht jedoch, dass sie trotz aller Hindernisse am Leben bleiben und langfristig auch ihre eigenen, von denen der Sozinianern abweichenden Traditionen bewahren konnten.

Bibliographie

BALÁZS, MIHÁLY (2003), About a copy of *De falsa et vera unius Dei... cognitione* (Additional data to the history of the English connections of the Antitrinitarians of Transylvania), Odrodzenie i reformacja w Polsce XLVII, 53–64.

- (ed.) (2008), Bibliotheca Dissidentium Répertoire des non-conformistes religieux des seizième et dix-septième siècles, vol. XXVI (Ungarländische Antitrinitarier IV. Dávid Ferenc) Baden-Baden: Bibliotheca Bibliographica Aureliana.
- (2005), Discussiones et concordia. Die Beziehungen zwischen polnischen und siebenbürgischen Antitrinitariern im 16. Jahrhundert, in: Lech Szczucki (ed.), Faustus Socinus in Polonia, Kraków: Polska Akademia Umiejętności, 147–161.
- (1996), Early Transylvanian Antitrinitrianism 1567–1571. From Servet to Palaeologus, Baden-Baden.
- (2000), György Enyedi zwischen Palaeologus und Faustus Socinus. Anmerkungen zum unbekannten György Enyedi, in: Mihály Balázs/Gizella Keserű (eds.), György Enyedi and Central European Unitarianism in the 16th to 17th Centuries: Papers Read in Kolozsvár-Cluj, September 1998 at the Conference György Enyedi and Central European Unitarianism in the 16th and 17th Centuries, Budapest: Balassi Kiadó, 15–22.
- (2013), Tolerant Country – Misunderstood Laws. Interpreting Sixteenth-Century Transylvanian Legislation Concerning Religion, The Hungarian Historical Review, New Series of Acta Historica Academiae Scientiarum Hungaricae 2, 85–108.

BALÁZS, MIHÁLY/GIZELLA KESERŰ (2013), Der siebenbürgische Unitarismus. Zum Forschungsstand, in: Ulrich A. Wien/Juliane Brandt/András F. Balogh (eds.), Radikale Reformation. Die Unitarier in Siebenbürgen, Köln–Weimar–Wien: Böhlau Verlag, 11–36.

BINDER, LUDWIG (1976), Grundlagen und Formen der Toleranz in Siebenbürgen bis zur Mitte des 17. Jahrhunderts, Köln–Wien: Böhlau.

BUDNY, SZYMON (1930), O urzędzie miecza używającem wyznanie zboru Pana Chrystusowego (1583), ed. Stanisław Kot, Kraków.

CZECHOWIC, MARCIN (1979), Rozmowy chrystiańskie, ed. Alina Linda/Maria Maciejawska/Lech Szczucki, Warsaw- Łódź: Państwowe Wydawnictwo Naukowe.

DÁN, RÓBERT (1982), Matthias Vehe-Glirius, Life and work of a radical Antitrinitarian, with his collected writings, Budapest/Leiden: Brill.

- (1987), Az erdélyi szombatosok és Péchi Simon (Die siebenbürgischen Sabbatarier und Simon Péchi), Budapest: Akadémiai Kiadó.

FEISCHMANN, STEFAN (2006), Szymon Budny: Ein theologisches Portrait des polnischen-weissrussischen Humanisten und Unitariers, Köln-Weiimar: Böhlau.

HORN, ILDIKÓ (2009), Hit és hatalom. Az erdélyi unitárius nemesség 16. századi története (Glaube und Macht. Geschichte des siebenbürgischen unitarischen Adels im 16. Jahrhundert), Budapest: Balassi Kiadó.

Kamieniecki, Jan (2002), Szymon Budny - zapomiana postać polskiej refrormacji, Wrocław: Wydawnictwo Uniwersytetu Wrocławskiego.

Kénosi Tőzsér, János/István Uzoni Fosztó (2002), Unitario-Ecclesiastica historia Transylvanica Liber I–II. Volume IV/1, ed. János Káldos, Budapest: Balassi.

Kanyaró, Ferenc (1905), Enyedi György unitárius püspök beszédeiből (Aus den Predigten des unitarischen Bischofs György Enyedi), Sárospataki füzetek, 161–166.

Keserű, Bálint (2000), Die ungarische unitarische Literatur nach György Enyedi (Über ideengeschichtlich relevante Werke aus der Zeit 1597–1636), in: Mihály Balázs/Gizella Keserű (eds.), György Enyedi and Central European Unitarianism in the 16th to 17th Centuries: Papers Read in Kolozsvár-Cluj, September 1998 at the Conference György Enyedi and Central European Unitarianism in the 16th and 17th Centuries, Budapest: Balassi Kiadó, 73–84.

Keserű, Gizella (2005), The Late Confessionalisation of the Transylvanian Unitarian Church and the Polish Brethen, in: Lech Szczucki (ed.), Faustus Socinus in Polonia, Kraków: Polska Akademia Umiejętności, 163–188.

Kruppa, Tamás (2013), Die Religionspoltik der Báthorys in den 1580er Jahren. Ein Versuch zur Verhinderung der protestantischen Religionspraxis (1579–1581), in: Ulrich A. Wien/Juliane Brandt/András F. Balogh (eds.), Radikale Reformation. Die Unitarier in Siebenbürgen, Köln/Weimar/Wien: Böhlau Verlag, 11–36.

- (2014), A kereszt, a sas és a sárkányfog. Kelet-közép-európai törökellenes ligatervek a Báthory-korszakban 1578–1597 (The cross, the eagle and the dragon's tooth. Plans for an anti-Ottoman league and battles against the Ottomans in the Báthory era 1578–1597), Budapest-Rome: Pázmány Péter Katolikus Egyetem Egyháztörténeti Kutatócsoportja.

Lubieniecki, Stanisław (1971), Historia reformationis Polonicae, Facsimile Ausgabe, ed. Henryk Barycz, Warsaw: Państwowe Wydawnictwo Naukowe.

Pietrzyk, Zdisław (1991), Szymon Budny, in: Valentin Koener (ed.), Bibliotheca Dissidentium Répertoire des non-conformistes religieux des seizième et dix-septième siècles. vol. XIII (Antitrinitaires polonais II, Baden-Baden: Bibliotheca Bibliographica Aureliana, 8–94.

Pirnát, Antal (1971), Arisztotelianusok és antitrinitáriusok. Gerendi János és a kolozsvári iskola (Aristotelianer und Antitrinitarier. János Gerendi und die Klausenburger Schule), Helikon XVII, 363–392.

- (1961), Die Ideologie der Siebenbürger Antitrinitarier in den 1570er Jahren, Budapest: Akadémiai Kiadó.

- (1982), Il martire i l'uomo politico (Ferenc Dávid e Biandrata), in: Róbert Dán/Antal Pirnát (eds.), Antitrinitarianism in the Second Half of the 16th Century, Budapest/Leiden: Brill, 157–190.

Rothkegel, Martin (2013), Jacobus Palaeologus und die Reformation. Antireformatorische Polemik in der verlorenen Schrift Pro Serveto contra Calvinum, in: Ulrich A. Wien/Juliane Brandt/András F. Balogh (eds.), Radikale Reformation. Die Unitarier in Siebenbürgen, Köln–Weimar–Wien: Böhlau Verlag, 91–134.

Růžena, Dostalová (ed.) (1971), Jacobi Chii Palaeologi Catechesis Christiana dierum duodecim, Warsaw: Państwowe Wydawnictwo Naukowe.

Szczucki, Lech (1982), Polish and Transylvanian Unitarianism in the Second Half of the 16th Century, in: Róbert Dán/Antal Pirnát (eds.), Antitrinitarianism in the Second Half of the 16th Century, Budapest/Leiden: Brill, 231–241.

- (1972a), Antytrynitaryzm w Europie wschodniej, Odrodzenie i Reformacja w Polsce 24, 161–171.
- (1972b), W kręgu myślicieli heretyckich, Wrocław: Zakład Narodowy im. Ossolińskich.
- (2005), Fausto Sozzini and his Heritage, in: Lech Szczucki (ed.), Faustus Socinus in Polonia, Kraków: Polska Akademia Umiejętności, 186–298.

Válaszúti, György (1981), Pécsi disputa (Die Disputation in Pécs), ed. Róbert Dán/ Katalin Németh, Budapest: Akadémiai Kiadó.

Varjas, Béla (ed.) (1970), Régi Magyar Költők Tára (Sammlung älterer ungarischer Gedichte) XVII. Jh. T.V, A szombatosok költészete (Die Poesie der Sabbatarier), Budapest, 483–518.

Williams, George H. (ed.) (1995), History of the Polish Reformation and Nine Related Documents, Mineapolis, MN: Fortress Press.
- (1990), Unterschiede zwischen dem polnischen und siebenbürgischen Unitarismus und ihre Ursachen, in: Wolfgang Deppert/Werner Erdt/Art de Gro (eds.), Der Einfluss der Unitarier auf die amerikanische Geistesgeschichte, Vorträge der ersten deutschen wissenschaftlichen Tagung zur Unitarismusforschung vom 13–14. Juni 1985 in Hamburg, Frankfurt am Main: Peter Lang, 33–57.

Borbála Lovas

On the Margins of the Reformation

The "Local" and the "International" in György Enyedi's Manuscript Sermons and Printed Works

Transylvania in the second half of the sixteenth century was anomalous in its stance on freedom of religion.[1] Following the collapse of the medieval Hungarian Kingdom, a new reformed Church emerged in the principality during the reign of the young Prince John Sigismund Szapolyai. At the Transylvanian Diet of 1568, the Edict of Thurda (Torda/Thorenburg)[2] was proclaimed, putting into law religious tolerance and freedom of conscience. Four "received" religions had equal rights in the territory: Roman Catholicism, Calvinism, Evangelical Lutheranism, and Anti-Trinitarianism (later known as Unitarianism).[3] Owing to the prince being influenced by his Italian physician Giorgio Biandrata, and by the first Anti-Trinitarian Bishop Ferenc Dávid, the Anti-Trinitarians used the young ruler's sympathy to establish themselves as the dominant religious group in Transylvania. Employing printing facilities in Alba Iulia (Gyulafehérvár/Karlsburg), and in Cluj-Napoca (Kolozsvár/Clausenburg), the Anti-Trinitarians played a leading role in ecclesiastical debates that influenced the political life of the principality. Cluj-Napoca, a royal free town, became both the residence of the Unitarian bishopric and the intellectual and ecclesiastical centre of the Transylvanian radical Reformation movement (Balázs: 2008, 17). A wide range of Unitarian works were published, including polemics, catechisms, doctrines, orations in Latin and the vernacular, and, notably, the first volume of the sermon collection of Ferenc Dávid (1569) dedicated to Prince John Sigismund.[4] With the death of

1 This study, originating from ongoing research into Humanism in East Central Europe at Eötvös Loránd University of Budapest, is supported by the Hungarian Academy of Sciences (MTA-ELTE Humanism in East Central Europe Research Group). I would also like to thank James Plumtree for his advice and comments.

2 For ease of understanding for an international reader, modern place names are used in the text, with equivalent names following in brackets.

3 For the Edict, and the ecclesiastical and political context, see István Pásztori-Kupán's analysis (2009, 167–176), and the more detailed perspective of Mihály Balázs (2013).

4 The single volume published shows signs of hurried production (Balázs: 2008, 233). Dávid, in the dedicatory epistle at the start of the volume, records the importance of the sermons being printed in the manner they were delivered (1569, [II]). The speed of the production suggests

the young and tolerant prince, the later volumes were not to be. The fortunes of the Unitarians changed. Strict publishing regulations in the 1570s severely limited the Unitarian output. Only practical literature for the pious, such as hymnbooks, catechisms, biblical stories in verse, and a handful of funeral orations were allowed to be published.[5] The new regulations favoured the Catholic and the increasingly powerful Calvinist Churches.[6] Moments when members of the Unitarian Church could take advantage of weakening censorship to publish important texts were rare.

Positions were also strengthened within the Unitarian Church itself. Following the imprisonment and death of Ferenc Dávid, the second bishop, the hardliner Demeter Hunyadi, with Biandrata, attempted to move the Church towards more conservative doctrinal ideas. The radicals, including the non-adorantists, were expelled, and clerics were coerced into signing the *Consensus ministrorum* (1579) and forced to remain silent. To the delight of his contemporary critics, in 1592 Hunyadi collapsed while delivering a sermon and died shortly afterwards. His successor, György Enyedi, continued the formulation of coherent Anti-Trinitarian ideas. Due to the lack of print, a variety of manuscripts were disseminated. Texts that would have been quickly printed, and even more quickly banned, were carefully collected and copied by hand in Transylvania. In addition to a rich corpus targeting a broad range of readers, exclusive scholarly Anti-Trinitarian works by such radicals as Jacobus Palaeologus, Matthias Vehe-Glirius, Johannes Sommer, and Christian Francken were circulated.

Less than five years into his role as bishop, Enyedi died on November 24 1597. Although he was a noted scholar, religious figure, teacher, translator of Boccaccio into Hungarian and of Heliodorus into Latin, the assessment of Enyedi, the dominant figure of the age,[7] has been greatly shaped by the curious publication history of a single work. Owing to a moment of political instability in the principality, the *Explicationes*, Enyedi's polemical Latin summary of arguments that refute the traditional interpretation of texts used in debates to demonstrate the

Dávid was intending the work – with references to significant Anti-Trinitarian works by Servet, Fausto, and Lelio Sozzini – not for preaching exempla, personal piety, or for posterity, but rather to be used in contemporary theological debates. The number of manuscript copies of the work in the following century suggests the work was moderately popular.

5 The censoring regulations are examined in depth by Mihály Balázs (1996). Carmen Florea (2002, 73–80), provides a short summary of the Unitarian publications, and includes an account of how print culture turned into a handwritten culture. Of the two hundred and fourteen vernacular sermons and sermon collections known to have been printed in Hungary up to 1655, Dávid's sermon collection and three funeral orations are the only Unitarian works (Maczák: 2008, 63–89).

6 The suppression of Unitarian book printing became total with the judgment of the eighteenth century Habsburg rulers. The unintended result was an even greater manuscript tradition.

7 For details about Enyedi's life see Káldos/Balázs: 1993, 11–18, Balázs/Káldos: 1997, 5–27, and the studies in Balázs/Keserű: 2000.

Trinity, was posthumously published in Cluj-Napoca in 1598.[8] It was banned the following year, and copies were confiscated and burnt by the order of Prince Sigismund Báthory. While suppressed in Transylvania, surviving copies of the work were widely circulated on the continent, and within a few years works were published, which mentioned or tried to refute Enyedi. From a brief mention in the writings of the theologian Christoph Pelargus (1605), Enyedi's printed text was increasingly discussed and refuted in print by a notable list of leading Lutheran and Calvinist theologians,[9] some of whom were supported financially by Transylvanian princes.[10] Given the international attention the *Explicationes* was receiving, Enyedi's Latin text was translated into Hungarian and published in two editions (1619, 1620),[11] and then reprinted in Latin, with errors, around 1670 in what has been assumed to be Groningen.[12] Owing to the international reactions to the work, modern scholars of the Protestant Reformation know Enyedi primarily through this single publication.

The response to Enyedi in Hungary by other religious factions followed sectarian lines. The Unitarian Church, diminishing in stature, was attacked by the Calvinists and the Lutherans, and, to a lesser extent, the Catholics. The increasingly dominant Calvinist Church, which was receiving support from the aristocracy, aggressively targeted the radical congregations for potential converts. Subsequently, Hungarian refutations of Enyedi appeared, written by the Calvinist elite who had been educated in Germany. As a consequence of this change in affairs, disputes and polemics against Enyedi were widespread. István Milotai Nyilas, court preacher to the Calvinist Prince Gábor Bethlen, dedicated his *Speculum trinitatis* (1622) to his patron, presenting Bethlen as the true destroyer of idolatry ([i–xxi]). Enyedi was a prime target. In a similar manner,

8 Unless otherwise noted, in this paper the title *Explicationes* refers to the first edition of the work published in Cluj-Napoca by the Heltai Printing Press. For recent studies of the *Explicationes* see: Simon: 2013; Simon: 2014; Simon: 2016.

9 Notable examples being Paraeus: 1609, Martin: 1614, Balduin: 1619, Thumm: 1620, Feuerborn: 1658.

10 A major figure was Johann Hienrich Alsted's younger colleague, Johann Heinrich Bisterfeld. His unpublished *Mysterium Pietatis Ostensum* focusing on the works of Fausto Sozzini and György Enyedi, is known to have existed owing to its appearance in the property list of Michael Halicius (Viskolcz: 2004, 75–76). Márton Szentpéteri (2012) has revealed the work was published as the second part of Bisterfeld's book, Sciagraphia symbioticae.

11 The 1619 edition, printed in Cluj-Napoca, did not receive the permission of the prince following its secret publication, and was subsequently banned. The 1620 edition, published with the help of Simon Péchi (one of the leaders of the Transylvanian Sabbatarians), was exactly the same as the earlier edition, but with the date altered and the place of publication omitted on the title page. The 1619 edition was still used inside the town walls, with only the 1620 edition allowed to leave Cluj-Napoca. For more details of the perils of the printer János Makai Nyírő, see Tóth: 1957, 589–599.

12 Another possible place of publication, printer and involved bookseller for the second Latin edition will be posited in a forthcoming publication by Lovas.

István Geleji Katona, supported by Prince György Rákóczi I, attacked in the most vitriolic way the *Explicationes* of the long dead bishop in his *Titok titka* (Secret of secrets), published in 1645.[13] Enyedi was, in Geleji's view, a dangerous enemy of the truth, a Judaiser, a Jew, an idiot, a pagan, and a speaker who spoke in a more godless manner than the Turks.[14] Attacks in print coincided with co-operation with Johann Heinrich Bisterfeld in order to establish the Calvinists in Cluj-Napoca, the heartland of the Unitarians, and to legally attack their rival's position in Transylvania.[15]

In comparison with the Calvinist broadsides, despite the fact that the Jesuits in Transylvania had long been urging for a refutation, the Catholic response was slower. A copy of the *Explicationes* had been sent to Rome in 1600 with this intention.[16] Alfonso Carillo, who transported the volume, suggested to his superior general, Claudio Acquaviva, to give the work to the leading theologians of the Counter-Reformation: Gregory of Valencia, and Robert Bellarmine.[17] No refutation was forthcoming. Jesuits under the protection of Gábor Bethlen had,

---

13 Other refutations of the *Explicationes* by Hungarians published abroad include Szentkirályi: 1619, Tályai: 1632, Almási: 1640, Jászberényi: 1662.

14 Geleji: 1645, 174–175: ("Elégvé tsudalni nem győzöm, hogy ezt az embert, az ő utánna tsetlő boltó szegény vakok illy igen imádják, mintha soha aszonyi állat-tol nálánál böltsebb e' világra nem született volt. Én, Isten látja, nem tapasztalok semmi óllyas mély böltseséget benne, hanem ugy veszem eszemben, hogy minden irása vagy szent irásvesztegetés, vagy penig oktalan agyaskodás, melly rész szerént tudatlanságból, s' rész szerént penig megáltalkodott gonoszságból, származott, ugy mint ki az igazságnak meg esküdt dühös ellensége volt"), 534: ("Gyanu fér hozzája, hogy semmit sem [tulajdonított az apostolok írásának], hanem a' szivében merő Sido volt, tsak hogy szintén ki-fakasztani nyelvével, és irásával nem merte"), 780–781: ("Ez igen veszett ügyű emberhez illendő habozás és nem irás magyarázás, hanem erőszakos tsigázás. Töri, faggatja a' tévelygő elméjét, s' fejét az igazsággal valo tusakodtában, tsak hogy ezt a' nevezetes, és világos irást, az ő kábolgyás képzésére tekerhesse, s' bötűköt egymástól szaggatja, diribeli, darabolja, és folyo rendeket el bontván tővel, hegyve állatja őköt öszve, és tulajdon, s' természet szerént valo jegyzéseket, idegen kedig szántszándékval olly homályos hálozásval, és tétovázásval, hogy alig veheti még az értelmes olvasois eszében, mit akarjon, és mi légyen értelme. De hamisság minden beszéde, egy sints igaz benne"), 1072: ("Hiszem Pogány ember volt ez? Pogányabbul beszéllett még a' Törököknél is, kik azt mondják, hogy az Istennek nintsen fia, mert nem volt soha felesége; holott ez az ördög tagja, az Istennek nemzése, és születése felől nem is ugy gondolkodik, mint az embereknek tiszta szaporodások, hanem mint a' leg-nemtelenb oktalan állatoknak fajzások felől. Oh gehenna tüzével megtisztitando tisztátalan lélek!..."). For Enyedi's use of Biblical texts and Hebrew sources, see Róbert Dán's important study on Reformation, Anti-Trinitarianism and the Hebrew language in Hungary (1973, 109–114); for the Transylvanian Sabbatarians, see Dán: 1987.

15 On the development of confessionalisation see Murdock: 2000 and Szentpéteri/Viskolcz: 2005.

16 The said volume is possibly the one now located in the Biblioteca Casanatense (Molnár: 2000, 238).

17 Lukács: 1969–1987/IV, 463: "12. Postscriptum - Ex Transylvania missus fuit mihi liber pestilens arianorum, quem V.ae P. transmitterem, ut nunc facio, dandum Ill.mo Bellarmino vel Patri de Valentia confutandum, quia plurimum nocet. Ego nec lege quidem potui".

for twenty years, written epistles countering Enyedi (Káldos/Balázs: 1993, 29–40), but were not supported by works in print. In 1626, Acquaviva responded by ordering György Káldi, the author of the first published Catholic Hungarian translation of the Bible (printed in Vienna in 1626), to produce such a text. Káldi, having been assigned rector of the collegium of Bratislava (Pozsony/Pressburg), was absolved of the work (Káldos/Balázs: 1993, 35–37). Káldi, however, continued with the condemnation of Enyedi's texts in sermons.[18] The first major – and complete – Catholic refutation of Enyedi's *Explicationes* was by the Jesuit Ambrosio de Peñalosa. The *Opus egregium*, written by the Spanish professor of theology at the Viennese College, was begun in 1629 and printed in 1635. Despite its length and detail, the work had little influence in Hungary. The Jesuits had, again, been officially banished from Transylvania, and pleas to have the work translated from Latin into Hungarian were considered a colossal waste of time and effort. A Hungarian translation finally appeared in the eighteenth century (Molnár: 2000, 242–243).

Less known to modern scholars is a major corpus of vernacular texts through which Enyedi himself was the participant in contemporary theological disputes. His dissemination of Anti-Trinitarian ideas to local Transylvanian audiences in his daily sermons has long been neglected by scholarship, in part owing to their survival only in copied manuscripts. Recent studies have established the structure of the sermon collection (Káldos/Balázs: 1993, 121–130; Káldos: 2013; Lovas: 2013b; Lovas: 2016a; Lovas: 2016b) and discovered new variants (Lovas: 2013a). The texts reveal the methods Enyedi and his later editors and copyists employed, focussing on the everyday sermons while incorporating the detailed scholarly theological explanations of the Unitarian articles of faith. Though his sermons were mostly not the target of internal and international debates, the history of the corpus is more complicated than that of the afterlife of the *Explicationes*. In addition to being the first Unitarian to produce a detailed and comprehensive articulation of the Church's beliefs, he is also the first Unitarian to have produced a sizeable composed sermon collection – albeit surviving only in later manuscript

18 It has long been suggested in Hungarian scholarship (cf. Bitksey: 1979, 24) that Káldi, in his first sermon on Pentecost Sunday (1631b, 719–728), third sermon on St Thomas' day (1631a, 119–127), second sermon on St Philip's and St Jacob's day (1631a, 478–485), referred to sermons delivered by Enyedi that he personally heard as a youth in Cluj-Napoca. Textual analysis however reveals that the Jesuit quoted from Enyedi's *Explicationes*, from either the Latin or Hungarian translation. These elaborated comments are supposedly the remaining parts of Káldi's unfinished refutation of Enyedi. Given Káldi's sermons were published in Habsburg territory (Vienna and Bratislava), it should be noted that the Jesuit was working in a different context. Notably, unlike texts of Ferenc Dávid and the other refuted errants, the published sermons of Káldi do not mark Enyedi's texts in the margin. The "pretender bishop of the Arians in Kolozsvár", as Enyedi is described, does not even appear in the index of the volumes.

copies. Only a dozen of the remaining copies and variants of the 213 individual sermons have been published.[19] As a consequence, the scholarly bias towards easily available printed materials has led to an understanding of the Transylvanian Reformation being weighed heavily towards the denominations less affected by the censorious printing regulations. An ongoing project to publish Enyedi's sermons will help rectify this omission.[20]

The collection has a complex textual transmission. No autograph manuscript survives. The remaining manuscript codices, located in Cluj-Napoca, Târgu Mureş (Marosvásárhely/Neumarkt), and Sárospatak, were almost all copied in small towns and villages in the principality, and are all dated between 1613 and 1696.[21] The absence of any clear connection between these surviving manuscripts suggests far more copies of the sermons existed.[22] The original period of composition was between 1592 and 1597, when Enyedi was bishop of the community. The sermons continued to be used as models in the century that followed his death. Some of the codices have dates and locations informing us where the sermons were delivered later; others show signs of editing – typically amendments and explanations. The collection employs a unique structure. While the sermons are individually numbered from one to two hundred and thirteen, the

19 Kanyaró: 1900, 30–40 (Sermon 115); Horváth: 1905, 161–166 (Sermon 94); Boros: 1910, 26–32 (Sermon 38); Balázs/Káldos: 1997, 85–221 (Sermons 1, 2, 42, 43, 53, 56, 60, 95, 170); Gabriella: 2004, 379–389 (Sermon 115); Szelestei N.: 2005, 116–120 (Sermon 108); Takács: 2011, 75–181 (Sermons 186, 187, 190, 193, 194, 195), Lovas: 2014, 376–387 (Sermon 93).

20 A four volume critical edition of the whole Enyedi sermon corpus by the author and the MTA-ELTE Humanism in East Central Europe Research Group is being published: *Enyedi György prédikációi 1-4*, ed. B. Lovas, Budapest: MTA-ELTE HECE – Magyar Unitárius Egyház, 2016–2019.

21 Codex of Sámuel Gyalai: 1617–1626, contains sermons 43, 50, 100; 3rd Codex of Kolozsvár: 1613, copied by Gyárfás Lisznyai, contains the second triacas (sermons 34–66) with some hiatus; Codex of Sárospatak: mid-17th c., unknown copyist, partly fragmented, contains sermons 93–116 and 123–124; Codex of Székelykeresztúr: 1629, copied by Gergely Fejérdi, contains 42 selected sermons (24 sermons from the second triacas, 13 sermons from the sixth triacas, 2 sermons from the 7th triacas); Codex of Marosvásárhely: 1642–1696, mixed copy, Sinfalva, Tordatúr(?), contains around a dozen selected sermons (4 from the first triacas, 3 from the second triacas, 1 maybe from the third now not known triacas, 2 from the fourth triacas and some yet unidentified sermons maybe of Enyedi); 4th Codex of Kolozsvár: 1621, unknown copyist, Nagyajta, contains the second triacas (sermons 34–66) with some hiatus; 1st Codex of Kolozsvár: beg. of 17th c., unknown copyist, contains the sermons 200–212 and the fragments of sermons 56 and 57; 5th Codex of Kolozsvár: mid-17th c., unknown copyist, contains the main part of the sixth triacas (sermons 167–195); Conciones vetustissimae: bef. 1642–1659, mixed copy, contains four sermons in Hungarian (Sermon 20, 185, 188, 191), and some sermons and drafts attributed to Enyedi in Latin; 2nd Codex of Kolozsvár: 1664, copied by János Bitai, Torockó, partly fragmented, contains 30 sermons from the 3rd triacas.

22 Some of these lost codices have been catalogued in Káldos: 2010, 189–190, 196, 202; Káldos: 2013, 89.

collection is divided into triacases – blocks with thirty-three sermons. Two of the manuscripts employ a centuria system, which is yet to be understood.[23]

The relationship between Enyedi's sermons and his "*Liber perniciosus*" (Vogt: 1738, 235) is one that has gone unnoticed. The theologians who attacked Anti-Trinitarian beliefs quoted the *Explicationes* in their sermons (with Hungarian authors also quoting the translation). No evidence suggests that any other writings by Enyedi were used in their critiques. This "international" Enyedi, seen through the *Explicationes*, has obscured modern understanding of the "local" Transylvanian context. Though his opponents did not appear to make the connection, Enyedi – or his publisher – made links between the printed text and the written sermons. The first edition of *Explicationes*, published fifteen years before the first known surviving manuscript of the sermons, contains printed marginalia mentioning sermon 210 by number: this proves the sermon collection was already in existence and that connections were being made between the sermons and the *Explicationes.*[24]

As the reception of the *Explicationes* illuminates the international debates, the reception of the sermons colour modern knowledge of the local disputes. The sermons reveal the bishop developing his arguments to address a larger audience. A former student of Enyedi, János Szilvási, who had converted to Calvinism from Unitarianism, attacked the bishop in an *oratio* at the Calvinist synod in Târgu Mureş.[25] Enyedi responded on the 17 October 1593 with a sermon delivered in the main Unitarian church in Cluj-Napoca. To engage with his former pupil and not merely his congregation, Enyedi sent the text of the sermon, which he had recorded in Latin, with an accompanying letter to Szilvási.[26] The autograph text testifies to Enyedi's linguistic abilities. He is likely to have delivered the sermon in Hungarian, with Latin notes, to the multilingual community of Transylvania.[27]

23 2nd Codex of Kolozsvár: 1664, 1: "Centuria Tertia Concionum Gyeorgii Enyedi". 1st Codex of Kolozsvár: beg. of 17th c., 1: "Concionum Georgii Enyedii Centureae[!] primae Triakas septima". Recent studies have revealed that while in the second case the copyist possibly used the term to represent a section of sermons of undefined number, the first case is clearly a mistake of the copyist owing to the codex containing the third triacas of the corpus. For further explanation see: Lovas: 2016a and Lovas: 2016b.

24 Enyedi: 1598, 26. This note is found in other editions: Enyedi: 1519, 1520, 37; and Enyedi: c. 1670, 26.

25 The text was published (Szilvási: 1591), but no known copy survives. The oratio concerned 1 Cor 1:4. Szilvási later converted to Catholicism.

26 Enyedi's sermon discussed Eph 4:1. For a detailed analysis of the Enyedi–Szilvási debate see Simon: 2009; Simon: 2016, 25–120, 340–345 etc.

27 As Carmen Florea (2002, 72) has shown, Enyedi was a special case in the Unitarian hierarchy in Cluj-Napoca: "With the exception of György Enyedi, the Church's superintendents [bishops] were also all elected to serve as the plebanus of Cluj, and, with the exception of John Erasmus [Erasmus Johannis], all preached to the Hungarian-speaking community in the town". In addition, it should be noted that in the principality of the Three Nations (Hun-

The same sermon exists, in Hungarian, in several variants, as number 60 in his sermon collection. Continuing the debate, Enyedi followed his sermon with a *Defensio* and a *Concionis examen*, where he criticised Szilvási's orations.[28] In contrast to his predecessor Ferenc Dávid who was permitted by the ruling prince to employ technology to disseminate texts of delivered sermons in order to aid the Unitarian position in local disputes, Enyedi relied on manuscripts. Notably, when Enyedi printed his arguments in the *Explicationes*, the local context was removed. Printing only the full text of the *Defensio* and parts of the *Concionis examen*, omitting sermon 60, Enyedi notes in his text that the arguments are taken from a dispute against someone concerning the divinity of Christ.[29] Enyedi's written response to a local debate with a former pupil was recast for his printed argument.

The relationship between the printed polemic and the handwritten sermon possibly reflects Enyedi's balancing of the local audience and the international one. In Enyedi's exegesis of Paul's letters to the Philippians in the *Explicationes*, he includes references to Heliodorus' *Aethiopica*, which he had translated from Greek to Latin and prepared for publication in 1592.[30] His exegesis influenced

garians, Saxons, Szeklers), the Unitarian Church had a bilingual community. Following set rules, the role of bishop was alternated between the Saxons and the Hungarians. Enyedi, having made a pact with the German Erasmus Johannis, who had been asked not to preach heretical ideas from the pulpit, preached instead. For more on Erasmus Johannis, see Dán: 1983.

28 All three texts can be found in the autograph Enyedi-Codex: bef. 1597, 1–37, 37–75, and 75–141. A copy of the texts are available in the Codex of Balázs Karácsonyi (manuscript, copy, Biblioteca Academiei Române, Filiala Cluj-Napoca, MS. U. 32). Given that the latter is a copy by another hand, the volume is less relevant to this study.

29 Enyedi: 1598, 123–124, on Luke 1:16: "Ea quae ad argumentationem ex hoc loco, pro Christi deitate confirmanda depromisolitam, cuidam mecum disceptanti aliquando respondi, hic repetam, & reponam".

30 The biblical section discussed in the *Explicationes* is Phil 2:5–11. Enyedi's translation of Heliodorus' *Aethiopica* was not published; it survives in only one late handwritten copy. Currently only part of the foreword, in Hungarian translation, has been published, though an edition is in preparation. Though Enyedi describes himself in his preface as the first Latin translator of the work, *Aethiopica* had been translated into Latin and published in Basel already in 1552 (and, later, Antwerp in 1556) by the Polish Jesuit Stanisław Warszewicki, then a pupil of Melanchthon. Enyedi did not merely translate Heliodorus' text, but also provided his text with quotations and references to the studies of Julius Caesar Scaliger, Marcus Antonius Muretus, Michael Neander, Vincent Obsopoeus, Nicephorus, Angelo Poliziano, Guilielmus Canterus, and Martin Crusius, to highlight qualities of the romance. In the later opinion of a key figure of the Counter Reformation, the Hungarian Jesuit Péter Pázmány, *Aethiopica* was listed among works deemed advisable to avoid and inappropriate for moral teaching owing to being capable of giving "offence to the youth", Heliodorus' work was placed alongside Epicurus, Ovid, and Terence (Bitskey: 1979, 62). Enyedi knows the French, Italian, Spanish, German, English translations, but he does not mention Warszewicki, nor Melanchthon. And as Berkes mentions, Enyedi also had to know the name of Warszewicki because of the Jesuit's connections to the Báthory family. As she suggests, the former

later scholars, from Erasmus Schmied, Lambert Bos, Jean Leclerc, Georg Raphael, Daniel Whitby, and Johann Jakob Wettstein in the seventeenth and eighteenth centuries, up to the twentieth century in the writings of Wilhelm Werner Jaeger and Adolf Jülicher.[31] The question arises whether this exegesis, with its noted classical erudition, was presented to his local Transylvanian audience. A fragmented copy of sermon 195 corresponds paragraph by paragraph with the elucidation in the *Explicationes*, but frustratingly ends before the *Aethiopica* reference is reached.[32] It does not seem too far-fetched to picture Enyedi preaching on the parallels between the letters of Paul and the geography of Heliodorus.

For Hungarians, the connection between delivered sermon and published polemic was strengthened by Enyedi's posthumous translators. Máté Toroczkai's printed Hungarian translation of the *Explicationes* (Enyedi: 1619, 191–192) inserted parts of two of Enyedi's sermons into the text, introduced chapter headings that refer clearly to the sermons, and printed references to the sermons,[33] although he did not adapt the material for print. Enyedi's statement that more would be told at a later date, a sign of oral delivery, is incongruously retained in Toroczkai's text.[34] Likewise, the second half of a sermon delivered with

---

translation did not escape Enyedi's attention, but he intentionally kept it quiet. (cf. Berkes: 2010; Berkes: 2011). Given that Enyedi dedicated his translation to the young Prince Sigismund Báthory, and mentioned his age and – following Melanchthon and the above-mentioned scholars – the didactic qualities of the work, the Unitarian bishop would have disagreed with Pázmány (Heliodori Aethiopicae: 1592, 3–5). The subject of the dedication, Prince Sigismund, however, would later be subjected to rebuke in Enyedi's sermons.

31 The long afterlife of Enyedi's writings was given greater breadth by the recently published research of József Simon (2014). Simon also suggests that Enyedi's contemporaries were indifferent to comparing the New Testament to classical secular novels. Reading Hungarian and international responses of that period, it is clear that while they scrutinised Enyedi's arguments and sources, none of them indicated the use of Heliodorus' Greek romance. The first notice appears a century later. Likewise, with the later authors, it is notable that Jülicher, who mentions Enyedi as Erasmus Schmied's source, admits that he was unable to examine Enyedi's *Explicationes* (Simon: 2014, 206), which remained in a comparatively large number of copies in European libraries in comparison to the average number of Hungarian and Transylvanian publications, because he could not find a single copy of the bishop's work.

32 Sermon 195, fragm. (Christus quomodo aequalis Deo; 5th Codex of Kolozsvár: mid-17th c., 148r–153v).

33 Beneath the exegesis of Jer 10:11 in the Hungarian translation is the note: "In concione 82. de his verbis ita loquitur. Idem G. Enyedi". The sermon variant of the chapter survives in a single copy, in the 2nd Codex of Kolozsvár (Causae durationis et ruinae impiorum; 1664, 150 [77v]). In a similar manner, the translated *Explicationes* has beneath the discussion of Mich 5:2 the note "Ex concione ejusdem G. Enyedi. 187". One copy of this section's sermon equivalent survives, in the 5th Codex of Kolozsvár (De Christi nativitate; mid-17th c., 101v–108v).

34 Enyedi: 1619, 192: "De erröl mászszor többet". As recently noted, Enyedi's reference in this twenty-line chapter is inserted in a paragraph of a sermon now numbered as sermon 16 (cf. Káldos: 2013, 110). This connection makes clear the status of the sermon, and supports the rearrangement of the sermon structure in the 2nd Codex of Kolozsvár. Sermon 16 should be put in place of Sermon 82 (16+33+33), and all the sermons from the first to third triacas

an *objectio-responsio* format, is similarly printed with an out of place "Amen".[35] Toroczaki included the sermons of Enyedi in the parts of the *Explicationes* that were frequently disputed by international readers, providing his vernacular Hungarian readers with more material to understand the ongoing debate. This feature, of supplementing the *Explicationes* with other writings by Enyedi, did not go unnoticed. While criticising Enyedi's work, Milotai Nyilas also targeted his publishers, noting that sections of his work had been thrown together by his successors.[36]

This treatment of Enyedi's work by his followers echoes the strange relationship among the bishop's writings. The cross-fertilisation of texts by the later editors and translators resembles Enyedi's own style of composition. In the aforementioned printed marginal reference to sermon 210, it has been shown that while the text of the *Explicationes* and sermon share the same idea, they were not copied from each other due to a divergence in tone and approach (Káldos: 2010, 190–194). In a similar manner, Enyedi incorporated his own translation of Heliodorus in his debate with his former student. It appears that the bishop was deliberately incorporating his different writings – his sermons, translations, and debates – into the *Explicationes.* A closer examination of the manuscripts of the sermon collection has further illuminated a feature of Enyedi's work that has been little noticed. The sermons and the *Explicationes* share a large number of identified sources,[37] suggesting the two productions, one for local listeners and the other for the international readers, were closely connected as Enyedi prepared them.

More exciting for the modern scholar are the shared textual parts that appear in the first edition of the *Explicationes* that are not identified in the published volume; these reveal tantalising alterations in presentation by Enyedi to suit the

---

subsequently moved. Correspondences between the two codices have already been noted (cf. Káldos: 2013; Lovas: 2013b), but closer analysis by the author of this paper has proved that the fragmented texts in the Codex of Sárospatak (containing the third triacas) correspond one by one with the sermons in the 2nd Codex of Kolozsvár. It should, however, be noted that the 2nd Codex of Kolozsvár contains only thirty sermons instead of thirty-three. For further information on the rearrangement of the corpus see: Lovas: 2016a and Lovas: 2016b.

35 Sermon 187 (De Christi nativitate; 5th Codex of Kolozsvár: mid-17th c., 108v).

36 "Megkandicsálta ezt Enyedi, es az mit ellene talahatot, ugyan Praedicatioban szerzette, az mint az ő Ivadéki, töb irasi köziben taszitották" ("Enyedi glimpsed this [about the birth and nature of Jesus], and what he found against it, wrote it up in a sermon, which was tossed among his other writings by his scions") (Milotai Nyilas: 1622, 327).

37 The identifying of Enyedi's sources is still in progress. In the manuscripts, the marking of sources in the margins is different not only in the printed format, but also among the individual manuscripts. Closer study can reveal the shared sources of the parallel texts, and so subsequently aid understanding of the manuscripts. Research into how the copyists, using their different strategies during the writing process, may have altered or omitted many of the references is currently in its early stages.

intended context. One concerns Enyedi's explication of a common feature of sixteenth- to seventeenth-century debates produced by Anti-Trinitarians: Psalm 2. In addition to resembling an earlier exegesis in the *Explicationes* on Ps 2:7 (1598, 56–63; 1619, 82–111), the text closely resembles three sermons surviving in two codices.[38] Almost three hundred lines, in which Enyedi criticises the doctrine of the Trinity combining typical Unitarian arguments with arguments from post-Biblical Hebrew polemics, closely correspond. It seems likely that the Hungarian sermons and the Latin treatise originated from a *dispositio*. The main difference – other than the language – is the employment in the sermons of the didactic topos of the mirror for princes. Enyedi asserts that monarchs that go against the will of God will be punished. Given contemporary concerns about the encroaching Ottoman threat, a reccurring theme in the talk of the *Regnum Christi* is a discussion of uniting with pagans. This social context is omitted in the *Explicationes*, which does not feature these elements. These political connotations, made the sermons easily adaptable by later preachers in the increasingly assaulted Unitarian minority for use against the monolithic Calvinist majority.

This local context explains the inclusion of another topos in the sermons: the image of a chosen people. Following the death of John Sigismund, the Unitarian Church lacked a ruler who would aid their religion. The princes, turning to Catholicism in Enyedi's time and Calvinism in the period following his death, did not assist the Unitarians. Mercantile, cultural, and educational connections with the Hungarian, German, Polish and Italian territories meant the Transylvanian Unitarians were familiar with the frequent Reformation analogy of Biblical Israel. Reformation authors frequently compared living rulers to exemplary figures such as Josiah, Moses, David, Gideon, and Solomon (Murdock: 1998). Owing to the marginalisation of the Unitarians, Enyedi compared Sigismund Báthory to the less popular Zedekiah, Jehoiakim, King of Judah, and even to Rehoboam, "the folly of the nation". Since copyists kept these complaints, a preacher was able to creatively substitute a contemporary ruler for the same result. Likewise, the status of Transylvania, as a tributary state of the Ottoman Empire, balanced between the Sublime Porte and the Habsburgs, was a problematic issue much emphasised in Enyedi's sermons. Using the Jewish-Hungarian parallel, and applying the common Reformation model of New Israel to Transylvania and the Unitarian community, the bishop wields the well-known analogies for confessional and territorial identities in a unique way. Nebuchadnezzar becomes a positive figure, used as an analogy for the Sultan, while the Transylvanian prince

38 The sermons in the 5th Codex of Kolozsvár: Sermon 192 (Frustra temunt contra Deum homines): 130v–136v; Sermon 193 (Quomodo Christus filius Dei): 136v–142r; Sermon 194 (De Regno Christi): 142r–148r. The sermons in the Codex of Székelykeresztúr: Sermon 192: 618 (518) – 634 (534); Sermon 193: 634 (534) – 643 (543); Sermon 194: 643 (543) – 656 (556).

is assigned the role of Zedekiah. Though Enyedi does not identify the prince by name, explicit references to the ruler's age make it apparent to his audience who is meant. In another dazzling use of biblical allegory, Enyedi presents the Habsburg Empire as Egypt.[39] Given the fluctuations in context, from the end of the seventeenth century these sermons became increasingly unadaptable.

One possibility is that the "local" was written earlier than the "international". The fragmented Codex of Sárospatak contains a sermon that appears – without any indication – in the *Explicationes.*[40] The connection is not immediately apparent, as the subject of the sermon is John 8:56, and for the *Explicationes* John 8:58. The latter, "I say to you, before Abraham was, I am", was an oft used text in international ecclesiastical debates. Placing the two Enyedi texts side by side, it becomes apparent that the hand-copied sermon and the printed text contain the same content, argument, and quotations, paragraph by paragraph. The philo-

39 For discussion of this analogy, see Lovas: 2012. A short paragraph of one of Enyedi's sermons will provide a clear impression of his crafting of Biblical comparisons (Sermon 53, 4th Codex of Kolozsvár: 1621, 70v; abbreviations have been silently expanded): "Sedechias kiraly az sok tanaczok miatt, keorwlle forgolodok akarattyabol, meg vete Nabugodonozort hwti ellen, s' az Aegyptombeli kirallyal keote frigyet, kit minden Nemzetseguel inkab kel vala gywleolniek az sidoknak, mert ott tartottak vala rabsagban, es ott nyomorgattak vala az eo eleieket. [...] Immar tekinczy ket fele, gondolkodgyal magadban a' mostani allapatunk feleol, lasd meg ha nem ezen linean vagyunke? A Nemet, (mikor velwnk frigye vala,) nem otalmazhatta meg Orszagunkat, mikeppen az elseo Joachim kiralyt Aegyptom. Az vtan Sedechias az eocze, megis oda keote magat, maga iol tudgya vala rosz voltokat, de bizony meg fizetenek neki erette. Am mig bekes leon Nabukodonozorral, addig sem Aegyptom, sem semmi Nemzetsegh nem mere bantani, nagy czyendessegben vralkodek, bekeseggel bira Orszagat 8. eszteneig. De mihelt onnat el hordola, nyaka szakada, mind Orszaganak s' mind eo maganak. Pogan vala Nabugodonozor, pogan a' teoreokis. De a' mint amaz tellyesseggel elfoglalhattya vala Sido Orszagot, ketszer, de megis io akarattyabol kiralt hagya ott az Sidoknak eo nemzetsegekbeol: Azonkeppen bizony kezeben volt Magyar Orszag es Erdely a' teoroknek, de megis kiralyt feiedelmet hagyott a' mi magunk Nemzetsegwnkbeol. [...] Sedechiastol czyak hwseget s adoot keuan vala Nabugodonozor. Mit keuan mi teollwnkis egyebet teoreok czyaszar?" (King Zedekiah, because of his many aldermen, and because of the will of the schemers, despised Nebuchadnezzar against his pledge, and made a league with the king of Egypt, who is most hatred by the Jews, because there were kept and oppressed their ancestors. [...] Now look around, and ponder in yourself concerning our present state, and see, whether or not we are in the same situation. The German, (when he had a league with us), could not save our country, just as the first king, Jehoiakim was not saved by Egypt. Then Zedekiah, his brother fastened himself on these, though he knew well that they were bad, and was paid well by them. But while he was at peace with Nebuchadnezzar, neither Egypt nor any other nation could harm them, and he was ruling in great tranquillity, and there was peace in his land for eight years. But as soon as he turned from them, his neck was broken, just like his country's neck. Nebuchadnezzar was pagan, the Turk is also pagan. But as he occupied entirely the Land of the Jews twice, but yet according to his benevolence left them a king in charge from their own nation, so likewise Hungary and Transylvania were in the hands of the Turk, but yet, he left a king, a reigning prince from our nation. [...] Nebuchadnezzar expected only loyalty and contribution from Zedekiah. What else does the Turkish emperor want from us?)

40 Sermon 93 (Codex of Sárospatak: mid-17th c., I/288–305).

logical analysis of the Bible's Greek text and conclusion are shared. The only omission is the beginning and the close of the sermon, and a statement by Enyedi excusing himself to the unlettered for speaking in a foreign language.[41] Given that the Hungarian sermon is closer to the *Explicationes* than the later Hungarian translation, it seems likely that Enyedi wrote for his local, less scholarly audience first, before engaging with the larger religious disputes that embroiled the continent. It also appears that the bishop, although writing on various subjects that would not be understood by all of his listeners, was yet considerate of their abilities.

The connections between the *Explicationes* and the sermon collection reveal how Enyedi presented Unitarian beliefs for local listeners and international readers. They illuminate how sermons delivered to a minority in a marginal principality became a central subject in continental polemics. It also shows how a regional bishop, whose Church was subjected to stringent state control, became a name to be mentioned in debate (even if his work was not properly identified). Notably, though the sermon collection themselves dropped out of usage due to later political and social upheavals in Transylvania, the parallel parts printed in the *Explicationes* continued to be quoted and disputed in tracts and Biblical explications as late as the early years of the twentieth century. Though this is in part due to appearing in print, it is also owing to Enyedi's continuation of the oral techniques in a different format. That a studious bishop, on the geographical border of European Christianity, repeatedly crossing the border between the written and printed and the silent and spoken word, could become a posthumous presence in later continental theological debates is testament to both Enyedi and the unique political context in which his works were produced and disseminated.

Bibliography

Manuscripts

Conciones vetustissimae (bef. 1642–1659), Biblioteca Academiei Române, Filiala Cluj-Napoca, MS. U. 262.

Enyedi-kódex [Enyedi-Codex] (bef. 1597), Biblioteca Academiei Române, Filiala Cluj-Napoca, Ms. U. 474.

Gyalai Sámuel prédikációgyűjteménye [Sermon collection of Sámuel Gyalai] (1617–1626), Cluj-Napoca, Biblioteca Centrala a Universitatii Victor Babes, MS. 1777.

41 "Az kik penigh irast nem tudnak, ne banniak, ha szokason kwuwl idegen nieluen kell it szollanom" (Codex of Sárospatak: mid-17th c., I/297; abbreviations silently expanded).

Heliodori Aethiopicae historiae libri decem (1592), Nunc primum in Latinam linguam conversi interprete Georgio Eniedino Transilvano, copied by S. Nemay in 1647, Biblioteca Academiei Române, Filiala Cluj-Napoca, MS. U. 1089.

Kolozsvári Kódex [1st Codex of Kolozsvár] (beg. of 17th c.), Biblioteca Academiei Române, Filiala Cluj-Napoca, MS. U. 737/I.

Kolozsvári Kódex [2nd Codex of Kolozsvár] (1664), Biblioteca Academiei Române, Filiala Cluj-Napoca, MS. U. 737/II.

Kolozsvári Kódex [3rd Codex of Kolozsvár] (1613), Biblioteca Academiei Române, Filiala Cluj-Napoca, MS. U. 737/III.

Kolozsvári Kódex [4th Codex of Kolozsvár] (1621), Biblioteca Academiei Române, Filiala Cluj-Napoca, MS. U. 737/IV.

Kolozsvári Kódex [5th Codex of Kolozsvár] (mid-17th c.), Biblioteca Academiei Române, Filiala Cluj-Napoca, MS. U. 737/V.

Marosvásárhelyi Kódex [Codex of Marosvásárhely] (1642–1696), Târgu Mureş, Biblioteca Teleki, Codex 0636.

Székelykeresztúri Kódex [Codex of Székelykeresztúr] (1629), Târgu Mureş, Teleki-Bolyai Library, Codex 0439.

Sárospataki Kódex [Codex of Sárospatak] (mid-17th c.), Sárospataki Református Kollégium Nagykönyvtára, Kt. 7.

Books published before 1800

Almási Porkoláb, Andreas (1640), Disputatio Theologica, De Tribus in unica Deitate Personis... adversus Pauli Samosteni, Photini, Socini Enyedini, horumque sequacium, vera ac ortodoxa sententia dilucide demonstratur ..., Franeker: Uldericus Balck.

Balduin, Friedrich (1618), Trinitatis Disputatio... Wittenberg: Helwig.

Enyedi, György (1598[1], c. 1670[2]), Explicationes locorum Veteris et Novi Testamenti, ex quibus Trinitatis dogma stabiliri solet, Auctore Georgio ENIEDIO superintendente ecclesiarum in Transylvania, unum Patrem Deum et eius Filium Jesum Christum per Spiritum Sanctum profitentium, 1st edition [Heltai]: [Kolozsvár]; 2nd edition [n.p.]: Groningen.

– (1619[1], 1620[2]), Az ó es vy testamentvm-beli helyeknek, mellyekböl az Háromsagról való tudománt szokták állatni, magyarazattyok, ENYEDI Gyeorgy, Erdély országban az egy Atya Isten, es az ő Sz. Fia, az Iesus Christus felől, Sz. Lélek által ki adatott tudomány-ban eggyező ecclesiáknak püspöke által deák nyelven iratott, Máté Toroczkai (tr.), 1st edition, 2nd edition [Heltai]: [Kolozsvár].

Ferenc, Dávid (1569), Első Resze az szent irasnac külön külön reszeiből vöt predicaciocnac az atya istenről, ennek kedig az ő fiaról az Ihesvs Christvsrol, es az mi öröcseguncnec peczetiről az szent lelekről. Gyula-Fehérvár: Vagnerus.

Feuerborn, Justus (1658) Posthumus Anti-Enjedinus, Giessen: Hampel.

Geleji Katona, István (1645), Titkok titka..., Gyulafehérvár: (typ. principis).

Jászberényi, P. Pál (1662), Examen doctrinae ariano-socinianae, London: Sumptibus Samelis Broun.

Káldi, György (1631a), Az Innepekre-valo Predikatzioknak Első Resze, Bécs/Pozsony: Rikeszt [et typ. Societatis Jesu].
- (1631b), Az Vasarnapokra-valo Predikatzioknak Első Resze, Bécs/Pozsony: Rikeszt [et typ. Societatis Jesu].
Martin, Jacob (1614), De tribus Elohim liber primus, photinianorum novorum et cum primis Georgii Eniedini blasphemiis oppositus, Wittenberg: Schurer.
Milotai Nyilas, István (1622), Speculum Trinitatis, Debrecen: Rheda.
Paraeus, David (1609), In Genesin Mosis commentarius, Frankfurt: Rhodius.
Pelargus, Christoph (1605), Admonitio de Arianis recentibus eorumque blasphemis dogmatibus, Leipzig: Francus.
Peñalosa, Abrosio de (1635), Opus Egregium De Christi Et Spiritus Sancti Divinitate, Nec Non SS. Trinitatis Mysterio. Contra Iudaeos, Photinum, Socinum, Eniedinum aliosque veteres & novos Arrianos, Vienna: Formica.
Szentkirályi, Benedictus (1619), Vindicatio locorum veteris testamenti... adversus Georgii Enyedini locorum ut vocat explicationes, Marburg: R. Hutwelcker.
Tályai Z., Martinus (1632), Disputatio Theologica Tertia De Persona D. nostri Iesu Christi ac duabus naturalis... Quarum vera unio personalis ex Sacra Scriptura adversus falsas Enjedini aliorumque socinianorum contradictiones demonstratur... Leiden: Ex Officina Bonaventurae & Abrahami Elzevir.
Thumm, Theodor/Johann Ulrich Rentz (1621), Apodeixis theologica, spiritum sanctum non per...: erroribus et corruptelis modernorum Photinianorum, inprimis Fausti Socini, Georgii Eniedeni, Christophori Osterodi, Valentini Smalzii etc. ad disputandum proposita, Tübingen: Werlinus.
Vogt, Johann (1738), Catalogus historico-criticus librorum rariorum, Hamburg: Christian Herold.

Secondary Sources

Balázs, Mihály (2013), Tolerant Country – Misunderstood Laws: Interpreting Sixteenth-Century Transylvanian Legislation Concerning Religion, Hungarian Historical Review 2, 1, 85–108.
- (2008), Ferenc Dávid, Bibliotheca Dissidentium vol. XXVI, Ungarländische Antitrinitarier IV., Baden-Baden & Bouxviller: V. Koerner.
- (1996), János Zsigmond fejedelem és a cenzúra, in: András Kovács/Gábor Sipos/Sándor Tonk (eds.), Emlékkönyv Jakó Zsigmond születésének nyolcvanadik évfordulójára, Kolozsvár: Erdélyi Múzeum-Egyesület, 21–30.
Balázs, Mihály/János Káldos (eds.) (1997), Enyedi György válogatott művei, Bucharest–Kolozsvár: Kriterion.
Balázs, Mihály/Gizella Keserű (eds.) (2000), György Enyedi and Central European Unitarianism in the 16th to 17th Centuries, Budapest: Balassi.
Berkes, Katalin (2011), Enyedi György és a zsiráf, Magyar Könyvszemle, 126, 381–386.
- (2011), Kikről hallgat Enyedi?: A Héliodórosz-fordítás előzményeihez, Acta Universitatis Szegediensis de Attila József nominatae: Acta Historiae Litterarum Hungaricarum, 53–59.

BITSKEY, ISTVÁN (1979), Humanista erudíció és barokk világkép. Pázmány Péter prédikációi, Budapest: Akadémiai Kiadó.

BOROS, GYÖRGY (1910), Enyedi György. Concio Ján. 12, 42, Unitárius Szószék (Székelyudvarhely), 1910/1-4, 26-32.

DÁN, RÓBERT (1987), Az erdélyi szombatosok és Péchi Simon, Budapest: Akadémiai Kiadó.

– (1973), Humanizmus, reformáció, antitrinitarizmus és a héber nyelv Magyarországon, Budapest: Akadémiai Kiadó.

– (1983), Erazmus Johannis "Világos bizonyítékai", Irodalomtörténeti Közlemények 87, 120–129.

FLOREA, CARMEN (2002), Shaping Transylvanian Anti-Trinitarian Identity in an Urban Context, in: Maria Crăciun/Ovidiu Ghitta/Graeme Murdock (eds.), Confessional Identity in East-Central Europe, Aldershot: Ashgate, 64–80.

GABRIELLA, H. HUBERT (2004), A régi magyar gyülekezeti ének, Budapest: Universitas.

HORVÁTH, CYRILL (1905), Enyedi György egyházi beszédeiből. III. Triac. Conc. XCIV., in: Cyrill Horváth (ed.), Sárospataki Füzetek, Sárospatak: Radil Károly, 161–166.

KANYARÓ, FERENC (1900), Enyedi György unitárius püspök beszéde, Keresztény Magvető 1, 30–40.

KÁLDOS, JÁNOS/MIHÁLY BALÁZS (1993), György Enyedi, Bibliotheca Dissidentium vol. XV, Ungarländische Antitrinitarier II., Baden-Baden/Bouxviller: V. Koerner.

KÁLDOS, JÁNOS (2010), Enyedi György prédikációinak szöveghagyománya, in: László Boka/Ildikó Sirató (eds.), Érték és értelmezés, Budapest: Gondolat/OSZK, 188–207.

– (2013), Enyedi György prédikáció-gyűjteményének szerkezete és a prédikációk textológiai vizsgálatának tanulságai, Erdélyi Múzeum 2013/1, 88–120.

LOVAS, BORBÁLA (2012), Erkölcs és identitás. Pogányság és kiválasztottság Enyedi György prédikáció-iban, in: Pál Ács/Júlia Székely (eds.), Identitás és kultúra a török hódoltság korában, szerk. Budapest: Balassi, 299–310.

– (2013a), Másolási stratégiák Enyedi György prédikációinak hagyományozódásában, Studia Litteraria, 2013/3-4, 79–94.

– (2013b), Non multa sed multum. Párhuzamos beszédek Enyedi György prédikációgyűjteményében, Erdélyi Múzeum 2013/1, 71–87.

– (2014), Textológiai és értelmezésbeli kérdések Enyedi György magyar nyelvű munkáiban. A prédikációgyűjtemény, PhD dissertation, ELTE.

LUKÁCS, LADISLAUS (1969–1987), Monumenta Antiquae Hungariae, I–IV. (1550–1600), Rome: Institutum Historicum S. I.

MACZÁK, IBOLYA (2008), A prédikációk szerepe és jelentősége a lelkiség-történeti kutatásokban, in: László N. Szelestei (ed.), Lelkiségtörténeti számvetés, Piliscsaba: PPKE BTK, 63–89.

MOLNÁR, ANTAL (2000), Sur la genése d'une polémique catholique contre Enyedi (Ambrosio Peñalosa: Opus egregium...1635), in: Mihály Balázs/Gizella Keserű (eds.), György Enyedi and Central European Unitarianism in the 16th–17th Centuries, Budapest: Balassi, 237–243.

MURDOCK, GRAEME (1998), The Importance of Being Josiah: An Image of Calvinist Identity, The Sixteenth Century Journal 29, 4, 1043–1059.

– (1995), International Calvinism, Ethnic Allegiance, and the Reformed Church of Transylvania in the Early Seventeenth Century, in: Maria Crăciun/Ovidiu Ghitta (eds.),

Ethnicity and Religion in Central and Eastern Europe, Cluj: Cluj University Press, 92–100.

– (2000), Beyond the Pale: International Calvinist Attacks against Unitarianism in Transylvania, in: Mihály Balázs/Gizella Keserű (eds.), György Enyedi and Central European Unitarianism in the 16th–17th Centuries, Budapest: Balassi, 245–252.

Pásztori-Kupán, István (2009), The Spirit of Religious Tolerance - A Transylvanian "extra calvinisticum"? in: Ábrahám Kovács (ed.), Calvinism on the Peripheries: Religion and Civil Society in Europe, Budapest: L'Harmattan, 155–179.

Simon, József (2009), Enyedi György (1555–1597) és a szillogizmus középfogalma, Világosság, 2009 ősz, 41–48.

– (2013), Aristotelismus, Nominalismus und Trinitätskritik. Die philosophischen Grundzüge der Explicationes Locorum Veteris et Novi Testamenti von György Enyedi (1555–1597), in: Ulrich Wien, András Balogh (eds.), Radikale Reformation - Die Unitarier in Siebenbürgen, Köln: Böhlau Verlag, 227–240.

– (2014), Zsákmány. Enyedi György esete Pál apostollal, Héliodórosszal és Werner Jaegerrel, Irodalomtörténeti Közlemények 118, 189–214.

– (2016), Explicationes explicationum: Filozófia, irodalom és egzegetika Enyedi György életművében, Budapest: Typotex.

Szczucki, Lech (1982), Polish and Transylvanian Unitarianism in the Second Half of the 16th century, in: Róbert Dán/Antal Pirnát (eds.), Antitrinitarianism in the Second Half of the 16th Century, Budapest, 231–241.

Szelestei N., László (ed.) (2005), Régi magyar prédikációk, 16–18. század, Budapest: Szent István Társulat.

Szentpéteri, Márton (2012), The Mystery of Piety Revealed and Defended: A Sequel to Johann Heinrich Bisterfeld's *De uno Deo?* Acta Comeniana 26, 89–98.

Szentpéteri, Márton/Noémi Viskolcz (2005), Egy református–unitárius hitvita Erdélyben 1641-ben, in: Heltai, János/Réka, Tasi (eds.), "Tenger az igaz hitrül való egyenetlenségek vitatásának eláradott özöne…" Tanulmányok XVI-XIX. századi hitvitáinkról, Miskolc: Miskolci Egyetem BTK, 93–102.

Szilvási, János (1591), Oratio Ioannis Zilvasii, Praemissa Disputationi Publicae, in Synodo Orthodoxorum Vngarorum Vasarhelyini celebratae, Anno 1591. mensis Janij die 13, Sibiu: Typis Joannis Henrici Cratonis, 1591.

Takács, Dániel (2011), Enyedi György krisztológiája hat prédikációjának elemzése alapján, MA thesis, ELTE BTK.

Viskolcz, Noémi (2003), Johann Heinrich Bisterfeld (1605–1655) Bibliográfia. A Bisterfeld-könyvtár, Budapest/Szeged: OSZK/Scriptum Rt.

V. Confessional Identity and Otherness

Magdalena Luszczynska

Inter-Faith Disputation, Christian Hebraism, or a Leadership Campaign?

The Multi-Dimensional Character of Marcin Czechowic's Anti-Jewish Polemics

1. Introduction

This paper discusses two anti-Jewish polemics composed in early modern Poland in the milieu of a radical Reformation group, known as the Arians or the Polish Brethren. In the mid-sixteenth century the Polish Brethren split from the Reformed Church, the "*ecclesia major*", forming a separate group, the "*ecclesia minor*". Due to their Anti-Trinitarian theology – the Polish Brethren questioned the dogma of Jesus' pre-existence – they were dubbed Arians. The name Arian, derived from Arius, a third-century Christian theologian who denied the divinity of Jesus, was given to the Polish Brethren by their opponents and was intended as a slander. Like Arius, the Polish Arians were considered heretics by the Catholic majority and by the Protestant Churches alike. This hostility led to the Arians' eventual expulsion from the country in 1658. Parenthetically, I am using the offensive name "Arian" for purely pragmatic reasons, as this is the term most commonly used in international scholarship.[1]

In the development of the Arian movement, one can distinguish three phases (Ogonowski: 1960). The first, from 1563, which marks the date of the earliest pronouncement of the group's separate identity, was characterised by ongoing discussions concerning the details of the Arian creed (for example, the Arian synods met in order to establish a unified stance on such matters as the hierarchy of divine persons or the Incarnation). The second phase, lasting from around 1566 for the next quarter of a century, was the era when foundational dogmas were agreed on, although the character of the movement and its group identity

1 The Arians would call themselves simply Christians, although there is a distinction here, too. The Arians referred to themselves by a neologism Chrystianie (Christians), derived from "Christ"" and coined in order to distinguish themselves from the Christians (pl. Chrześcijanie), derived from "chrzest" or "baptism". For further discussion on the terminology cf. Wilczek: 1994, 10–11.

were still crystallising. This second phase can be called "Arianism proper", as opposed to the "proto-Arianism" of earlier years. The final phase came about in the late nineties of the sixteenth century, when an Italian "heretical" theologian and religious refugee, Fausto Sozzini (1539–1604), became the leader of the movement. This brought about a significant redefinition of Arian ideology and doctrine; the movement abandoned the most radical of its social doctrines, and shifted towards humanistic rationalism, becoming what scholars like to see as a forerunner of the Enlightenment. Under this new leadership, the Polish Brethren came to be known as the Socinians.

The Arians have been a subject of scholarly investigations for decades. Polish researchers have focussed on editing and publishing Arian sources, on composing monographs outlining the history of the movement and biographies of the leading figures in the Polish Brethren Church and, most recently, on analysing the social and philosophical ideas of the sect. The most current and thorough survey of the historiography of the Arian movement has been presented by Piotr Wilczek (Wilczek: 2007). Wilczek demonstrates how changing research trends in Polish academia have influenced the treatment of the subject. To begin with, he identifies the way in which philological-historiographical concerns dominated the research of pre-war historians, whose works, although impressively thorough and systematic, were nevertheless more analytical than synthetic in their approach. The subsequent post-war period in Polish academia was inspired by Marxist-reductionist methodology and brought little new insight. Only in the late 1960s did this ideological bias give way to new, synthetic investigations into the philosophy and history of the movement. Despite this sustained academic treatment, the subject still continues to generate questions that have not been addressed and remains in need of new scholarly perspectives.

English-speaking scholarship, on the other hand, has been far less preoccupied with the idiosyncrasies of the movement. Anglophone historians of ideas have typically regarded the Arians in a broader perspective, either as one of the expressions of the pan-European radical Reformation (Williams: 1962), or as a stage in the development of the Unitarian Church (Wilbur: 1953). Both, the Polish and the English-language scholarship have tended to give much more attention to the latter, Socinian phase of the Arian movement.

What is underrepresented in scholarly literature on Arianism are studies of the early phase of Arian history, as well as analyses of previously unexamined aspects of the Polish Brethren's thought and writings. This paper attempts to address this lacuna. My research investigates the identity of the Arian movement at the time it was taking shape, that is, in the phase that I call "Arianism proper". I explore the ways in which the self-definition of the young Church as well as the personal identity of its creators were construed, i.e. how the Arian leaders regarded and represented themselves and their co-believers. To this end, I examine writings of one of the leaders of the movement, Marcin Czechowic, an Arian minister, ideologue and prolific writer, who sought to give the movement a unified face, and to fashion himself as its leader. I investigate how these two agendas were pursued through Czechowic's use of Jewish imagery and by introducing into Arian literature a Jewish character, who plays the rhetorical role of the "ultimate Other". I also show how the traditionally Christian genre of anti-Jewish polemics was adopted into Arian literature and thus, how it acquired new shapes and functions.

2. Arian-Jewish Polemics

Typically, the use of Jewish imagery in the works of the other early Arian writers drew upon lingering stereotypes and did not engage with Judaism per se. In fact, in their endeavour to reinterpret Christian theology and ethics, the Arian writers rarely distinguished between Biblical Israelites and contemporary Jews, and if they did, the latter were not their concern. In this respect, the two texts by Czechowic that I analyse are strikingly exceptional: both of them discuss Jewish theology and practices in depth, refer to Rabbinic literature, and, most importantly, give voice to contemporary Jewish figures. In the following paragraphs, I shall analyse the two texts, highlighting their rhetorical idiom. I shall argue that in each case the genre of Arian-Jewish polemic served as a tool for achieving a different socio-political aim.

Marcin Czechowic was one of the most influential thinkers in the formative years of the movement and the leader of what later became the mainstream of the Arian Church. Born and raised a Catholic, Czechowic pursued an ecclesiastical career and became a Catholic priest. However, having acquainted himself with Protestant thought, he turned first to Lutheranism, then to Calvinism, only then to become one of the leaders of the separatist movement, the Arians. From the early days of the movement, he was one of the most active Arian ministers and in 1570 he became the leader of the Arian centre in Lublin.

The first of the texts to be discussed is part of Czechowic's main work, which was written in 1575 and entitled *Christian Discussions* (*Rozmowy chrystianskie*). This was by far his greatest political and literary success. The book was commissioned by the Arian congregation and served as the first compendium of the group's ideology, practice, and ethics. As such, it has been seen as an attempt to provide a unified stance on major dogmatic points and thus to consolidate the young Church.

In writing *Christian Discussions*, Czechowic chose to present his teachings in the form of a dialogue, which he considered the most appropriate for educational reasons (and apparently, also, for reasons of propaganda):

> Learned and reasonable men among the Greeks, the Latin authors, other nations, and among us, the Polish, have tended to present their books in such form that it seems that two, three, or even more [characters] would dispute with one another, even if in fact that was not the case. They do so because this way the matters are more easily understood by the simple ones. I followed their way of writing[2](Czechowic: 1581, 7).

Christian Discussions was not the first time that Czechowic had made use of this literary form to expound on his doctrine. His 1564 literary debut, *A three-day conversation* (*Trzech dni rozmowa*) was also written as a dramatised discussion, this time between a Protestant (*Ewangelik*), a Catholic (*Papieżnik*) and a Christian (*Chrystijan*), who voices Czechowic's own stance. In this, he presented, among other things, his views on infant baptism. As Lech Szczucki argues (Szczucki: 1986, 96), it also contained the roots of all aspects of his later theology.

Christian Discussions is composed as a set of thirteen fictional conversations between an Arian master (Czechowic's porte-parole) and a student. These dialogues are divided into three parts: two sections entitled *Christian Chats* (*Gadki chrystiańskie*), which begin and end the work, are separated from one another by a polemical part named *Jewish Chats* (*Gadki żydowskie*). The pretext given for this tripartite structure is the storyline: the Student, having been the "victim" of an unexpected polemic with the Jews (who proved troublingly convincing), asks the Master to provide him with directions on how to conduct a successful disputation in case he has to face such opponents again. The result – *Jewish Chats* – is a set of lessons on anti-Jewish rhetoric, wherein the Student takes on the role of the Jews and the Master defends the Christian position. *Jewish Chats* begins with the Master answering the issues which were, allegedly, originally raised by the Jews. This opening section is followed by a part in which the discussion turns to the foundations of Christian-Arian theology. When read as a separate entity, *Jewish Chats* is the first Arian anti-Jewish polemic and here I will be concerned with this section of Czechowic's Arian catechism.

The second text to be analysed here, *A written response of Jacob the Jew of Bełżyce to which the said Marcin Czechowic replies* (*Odpis Jakuba Żyda z Bełżyc*) was published eight years later, in 1581. It is also written in the form of a dialogue, this time between Czechowic himself and a local Jew, Rabbi Jacob. The way Czechowic presents the genesis of the book is that Rabbi Jacob, with whom he claims to have been in constant contact, had read *Christian Discussions* (or at least the *Jewish Chats* section) and, insulted by the way the elements of Jewish religion had been portrayed, wrote to the Arian author in response. Jacob's letter was divided into four parts: an Introduction followed by three thematic sections (On the Talmud, On Sabbath, and On Circumcision). Czechowic further sub-

2 All quotations from the primary sources are my translations.

divided Rabbi Jacob's response into chapters and appended his own responses to each of them, making it a basis for the work in question.

There are two main reasons to juxtapose these texts. Firstly, one cannot but notice their structural dependence. For both are written in the unusual form of an Arian-Jewish encounter. As I have mentioned above, Czechowic appears to be the first (and to the best of my knowledge, the only) Arian author to make use of this literary genre. Moreover, whilst *Jewish Chats* claims to be a disputation manual (in which the Master guides the Student how to respond to the Jews), the second work, *Odpis*, is a disputation proper, attempting to realise the model proposed in the former work. The second reason to compare the two polemics is the correlation of their plotlines and themes. We are told that Rabbi Jacob's letter is a reaction to the matters discussed in *Jewish Chats*. Therefore, the second text, *Odpis*, remains in an intertextual dialogue with the first. This two-fold correspondence notwithstanding, I argue that in each case Czechowic chose to write an anti-Jewish polemic for different reasons, which I shall outline below.

3. Analysis and Comparison

3.1 *Jewish Chats:* An Internal Arian Dispute Framed as an Anti-Jewish Polemic

Despite its title, *Jewish Chats* is not concerned exclusively with Jewish issues. Lech Szczucki, the author of Czechowic's biography, who was also the first scholar to analyse the text, noted that discernible Christian threads were added in a seemingly artificial, arbitrary fashion (cf. Szczucki: 1964, 91). I propose that the combination of Christian and Jewish matters is not coincidental or "artificial", but is a conscious choice of the author. I argue that *Jewish Chats* can be divided into two distinguishable thematic parts. The first part is devoted to an account of the polemical strategy that the Student should master and to its implementation, thus providing a response to the initial anti-Christian accusations of the Jews. Hence, the beginning of the dialogue resembles a typical Christian-Jewish polemic. The second part, much longer and more sophisticated, deviates from the initial Jewish anti-Christian arguments in order to focus on the fundamentals of Christian belief and to present a defence of Arian Christology.

This bipartite structure of the work invites the application of a conceptual approach to help analyse the author's rhetorical strategy and shed light on his agenda. Historical Dialogue Analysis (HDA), a relatively new branch of linguistic inquiry which employs linguistic-logical methodology to analyse historical texts, appears to be a suitable choice. One of the most successful implementations of HDA research principles is a typology of polemical encounters proposed by Marcelo Dascal, a philosopher at Tel Aviv University. Dascal conducted logical and linguistic analysis of the form, sequence and function of rhetorical moves used in various historical documents. He took into account the scope of disagreement, the ways the parties tried to resolve it, and their ultimate goals. Thus, he defined three ideal types of polemical exchanges: discussion, dispute, and controversy (cf. Dascal: 2004, 3–20). Not only does each of these categories involve a specific strategy and aspire to reach a different goal, but it also manifests itself in specific socio-historical conditions.

The first type, discussion, revolves around a particular problem and aims at a rational resolution, typically by providing factual, verifiable proofs. Having encountered a problem, the polemicists recognise its source and try to address it through a search for rational solutions. Contrarily, a dispute is a far more all-encompassing event. The adversaries' positions are rooted in radically different principles and reinforced by the conviction that the opponent's stance is not a one-off mistake but the result of an entirely erroneous worldview. There is little hope for reaching an agreement. The opponents' goal is not a solution but a dissolution, and the real aim of the contenders is to win over the audience. As a result, rational argumentation is almost entirely absent, and replaced with accusations of stubbornness, illness, inborn inability to understand the truth and the like. The third category is controversy, which unlike the two former types of discourse, cannot be either solved or dissolved; rather, the successful end would be a resolution reached by working out a middle ground that can be accepted by the contenders. Since the latter category is irrelevant to the case at hand, we shall focus on the former two.

Each type of polemical encounter employs specific rhetorical moves and aims at a different goal. Polemicists engaged in a discussion tend to provide factual proofs in order to convince the opponent and reach the objective truth. Disputants would rather resort to techniques intended to destroy the opponent, embarrass them, leave them speechless, or otherwise prevent them from defending their position any further. Such manipulation aims at victory, proving to the audience that the opponent is wrong, untrustworthy, evil, or simply ignorant. Finally, controversy is also associated with arguments that appeal to emotion rather than reason, however their ultimate aim is to persuade and convince the audience. Arguments may therefore appeal to shared fears or lingering stereotypes or provide premises that compel the audience to draw desirable conclusions.

When employing these three types to analyse religious polemics, Dascal argues that application of a given rhetorical strategy depends (among other things) on the religious divide between the disputants. Thus, if one classifies religious polemics as either intra-faith (between members of the same religion), inter-faith (between adherents of different religions) or extra-faith (polemics in which one of the parties does not subscribe to any religion), one is likely to find that this categorisation tends to parallel the tripartite typology outlined above.

This classification allows one to describe and understand the shift between the two parts of *Jewish Chats.* At first sight, *Jewish Chats* seems like a variation on the classical themes that feature in Christian-Jewish polemics.[3] Although the actors are not the typical *dramatis personae* – that is, not a Jew and a Christian, but a Master and a Student, the latter is in fact a mouthpiece for the Jews. The flow of argument does not divert much from the traditional ancient and medieval discourse. The Student opens by recalling how the Jews boast about their status as the chosen people, their certainty of a covenant with God, and their devotion to the Law, for which they were ready to be killed. Jewish arguments against Christianity include the criticism of the New Testament, which they held to be a novelty, contravening the sacred, God-given lore. The student complains: "[They criticised us for many reasons:] firstly, that our Christian faith is new and in conflict with their, ancient one" (Czechowic: 1575, 67b). Other anti-Christian charges levelled by the Jews include Christian polytheism and worship of invented deities, as well as the multiplicity of different denominations and heretical ritual practices in churches. Last but not least, the Jews are reported to be spreading blasphemies against Jesus:

> Were that Jesus of yours indeed the promised Messiah, or as you put it, the Son of God, he would not have contradicted God's will but he would have fulfilled it. Thus, he would have kept the divine lore given once through Moses and would never have let go of the books of the Scripture, since this is what God had ordered individually to all of his Messiahs and Kings (Czechowic: 1575, 68b–69a).

The Master's response follows the lead of anti-Jewish polemical tradition too. The rabbinic reading of the Bible is criticised for spiritual blindness that misses the hidden truth and takes literally, symbols, figures, and the true meaning:

> [the Jews] refuse to see in their Torah anything but the letter or, so to speak, the superficial, carnal worship described by Moses; holding on closely to the shadow, they see no body; taking pride in the body, they notice no spirit, which is more worthy of attention (Czechowic: 1575, 83b).

The second pillar on which the Master rests his argument is the contention that Old Testament commandments were not eternal. The observance of the Sabbath holiday is said to have been abolished with the coming of Jesus. Circumcision, a rite concerned with the flesh is finite, temporary and as circumstantial as anything related to bodies. Circumcision is rightly understood as a seal of a contract of Abraham with the Divine, yet the object of the contract was the land of Canaan:

3 For a brief survey of themes and bibliography see Lasker: 2006

> Therefore, one of the reasons why this superficial circumcision of flesh has been invalidated is that God had fulfilled his promise by granting Abraham and his descendants the land [of Canaan], which they, stubborn and unruly [people], lost due to their bad temper (Czechowic: 1575, 74 b).

Since the Jews lost the land and the covenant with God was abrogated, continuing to preserve only its seal – the circumcision of flesh – is pointless.

This tally of examples shows how, despite the fact that both parties claim to derive their arguments from the Bible alone and to buttress them with scriptural proof texts, there is no prospect for agreement. The interpretation of the scriptural data brings the Master and "the Jews" to different conclusions, because both exegeses are rooted in separate traditions and are a part of two incongruent worldviews. This results in both parties resorting to irrational accusations: the Jews, as the Student reports, shout and interrupt ("[they would not let me speak,] talking themselves, yelling in unorderly fashion, mixing earth with heaven, they shout and refuse to hear out anyone, even if he was to speak words of gold" Czechowic: 1575, 68a); the Master on his part calls them "stupid, blind, and stubborn in their mistaken ways" (Czechowic: 1575, 129a). The author of the text ensured that the ideological divide between the opposed sides is presented as clearly as possible. Since the text is directed to a very specific readership, the community of the Polish Brethren whose ideology is represented by the Master, this initial arrangement seems calculated to bring a result. The author of the polemic sets the roles of the *dramatis personae:* the Jews, who dismiss the Christian belief system and ways of reasoning from the outset, play the role of a villain who is destined to lose the argument. We are therefore presented with a classic example of a dispute between two religions.

However, the latter part of the polemic is transformed; to use Dascalian terminology, the dispute turns into an intra-faith discussion. The change in the character of the polemic is distinguishable by the modification of style, the attention given to different themes, and, indeed, by the apparent metamorphosis of the interlocutors taking part in the discussion. To begin with, the subjects change. The questions that the Student asks aim now to establish how Christian theological difficulties should be dealt with. Thus, the Student asks the Master to expound on the nature of Jesus:

> You certainly have no doubts that there is only God [who] is the Lord of heavens and earth, because only He is the Creator of all, the Lord, and the Maker. Then your Jesus, being only a human, cannot be the Lord of heavens, since he did not create it. Making him the Lord in heavens, not only do you create two gods, but you also deny God, refusing His rule over you (Czechowic: 1575, 123a).

The Student also quotes the puzzling question of the Incarnation, and undermines the authority of the New Testament by showing its internal contradictions:

> Thus say the Jews (...): if Joseph, Mary's husband, was not Jesus' father, how can then Jesus be a true descendant of David, given that your Gospels do not trace his lineage to Mary's [ancestors] but to Joseph's (Czechowic: 1575, 145b).

Even more à propos is another purportedly Jewish argument brought up by the Student:

> They take the words "The Holy Ghost shall come upon thee'"(Lk 1.35) and verse 31 "behold, thou shalt conceive in thy womb" and say that it means "into your womb you shall allow the Son of God, the eternal and holy spirit, who spoke to the forefathers" (...) and they add that one cannot allow in anything what has not existed before, so the maiden could not have conceived a son if the son had not existed beforehand. And they add for support Matt 1:18: "When as his mother Mary was espoused to Joseph, before they came together, she was found with child of the Holy Ghost". (...) Doing so, they stretch [the meaning of] the word *ex* or *ek* (of), as in "of the Holy Ghost" trying to support their entire argument [about the pre-existence of Jesus] on the claim that nothing could exist if it did not originate from something – *ex*, that is, out of something, and they wish to understand *ex* to be the Holy Ghost, that eternal, pre-existing Son of God from whom Jesus is supposed to have been born (Czechowic: 1575,156 b).

This "Jewish" argument aims at demonstrating that the Son of God existed before the birth of Jesus, who was an incarnation of an eternal divine person. It is hard to imagine that an adherent of the Mosaic faith would be preoccupied with demonstrating the pre-existence of Jesus. Evidently these questions do not reflect views of the Jewish polemicist, but rather address the issues that constituted the main source of discord at the early Arian synods.

Not only do the Student's questions change, but the difference between the two parts of *Jewish Chats* is also discernible in the style of answers that the Master gives. To begin with, the Master's argument appeals much less to stereotypes and emotions, and is contingent on objectively verifiable proof texts. He focuses on providing abundant evidence from Scripture and other external sources. For example, when discussing the Virgin Birth, or the pre-existence of Jesus (which he denies), he provides a detailed etymological analysis of biblical terms in the original languages, Hebrew and Greek, to legitimise his exegesis.

Secondly, the Master supports his point with a variety of source material. He employs Jewish texts, such as the Talmud, Rabbinic commentaries, and Midrash, but also a variety of Christian texts, including the Epistles and Gospels (in Greek and Latin translation), and the commentaries of a contemporary French Humanist, François Vatable. Apparently, Czechowic's Master assumes that his interlocutor is familiar with the Christian Hebraist's library. Yet, if the Master's interlocutor were a Jew, as we were earlier told, then Czechowic's buttressing his point with Christian texts would have to fail as a rhetorical strategy.

The shift in the polemical style discernible through close reading of *Jewish Talks* also begs for closer examination. Application of the theoretical model proposed by Dascal helps to pinpoint precisely how the change in types of arguments and the shift in polemical goals occurs in the course of *Jewish Chats.* The tactical shift between the first and the second part of Jewish Chats marks a two-fold change. First, from a disputation, that is, a verbal contest that aims at deriding the opponent, the polemic turns now into a discussion, which is designed to win over the interlocutor (and the audience) by providing them with objective, convincing evidence. Secondly, an inter-faith encounter between a Christian-Arian theologian and a stereotypical Jew, whose stance is recounted by the Student, is replaced by an intra-faith exchange. The new opponent comes from the same exegetical tradition, but seems to be holding radical, and, according to the Master's standards, mistaken and heretical views that can be classified as "Judaising". In other words, Czechowic's Master takes issue no longer with the Jews, as he did in the first part of the polemic, but with "new, uncircumcised Jews" (Czechowic: 1575, 148a): ideologues of the Arian movement who would oppose Czechowic's views.

The fact that *Christian Discussions*, including *Jewish Chats*, was directed against radical Arian ideologues has been suggested beforehand. What has not been analysed is Czechowic's skilful deployal of the traditionally Christian genre of an anti-Jewish polemic, as well as his use of the character of the Jew – the ultimate Other – to conduct this intra-faith dispute. Through conflating the Jewish anti-Christian arguments of the first part of the *Jewish Chats* with the ideology of his Arian opponents in the second part, Czechowic makes use of lingering anti-Jewish prejudice in order to discredit his opponents.

3.2 *Odpis:* Creating Personal Identity and Legitimising Leadership

The second anti-Jewish polemic I discuss here, *Odpis*, although showing obvious affinities to Czechowic's earlier work, also reveals significant differences, both in form and in its cultural meaning.

In the introduction to the work, Czechowic declares that the main purpose of the text is threefold: to convince the Jew he talks to (if such be the will of God), to teach true Christianity, and last but not least, to protect simpletons who are in danger of being convinced by the Jews. Czechowic declares:

> I used his [Jacob's] writing against me in order to serve God's glory and Christ; to convince and, if such is God's will, to gain this Jew and others; to give testimony to our true Christian devotion [derived] from the Scripture; to save the fearful and labile simpletons from the many sneaky and deceptive New Jews and to keep them [the simpletons] in the true Christian faith (Czechowic: 1581, 4).

Even though the intended audience and the polemical agenda of the two anti-Jewish polemics authored by the Arian theologian are similar, the rhetorical strategy used is different in each of the texts.

To begin with, the choice and organisation of subjects differs significantly. The elements of Jewish practice – the authority of the Talmud, celebration of the Sabbath and the ritual of circumcision, which received very little attention in *Jewish Chats*, and gave room to the "Christian" topics – become in *Odpis* the main focus of the discussion. This could be attributed to the genesis of the text, namely to the fact that Czechowic has "dramatised" a letter of his Rabbi–friend, and so the thematic order was imposed on him. This would not be the first time Czechowic had done his. Such a strategy informed the structure of one of his first works, a short text entitled *Votum ... on baptising babies* (*Wotum ... na pytanie, jeśli grzech niemowiątka krzcić albo nie*). The text was composed in the immediate context of a discussion on infant baptism that took place at a synod in Vilnius on 26–27 January 1564. As the title suggests, *Votum* is Czechowic's reaction to a text composed by an Arian minister, Wędrogowski. It outlined his criticism of infant baptism and was distributed among co-believers. The pamphlet, dubbed by Czechowic as Wędrogowski's *votum* (i.e. declaration), was meant not only to explain the author's stance on the matter, but also, to disprove his opponents' position. Given its belligerent tone, as well as its political importance, Czechowic felt obliged to respond. Czechowic's work was therefore an rearrangement of competing views into a conversational format (as Czechowic puts it: "you should know, Reader, that this *Votum* is to be found in full, but was divided into parts for the sake of Marcin's response"). In this sense, *Votum* as a literary composition serves a paradigm for the later *Odpis*.

However, one needs to remember that unlike Wędrogowski's open and widely-distributed declaration, Rabbi Jacob's letter was a piece of personal correspondence, whose content was known only to the sender and to the addressee. Czechowic's role as the ultimate author and editor of the original letter therefore remains undeniable.

The second difference, which one can see from a casual inspection of the book, is the amount and the type of texts quoted. Apart from the Jewish Bible, an unquestionable authority recognised by both parties, Czechowic refers to the Targumim (Aramaic translations of the Bible), Midrash collections, and major Rabbinic commentaries. He mentions (and condemns) Jewish anti-Christian compositions such as *Toldot Yeshu* (a Jewish satirical rewriting of the Gospels) or the *Nizzachon* texts (anti-Christian polemical handbooks). He knows of *Sefer ha-Kuzari* by Yehuda ha-Levi, and feels at ease quoting Talmudic stories (for example, he devotes much room to the Bar-Temalion story, which he takes to be a proof-text for the satanic origin of Jewish commandments. Cf. Akhiezer: 2006, 457). Last but not least, he conducts detailed grammatical analyses of the Hebrew terms, and in one place he even goes as far as to show off knowledge of cantillation signs and their function in the text:

> The prophecy in chapter 2 (Hos 2:13) reads והשבתי כל משושה חגה חדשה ושבתה וכל מועדה -Wehiszbbati kal meszoszah [sic] chagach, weszabbatta wekol mohadah -That is: "I cause all his joy to cease'" and here there is a division. [This is] because there is a double line that you call זקף קטון zakoph katon above ש in the word משושה meszoszah (Czechowic: 1581, 219).

Unlike in the second part of the *Jewish Chats*, *Odpis* contains almost no references to the Christian canon.

Thirdly, not only the quantity, but also the style of the references to Jewish literature is worth noticing. Almost all of the above-mentioned texts are quoted in three languages. Czechowic inserts citations in Hebrew, appends each quotation with a transliteration according to the Polish phonetic system, and finally provides his readers with a translation into Polish. Parenthetically, this approach to quoting must have been useful for the "Arian simpletons" who read Czechowic's work, but it is even more helpful to a contemporary reader interested in the sources which Czechowic made use of when composing his work. In fact, inconsistency in transliteration, cases of misreading, spelling mistakes, and other errors leave one rather underwhelmed.

Finally, Czechowic also exhibits knowledge of Jewish ritual practices. This comes across in his repeated criticisms of the traditional observance of holidays, which he holds are unbiblical. He makes references to Jewish language practices (such as the use of "*hay Adonai*" expression – a customary oath, which he finds blasphemous[4]), and discredits Jewish folk beliefs. Interestingly, he also disparages popular Christian anti-Jewish myths, such as the blood libel and desecration of the host:

> [...] regarding blood, which all Jews need: I would not know for what kind of purification [would they use it], the same concerns the Papists' wafer – I do not believe in that. It is a mistake and fabrication (Czechowic: 1581, 133).

Perhaps the most interesting aspect of this anti-Jewish polemic is that despite his heavy emphasis on Jewish literature, Czechowic's actual knowledge of the Hebrew language was rather limited. Although he spent a year in Leipzig, where he took a course in Hebrew, this was apparently not enough to enable him to read primary sources independently. In fact, as noted above in passim, his Hebrew passages contain mistakes that reveal that his expertise was not as extensive as he would like us to believe.[5] Moreover, not only his Hebrew quotations, but also his

4 For Christian mocking of the expression Hay Adonay (rendered as caiadonai) in Italy see Harrán: 2008, 427–463.

5 Rosenthal discussed Czechowic's most conspicuous mistake, where Czechowic misquotes a

analysis of Talmudic fragments are taken from works by Latin Hebraists, often verbatim. For example, both Czechowic's comprehensive lecture on the structure of the Talmud, as well as his rendering of the story of Bar-Temalion are taken from the work of an Italian Hebraist, Pietro Colonna Galatino (1460–1540).[6] At times marginal notes point to the texts he had gathered information from, but in most cases he does not reference his sources.

Let us recall that in the introduction Czechowic declares that the main purpose of the text is to protect simpletons who are in danger of being convinced by the Jews, and to teach true Christianity. The main target readership is therefore the Arian community, and the goal is Arian apologetic and polemic with any non-Arian creed and praxis. Given that the text is meant to serve the Arian reader, and in particular, the simple-minded adherents of the Arian doctrine, and that quoting Hebrew did not, most probably, come effortlessly to him, this analysis begs the question: Why is Czechowic so preoccupied with proving his familiarity with Jewish tradition? Why is it so important to him that he even gives quotes in Hebrew?

I argue that this display of knowledge of Judaism, Jewish literature, and Jewish customs was part of a conscious strategy of creating his own persona, and perhaps even a sixteenth-century version of a leadership campaign.

When approaching the interrelation of a literary text, especially one in which the author presents himself as one of the *dramatis personae*, and the intellectual biography of the author in question, it is helpful to consider Paul Ricoeur's investigation into the "narrative unity of personal life". Ricoeur proposes looking into the way personal identity is construed and expressed through narrative. His proposition comprises three postulates. Firstly, he advocates shifting attention from a nominalised way of understanding the self, that is through the use of the pronoun "I", to a reflexive understanding, wherein the "I" becomes an object of a noun (in the original French the difference is between the nominal "je" and reflexive "se" or "soi").

His second postulate is to resolve a difficulty posed by the ambiguity inherent in the definition of the term identity, or the self. Ricoeur observes that the Western philosophical tradition offers two conflicting definitions. The first understanding stems from the Cartesian cogito, and it begets a concept of identity that Ricoeur calls "selfhood" or *ipse-self.* According to this tradition, personal identity is not linked to an unchangeable core, but is recreated time and again through one's actions. In other words, the meaning of "I" can be captured in an

---

Talmudic verse and merges two statements into one, which leads to mis-translation. Cf. Rosenthal: 1966, 89–90.

6 Cf. Galatino: 1561, 419. The Christian Hebraist works of which Czechowic availed himself, as well as his linguistic studies, will be discussed in my forthcoming article.

answer to a context-dependent question *who (did x)?* The second conception of the self originates in philosophical tradition that broke away from Cartesian ontology and is epitomised in the thought of Friedrich Nietzsche. According to this school of thought, the self is a coherent, consistent set of characteristics over time, which Ricoeur calls the *idem-self*, or "sameness". The character of the self is therefore discernible through the analysis of what the self consists of, and what it is like, rather than what it does. Marrying the two conceptions of the self, Ricoeur defines personal identity as essentially a narrative attestation: "narrative constructs the identity of the character, what can be called his or her narrative identity, in constructing that of the story told. It is the identity of the story that makes the identity of the character" (Ricoeur: 147–148).

In other words, the act of self-narration is indispensable for building one's personal identity (which comprises both the ipse- and the idem-selves). This narration can be accomplished in the presence of and dialectical relation with the (narrative) other. Thus, Ricoeur posits the third postulate on which rests his hermeneutics of the self, which is also verbalised in the maxim-like title Ricoeur gave to his work: *Oneself as Another.* The conjunction "as", explains the author, assumes the role of both a comparison marker (like its function in the phrase "bright as the Sun") and of an expression of implication (meaning "inasmuch as").

When applied to the reading of *Odpis*, this theoretical framework enables us to uncover another stratum of Czechowic's work. Arguably, Czechowic used an epistolary conversation, in which one of the characters bears his name, in order to present (and indeed, create) a very particular self-portrait. His literary persona emerges through comparison with the "other" – a Jew, but is also created (or unveiled) in the process of conversation.

In his first major work, *A three days conversation*, Czechowic puts in the mouth of a Christian (with whom he identifies himself) the following assertion:

> There are some who say, and mostly in front of ignoramuses and simpletons, that all other books are worthless except for the Bible, but even about it (the Bible), they care little. They do so in a subtle fashion, as they have found an excuse for their carelessness and for their lack of enthusiasm to study. However, no matter how much people were to stray in their writing, a diligent reader may find in their writing something that will comfort him and will make him more prudent. Thus indeed Augustine and Jerome did, when they instructed the reading of heretical books and confessed that they too had read them. Thistle, nettle, and datura are all evil and poisonous herbs, and yet a bee makes good honey out of them, by using what is good and leaving out what is bad. A true and diligent teacher should do likewise. Especially, holding always onto the Bible as a yardstick, he should read these and those and reason by God's Word whether they write correctly or wrongly. Not like many, who disdain books: a Papist – the books of a Lutheran, and a Lutheran together with the Papist – ours. They close in front of

> themselves the gates to knowing God and they have contempt for God's gifts and the means by which he admonishes them (Czechowic: 1578 b, 29–30).

One's true wisdom can therefore be strengthened, despite, or perhaps, precisely through, reading one's opponents' writings. It seems that the effort made in showing his familiarity with Jewish texts is an implementation of this principle. Czechowic has no doubt that his understanding of the divine truth originates in divine inspiration:

> The Lord God willed, in His fatherly grace, to show me alone, [chosen from] amongst many others and greater ones, Antichristian errors; to lead me away from His deadly trial; and to grant me the salutary knowledge of His Son, Jesus (Czechowic: 1575, iv a-b).

His engagement with Judaism can only "produce honey out of poisonous herbs". His faith is so well-grounded that he is able to use Jewish texts in a disputation in order to convince those who consider them valuable (be it real Jews or "Judaising" radical Arians) yet without jeopardising his own belief. In this way, Czechowic fashions himself as a true Christian and an inspired exegete, whose knowledge is a result of epiphany, as well as a skilled, bold polemicist.

To answer why enhancing his self-portrait would be so important to Czechowic, one needs to consider the socio-historical context in which *Odpis* was conceived. Having rejected the authority of the well-established Church hierarchies, the Radical Reformers, and the Arians among them, renounced what had been the prevalent type of authority. Now, knowledge and charisma became the core qualities of the leader, and their display a way of claiming such leadership. The traditional sociological model of authority proposed by Max Weber distinguished three ideal types: traditional, charismatic, and legal-rational (Weber: 1968). In other words, he defined legitimacy as a belief that those in the position of power are rightly elevated. The bases of such conviction are rooted either in a shared will to preserve traditional power structures, in appreciation of the given leader's personal traits, or in the position that he or she was entrusted. Since Weber's theory, the concept of legitimacy has been stirring discussions and controversies in generations of social scientists. As François Bourricaud ironically observed, "Ideologists fluctuate between an obsession with legitimacy and the cynical thesis that there is no such thing as legitimacy" (Bourricaud: 1987, 57). Consequently, scholarly attention has shifted to a related concept of legitimisation, understood as continuous human action rather than an acquired characteristic. "What characterises government, in other words, is not the possession of a quality defined as legitimacy, but the claiming [of it] the activity of legitimation", explains Rodney Baker (Baker: 2001, 14). Baker denounces legitimacy as a fiction, a metaphor that is irrelevant to describe any government and serves exclusively as a normative description of authorities (that is, in a discussion about whether a given leader and his decision are justified or not). On the other hand, the notion of legitimation presents itself as a valuable analytical tool in any empirical research enquiring into the character of government – be it sociological, or be it historical. Conceived of this way, legitimation is an active, politically charged form of communication, carried out on a regular basis by any ruler. It takes many forms and is akin to what Goffman described as presentation of self (Goffman: 1959). Accordingly, legitimation is an ongoing performance that aims at and results in the creation and validation of the leader's personal identity. This process is possible through the leader's identification with a set of desired values that are at the same time held in high esteem by the community who play the role of both the audience and the judges of the performance.

Ostensibly, Czechowic's fashioning himself as a biblical scholar and a fine polemicist is not only a response to Rabbi Jacob's critique of his earlier work, but has a deeper, inward-looking dimension to it. Since legitimisation of political leadership and creation of identity through literary creation are two inseparable sides of one coin and since both can be achieved in a process of self-narration, Czechowic's polemic with the Jew becomes a tool for constructing a self-portrait, something which can be seen at the same time as a way to validate and legitimise his charismatic authority.

4. Conclusions

This paper has aimed to shed light on two texts that can be classified as Christian–Jewish polemics. Even though anti-Jewish rhetoric and literature has had a long and well-established place in Christian apologetic discourse, Arian literature typically did not engage itself with conducting polemics with the representatives of the Mosaic faith. Czechowic's two texts are conspicuous exceptions.

However, a closer examination of the two polemics revealed that the Jews were not the target of Czechowic's writings. The use of anti-Jewish literature for internal reasons is not unprecedented. Composing an anti-Jewish polemic with the aim of disparaging errors of co-believers is a phenomenon known from the earliest days of Christianity. The two anti-Jewish polemics authored by Czechowic deserve attention since they represent the variety of goals that can be achieved by the use of a traditional Christian genre.

The first text, *Jewish Chats*, was composed at a time when the most urgent task that the leaders of the Arian movement faced was to establish unified doctrine. *Jewish Chats* is a part of a catechism, written in order to provide a unified stance on ideological matters for the young, diverse, uncoordinated movement in the making. Czechowic was acting as a representative of the mainstream of the Arian Church, and thus one of his primary goals was to discredit the extreme tendencies within the movement.

Odpis was composed at a time when the movement's ideology was more consolidated,[7] yet Czechowic had begun to lose the relatively strong position he had enjoyed until then. In fact a few years after *Odpis* was composed, Czechowic lost the position he was holding, to a new arrival on the Arian stage – Fausto Sozzini. Sozzini was an Italian theologian, the nephew, student and continuator of the teaching of another great thinker and Hebraist, Lelio (Laelius) Sozzini. Fleeing the danger of religious persecutions, Fausto Sozzini left Italy and eventually settled down in Cracow in 1579, two years before *Odpis* was published (George Williams, one of the foremost historians of the Reformation, considers this date epochal for Polish Arianism, calling it "the advent of Sozzini"; cf. Williams: 1962, 746).

In *Jewish Chats*, the polemical use of a Jew as a symbol of difference within the Arian community and the intra-faith disputation between a Christian and a Jew therefore becomes the framework for an inter-faith dispute between two streams of Arian thought. Anti-Jewish polemic as a genre offered a way to disparage opponents' arguments by presenting them as "Jewish". Anti-Jewish polemic was therefore a tool for promoting the desired version of Arian Christianity, and for moulding the group identity of the young Church.

I therefore propose that Czechowic's goal of using the genre of anti-Jewish polemic in *Odpis* was more personal. One of the reasons why he made such a great effort to convince the readers of his familiarity with the ways of Jews, even though his actual knowledge of Hebrew was very limited, was his self-promotion as a Christian Hebraist. In *Odpis*, he depicts himself as a scholar who is as knowledgeable about Judaism as the Jews themselves, if not more so.

Although a sixteenth-century Polish reader could avail themselves of anti-Jewish polemic published in his or her native language, such texts were in most cases translations of Western-European anti-Jewish literature. The two polemics conceived by Czechowic and discussed here therefore constitute two rare, original specimens of the genre. Their value for scholarship is twofold. On the one hand, they show how the Arian discourse, although considered heretical and foreign to Catholic propaganda, followed the well-trodden path of Christian use of the "hermeneutical Jew" for their own internal purposes. On the other hand, given their inward-looking agenda, which is disguised by the literary form of inter-faith disputations, they offer an invaluable insight into the methods that the Arian leader used to forge Arian identity. This makes them potent and fascinating objects of research.

7 As a result of the Lusławice agreement in 1575–1578, the ditheists joined the Unitarian camp, accepting its ideology. Cf. Wajsblum: 1928, 52–53; Urban: 1956, 109.

Bibliography

AKHIEZER, GOLDA (2006), The Karaite Isaac ben Abraham of Troki and his Polemics against Rabbanites, in: Daniel J. Lasker/Matt Goldish/Boaz Huss/Chanita Goldblatt (eds.), Tradition, Heterodoxy and Religious Culture: Judaism and Christianity in the Early Modern Period, Beer-Sheva: Ben Gurion University of the Negev, 437–468.

BAKER, RODNEY (2001), Legitimating Identities, New York: Cambridge University Press.

BOURRICAUD, FRANÇOIS (1987), Legitimacy and Legitimization, Current Sociology 35, 57–67.

CZECHOWIC, MARCIN (1581), Odpis Jakuba Żyda z Bełżyc na dyjalogi Marcina Czechowica, na który zaś odpowieda Jakubowi Żydowi tenże Marcin Czechowic, Cracow: Aleksy Rodecki.

– (1575), Rozmowy christianskie, które z greckiego nazwiska dialogami zowią, a ty je nazwać możesz wielkim katechizmem, w których są rozmaite gadania o przedniejszych artykułach wiary christiańskiej, Cracow: Aleksy Rodecki.

– (1578a), Trzech dni rozmowa o niektórych artykułach tych czasów wzruszonych, a zwlaszcza o nurzaniu niemowiątek, w której się wiele potrzebnych rzeczy (nie jedno k temu sakramentowi, ale i ku innem sprawam należących) z Pisma Ś. a and to z dawnych teologów i z rozmaitych autorow przywodzi i rozbiera, Wieliczka: Jan Karcan.

– (1578b), Wotum, albo zdanie ministra zboru wileńskiego Mikołaja Wędrogowskiego na pytanie: Jeśli grzech niemowiątka krzcić albo nie? Przestroga na to Wędrogowskiego Wotum Marcina Czechowicza, Wieliczka: Jan Karcan.

DASCAL, MARCELO (2004), On the Uses of Argumentative Reason in Religious Polemics, in: Theo L. Hettema/Arie van der Kooij (eds.), Religious Polemics in Context, Assen: Royan Van Gorcum, 3–20.

GALATINO, PETRUS COLONNA (1561), Opus toti christianae reipublicae maxime utile, de arcanis catholicae veritatis, contra obstinatissimam Iudaeorum nostrae tempestatis perfidiam. Ex Talmud, aliisque Hebraicis libris nuper excerptum: et quadruplici linguarum genere eleganter congestum, Basel: Hieronymus Suncinus.

GOFFMAN, ERVING (1959), The Presentation of Self in Everyday Life, Garden City, NY: Anchor.

HARRÁN, DON (2008), "Adonai con voi" (1569), a Simple Popular Song with a Complicated Semantic about (What Seems to Be) Circumcision, in: Maria Diemling/Giuseppe Veltri (eds.), The Jewish Body: Corporeality, Society, and Identity in the Renaissance and Early Modern Period, Leiden: Brill, 427–463.

LASKER, DANIEL J. (2006), Jewish Anti-Christian Polemics in the Early Modern Period: Change or Continuity? in: Chanita Goldblatt/Howard Kreisel (eds.), Tradition, Heterodoxy and Religious Culture: Judaism and Christianity in the Early Modern Period, Beer Sheva: Ben Gurion University of the Negev, 469–488.

NIRENBERG, DAVID (2013), Anti-Judaism: The Western Tradition, New York/London: W.W. Norton & Company.

OGONOWSKI, ZBIGNIEW (1960), Socynanism polski. Warsaw: Wiedza Powszechna.

RICOEUR, PAUL (1992), Oneself As Another. Chicago: The University of Chicago Press.

ROSENTHAL, JUDAH M. (1966), Marcin Czechowic and Jacob of Bełżyce: Arian-Jewish Encounters in 16th-Century Poland, American Academy for Jewish Research, Proceedings of the American Academy for Jewish Research 34, 77–97.

Ruether, Rosemary Radford (1974), Anti-Judaism is the Left Hand of Christology, New Catholic World, 217, 12–17.

Szczucki, Lech (1964), Marcin Czechowic 1532–1613. Studium z dziejów antytrynitaryzmu polskiego XVI wieku, Warsaw: Państwowe Wydawnictwo Naukowe.

– (1993), Nonkonformiści religijni XVI i XVII wieku: Studia i szkice, Warsaw: Polska Akademia Nauk. Instytut Filozofii i Socjologii.

– (1986), Szymona Budnego relacja o początkach i rozwoju anabaptyzmu w zborze mniejszym, Odrodzenie i Reformacja w Polsce, 31, 93–109.

Urban, Wacław (1956), Losy braci polskich od założenia Rakowa do wygnania z Polski, Odrodzenie i Reformacja w Polsce 1, 103–139.

Wajsblum, Marek (1928), Dyteiści małopolscy, Reformacja w Polsce 5, 32–97.

Wilbur, Earl Morse (1953), Our Unitarian Heritage. An Introduction to the History of the Unitarian Movement. Boston, MA: Beacon Press.

Wilczek, Piotr (1994), Erazm Otwinowski: Pisarz ariański, Warsaw: Gnome books.

– (2007), Polonice et Latine: Studia o literaturze staropolskiej. Katowice: Wydawnictwo Uniwersytetu Śląskiego.

Williams, George H. (1962), The Radical Reformation. Philadelphia, PA: The Westminster Press.

Weber, Max (1968), Economy and Society: an Outline of Interpretive Sociology. New York: Bedminster Press.

Joanna Partyka

British Protestants and Women's Freedom to Write

Scholars who are interested in women's literacy and their role in the culture of the sixteenth and seventeenth centuries observe that in Britain then:

> for the first time significant numbers of women from diverse social ranks were able to read. A small proportion of them also began to write and publish, more than 300 authors producing over 800 first editions (Wheale: 2005, 110).

The aim of this paper is to connect this interesting phenomenon to the Puritan tradition of journal-keeping and to the Quaker movement which was open to female preachers. The spiritual diary played an important role in self-examination. Indeed, manuals instructing on how to write such a diary were also addressed to women. Quaker women were obliged to write down their prophetic judgments. It seems that some of these women made use of that concession to write in order to create literature. To show this I will mention, among others, Lucy Hutchinson, Anne Dudley Bradstreet (both Puritans), Lady Anne Clifford, Lady Margaret Hoby, the oldest known British female diary-keeper, Margaret Fell, the "mother of Quakerism", and the first woman to become a Quaker minister, Elisabeth Hooton.

Women were not always allowed to write, although there always were the proverbial exceptions confirming the rule. Despite many barriers and male prejudices, as well as thwarted access to knowledge which often prevented active participation in culture, there were female authors to be found in various European countries already in the Middle Ages. It seems that throughout the centuries the difference between "male" and "female" writing consisted primarily in that women's literature aroused amazement and objections even if it was by no means of any distinction. It was interpreted as a manifestation of revolt against the recognised norms. A woman who took to writing, for whatever reason, resolved to exit the territory meant for a wife and a mother. Juan Luis Vives (1492–1540), the author of the first pedagogical work providing a detailed plan of education for girls, *De institutione feminae christianae* (1523), did not consider it essential to teach them how to write, although he did suggest that women should know Greek and Latin in order to be able to read in those languages. He says: "When she is taught to read, let her peruse books that impart instruction in morals; when she learns to write, do not have her imitate idle verses or vain and frivolous ditties [...] " (Vives: 2000, 71). The Spanish humanist was a tutor in the service of the Queen of England, Catherine of Aragon, as the preceptor of her daughter Mary. To Vives, an educated woman meant a loving mother involved in the education of her daughters, and an obedient wife constantly busying herself around the home and the household, under no circumstances engaging in public affairs. As he observes:

> If she is a good woman, it is best that she stay at home and be unknown to others. In company it is befitting that she be retiring and silent, with her eyes cast down so that some perhaps may see her, but none will hear her (Vives: 2000,72).

The reading of ancient authors was intended to serve self-improvement, whereas the reading of Scripture and the writings of the Fathers of the Church, even in the original, was to teach women a proper religious attitude, and the reading of housekeeping and child-raising manuals to teach them to be good and thrifty housewives and careful mothers. Thomas More (1478–1535), Vives' contemporary and friend, believed that education was to ensure spiritual autonomy for women, develop their ability to make independent decisions and distinguish between good and evil. Pamela Joseph Benson writes,

> [More] was a profeminist educator who gave his female students spiritual and ethical autonomy which the hierarchy of marriage did not require them to sacrifice or compromise. More was an anomaly among Renaissance educators because he did not place woman in a dilemma (Benson: 2010, 158).

However, More's Latin poem which reflects his opinion on female education – *Versus iambici dimetri brachycatalectici ad Candidum, qualis uxor deligenda* (To Candidus: How to choose a wife. A Poem in Iambic Dimeter Brachycatalectic) – is quite paradoxical. As Cousins suggests,

> [...] the association between female education and women's domestic confinement was confirmed by More with an emphasis quite distinct from either Erasmus or Vives, and one suggesting that the allegedly ideal woman's contribution to the common weal will in most cases be of very private significance: the female humanist, in fact, as perfect *mulier economica* (Cousins: 2009, 81).

The Protestant Richard Mulcaster wrote in the treatise *Positions Concerning the Training up of Children* (London, 1581) that young English women should follow a specially prepared curriculum aimed at making them "read plainly and distinctly" as well as "write faire and swiftly":

> And is not a young gentlewoman, thinke you, thoroughly furnished, which can reade plainly and distinctly, write faire and swiftly, sing cleare and sweetely, play wel and

> finely, understand and speake the learned languages, and those toungues also which [182] the time most embraseth, with some Logicall helpe to chop, and some Rhetoricke to brave. Besides the matter which is gathered, while these toungues be either learned, or lookt on, as wordes must have seates, no lesse then rayment bodies. Were it any argument of an unfurnished maiden, besides these qualities to draw cleane in good proportion, and with good symmetrie? Now if she be an honest woman, and a good housewife to, were she not worth the wishing, and worthy the shryning? and yet such there be, and such we know" (Mulcaster: 1994, 181–182).

In the Catholic Europe of the sixteenth and seventeenth centuries, future queens, ladies-in-waiting and nuns of certain monastic orders were allowed to acquire education. A convent was one of few places where women learned not only to read, but also to write, frequently also in Latin. Books were put in their hands in order to make it easier for them to pray and form a religious attitude. This constant presence of the book in nuns' life made it habitual for them to make use of the written word, and sometimes induced them to reach for the pen. Certain monastic rules actually required the nuns to master the art of writing. As a result, in Catholic countries, both in the Middle Ages and in modern times, monasteries were a place where women could nurture their literary talents, which may be interpreted as a form of freedom. What is more, in a convent women had an opportunity to gain a kind of social identity. Women who did not feel free in the family – since they were subject to various restrictions on the part of their fathers, brothers, husbands, and even sons – had an opportunity, paradoxically, to get a taste of freedom behind the walls of a convent, which was always associated – today perhaps even more than in the seventeenth century – with closure, isolation, separation from the world. The dissolution of the monasteries by Henry VIII (1535–1540) not only significantly affected economic life in England and the English landscape, but also the lives of religious women. It resulted in the disappearance of the monastic environment, where women could count on a special type of freedom, the freedom to write (although it should be emphasised that in England female orders were totally subordinated to male authority and did not offer such opportunities as in Italy, France or Spain). It is symptomatic, for example, that in the seventeenth century many female religious writers in the Iberian Peninsula, if not the overwhelming majority of them, were involved in creative activities behind the cloister walls. Some of them went there with their talents already formed, others did not have such ambitions at the beginning, but were trained in writing skills (sometimes virtually drilled) by their confessors, in accordance with the Council of Trent's recommendations for nuns to write their autobiographies. Therefore, they were frequently set to writing under force, although with time, when they reached a certain level of skill, this occupation ceased to be a mere duty. Today's researchers are most interested in exactly what did not arise from duty and what therefore may be evidence of female aspirations for freedom. Whether it was autobiographical notes or religious poetry, the writing nuns smuggled their own feelings and intuitions, their own perception of the world, in these texts written to order. And so, paradoxically, in convents women were allowed to break the fetters of silence they were doomed to obey according to Scripture and the Church Fathers. Some of them entered the space traditionally reserved for men, writing treatises, encyclopaedias or composing exquisite classical poems in the "male language", i. e. in Latin. Upon the emergence of Protestantism in England, freedom to write was gained by lay, mostly Puritan and Quaker women, and therefore the circle of female writers was greatly expanded. The ability to write became a virtue, and even a necessity.

Puritan religosity imposed on both men and women the duty of spiritual self-improvement, at the same time offering an instrument facilitating self-examination and self-control. This was a systematically kept spiritual journal which enabled the examination of the soul and the correction of subsequent behaviour in accordance with the divine commandments and recommendations. Detailed instructions were published in England in the mid-seventeenth century on what a spiritual diary was to look like. John Beadle's (1595–1667) *The Journal or Diary of a Thankful Christian* was published in 1656, and a similar instruction entitled *Prima, the First Things in Reference to the Middle & Last Things* had been written earlier, in 1654, by Isaac Ambrose (1604–1664), and published in 1674, ten years after the author's death, in the collection of *Complete Works.* This manual of Beadle, an Essex minister, has 184 pages, and is divided into eight chapters, which explain the benefits of keeping a diary and provide detailed guidelines on how such a diary is to be kept. In the introduction "To the Reader" Beadle explains the importance of keeping a spiritual journal:

> We have our State Diurnals, relating the National affairs. Tradesmen keep their shop books. Merchants their Accompt books. Lawyers have their books of presidents. Physitians their Experiments. Some wary husbands have kept a Diary of dayly disbursements. Travellers a Journall of all they have seen, and hath befallen them in their way. A Christian that would be exact hath more need, and may reap much more good by such a Journall as this. We are all but Stewards, Factors here, and must give a strict account in that great day to the high Lord of all our wayes, and of all his wayes towards us (Beadle: 1656, b^{v}).

As Murray observes,

> […] Beadle's instructional manual helped to popularize the already well-known practice of diary-writing among every level of the faithful and also to emphasize it as an important component of Puritan spirituality and Christian devotion […]. The Puritan diary or a "Register-book for conscience", as Beadle calls it, […] was used as a confessional vehicle or more specifically as a replacement for the Catholic sacrament of auricular confession which had given pre-Reformation generations a spoken assurance of forgiveness (Murray: 2013, xxxv–xxxvii).

A spiritual diary was to serve exclusively the personal needs of the writer. Therefore it could be a place for honest introspection and women scrupulously made use of that fact. What is more:

> Puritanism and gender interacted in dialectical fashion in seventeenth-century England and changed one another significantly as a result of that interaction. Such Puritan strategies as reliance on the experience of the individual, extensive use of literacy, and infusion of spiritual issues into all activities deeply affected women's spirituality and their conventional roles in the community. At the same time, changes in the traditional practices of gender altered the Puritan experience (Willen: 1992, 561).

Here we should add that the spiritual diary was not "the only form of writing that early modern women could pursue without ever having to excuse themselves for doing so" – as Effie Botonaki wrongly argued in her article on English women's spiritual diaries (1999, 4) having forgotten about translations of religious works, e.g. the lives of saints translated by Catholics, which were in demand and which were frequently done by women. Nevertheless, it seems that keeping spiritual diaries was quite popular among British Puritan women. Some of these journals were exclusively devoted to religious life, like that of the Countess of Warwick's diary which "mentions little about anything except prayers and thanks to God" (Macfarlane: 1970, 8), while others provide a real spectrum of everyday women's life.

What did female spiritual diaries look like in practice? Here is a handful of examples. The oldest journal which was meant to help its author to preserve inner discipline comes from the turn of the sixteenth and seventeenth centuries, and belonged to Lady Margaret Hoby (1571–1633). The diary was edited in 1930 by Dorothy M. Meads. In the introduction to the text Meads ascertains,

> Where and how Margaret Dakins acquired her ability to read and write, keep accounts, sing, and play the "alpharion", her knowledge of household and estate management, of surgery and salves, all which her diary shows her to have practiced, there exists no definite indication (Meads: 1930, 5).

We learn from the diary that Hoby spent a majority of her day on visits to church, praying and talking to her chaplain. However she also tended to the garden, kept daily accounts, looked after the kitchen, did needlework, rode on horseback and fished, paid visits and entertained guests, went for walks and read a great deal. In her husband's absence she also coped with the huge estate on her own. It is significant, that Lady Hoby could not open up even before herself or examine the state of her soul, as was recommended half a century later by the authors of the above-mentioned guides to diary writing. As Meads points out:

> Her daily personal record is very introspective yet she shows no real capacity for self-knowledge or ability in self-analysis, for she sets down more or less conventional religious expressions of self-disparagement (Meads: 1930, 47).

The Puritan formation of this earliest known British woman allowed her only to express frequent self-criticism as required by convention. It is worth mentioning that apart from her journal, Margaret also kept a commonplace book, a table book and a sermon book in which she noted down the sermons she listened to.

The next female diary keeper Anne Clifford, Countess of Pembroke (1590–1676), "known as one of the most important female writers of the seventeenth century and one of the era's most prolific, dedicated, and artful self-documenters" (Acheson: 2007, 9), kept journals throughout her long life, although unfortunately only a small part of her diaries has survived. Arthur Ponsonby (1927, 50) points that "it is excellent diary writing, detailed, natural and spontaneous". Apart from diaries, Anne left behind also a biography of her parents and an autobiography based on her journals. It is noteworthy that Anne wrote a lot about herself, including among other things the conflicts with her first husband who clearly did not care much for her: "After supper my Lord and I walked before the gate where I told him how good he was to everybody else and how unkind to me" (Clifford: 2007, 178). From time to time she is tormented with guilt with respect to her husband whom she constantly complains about. However, she feels lonely "like an owl in the desert" (Clifford: 2007, 83) since her "Lord" time and again departs for long journeys. In addition he does not reply to her letters: "I wrote not to my Lord because he wrote not to me since he went away" – she excuses herself (Clifford: 2007, 135). After each return of her husband Anne can hardly hide her bitterness, though she overcomes resentment and makes peace: "[…] my Lord […] assured me how kind and good a husband he would be to me" (Clifford: 2007, 91), "My Lord and I were never greater friends than at this time" (Clifford: 2007, 93). The journal also contains a record of her offences against God: "[…] yesterday I forgot that it was fish day and ate flesh at both dinners" (Clifford: 2007, 105). Clifford was not a Puritan, although she was brought up in a strict and religious atmosphere and she explicitly stressed her Protestant convictions: "About this time I began to think much of religion and do persuade myself that this religion in which my mother brought me up in is the true and undoubted religion, so as I am steadfastly purposed never to be a papist" (Clifford: 2007, 144).

Lady Grace Sherrington (1552–1620), wife to Elizabeth I's courtier, Anthony Mildmay, was the author of a volume of meditations (ca. 900 pages) and an autobiography, which is "among the most personally revealing writings […] by a Renaissance Englishwoman" (Martin: 1994, 33). She was raised in a family of Puritan traditions, and she clearly expressed the aim of her meditations: "This book of my Meditations is the consolation of my soule, the joye of my hart & the stabilitie of my mynde" (Mildmay: 1994, 49[30[1]]). The personal notes she left

1 The number in square brackets refers to the pagination of the manuscript.

behind constitute a combination of a journal with a household book. As we learn from her records, Grace was a medical practitioner and apart from noting down current events she also collected prescriptions and medical recommendations in her book:

> every day I spent some tyme in the Herball and books of phisick, & in ministering to one or other by directions of the best phisitions of myne acquaintance & ever god gaue a blessing therevnto" (Mildmay: 1994, 60 [46]).

Lady Grace Mildmay was aware of her writing skills and the practical value of her writings. As she wrote,

> All these things coming into my mynde, I thought good to set them downe vnto my daughter, and her children, as familiar talke and communication with them, I being dead, as yf I were aliue (Mildmay: 1994, 42[4]).

Puritan ladies frequently wrote, and even published, instructions addressed to their fellow women on how to make everyday self-examination. As Botonaki highlights:

> In doing so, they were occupying the authoritative position of the male authors of such books, sharing the privilege of offering spiritual guidance, and outlining the devotional routine of their fellow believers (Botonaki: 1999, 7).

Susannah Hopton (1627–1709), an author of many devotional works, in the *Daily Devotions consisting of Thanksgiving, Confessions, and Prayers, by an Humble Penitent*, a spiritual guidebook for men and women which appeared anonymously in 1673, suggests that every evening the following questions be put to oneself:

> How have we spend this day, how has it past, from our down-lying to our uprising, to the first hour, the third, the sixth, the ninth, to the Evening, to this hour; where was each hour spent, and with whom, and in what employment? (Hopton: 1717, 395)

Similar instructions, although even more elaborate, are contained in a devotional book entitled *A Method of Devotion Or Rules for Holy & Devout Living, with Prayers on Several Occasions, and Advices and Devotions for the Holy Sacrament* (London 1709) by Puritan Elizabeth Burnet (1661–1709). Burnet was also a quite prolific author of dialogues, letters and meditations. She consciously used her literary gift to teach the practice of piety in everyday life addressing her advice both to men and women without making any discrimination (cf. Burnet: 1713).

It is worth noting that when writing down their spiritual diaries women often listed the benefits that were brought to them. Elizabeth Bury (1644–1720), for example, used to claim that "She found it of singular Advantage to her self, to observe this Method; and would often say, that were is not for her Diary, she would neither know what she was, or what she did, or what she had" (Bury: 1721, 13). Sarah Savage (1664–1752) confessed:

> August 1686. I have had it in my thoughts to do something in the nature of a Diary, being encouraged by the advantages others have gained thereby, and the hope that I might be furthered by it in a godly life, and be more watchful over the frame of my heart when it must be kept on record" (Savage: 1819, x).

Having analysed sixteen spiritual diaries of English Protestant women, Effie Botonaki finds that

> Most of the [...] diaries are testimonies of the struggle between what their authors had to do (according to the instructions of the manuals) and what they were emotionally and physically able to do in regard to their devotional duties. However, in spite of the intense spiritual pressure these women were under, they had – for the first time ever – the authority to evaluate, approve, and condemn their own conduct (Botonaki: 1999, 11).

The freedom to evaluate their own actions and to mete out punishment for their misdeeds was here combined with the freedom to write. Botonaki concludes her article as follows:

> While assuring these women that they were walking on God's path, spiritual diary writing enabled them to slip into forbidden shoes: those of the male spiritual guide, merchant, and lawyer. This liberation from culturally enforced gender roles and rules of conduct – even if only within the pages of a diary – is one of the reasons that many seventeenth-century women became zealous diary keepers (Botonaki: 1999, 21).

A historian of religion Amanda Porterfield asks, "what attracted women to Puritanism?" as it is often emphasised that Puritan theology was patriarchal and oppressive for women. According to her,

> Puritan theology and Puritan preachers attracted women not only because they offered women symbols of emotional gratification, but also because Puritan theology and Puritan culture enabled women to exercise an indirect, often public and deliberate authority (Porterfield: 1991, 199).

An example may be Lucy Hutchinson (1620–1681), a Puritan writer, the biographer of her husband Colonel John Hutchinson, and the translator of the complete text of Lucretius' *De rerum natura* into English. There are many indications that her husband's biography was just a pretext to express herself: "[...] her glowing portrait of his life is better understood", writes Porterfield, "as an autobiographical account of her feelings than as a realistic portrayal of him" (1991, 201).What is more, the portrait appears to be perfect from the literary point of view. Those observations lead Porterfield to the following conclusion: "images of female piety [in Puritan culture] were primarily attractive as aids to obtaining authority" (1991, 202).

Another example of a Puritan woman who was a writer of a great renown even in her own day, as well as the first American female poet to be published, was

Anne Dudley Bradstreet (1612–1672) – incidentally, the only female writer to be included in an extensive monograph *Meet the Puritans – With a Guide to Modern Reprints* by Joel R. Beeke and Randall J. Pederson (Reformation Heritage Books, 2006). The title of the second edition of her poems reveals her great erudition: *Several Poems compiled with great variety of Wit and Learning, full of Delight; wherein especially is contained a compleat Discourse, and Description of the Four Elements, constitutions, ages of man, seasons of the year. Together with an exact Epitome of the three first Monarchyes, Viz, the Assyrian, Persian, Grecian. And beginning of the Romane Common-wealth to the end of their last King: With diverse other pleasant & serious Poems, by a Gentlewoman in New-England. The second Edition, Corrected by the Author and enlarged by an Addition of several other Poems found amongst her Papers after her Death.* It is worth emphasising that Bradstreet was fully conscious of her position as a female writer, as she wrote:

> I am obnoxious to each carping tongue
> Who says my hand a needle better fits.
> A Poets pen all scorn I should thus wrong.
> For such despite they cast on Female wits:
> If what I do prove well, it won't advance,
> They'l say it's stoln, or else it was by chance (Bradstreet: 1678, 4).

Let us now move on to women connected to the Quaker movement. Quakers travelled around the country as travelling preachers and missionaries, preparing sermons and preaching on their own. Since Quakers commanded all records relating to their preaching activities, as well as personal notes evidencing improvement of contacts with God in meditations, to be preserved and kept,[2] modern researchers have at their disposal an inimitable source of information on public activities of English women in the sixteenth and seventeenth centuries. Quaker women, frequently with male consent, often became involved in the religious debates of that time. Priscilla Cotton and Mary Cole, co-authors of a manifesto/proclamation of 1655 entitled *To the Priests and People of England*, were Quakers. The authors declare themselves therein in favour of women's right to preach and actively participate in Church life, including the right to accept new members and elect ministers. According to Paul Salzman (2000, xxii), "*To the Priests and People of England* forms part of a continuing debate, not only amongst Quakers, on the position of women within religious discourse". The most famous defender of women's right to preach was the Quaker Margaret Fell (1614–1702), the author of a pamphlet *Women's Speaking Justified, Proved and Allowed of by the Scriptures* (1666). Terry S. Wallace who edited the works of Fell claims: "Feminist historians have recognized it as a key document, one of the first

2 In 1672 the Quakers decided to collect and preserve their writing.

by a woman, in the evolution of woman's vision as an equal partner with man" (Wallace, 2009, 57). Let us quote a significant passage of Fell's manifesto: "the Church of Christ is a woman, and those that speak against the woman's speaking, speak against the Church of Christ, and the Seed of the woman, which Seed is Christ" (Fell: 1992, 366).

Gerardus Croese, the author of the *General History of the Quakers*, six years before Fell's death described her life as follows,

> [Margaret Fell] totally forsook the Reformed Churches, dedicating her self entirely to be a Member of the Quakers Society, and spending all her time in their Company. Her Husband loved her exceedingly, and was much taken with her Piety, so that she could easily obtain of him this favour, that her House might be a Receptacle for Fox and his Colleagues, and also a place of Meeting for all the Society to Assemble in together, as oft as they would, for the Publick Performance of Sacred Duties; as indeed it was, and continued so after his death, till the death of Fox her second Husband. Not long after her Conversion to this new Religion, she began to abandon her Distaff and Womanly Instruments, betaking her self to Preach and Teach, Instructing the People not only Viva Voce, but by several Books wrote and published by her; by which means she gained many Proselytes. And after this time her House and Family became, as it were, a School and Nursery for all that Sect, both Hearers, Preachers, and Students, of both Sexes (Croese: 1696, 46).

Another famous Quaker woman, Elisabeth Hooton (1600–1672), was described by Croese as "the first of her Sex among the Quakers who attempted to imitate Men and Preach" (1696, 37; cf. Manners: 1914). The authors of *A Biographical Dictionary of English Women Writers 1580–1720* noted that about a third of the writers in their *Dictionary* (ca. 200) were Quakers (Bell/Parfitt/Shepherd: 1990). They published sermons, works of a prophetic nature, proclamations, autobiographies, doctrinal disputes with Anglicans and Baptists, polemics, biographies, journals, poems, testaments, appeals for tolerance addressed to political leaders and open letters. The "Mother of Quakerism", Margaret Fell, "in a period when other women writers appeared in print rarely, anonymously, apprehensively, or only posthumously, [...] eagerly sought print for her polemical works while maintaining an extensive manuscript circulation of letters to Friends", writes Judith Kegan Gardiner (1995, 43). Quaker women actively participated in public life, and even sacrificed family life spending long periods of time away from home, constantly travelling as preachers and missionaries. They were also sometimes put in prison and persecuted in various ways. The authors of the *Dictionary* emphasise that the Quaker movement allowed women to take part in public life, and also encouraged the writing of women from lower social strata, who would have remained illiterate if not for their religious passion. "It seems clear that Quakerism offered particular opportunities for women to act and to write as part of the action" – we read in the Foreword to the *Dictionary* (1990,

262). The authors wonder: "What was it about Quakerism, of all the Civil War sects, that led so many women to write and publish their writing?" (1990, 260). The answer seems to be simple in the light of what has been said already: the Quakers quickly developed a broadly conceived understanding of the social and political activity of women. The spirituality of Quakerism was free from gender stereotypes. It also opened up an opportunity for women to cross/overcome class barriers. Quakers also appreciated the value of printed matter as an effective medium of propaganda, which benefitted women who could rarely publish their texts in print. As a result:

> a considerable number of women made themselves heard as part of radical religious sects that flourished during the period of the Civil War. [...] [Quakers] provided the largest number of women religious writers in the seventeenth century" (Salzman: 2000, xxii).

Let us note that both Puritanism and Quakerism perceived writing as a duty, and Puritan and Quaker women treated their activity in this field exactly as such. Since, however, "whatever the topic of her writing, a woman has to justify her action" (Bell/Parfitt/Shepherd: 1990: 249), Protestant women justified their activities which were not literary by appealing to duty. It is worth mentioning also the authors of poems or poetic anthologies, who were well aware of their abilities. These include Aemilia Lanyer (1569–1645), "one of the first women writers in early modern England to claim a professional poetic voice for herself" (Miller: 2009,144), who in 1611 published a Latin poem *Salve Deus Rex Judaeorum*, dedicated "To all Vertuous Ladies in generalle" (cf. Lanyer: 1993, 12), as well as a country poem *The Description of Cook-Ham* dedicated to Anne Clifford and her mother. Another is Mary Chudleigh (1656–1710), the author of panegyric poems written in praise of women (cf. Olive: 2002). It is also noteworthy that it was in England, in 1582, that the first anthology of women's religious writings – prayers and devotional works – in Europe, *The Monument of Matrons, Containing Seven Several Lamps of Virginity*, with over 1500 quarto pages, was published by Thomas Bentley (cf. King: 2005).

In conclusion, I would like to share a certain doubt, only to try to dispel it immediately. Spiritual diaries written by Puritan women and the sermons and meditations of Quaker women were as "private" as they were "public" and were written merely out of a sense of duty. As the authors of *A Biographical Dictionary of English Women Writers* (1990, 256) observes:

> The categories of "private" and "public" prove to be a false distinction: all these kinds of writing, including the apparently "personal" spiritual autobiography, are the product of engagement in public church practices, and the majority of the sectarian women whose names we record as writers were, primarily, church activists whose writing was part of that work.

Female religious "activists" performed their work in this way, whereas Puritan women were requested to engage in individual contact with God, being offered a tool in the form of a spiritual journal. May duty be considered as a manifestation of freedom? Paradoxically, it seems so. English Protestant women clearly liked that duty and readily joined radical religious sects. Not all texts written by English Protestant women were a manifestation of religious duty. A pen put into female hands could also serve other purposes. Even if women did not fully exercise that freedom, they enjoyed it. Paraphrasing the already quoted title of Margaret Fell's work, I would like to conclude with a phrase which – I think – aptly illustrates the phenomenon described here: *Women's Writing Justified.*

Bibliography

ACHESON, KATHERINE O. (ed.) (2007), The Memoir of 1603 and the Diary of 1616–1619, Peterborough: Broadview Editions.

BEADLE, JOHN (1656), The Journal or Diary of a Thankful Christian, London: E. Cotes.

BELL, MAUREEN/GEORGE A.E. PARFITT/SIMON SHEPHERD (eds.) (1990), A Biographical Dictionary of English Women Writers, 1580–1720, Boston, MA: C.K. Hall.

BENSON, PAMELA J. (1992), Invention of the Renaissance Woman: The Challenge of Female Independence in the Literature and Thought of Italy and England, Pittsburgh, PA: Pennsylvania State University Press.

BOTONAKI, EFFIE (1990), Seventeenth-Century Englishwomen's Spiritual Diaries: Self Examination, Covenanting, and Account Keeping, The Sixteenth Century Journal 30, 1, 3–21.

BURNET, ELIZABETH (1713), A Method of Devotion Or Rules for Holy & Devout Living, with Prayers on Several Occasions, and Advices and Devotions for the Holy Sacrament, London: Joseph Downing.

BURY, ELIZABETH (1721), An Account of the Life and Death of Mrs. Elisabeth Bury, Who Died, May the 11th, 1720. Aged 76. Chiefly Collected out of her Own Diary. Together with her funeral sermon, preach'd at Bristol, … By the Reverend Mr. William Tong, and her elegy, by the Reverend Mr. J. Watts., ed. Samuel Bury, Bristol: J. Penn.

CLIFFORD, ANNE (2007), The Memoir of 1603 and the Diary of 1616–1619, ed. Katherine O. Acheson, Peterborough: Broadview Editions.

CORNS, THOMAS N./DAVID LOEWENSTEIN (eds.) (1995), The Emergence of Quaker Writing: Dissenting Literature in Seventeenth-century England, London: Frank Cass and Company.

COUSINS, A.D. (2009), Humanism, Female Education, and Myth: Erasmus, Vives, and More's "To Candidus", in: A.D. Cousins/Damian Grace (eds.), A Companion to Thomas More, Cranbury: Associated University Presses, 77–94.

CROESE, GERARDUS (1696), General History of the Quakers Containing the Lives, Tenents, Sufferings, Tryals, Speeches, and Letters of All the Most Eminent Quakers, Both Men and Women, from the First Rise of that Sect, Down to this Present Time; Collected from Manuscripts, London: John Dunton.

DUDLEY BRADSTREET, ANNE (1678), Several Poems Compiled with Great Variety of Wit and Learning, Full of Delight, Boston: John Foster, online, http://digital.library.upenn.edu/women/bradstreet/1678/1678.html#3.

FELL, MARGARET (2009), A Sincere and Constant Love: An Introduction to the Work of Margaret Fell, ed. Terry S. Wallace, Richmond, IN: Friends United Press.

– (1992), Women's Speaking Justified, Proved and Allowed of by the Scriptures [1666], in: Charlotte F. Otten (ed.), English Women's Voices, 1540–1700, Miami, FL: Florida International University Press, 363–378.

GARDINER, JUDITH KEGAN (1995), Margaret Fell Fox and Feminist Literary History: A "Mother in Israel" Calls to the Jews, in: Thomas Corns/David Loewenstein (eds.), The Emergence of Quaker Writing: Dissenting Literature in Seventeenth-Century England, London: Frank Cass and Company, 42–56.

HOBY, MARGARET (1930), Diary of Lady Margaret Hoby 1599–1605, ed. Dorothy M. Meads, London: Routledge.

HOPTON, SUSANNAH (1717), A Collection of Meditations and Devotions … By the first Reformer of the Devotions in the ancient way of Offices [Susannah Hopton]; Afterwards Reviewed and Set Forth by the Late Learned Dr. Hickes. London: N. Spinckes, M.A.

KING, JOHN N. (2005), Thomas Bentley's Monument of Matrons: The Earliest Anthology of English Women's Texts, in: Pamela Joseph Benson/Victoria Kirkham (eds.), Strong Voices, Weak History: Early Women Writers and Canons in England, France, and Italy, Ann Arbor, MI: University of Michigan, 216–238.

LANYER, AEMILIA (1993),The Poems of Aemilia Lanyer: Salve Deus Rex Judaeorum, ed. Susanne Woods, Oxford: Oxford University Press.

MACFARLANE, ALAN (1970), The Family Life of Ralph Josselin, a Seventeenth-Century Clergyman. An Essay in Historical Anthropology, Cambridge: Cambridge University Press.

MANNERS, EMILY (1914), Elizabeth Hooton, First Quaker Woman Preacher (1600–1672), annot. Norman Penney, London: Headley Brothers.

MARTIN, RANDALL (ed.) (1994), The Autobiography of Grace, Lady Mildmay, Renaissance and Reformation 30, 1, 33–82.

MEADS, DOROTHY, M. (ed.) (1930), Diary of Lady Margaret Hoby 1599–1605, London: Routledge.

MILDMAY, GRACE, LADY (1994), The Autobiography of Grace, Lady Mildmay, ed. Randall Martin, Renaissance and Reformation 30, 1, 33–82.

MILLER, NAOMI J. (2009), (M)other Tongues: Maternity and Subjectivity, in: Marshall Grossman (ed.), Aemilia Lanyer: Gender, Genre, and the Canon, Lexington, KY: University Press of Kentucky.

MULCASTER, RICHARD (1994), Positions Concerning the Training up of Children, Toronto: University of Toronto Press, online, http://members.tripod.com/bible_study/courses/training/positions.html.

MURRAY FRY, GERMAINE (2013), A Critical Edition of John Beadle's *A Journall or Diary of a Thankfull Christian*, London: Routledge.

OLIVE, BARBARA (2002), A Puritan Subject's Panegyrics to Queen Anne, Studies in English Literature, 1500–1900, 42, 3 (Restoration and Eighteenth Century), 475–499.

PONSONBY, ARTHUR (1927), More English diaries. Further Reviews of Diaries from the Sixteenth to the Nineteen Century with An Introduction on Diary Reading, London: Methuen.

PORTERFIELD, AMANDA (1991), Women's Attraction to Puritanism, Church History 60, 2, 196–209.

SALZMAN, PAUL (ed.) (2000), Early Women's Writing: An Anthology 1560–1700, Oxford: Oxford University Press.

SAVAGE, SARAH (1819), Memoirs of the Life and Character of Mrs. Sarah Savage, Eldest Daughter of the Reverend Philip Henry A.M., ed. J.B. Williams, London: Ogles, Duncan, and Cochran.

VIVES, JUAN LUIS (2000), The Education of a Christian Woman: A Sixteenth-Century Manual, ed. Charles Fantazzi, Chicago: University of Chicago Press.

WALLACE, TERRY S. (ed.) (2009), A Sincere and Constant Love: An Introduction to the Work of Margaret Fell, Richmond, IN: Friends United Press.

WHEALE, NIGEL (2005), Writing and Society: Literacy, Print, and Politics in Britain, 1590–1660, London: Routledge.

WILLEN, DIANE (1992), Godly Women in Early Modern England: Puritanism and Gender, The Journal of Ecclesiastical History 43, 4, 561–580.

Paweł Rutkowski

Papists, Frogs and Witches

Representing Quakers in Seventeenth-Century England

It is a commonplace to say that Quakers, the English religious movement founded in the mid-seventeenth century by George Fox, had an exceptionally bad press from their contemporaries. The custom of describing Quakerism as "a dung-hill of errors and heresies" (Clapham: 1656, A^2), "gangrene" (Jenner: 1670, Av), "spiritual plague" (Baxter: 1656, B) and the like was a standard non-Quaker way of writing about them and discloses the genuinely strong emotions that the new religious group evoked from the very beginning – emotions much stronger than in the case of other sects that appeared, quite numerously, at the time in England as a result of the religious toleration policy pursued by the Cromwellian regime.[1] The Anglican and Presbyterian majority, surprised and horrified by the unprecedented sectarian explosion, tended to single out Quakers, who were considered by many the "worst" and most dangerous of all recent religious novelties. In practice, Quakerism became the face of English sectarianism, as it was supposed to be a "medley" or "the common sink of all the heresies of our times" (Farmer: 1657, 28; Clapham: 1656, 62; Jenner: 1670, 20; *Parallel:* 1700, 1). In similar vein, Quakerism was also compared to a "serpent" that devours all other errors in order to grow and "become a dragon" (Clapham: 1656, 62). Such judgments concerned a set of peculiar Quaker beliefs, which the mainstream Protestants found absolutely "abominable" and "monstrous". These controversial doctrines included immediate inspiration and contact with God (the famous "inner light"); disregard for the Scriptures as the chief source of revelation; possibility of attaining the state of sinless perfection here and now; rejection of traditional forms of worship, priesthood and oath-taking; and radical

1 The "monster of toleration", as Thomas Edwards put it (1646, 64), shocked the traditionalists of all sorts who were certain that there was "nothing more pernicious to mankind and human society" as it was in fact a "propagation of false religions" (Prynne: 1655, 15). In desperation, they even addressed Cromwell to "put some restrictions onto that (almost) boundlesse tolleration now amongst us" to protect Christianity and the Church from "filthy and abominable errours" (Clapham: 1656, n.p., 62).

social equality hardly understandable in a highly stratified society (Moore: 2000, 51–111).

Confusion and concern caused by virtually everything Quakers professed or did gave birth to the hostile rhetoric prevailing in contemporary anti-Quaker texts. Their authors used a variety of strategies in order to attack and cope with the new adversary. They tried to demonstrate, or at least suggest, that Quakers were either Papists in disguise, or witches dabbling with black magic, or they attempted to dehumanise them by implying that their controversial behaviour made it possible to associate them with animals. These three ways of representing Quakers often merged and reinforced one another, thus emphasising even further the negative image of the religious movement in the English popular mind.

The function of the anti-Quaker pamphlets, however, was not simply to offend and discredit their opponents. They were also supposed to provide an interpretive and explanatory framework in which Quakers could be placed and thus classified. It was thought necessary as Quakers seemed so shockingly different and alien that they had to be first "translated" into something more familiar to be understood at all. Puzzled by the rise of Quakers, many Protestant authors, trying to fathom the mystery of the new sect's origin, claimed that they had come from Rome. Such an apparently bizarre opinion was in fact consistent with the master conspiracy theory, widely accepted in England at the time, according to which the Roman Church, as Protestant England's arch-enemy, was always ready and willing to destroy it in order to restore Catholicism. In consequence, the Pope and his men were believed to be ultimately responsible for everything that could do harm, actually or potentially, to good English Protestants. It was the universal fear of "Popery" that triggered a popular belief that the sudden arrival of so many sects in England – Baptists, Ranters, Diggers, Adamites, Muggletonians, Fifth-Monarchists, Seekers, and so on – was for certain the evil-doing of Rome. It was because the Pope wanted to divide the English people and draw them from the Church of England, thus weakening and compromising the Protestant faith and Church. The anti-Quaker texts invariably stressed and argued that Quakers were part of the scheme, too.

William Prynne was one of those who firmly insisted that the sect was no doubt set up by the Pope's emissaries, Franciscans and Jesuits, "sent from Rome to seduce the intoxicated giddy-headed English nation" (Prynne: 1655, title page). To demonstrate it, he mentioned a testimony of a certain Mr. Coppinger, an Irishman who, while attending a Quaker meeting in London in 1653, allegedly met two members of the Franciscan order he had seen formerly in Rome. The two friars "were now become chief speakers amongst the Quakers", which only confirmed that the sect was not only founded but also controlled from within by Catholics (Prynne: 1655, 3; Clapham: 1656, 65–66; Baxter: 1656, C^{2}, C^{3}–C^{3}v, 142). Quakers also resembled Franciscans as far as their behaviour and appearance were concerned. In their missionary work they were supposed to use the methods of the greyfriars, reaching their potential supporters as itinerant preachers and usually travelling by two. What is more, their apparel was modest and some of them wore "rough Haircloth and Cords about their bodies, like the Franciscan Cordiliers", which was "a very probable Evidence, that they were spawned from them" (Prynne: 1655, 5, 37).

To demonstrate that Quakers were linked with the Society of Jesus as well, the polemicist Thomas Jenner referred to an English Jesuit, who once confessed that he "came over [to England] to propagate the Roman Faith". In order to attain his goal he made use of "people called Quakers", who "did their [i. e. Jesuits'] work at the second hand" (1670, 166). The sectaries may have been unaware of their true origin, as their founding fathers tended to conceal their identity, at the beginning at least, to "catch the silly people" (Prynne: 1655, 8). This, however, did not change the fact that Quakers, shaped by their founders, as their adversaries thought, adopted and used the ways commonly ascribed to Jesuits. In a literary dialogue between a Jesuit and Quaker from 1674, the former offered the latter his Machiavellian advice on how to deal with opponents: "vilifie your Adversaries, fling Dirt enough, some will stick; Let your words be like the Devils Oracles, capable of two or three Senses: the Art of Equivocation is absolutely necessary at a pinch". The tip was shrugged off by the Quaker, for whom it was merely a dull and redundant repetition of what all the Quakers had already well known and put into practice (*Quakers Pedigree:* 1674, 8). This was an allusion to the Church of England ministers being pitilessly attacked by Quakers, who, for instance, were wont to interrupt individual parish vicars' sermons or services in order to openly challenge them. The allegedly Jesuit-like strategy of slander was supposed to be part of the "grand design", whose ultimate destructive goal was to "decry and unhinge" the whole system of the Anglican ministry and ordinances (Jenner: 1670, b^2; Deacon: 1656, 9). The target was indicated by nobody else but the Papists (and the Devil, for sure) who knew well enough that men deprived of their pastors would be "like a Dog that hath lost his Master, and therefore will be ready to follow any body that first whistleth to him" (Baxter: 1656, Cv).[2] One of the chief arguments used by Quakers in their struggle with the Church of England and its ministers was their categorical assertion that no denomination in history – apart from themselves – had been a "true" Christian Church. This claim, particularly

2 Interestingly, Baxter observed that the present campaign against Anglican clergymen was modelled on the first Protestant Reformers' ideological war, now imitated by the Catholics, who: "remember yet that it was the disgracing of the Popish Clergy, partly by their own notorious ignorance and viciousness, and partly by our perswading men that the Pope is Antichrist, which was the main advantage which the Reformers had for the ruining of the Papall Kingdom; And therefore they would, partly in Policy, and partly in Revenge, attempt the destruction of our Churches by the same means [...]" (1656, Cv).

offensive and infuriating for their opponents, was just another thing Quakers were thought to have borrowed from the Papists, who also maintained that Protestant congregations were "no true Churches" (Baxter: 1656, 26).

Quakers were therefore suspected to be Rome's fifth column, whose actions – regardless of whether they were fully conscious of that or not – were supposed to subvert English Protestantism. Such suspicions were fuelled by stories about Quakers contacting Catholics, like the one about Samuel Fisher, who in his missionary zeal went to Rome in 1660 to testify the truth to some cardinals and, possibly, the Pope. His foreign expedition was noted on his return home but to opponents of Quakerism the most important aspect of the whole affair was that Fisher had *not* been arrested in Italy. "Could a Protestant Minister – asked rhetorically Thomas Jenner – have given his Testimony against the Pope in Rome, and have, notwithstanding, escaped the Inquisition?" The incredibly lucky escape of the Quaker from the lion's den could be accounted for in one way only: "the Pope so well knows what Tools the Jesuits use to work withall, that (for his own interest) he can bear a few hard words from those that ignorantly do his work in England" (Jenner: 1670, b^{3}v). Another source bluntly suggested that Fisher "went to Rome, not so much to Convert the Pope, as to fetch Instructions" (*Quakers Pedigree:* 1674, 7).[3]

The idea that Quakers were in fact secret agents, or at least useful instruments, of the Pope went together with a "discovery" that Quakerism was closely akin to Catholicism in its doctrine and forms of devotion. As Prynne claimed,

> It is the observation of many learned intelligent Protestants who have pried into the opinions and Practises of all our late New Sects, That in their Books, Writings, Speakings, Preachments, Practises, are interlarded, and mixed with some Jesuiticall and Popish Tenents, opinions, Ceremonies and Practises; by which we may as visibly discover a Jesuit, a Popish Priest or Fryer in them, as we may a Lion by his paw (1655, 7).

Since Quakers failed to adhere closely to the classical Protestant dogma of justification and accepted the value of good works, their theology was declared inherently papist (Clapham: 1656, 24–25, 57; Gaskin: 1660, 38; Jenner: 1670, b^{3}v; *Quakers Pedigree:* 1674, 5). So was their Arminian concept of universal salvation as well as an opinion that the testimony of the Bible was of secondary importance in comparison with God's voice heard in the believer's heart. Thus denigrating the Bible as the living Word of God – which was particularly appalling for all *sola scriptura* Protestants – Quakers simply repeated the Papists' "main errour [that] lieth in the contempt of the Scriptures" (Baxter: 1656, 26).

3 Anti-Quaker writers focussed on Fisher's case, but they did not mind that their explanation of sparing the Quakers by Roman Catholics was weakened by other relations in which Quakers were imprisoned and even tortured by the Inquisition. See e.g. P[errot]: 1661 or Evans: 1662.

According to Richard Baxter, the constitutive feature of Quakerism – "the very Master-sinne in them" – was spiritual pride manifesting itself, for instance, in that "they set up themselves so far above all the people of God on earth" and "damn all the Church and people of God for this 1600 Years at least" (1656, B^3v–B^4v). Quakers were accused of being so haughty that they dared to believe in their being even "fuller of the Spirit" and having "more knowledge and stronger faith" than the Apostles themselves (Gaskin: 1660, 82).[4] Such outrageous arrogance led to Quakers' belief in their own congregation's exclusive infallibility that was, as Baxter put it, "the pillar of their Kingdom and the matter-point of their New Religion" (1656, 9; Bradshaw: 1656, 8). Quakers' sectarian autarchy and self-importance – a trait of each religious movement at the early stage of its development – was, inevitably, associated, or rather identified, by their Protestant adversaries with the Catholic doctrine of papal infallibility (Baxter: 1656, 9). As John Gaskin said,

> [Y]ou Quakers have such an infallible knowledge, that you cannot erre; but we can smell from whence you sucked this poyson, even from your Father the Pope, the great Antichrist, who only claimeth this infallible Spirit (1660, 82).

Another symptom of the unbounded pride commonly ascribed to Quakers was their "Conceit of perfection attainable in this Life" (*Quakers Pedigree:* 1674, 5; Gaskin: 1660, 1). Discussed in Quaker writings, the idea that it was possible to live without sin and keep the commandments to the letter raised extreme emotions. It was not only because such moral perfectibility available for humans here and now appeared totally preposterous and fantastical but also because it was considered just another version of (equally false) Catholic sainthood. So, when Quakers aspired to being "holy, just, good and free from sin", they actually followed in the footsteps of Popish saints like St Francis (Prynne: 1655, 6) or innumerable Roman "Nuns, Monks and Hermites" believing that perfection could be attained by "casting off worldly callings, Emploiments, Relations after the flesh, and propriety" (Baxter: 1656, 27).

Quakers were denied originality even in their attachment to "inner light", the central doctrine of their religion. Being essentially an immediate divine revelation, it was apparently mixed up and identified with the Catholic theological notion of natural reason, with which all humans were equipped to help them make moral judgments and decisions. Richard Baxter – as a Protestant emphasizing human ultimate dependence on individual faith, the Word of God and

4 Shocked by what he must have taken for blasphemous impudence, John Gaskin further wondered: "what a most horrid uncharitable thing it is, to judge all the Protestant Churches, before you sprang up, to be false Heretical Churches; for then Christ had no Church for sixteen hundred yrs, for there were none of your opinions heard of while these late years, and then Christ was a head without a body" (1660, 103).

divine grace – condemned both Catholics and Quakers for their supposedly common belief in "the sufficiency of the common-light that is within them". This concept was spread by who else but Jesuits, who "would [earnestly] perswade us that there is a light in every mans conscience", thus making people delude themselves that achieving salvation was "in mens own power" (1656, 8, 27). However, references to the inward light were primarily used to demonstrate that Quakers were merely idolaters: they were supposed to idolise the light, in exactly the same manner as Catholics, according to Protestant propagandists, worshipped material objects and images. As Gaskin put it,

> [D]o not the Quakers set up idols in their hearts, when they set up their inward works in the room and place of Christ? [...] obeying a light within them? and is not this to make an idol of their own works; which is worse then the Papists Images made of wood and stone? [...] and do not they thereby Idolize themselves? (1660, a^3v–a^4).

In another pamphlet there was a similar comparison:

> For if she [i.e. the Church of Rome] set up Material external Images: [...] [Quakers] set up an Idea, or an Internal Image to Idolise, and attribute Divine Honour to a Created natural light (*Quakers Pedigree:* 1674, 5).[5]

Quakers were also compared to Catholic clergymen and saints as far as the ecstatic side of their devotion was concerned. Their "extraordinary sudden extravagant Agonies, Trances, Quakings, Shaking, Raptures, Visions [...] Revelations, Illuminations", as it was enumerated, were considered "the very same in form and substance" as similar phenomena associated with "Popish Saints, Fryers, Priests, Jesuites, Nunnes, recorded in the lying Legends and lives of their Romish Canonized SAINTS" (Prynne: 1655, 7, 10; Baxter: 1656, C^2). Quakers' "trembling" could be, for instance, traced back to violent fits of Ignatius Loyola, tormented thus by devils, as his biographers testified (which by the way gave a clue about the demonic nature of the sectaries' trances) (Prynne: 1655, 21–23). Similarly, their visions of the afterlife – as those of one John Lawson – possibly had a precedent in tales about "the Saints of old", who, reportedly, had been in Heaven and Hell before their death (Ives: 1656, 22–23). The source of Quakers' religious "enthusiasm" was then the Catholic hagiographic tradition. Overall, their piety – defined as "their despising the fashions of the world, and contemning the honours and pleasure thereof [...] frequent fasting and neglecting of the body, their sober and austear carriage and deportment amongst men, with their willingnesse to suffer for their way" – had also their roots in charlatanry of "the Popish Monks and Friars", whose "pretended austerity and strictnesse of life and such like things" were intended to delude and attract gullible people (Clapham: 1656, 49).

5 See also Wigan: 1665, 49 and Jenner: 1670, cv.

The anti-Quaker writers' intention was to warn their readers that the Pope was really the "Founder" and "Ghostly Father" of Quakers and that by joining the sectaries one became, in one way or another, a Papist (Deacon: 1656, 6, 9; Jenner: 1670, 166).[6] Thomas Jenner, in order to emphasise the monstrosity of such a treacherous transformation, compared Quakers and their religion to "the Cockatrice, that sprang out of the root of the Romish Serpent" (1670, b^{3}v). It was one of innumerable animal similes and metaphors used in the ideological war in the times of the Reformation, virtually by all sides of the religious strife. Quite often, bestial epithets, first reserved by English Protestants for Catholics, were later on, when need arose, also applied to smaller heterodox denominations. Destructive locusts, for instance, which originally meant Jesuits,[7] then came to signify Quakers destroying the Church in the same manner "as Locusts destroy the fruits of the earth" (Morris: 1655, 1; Bradshaw: 1656, 4). Similarly, William Prynne called Jesuits and Franciscans "Romish Frogs" producing their "Spawne", that is, Quakers (1655, 1, 36; Baxter: 1656, 9). Samuel Morris also agreed that members of the sect were "of the same brood" as frogs better known as "Jesuites and Seminary Priests", and, additionally, gave reasons why they may be "fitly" compared to these water creatures:

> 1. As frogs delight in filthy lakes and puddles, so the Quakers delight in their false Doctrines, teaching the Traditions of men, and so walk on in their wickedness [...]
>
> 2. As frogs make a great croking in marish grounds, so the Iesuites, Seminary Priests and Quakers, by their sweet and fair words, get themselves favour in such Gentlemens house, where they can have entertainment (1655, 1–2).

Although the extended simile above clearly reveals the author's everyday knowledge of the common amphibians' customs, the image of Quakers as frogs had in fact a Biblical origin. Representing religious opponents in this way was usually based on the vision recorded in the Apocalypse: "And I saw three vncleane spirits like frogs come out of the mouth of the dragon [...] [that were] the spirits of deuils" (Rev 16:13–14), the dragon being usually interpreted as the Pope and demonic frogs as his servants of various kinds. Incidentally, the aforementioned locusts came from the same source: in his apocalyptic vision St John saw swarms of locusts coming out of the bottomless pit in order to kill the sinners and torment the saints (Rev 9:2–3).

Most of the other animal epithets used in the anti-Quaker pamphlets came from the Bible too. Quakers were then called "ravening wolves in sheep's cloth-

6 For the manner in which Quaker authors tried to refute their opponents' arguments and demonstrate that they should not be identified with Catholics, see Fox: 1654, Evans: 1662 and Moon: 1674.

7 "Jesuits from Rome spread like locusts over most parts of the Nation to make State and Church shake and tremble" (Prynne: 1656, 2; Quakers Pedigree: 1674, 3).

ing" (Bradshaw: 1654, 5; Clapham: 1656, 50; cf. Matt 7:15), "subtil foxes [that] seek to destroy the Vines of Christ's Vineyard" (Deacon: 1656, n.p.; cf. Cant 2:15), "a Generation of Vipers [...] sprung up amongst us" (*Devil:* 1656, A^2; cf. Matt 3:7, 12:34, 23:33; Luke 3:7), "sinful worms" (Clapham: 1656, 40), "scorpions [...] [that] sting the soul" (Morris: 1655, 2; cf. 1 Kings 12:11; Rev 9:5, 10), not to mention ubiquitous "serpents". Admittedly, such offensive names given to Quakers were quite conventional, making use of their negative connotations known from centuries of Biblical exegesis, and thus losing at least some of their insulting power. "Devaluation" of Biblical animal insults may have been also a consequence of the fact that the same supply was in constant use by all participants of the religious struggle at the time, including Quakers themselves. Noteworthy, is the fact that all anti-Quaker pamphleteers stressed the Quakers' own abusive language. Shocked and hurt to the quick by their "railing", in his refutation of Quakerism Baxter decided to present a sample of epithets (including references to animals) he himself was called by members of the sect: "Thou Serpent, Viper, thou Childe of the Devil, thou Son of perdition, thou dumb dog, thou false hireling, thou false Liar, Deceiver, greedy dog, thou ravening Wolf, thou cursed hypocrite" (Baxter: 1656, 1).[8]

More acute and, arguably, more effective verbal attacks on Quakers, consisted not in employing threadbare animal metaphors but in demonstrating that what they did, and how they behaved, made them resemble animals so much that they were practically shedding their humanity. Quakers' supposed beastliness was exemplified by ecstatic trances into which they fell during their meetings. As it was claimed, in their fits the enthusiasts, apart from quaking terribly, used to shriek, roar and howl "like Dogs". The nerve-racking noise not only frightened human witnesses but also compelled "the dogs to bark, and swine to cry, and cattle to run about" (*Devil:* 1656, B; Jenner: 1670, 158). The fact that Quakers made sounds that were normally emitted by beasts was even more clearly emphasised in the story of Mary White, a girl who in her trance, apart from suffering from usual fits, also uttered "strange out-cries, as barking like Dog, lowing like a Cow, &c." (Deacon: 1657, 20). The emphasis placed here – and in similar cases – on shocking animal-like behaviour served to point out the not entirely human status of Quakers.

Quakers were also commonly accused of leading promiscuous lives in defiance of established moral standards. Prynne's malicious report that: "some of

8 George Fox used animal imagery not only to attack his adversaries but also to sharply distinguish members of his movement from anybody else. He preached that it was necessary to separate "the sheep from the goats, and the lambs from the wolves [...] the Kytes from the Doves [...] putting a difference between the precious and the vile, betwixt the holy and unholy" (1654, 8–9). The same strategy of distinction was used by the Quaker James Naylor, who, when interrogated, compared himself to a lamb and his enemies to wolves (Impostor: 1656, 18).

them [...] [had] been lately taken shaking with their female Proselites between the Sheets in a warme bed, as I am credibly informed" (1655: 23) was by no means exceptional in the anti-Quaker writings. Such rumours usually concerned leaders of the movement – e.g. James Nayler was alleged to practise a kind of free love with many women (*Relation:* 1656, 5–6) – but the reputation of rank-and-file members also suffered. In consequence, it was often claimed that Quakers' meetings regularly turned into orgies, during which, as it happened once in Yorkshire, "they all very lovingly [...] went to bed together in the straw stark naked, save what men and women were in beds". Such outrageous sexual licence was quite naturally compared to the behaviour of animals, as it was befitting "swine in a stye", rather than humans (Deacon: 1657, 49).[9] Quakers could even further degrade themselves by practising zoophilia, which at the time was considered one of the worst and most hideous sins and crimes, as offenders acting *contra naturam* undermined and betrayed their own humanity (Thomas). To show that Quakers were particularly prone to bestiality their adversaries publicised, whenever they could, stories about how low they had, repeatedly, fallen. John Deacon, for example, readily informed his readers about a certain Birch, "who was seen in the act committing Buggery with a mare, and for it fled" (1657, 20), and John Denham published a satirical ballad entitled *A relation of a Quaker, that to the shame of his profession, attempted to bugger a mare near Colchester* (1659, 1).[10]

The critics of Quakers also claimed that their beastly nature clearly manifested itself in that they rejected social norms and manners accepted by everybody else. As "enemies against civility and good manners", they failed to acknowledge class differences by refusing, for instance, to take off hats in front of their social superiors. Unlike any other nation "under the whole Heavens" they failed to "give civil honour and respect" to people of higher rank and, furthermore, refused to "shew outward tokens of love and courtesie to their equals". For that reason, Quakers relegated themselves to a very low position in the hierarchy of civility and humanity, their place being even lower than that of "savage Indians", who had their own social rules and dutifully adhered to them (Clapham: 1670, 66). Bradshaw believed that Quakers, through their basic "incivility", severed links with the rest of mankind altogether, which automatically placed them among "the bruit beasts that are led with sensuality as utterly void of rationality" (1654, 6). Elsewhere Clapham mentioned an imprisoned Quaker who, having nothing else to eat, found "a place neer the grate, where were many ugly spiders, of which he took and did eate till he was satisfied thereby as well as if he had eaten of the

9 For historical recurrence of accusations of orgiastic behaviour brought against heterodox religious groups, see Eliade: 1976, 69–92 and Cohn: 2005, 1–15, 35–50.

10 See also Gilpin: 1655, 20–21.

wholesomest food in the world" (1656, 45). The story was presented as the one circulating among Quakers, who in this way reassured themselves that they could work miracles, too (in this case, by satisfying hunger with what could hardly be called nourishing food). However, for Clapham, whose primary goal was to expose false saints' false miracles, this may have been merely a tale about a Quaker who broke just another social convention and taboo – as he and his fellow-sectaries were wont to do – eating utterly obnoxious food suitable perhaps for birds and rats but definitely not for humans.

In the anti-Quaker literature, understandably, much attention was paid to the early Quakers' practice of presenting themselves and preaching to the public without clothes. In 1657 John Deacon wrote about a man who "came stark naked to the Market-crosse in *Kertby-more*, and there stood speaking in that posture to the people, with this excuse, *That he stood naked by the command of the spirit, that he might speak the naked truth* [...]" (1657, 42). The quoting of the Quaker's own words corroborates that for the Friends such exposure was an act of obedience to their internal prophetic spirit and a spectacular sign of their innocence and truthfulness (Carroll: 1978, 76–83). However, for the beholders as well as anti-Quaker writers, outraged by such an unthinkable violation of the social taboo, "running naked in the streets and markets" was a visible manifestation of their "uncouth passions" and promiscuity (Jenner: 1670, 16, 18; Clapham: 1656, 52), which only confirmed the Quakers' well-established reputation of being a band of libertines. As in the case of their refusal to accept the traditional system of class relations, their public nudity put them on a par with "the poor Indians that go naked" for their savagery and lack of culture (Clapham: 1656, 35) and, naturally, with animals – it was surely considered "most odious and beastlike" for a human to do without apparel (*Devil:* 1656, A^4). Only someone really uncivilised and brutish in one's nature could want to offend other people's eyes and sense of decency in this manner.

The English were astonished by the rise of Quakerism and even more by its conspicuousness. Its relative popularity and ability to recruit new members was so annoying that some people thought that there must be some witchcraft and sorcery involved (Reay, 399). Charging Quakers with practising magic was quite "natural" for two reasons. Firstly, it agreed with the popular conviction many Protestants held that Roman Catholicism was nothing but "Sorcery, Abomination and Witchcraft" (*Quakers Pedigree:* 1674, 3). Protestant writers, from the very beginning of the Reformation, argued, as came up again and again in the debate over Quakerism, that,

> Enchantments, Sorceries, Charmes, Fascinations and Exorcismes are very frequent amongst Popes, and Popish Priests, Monkes, Fryers, Jesuites [...] [and that the] Popes were all most infamous Magicians, Sorcerers, and Inchanters [...] (Prynne: 1655, 8).

Many Jesuits were thought to have learnt "the art of Sorcery and Magick", eventually becoming "Arch-Magitians".[11] Logically, they were imitated by Quakers, their faithful disciples, who were supposed to enthusiastically study and practise their Catholic masters' black art (Prynne: 1655, 24).

The other reason for accusing Quakers of sorcery was that it had been customary for centuries to associate heresy, understood as opposition to true religion, with magic. Fox's followers were often nicknamed Jannes and Jambres (Prynne: 1655, 1; *Devil:* 1656, Av; Wigan: 1665, B; Jenner: 1670, b^4), after two Egyptian sorcerers who challenged Moses and Aaron, trying (in vain) to show the superiority of their magical tricks over God's power (cf. Exod 7:8–12). The then much-quoted Gospel reference to the story – "Now as Jannes and Jambres withstood Moses, so do these also resist the truth: men of corrupt minds, reprobate concerning the faith" (2 Tim 3:8) – was thought to apply to Quakers exceptionally well, not only because it described the nature of their sectarian movement so accurately, but also because it highlighted their magical associations. The anti-Quaker texts, however, primarily focussed on the figure of Simon Magus, a contemporary of the Apostles (Acts 8:9–24), who in the Christian historical memory was recorded as both the first heretic and a powerful magician (Clapham: 1656, 44, 79; Prynne: 1655, 8). He was thought to have used magic to bewitch the people of Samaria and turn them into his followers. According to their critics, Quakers were Simon's true disciples following in his footsteps, and their leader, George Fox, often compared to him, could be found "not only to equal, but in many things to exceed that [ancient] Arch-Heretick" (Hallywell: 1673, 3).[12] Fox's undoubted charisma resulted in rumours that the influence he had on others was really an effect of using magic. He was supposed to "bewitch people, by staring them in the face [and] taking them by the hand" (Farmer: 1657, 41), as in a relation about how he once came into "the company of a Gentlewoman, laid his hand on her forehead, after which she immediately became a Quaker for a certain time, who before had been much against it", all this being "related from the Gentlewomans own mouth" (Jenner: 1670, 160). Fox repeated the trick at Castledermot, Ireland, where he visited a certain Mr Wright "whose wife had for a long time refused to go to the Quakers Meeting, or hear them". This

11 To prove it, William Prynne related a story of the Jesuit Pierre Coton, a councillor of Henry IV of France, who was to be "an Arch-Magitian, and the best skilled in this black art of any of their Society". Coton, "as the Jesuites themselves affirmed, [...] had a Magycal Glasse, wherein he would plainly represent to the King whatever he desired to know; and that there was no thing done or consulted so secretly in the most Private Cabinets of other Monarches, which he could not disclose and reveal by the help of that constellated or rather condiabolated Glasse" (1655, 23–24).

12 According to the anonymous author Quakers could also be called pupils of "Menander, Cerinthus, Basilides, Carpocrates, Sabellius, Novatus, Arius, or any of those old condemned Hereticks" as well as men dabbling with magic (Parallel: 1700, A^4, 2).

time he "spoke with her, taking her by the hand, and [...] she without any further arguments, immediately turned an absolutely professed Quaker" (Jenner: 1670, 162).

Although it was Fox that was perceived as the chief practitioner of Quaker magic, his followers were believed to be capable of such feats as well. Encounters with Quakers were always potentially dangerous, as they by custom bewitched those who, out of reckless curiosity, attended their meetings (*Devil:* 1656, B). Such unfortunate visitors fell easy prey to their unscrupulous hosts, which was demonstrated by the anecdote about a certain Stephens, who went to Quakers' meeting in London with the intention to oppose their teachings.

> [A]t his first coming, he did till one of them, taking him by the hand, and rubbing his wrest very hard; which put him to very sore pain; and so altered his resolution, that he was so transformed by their inchantments, that he since confessed, that should any one whatsoever, have dared to oppose or resist them [...] he would have stab'd them to the heart, whatsoever had come of it (*Impostor:* 1656, 50).

Apart from poor Stephens – who, as it was suggested, had eventually ended "stark mad" – there were also other victims, like "a great Professor of Religion, a man of good parts, but something given to Novelties", who went to hear the Quakers and was

> presently bewitched by them, that he ran up and down the Town in a confused manner, crying out very blasphemously; *I am the Way, the Truth, and the Life*, and thus he continued for the space of two or three moneths, sometimes running naked about the streets in the night [...] (*Devil:* 1656, B).

That such unnatural and shocking conversions were possible was testified by the Bible itself: Quakers' victims were very much like the ancient Galatians who had been asked and reprimanded by St Paul in his epistle (Gal 3:1): "who hath bewitched you, that you should not obey the trueth?" (Jenner 1670: 175; Prynne: 1655, 8).

Bewitchment could be effected not only through touch and look but also through more tangible means. "[T]hese Quakers", claimed Prynne, "use inchanted Potions, Braclets, Ribons [...] to intoxicate their Novices and draw them to their party" (1655, 8), which further confirmed their affinity with witches, traditionally using such *materia magica.* Even their leader, besides his "hypnotising" powers, was supposed to resort to such methods, as was suggested in a story about how Fox, paying for his new clothes, gave the tailor's apprentice a piece of money wrapped in paper. The young man put it in his pocket and then for many hours felt compelled to return to Fox so much that he had to be physically restrained. Only when the bundle was taken out of his pocket and thrown into fire was he "at quiet" and never desired to visit Fox any more. For the narrator it was quite obvious that the incident looked "like something of Sorcery or Witchcraft" (*Parallel:* 1700, 2).

John Gaskin expressed an opinion, shared by many, that the deliberate use of enchanted objects or drinks were also responsible for "quaking fits" that were a trademark of Quakers (1660, 10). The ecstatic behaviour, an indispensable element of their meetings, was then an effect of bewitchment and, furthermore, it was almost unanimously identified with demonic possession, one of the harms traditionally done by witches to their neighbours. According to their opponents, Quaker enthusiasts, when in trance, behaved and looked exactly like demoniacs possessed by the devil: they fell on the ground, their limbs violently trembled, mouths foamed, bellies swelled and faces were repulsively contorted (Gaskin: 1660, 106; Jenner: 1670, 16; Ives: 1656, 5, 14). In order to demonstrate that Quakers were really possessed, Jenner related how an Anglican (?) minister came to the sectarian meeting in Durham and prayed there in the name of Christ. In a moment, all Quakers, in a beast-like manner, "roared in a hideous manner, howling, squeeking, yelping, roaring and with humming noise"; they also started shaking terribly and even asked the clergyman if he had come to torment them (Jenner: 1670, 16). Needless to say, such an unexpectedly violent reaction was characteristic for demoniacs – and demons inside them strongly averse to all holy names – who were subjected to the ritual of clerical exorcism.

There were also other analogies drawn between the beliefs and practices of Quakers and those traditionally ascribed to witches. According to Jonathan Clapham, Quakers could be called "manifest confederates of Satan" because they, just like witches, "cast down the holy Ordinances of God's worship and service", "turn[ed] their backs off the Ministry of the Word", and "cast off prayer to God" (Clapham: 1656, 38, 43). It was legitimate to compare Quakers to witches, because their new forms of devotion – just like the witches' Sabbath – seemed to be just a mockery and defiant reversal of all Christian rituals. No wonder that from time to time Quakers were directly, and formally, accused of taking part in diabolic gatherings (Reay, 396). In such cases they really served as "surrogate witches" (Elmer, 156) taking over crimes specifically related to witchcraft, as happened in 1659 in Dorset, where two women, former Quakers, confessed that they had taken part in the witches' meeting, during which they paid homage to the Devil and copulated with him (Jenner: 1670, 160–161).[13] In the context of distinctly English understandings of witchcraft – Sabbath excesses being rather a foreign import – Quakers could not avoid being associated with familiar spirits in the animal form. A certain William Spenser recollected how, while sleeping with a Quaker in one bed, he heard something hissing or humming about his com-

13 Deacon said that some Quakers even murdered a child although they did not commit such a hideous crime in order to produce a magical ointment, as witches used to do, but because in this way they wanted to show that they were capable of reviving it. However, their supernatural powers turned out to be delusive and, eventually, they were executed for the murder (Deacon: 1657, 49).

panion's head. He was afraid but, calmed down by the man, ignored the sound. However, when it was repeated – and when the Quaker "did blow like the hissing of a Goose several times towards his mouth" – he leapt out of the bed "crying for a light to guide and conduct him forth". The mysterious hissing creature, apparently of demonic nature according to Spenser, remained unidentified (Jenner: 1670, 158). In another widely reported case, John Gilpin, a man possessed after attending the Quaker gathering, was then accompanied by two spirits in the likeness of swallows that came and went through the chimney (later they changed into two butterflies) (Gilpin: 1655, 8–10). The popular imagination also attached an animal attendant to George Fox, who was said to ride a huge black, obviously demonic, horse that allowed him to be in two distant places at the same time. In his journal Fox indignantly registered this persistent popular rumour that transformed him into a stereotypical sorcerer (Penney: 1911, 38).[14]

All such Quakers-as-witches accounts were modelled on stories common in the era of witch hunts and witch trials; stories about the evil eye, magical touch, harmful artefacts, demonic servants that enabled witches to break their victims' wills and subdue them to serve their own interests. Such an appropriation of witchcraft motifs – in the English cultural milieu effectively combined with animal ones – apparently helped demonise Quakerism as well as explain its seemingly incomprehensible attractiveness and the appeal of its leaders.

The appearance of Quakers on the English religious scene came as a shock. The anti-Quaker authors, having identified them as dangerous enemies, strove very hard to discredit them. At the same time, they grappled with the problem of how to classify them properly, as they seemed so radical and so different from other religious groups. The method applied was to place their novelty in the web of already familiar concepts and meanings, which resulted in identifying Quakers with Catholicism and witchcraft, two very well-known threats that everybody in England had been long accustomed to and were able to cope with. The concomitant phenomenon was association of the sect's members with animals and immoral animal-like behaviour, which effectively led, at least partially, to dehumanization of the Quakers' image. Extensive joint use of the three, particularly offensive interrelated labels – papists, animals, witches – was a combination that built up a sense of the almost apocalyptic danger which was allegedly posed by the sectaries and helped justify the persecution that they were subject to. Such hostile representations were largely a response to Quakers' radicalism. When, towards the end of the seventeenth century, their uncompromising stance started to change – they gave up their ecstatic enthusiasm and stopped denying the

14 A black demonic horse serving a magician was an old cultural scheme well known and used since at least the Middle Ages. Fox's predecessors were, for instance, the alchemist Michael Scot (Brown: 1897, 218–219) or Johannes Teutonicus (Heywood: 1635, 253).

legitimacy of other Churches, for instance (Moore, 214–228) – the abusive terms, now considered no longer necessary, became rarer. Naturally, they were not dismissed altogether overnight – too many acrimonious words had been written and said by the two opposing parties – but, since Quakers gradually conformed to norms of the post-revolutionary pluralist religious settlement, they could finally be granted at least a dose of respect.

Bibliography

A Parallel between the Faith and Doctrine of the Present Quakers and that of the chief hereticks in all ages of the Church And also a parallel between Quakerism and popery, (1700), London: John Nut.

A True Relation of the Life, Conversation, Examination, Confession, and Iust Deserved Sentence of James Naylor the grand Quaker of England. Who for his blasphemous & abominable opinions, & practises, was whipt at a carts-taile, from Westminster to the Royall-Exchange in London, December the eighteenth 1656 and thereto stand in the pillory, and to have the letter B set upon his fore-head, and to be burnt through the toung with a hot iron, and to be kept in prison during life, without being allowed any sustenance, but what he shall earne with his owne labor, (1656), London.

Baxter, Richard (1656), The Quakers Catechism, or, The Quakers questioned, their questions answered, and both published, for the sake of those of them that have not yet sinned unto death; and of those ungrounded novices that are most in danger of their seduction, London: A.M.

Bradshaw, Ellis (1656), The Conviction of James Naylor and his lack spirit demonstrated from his own confessions, lyes, evasions, and contradictions in the maine points of doctrine by him held forth against the truth in answer to a book of his called Wickednesse weighed: the which was writt in answer to a little treatise called The Quakers quaking principles examined and refuted, London: M.S.

– (1654), The Quakers vvhitest divell unvailed, and their sheeps cloathing pulled off, that their woolvish inside may be easily discerned in answer to a letter subscribed Iames Naylor, a professed Quaker, [London:] S.I.

Brown, James Wood (1897), An Enquiry into the Life and Legend of Michael Scot, Edinburgh: David Douglas.

Carroll, Kenneth L. (1978), Early Quakers and "Going Naked as a Sign", Quaker History 67, 2, 69–87.

Clapham, Jonathan (1656), A Full Discovery and Confutation of the Wicked and Damnable Doctrines of the Quakers. As also, a plain vindication and confirmation of sundry fundamental points of the Christian religion, denyed or corrupted by the enemies of the truth in these times. Published for the benefit of such weak Christians, who are not so able to discover and oppugne the dangerous doctrines of subtil seducers when coloured over with fair words and pretences, and so are more apt to be taken in their snares. Whereunto is annexed an excellent discourse proving that singing of Psalmes is not only lawful, but an ordinance of God, London: T.R & E.M.

COHN, NORMAN (2005), Europe's Inner Demons: The Demonisation of Christians in Medieval Christendom, London: Pimlico.

DEACON, JOHN (1657), An Exact History of the Life of James Naylor with his parents, birth, education, profession, actions, & blaspheemies [sic]. Also how he came first to be a Quaker, and received his commission from heaven (as he saith) when he was in the field at plow. Taken from his own mouth. With the doctrines, tenets and practises of some other of the same sect, London.

– (1656), A Publick Discovery of a Secret Deceit. Or, The man of sin unmasked, his sheeps-clothing of glorious pretences pulled off; and his wolvish inside set forth in its colours. Where may easily be discerned Satan transformed into the resemblance of an angel of light, in that sect or society commonly called Quakers. Being nineteen quaeries, directed to their speakers at the Bull and Mouth neer Aldersgate: and answered by that grand fomenter of heresie, James Nayler. With a reply thereunto, and fourteen queries more returned by him unto me, fully answered: and twenty four more proposed, London.

– (1656), The Grand Impostor Examined, or, The life, tryal and examination of James Nayler the seduced and seducing Quaker: with the manner of his riding into Bristol, London.

DENHAM, JOHN (1659), A relation of a Quaker, that to the shame of his profession, attempted to bugger a mare near Colchester, London.

EDWARDS, THOMAS (1646), Gangraena: or A catalogue and discovery of many of the errours, heresies, blasphemies and pernicious practices of the sectaries of this time, vented and acted in England in these four last years: as also, a particular narration of divers stories, remarkable passages, letters; an extract of many letters, all concerning the present sects; together with some observations upon, and corollaries from all the fore-named premisse, London.

ELIADE, MIRCEA (1976), Occultism, Witchcraft and Cultural Fashions. Essays in Comparative Religions, Chicago: Chicago University Press.

ELMER, PETER (1996), "Saints or Sorcerers": Quakerism, Demonology and the Decline of Witchcraft in Seventeenth-Century England, in: Jonathan Barry/Marianne Hester/Gareth Roberts (eds.), Witchcraft in Early Modern Europe: Studies in Culture and Belief, Cambridge: Cambridge University Press, 145–179.

EVANS, KATHARINE (1662), This is a short relation of some of the cruel sufferings (for the truths sake) of Katharine Evans & Sarah Chevers in the inquisition of the isle of Malta who have suffered there above three years by the Pope's authority, there to be deteined until they dye: which relation of their sufferings is come form their own hands and mouths as doth appear in the following treatise, London.

FARMER, RALPH (1657), Sathan Inthron'd in his Chair of Pestilence. Or, Quakerism in its exaltation. Being a true narrative and relation of the manner of James Nailer (that eminent Quaker's) entrance into the city of Bristoll the 24. day of October, 1656. With one man going bare-headed before him: and two women; one on one side, another on the other side of his horse, holding the reines, and leading him. Singing, Hosannah, and Holy, Holy, Holy, Lord God of Israel. Together with some blasphemous letters found about him, with their examinations thereupon, in this city, and other considerable passages, and observations. Whereto is added a vindication of the magistrates and inhabitants of this city, in reference to the nestling of these Quakers amongst us. With a declaration of the occasion, rise and growth of them in this city, London.

Fox, George (1654), The trumpet of the Lord sounded, and his sword drawn, and the separation made between the precious and the vile; and the vineyard of the Lord dressed by his own husbandmen, and the dead trees cut down, and all the mystery of witchcraft discovered in all professions: by them who have come thorow great tribulation, whose garments have been washed in the blood of the lamb; who are accounted as the off-scowring of all things for Christs sake, scornfully called by the world Quakers, London.

Gaskin, John (1660), A Just Defence and Vindication of Gospel Ministers and Gospel Ordinances against the Quakers many false accusations, slanders and reproaches. In ansvver to John Horwood his letter, and E.B. his book, called, A just and lawful tryal of the ministers and teachers of this age, and several others. Proving the ministers calling and maintenance just and lawful, and the doctrine of perfection by free justification, preached by them, agreeable to the scriptures. VVith the Quakers objections answered. And the Quakers perfection by hearkning to, and obeying a light within them, proved contrary to the scriptures. And their practices in ten particulars proved contrary to the commands and examples of Christ and his apostles. By a lover of gospel ministers and gospel ordinances, London: W.G.

Gilpin, John (1655), The Quakers shaken, or, a warning against quaking. Being I. A relation of the conversion and recovery of John Gilpin, of Kendall in Westmorland, who was not only deluded, but possessed with the devill. II. A vindication of the said John Gilpin, from the aspersions of the Quakers. III. Twelve lying blasphemous prophecies of James Milner of Beakly in Lancashire; delivered by him Novemb. 14, 15, 16. IV. A relation of a horrid buggery committed by Hugh Bisbrown, a Quaker, with a mare. V. A relation of one Cotton Crosland of Ackworth in York-shire, a professed Quaker, who hanged himself, London: S.G.

Hallywell, Harry (1673), An account of familism as it is revived and propagated by the Quakers shewing the dangerousness of their tenets, and their inconsistency with the principles of common reason and the declarations of Holy Scripture, London.

Heywood, Thomas (1635), The Hierarchie of the Blessed Angels. Their Names, Orders and Offices. The fall of Lucifer with his Angells. London: Adam Islip.

Ives, Jeremiah (1656), Innocency above Impudency: or, The strength of righteousness exalted, above the Quakers weakness and wickedness; in a reply to a lying pamphlet, call'd Weakness above wickedness: published by J. Nayler, in answer to a book, entituled, The Quakers quaking. By which his notorious lyes are made manifest, and the truth of the said book justified, London: J. Cottrel.

Jenner, Thomas (1670), Quakerism anatomiz'd and confuted wherein is discovered their manifold damnable errors, taken (for the most part) from their own mouths and pens, with a confutation annexed. As also their vain principles, pernicious practises, and blasphemies (denying the Lord that bought them) evinced: also the Holy Scripture, worship and ordinances vindicated: the whole discourse being grounded upon II Pet. II. 1, 2, 3, [Dublin].

Moon, John (1674), A Jesuitical Designe Discovered: in a piece called, The Quakers pedigree; or, A dialogue between a Quaker and a Jesuit, &c., London.

Moore, Rosemary Anne (2000), The Light in Their Consciences: Early Quakers in Britain 1646–1666, University Park: Pennsylvania State University.

Morris, Samuel (1655), A looking-glasse for the Quakers or Shakers. And their follovvers, wherein they may behold their errours, acknowledge their false doctrines, and be converted. Written for the comfort of all true Protestants, and daunting of the Quakers, Jesuites, seminary priests, and all their cursed crew, who do oppose the church and Gospel of our Lord Iesus Christ, London.

PENNEY, NORMAN (ed.) (1911), The Journal of George Fox, Cambridge: Cambridge University Press.

P[ERROT], J[OHN] (1661), A na[r]rative of some of the sufferings of J.P. in the city of Rome, London.

PRYNNE, WILLIAM (1655), The Quakers unmasked, and clearly detected to be but the spawn of Romish frogs, Jesuites, and Franciscan fryers; sent from Rome to seduce the intoxicated giddy-headed English nation, London.

REAY, BARRY (1980), Popular Hostility Towards Quakers in Mid-Seventeenth-Century England, Social History 5, 3, 387–407.

The Devil Turned Quaker, or, The damnable, divellish, and accursed doctrines and designes of these desperate, deluded, and deluding people called Quakers their damnable opinions and horrid blasphemies touching the person and deity of our blessed Lord and Saviour Jesus Christ: especially the divelish practices and accursed blasphemies and opinions of one James Neyler, (1656), London.

The Quakers Pedigree: or, a dialogue between a Quaker, and a Iesuit who at last become reconciled, as (holding in a great measure) the same principles; wherein is shown how the mystery of Quakerisme was first hatcht by the Jesuites: by what arts, and for what design it was set on foot in England; and by what means it hath been propagated since, and is still defended. With their contrivance for the carrying it on for the future, (1674), London.

THOMAS, COURTNEY (2011), "Not Having God Before his Eyes": Bestiality in Early Modern England, The Seventeenth Century 26, 1, 149–173.

WIGAN, JOHN (1665), Antichrist's Strongest Hold Overturned: or, The foundation of the religion of the people called Quakers, bared and razed in a debate had with some of them in the castle at Lancaster, and in an additional account of the light within. Wherein is shewed, 1. That their first principle is a lye. 2. That their Christ is not the true Jesus. 3. That their idolatry is worse and more dangerous then Jeroboam's or the Papists. 4. That their principle denies the great mystery of godliness, departs from the faith, and leads to give attendance to the doctrine of daemons. Here also is shewed the occasion of their rise and growth, together with the right way of discovering their secret delusions. Lastly, the best things that the best of this people pretend to own, are here mentioned and allowed, London.

Jakub Koryl

Sources of Community

Mythical Groundwork of Early Modern Identities

1. Introduction: Distinguishing between *What* and *How*

This paper is principally analytical rather than descriptive. It discusses the conditions of possibility that at the turn of the late Middle Ages and early modern period provided collective beings with the necessary groundwork for making the features which distinguish one community from another. By discussing the conditions of possibility this paper will not focus on specifying *what* the particular being is, but *how* that collective being exists. That slight difference between *what* and *how* is of the utmost importance. If we want to say something reasonable about the origins of majorities and minorities as collective entities endowed with the attribute of consciousness, then we must first recognise their metaphysical ground. Namely, which understanding of being and which concept of truth underlies the development of early modern diversified identities?

With regard to *how* I am not concerned with the essence of collective being but with the so-called "essential swaying" (*die Wesung*), to use a term coined by Martin Heidegger (Heidegger: 1989, 260, 286–289, 484–486). To distinguish between *what* and *how* means to contrast the static meaning of essence (*das Wesen*) with an essential swaying, which opens itself up only in the historical process of acting out. By means of asking *what* we inquire into nothing but the essence, that is *what* makes a particular entity what it *is*. Through asking *what*, the entity is placed at our disposal and becomes an object of description. Thus collective entity can be calculated and precisely measured, its condition firmly objectified. In practice, this implies a factual analysis, which informs us objectively, and in fact also quantitatively, what majority and minority are. It only tells us which value is bigger or smaller than another. For example, five is less than six. With regard to the early modern period such an analysis actually tells us nothing about collective identity.

On the other hand "essential swaying" couples *what* and *how*, and in consequence gives us a richer and truly essential representation.[1] To enquire into the *how* of collective being and its consciousness, is to unfold the diversity of that being's manifestations throughout history. This process consists of disclosure, and revelation through collective being. Due to constantly changing conditions self-conscious entities always seek to establish their own spheres of acknowledgement, and constantly require self-confirmation and self-assertion. Instead of a static set of quantitative and qualitative features, the question *how* can reveal the principle that endows entities with the attribute of consciousness. For this reason I will not discuss at length any particular historical majority or minority.

This paper aims to answer four questions and eventually to lead to a discovery of the metaphysical ground of the early modern period. By the metaphysical ground of that era I mean the unprecedented kind of relationship between humans and reality, and the specific role of man in such a relation, namely *how* man becomes himself and *how* he assumes his privileged position in confrontation with politically and religiously disintegrated reality. Each of the four questions is focussed on the different aspect of the metaphysical ground. Firstly, *how* myth impacts on the sense of community? Secondly, under what circumstances the "notion of identity" (=) was replaced by "the identity of notion", that is *how* the metaphysical inquiry into substance was replaced by the introspective need of self-assertion. Thirdly, *how* identity allows us to discuss majorities and minorities as different, juxtaposed but self-conscious collective beings? Fourthly, and finally, *how* is it possible to recognise the conditions that make a difference between majority and minority? Was such difference comprehended quantitatively or qualitatively? The first two questions are concerned with *how* man exists and *how* is he able to know himself, while the third and fourth with *how* the truth

1 "Wenn wir nach dem »Wesen« fragen in der gewohnten Fragerichtung, dann steht die Frage nach dem, was ein Seiendes zu dem »macht«, was es ist, somit nach dem, was sein Was-sein ausmacht, nach der Seiendheit des Seienden. Wesen ist hier nur das andere Wort für Sein (verstanden als Seiendheit). Und demgemäß meint Wesung das Ereignis, sofern es sich in dem ihm Zugehörigen, Wahrheit, ereignet. Geschehnis der Wahrheit des Seyns, das ist Wesung; [...] Wesen wird nur vor-gestellt, ἰδέα. Wesung aber ist nicht nur die Verkoppelung von Was und Wiesein und so eine reichere Vorstellung, sondern die ursprünglichere Einheit jener beiden", (Heidegger: 1989, 288–289. See also Heidegger: 1977, 86–87: "Das Erkennen als Forschung zieht das Seiende zur Rechenschaft darüber, wie es und wieweit es dem Vorstellen verfügbar zu machen ist. Die Forschung verfügt über das Seiende, wenn es dieses entweder in seinem künftigen Verlauf vorausberechnen oder als Vergangenes nachrechnen kann. In der Vorausberechnung wird die Natur, in der historischen Nachrechnung wird die Geschichte gleichsam gestellt. Natur und Geschichte werden zum Gegenstand des erklärenden Vorstellens. Dieses rechnet auf die Natur und rechnet mit der Geschichte. [...] Diese Vergegenständlichung des Seienden vollzieht sich in einem Vor-stellen, das darauf zielt, jegliches Seiende so vor sich zu bringen, daß der rechnende Mensch des Seienden sicher und d. h. gewiß sein kann".

of reality is measured, or, to be more specific, *how* man gives measure to the truth.[2]

Before answering these four questions in the following three chapters of the analytical part I will now, in the descriptive section, comment briefly on a number of historical sources. These were taken chiefly from German history in order to provide supporting evidence for the issues discussed in the analytical section and to introduce the reader smoothly into the above-mentioned questions.

2. Descriptive approach: model histories of a community

On February 1546 in All Saints' Church in Wittenberg the funeral ceremony of Martin Luther took place. The ceremony was accompanied by funeral orations. Luther was honoured with a posthumous tribute in German by Johannes Bugenhagen and in Latin by Philipp Melanchthon. Upon his death Luther was acclaimed by Bugenhagen as "the God-sent Reformer of the Church".[3] Although Melanchthon's sermon was far more sustainable and sober, he drew the same conclusions: "Luther is included in that most beautiful multitude of excellent men whom God sent to unite and restore the Church [...] chosen by God for the renewal of the Church". Melanchthon's speech was also an expression of gratitude: "We thank you, all-powerful God [...] for protecting the ministry of the Gospel and for having renewed it now through Luther".[4]

The funeral orations delivered by Bugenhagen and Melanchthon provide us with three representative factors, crucial for the development, subject matter and functions of collective thinking. These three factors set out by Bugenhagen and Melanchthon are: 1) the precedence claimed by the German nation over other communities in the renewal of the Church; 2) the historical continuity of positive changes, crowned finally by Luther as *the God-sent Reformer of the Church*; 3) the *Lutheran Reformation* as a counter-measure against the Romanisation of Christianity. As such both authors proclaim the so-called German "separate way" (*Sonderweg*) discussed so much in contemporary scholarship.

Bugenhagen and Melanchthon convincingly demonstrate that history exists as a significant record for the next generations only if it is written down and

2 I follow here the footsteps of Heidegger's analysis on the way how "eine metaphysische Grundstellung" can be determined. See Heidegger: 1997, 136–137.

3 Bugenhagen: [1546], A3^{r}: "von Gott gesandten Reformatorn der Kirchen".

4 Melanchthon: 1843, 728, 731, 733: "est igitur illi pulcherrimo agmini summorum virorum, quos Deus ad colligendam et instaurandam Ecclesiam misit [...] a Deo ad Ecclesiae instaurationem delectum [...] Gratias agimus tibi omnipotens Deus [...] servas Evangelii ministerium, et nunc quoque per Lutherum instaurasti".

transcribed; that is, idiosyncratically understood and constantly reconsidered according to changing motivations. In his remembrance speech Melanchthon supplies us with the first guideline for recognising the qualitative character of the notion of majority. For to the question of who should keep in mind Luther's contribution, Melanchthon gives a clear answer: "righteous minds will always [...] praise his labours, faith, constancy and other virtues; and his memory will be most dear to all who are good".[5] Cherished by a qualitatively determined group of people (*bonae mentes, boni omnes*), collective memory becomes essential for the construction of a so-called "separate consciousness". Such consciousness establishes a sense of what is *ours* and typical *for us*, and eventually acknowledges among the community a duty to maintain this sphere against what is foreign or strange, namely against *malae mentes* and *mali omnes.*

The collective memory of the majority (*memoria bonis omnibus*, to use Melanchthon's phrase) gives community a source for self-identification, and it is only memory that justifies historical sources by endowing a particular group with a privileged role in the teleology of history. According to Bugenhagen, the beneficiaries of Luther's efforts were "all the churches of Christ in the German lands and numerous other nations".[6] This precedence given to the German nation was quaint, yet considered. It did not refer to an innovation first introduced by Luther, for novelty has always been accompanied by the *odium* of heterodoxy. For this reason, Bugenhagen assessed Luther's contribution in a prudent way as the culmination of the long history of Christian striving for reform. It is significant that he completely sidestepped the Catholic chapter of that history. According to him, if there were any precedents for renewal, these attempts were all suffocated by the Roman Catholic Church, and not supported by them. Thus Luther became a direct successor to John Hus who a century before had lost the battle for the truth.[7] In this struggle it was Luther who had finally overcome the tyranny of the Pope, and freed a significant part of the Christian flock from the disastrous Romanization. Bugenhagen's conclusions are clear: Luther's efforts signified a new apprehension and purification of the ancient truth, which had long been overshadowed by Roman Catholic precepts and authorities.

5 Melanchthon: 1843, 727: "bonae mentes semper statuent: [...] ipsius labores, fidem, constantiam, et caeteras virtutes laudandas esse, ac memoriam eius bonis omnibus charissimam esse".

6 Bugenhagen: [1546], A2^{v}: "durch welchen er uns allen, und allen Kirchen Christi in deutschen Landen, auch vielen in fremden Nationen, unaussprechliche Gaben und Gnade erzeiget hat".

7 Bugenhagen: [1546], B1^{v}: "Aber in dieser Betrübniß sollen wir auch billig erkennen Gottes Güte und Barmherzigkeit gegen uns, und Gott danken, daß er nach hundert Jahren von dem Tode des heiligen Johannes Huß (welcher um der Wahrheit willen getödtet ist Anno M. CCCC. XV.) balde uns erwecket hat, durch seinen Geist, diesen theuren Doctor Martin Luther, wider die antichristliche Lehre des leidigen satanischen Papsts".

However, as early as the year 1518, Luther had explicitly denied the significance of being a *Reformer*. By saying that "only he himself who has created the ages, knows the time of this Reformation",[8] Luther was not only refusing to be cast in the role of *Reformer*, but, most importantly, was also pointing out that the anticipated renewal of Christianity was the task of God's grace more than anything else. As a matter of fact, however, both the credit that Bugenhagen and Melanchthon gave to Luther and the latter's self-restraint were two sides of the same coin. One concerned a community sharing the distinctive set of beliefs epitomised by Luther, and the other the kernel of the Pauline nut.

However, Luther's writings from 1520 prove that his self-restraint did not mean that he played down or overlooked the social relevancy of his theological reconsiderations. His early disputes with Rome covered three different anti-Roman beliefs which he shared with his fellow German countrymen: 1) at the administrative level Luther disapproved of the curial policy, which robbed the German people of their money and dignity for Roman convenience alone; 2) at the cultural level he strove for a renaissance of the German nation from the barbarity he perceived in Rome; 3) at the doctrinal level he revealed the widespread misinterpretations of Roman theologians. In a memorandum addressed to the nobility of the German nation and the Emperor Charles V, Luther, on behalf of his fellow countrymen, chose his words so carefully that they became, over the next 400 years, a recurring theme of German national consciousness. In particular, this was true of German identity and Christian freedom. Moreover the address was delivered in *Hochdeutsch*, a genuine German tongue.

Referring to the abuse of authority and doctrinal monopoly, Luther held that "the Romans have used them for a long time to make us idiots and [people] of a fearful conscience".[9] Thereby Romanists, by surrounding themselves with "three walls" of secular and religious tyranny, have acted as a gag on German freedom, and are no longer able to reform (*reformieren*) corrupted Christendom.[10] It follows that the abuses of papal authority were based on an unconcealed conviction of Roman cultural superiority over the German nation and land. For Luther this myth of spatial backwardness explains the arrogant attitude of the Holy See toward the German people: "we are Christ's vicars", the Romans would say in order to justify their behaviour, "and the shepherds of Christ's sheep. The silly drunken Germans must resign themselves to it. [...] They want Germans to

8 Luther: 1883d, 627, l. 30–31: "Tempus autem huius reformationis novit solus ille, qui condidit tempora".

9 Luther: 1888a, 414–415: "damit uns nu lange zeit die Romer habenn schuchter und blod gewissen gemacht".

10 Luther: 1888a, 406, l. 21–23: "Die Romanisten haben drey mauren, mit grosser behendickeit, umb sich zogen, damit sie sich biszher beschutzt, das sie niemant hat mugenn reformierenn, dadurch die gantz Christenheit grewlich gefallen ist".

remain naive fools and continue paying the money to satisfy their unspeakable avarice".[11] It soon became clear that Charles V, the titular ruler of the German Reich, was "shamelessly trodden under foot and oppressed by the Popes", to quote Luther's own admonishment to the newly elected Emperor,[12] since he merely served the Roman interests. Luther was actually the first to recognise the disturbing incoherence, later objectified by Friedrich Schiller, of the fact that the German Reich and German nation were not one and the same entity.[13] Consequently, such German national consciousness became the principal attribute of a collective being (Luther and Ulrich von Hutten spoke of *deutsche landt und Nation*) which was founded upon mythical imponderables, regardless of actual political achievements.

In this politically-disintegrated Reich, Luther was considered both a religious and political prophet and placed by his followers at the forefront of the *reformation.*[14] This German myth of the Lutheran Reformation, first verbalised around 1520 and repeated over the next 400 years, aimed at shaping the collective identity of the German nation. It should be emphasised, however, that not only German specificity became the decisive bond of that community. For struggles with Rome and the Romanization of politics, faith, culture and society were equally important; in some cases even predominant, as for instance in Hutten's dialogue *Arminius.* His deliberate reassessment of German mythology and Roman historiography, with regard to Arminius in particular, emphasised the pivotal feature of anti-Roman hostility that ought to distinguish real Germans from those oppressed by the Romans. According to Hutten, Arminius "revived a Germany that had been thoroughly trampled and torn in pieces".[15] The myth of Arminius, as the *liberator Germaniae*, provided the pattern for future conduct, and integrated individuals who had been torn apart into a self-conscious community.

Taken directly from Roman historiography, Arminius' portrait was developed by Hutten into a vivid, stimulating image of values giving organised existence to a collective, yet separate, consciousness. Characterised by contrastingly marked

11 Luther: 1888a, 417, l. 8–9; 419, l. 2–3 "darnach sagen, wir sein Christi Vicarii und hirten der schaff Christi, die tollen, vollen Deutschen mussens wol leyden. [...] meynend, die tollen Deutschen sollen unendlich todstocknarn bleyben, nur ymer gelt geben, yrem unauszsprechlichem geytz gnug thun".

12 Luther: 1888a, 405, l. 35–36: "deutscher keyszer szo jemerlich sein von den Bepsten mit fussen tretten und vordruckt".

13 Schiller: 1916, 13: "deutsches Reich und deutsche Nation sind zweierlei Dinge". See also Böckenförde: 1995, 129–154.

14 Pettegree: 2015, 254 openly labels Luther, on account of his actual impact in the German Reich, "the nation's pastor".

15 Von Hutten: 1860, 412, l. 30–31: "ego penitus proculcatam et discerptam brevi Germaniam restitui".

out features, these common historical figures make up a web of distinguishing signs which enable entities to recognise themselves as being separate and unique. The deliberate retelling of this myth revived ancient German identities and spurred the community into emancipatory action, since it was Arminius who "evoked the memory of freedom",[16] and, as such, met the highest expectations of his early modern descendants who were subjugated by the same, common enemy. German by birth, most free and invincible by his deeds, Arminius became the most genuine embodiment of Germanness (*Germanissimus*), as Hutten himself concluded.[17]

Only in confrontation with Romanness did being a true German, or Germanness itself, gain full and positive clarity. Hutten, however, went even further. His interpretation of ancient history proves that particular heritage does not constitute a collective identity by itself, but rather the most relevant factor socially is "ethnic boundary", to use a term introduced by Fredrik Barth.[18] This means that a community seeks its self-assertion and self-apperception by way of interaction with different, foreign communities. A boundary establishes a demarcation line that defines both internal and external interactions – it involves, as Barth points out, criteria for regulating affiliation and exclusion. "Those who were paying the tribute to foreigners", Hutten openly declared, "I did not consider to be Germans, nor those who allowed other shameful proposals to be imposed on them".[19] In brief, *we* does not mean *you*, *our* does not mean *yours*. Therefore Romanization was neither an abstract concept nor an imaginary threat. In the collective consciousness it had specific significance. Luther's warning, "let us watch, for the German land will soon become like Italy",[20] is perhaps the most glaring illustration of Romanization understood as an administrative, religious and cultural assimilation of the German nation. In a similar manner and for comparable reasons, Hutten was hoping that "soon not even a trace of the Romans would be left in Germany, even the remembrance [*memoria*] would be erased".[21]

An excellent typology for the multi-layered phenomenon of Romanisation was introduced by Helmuth Plessner in his book *Belated Nation* (1974, 52–56).

16 Von Hutten: 1860, 415, l. 12: "libertatis memorem retinui". See also Mertens: 2004, 96–100.

17 Von Hutten: 1860, 416, l. 14–16: "huic negotium do, ut in foro, plateis, circo, triviis et ubiubi hominum ac dearum frequentia est, pronunciet Arminium Cheruscum liberrimum, invictissimum et Germanissimum".

18 Barth: 1998, 15. See below.

19 Von Hutten: 1860, 413, l. 21–22: "neque pro Germanis habui qui tributa exteris penderent aut aliis conditionibus obnoxios teneri se paterentur".

20 Luther: 1888a, 416, l. 28–29: "aber sehen wir zu, deutsch landt sol bald dem welschen gleich warden".

21 Von Hutten: 1860, 413, l. 25–27: "paulo post ne ullae in Germania Romanorum saltem reliquiae superessent, pene memoria aboleretur".

According to Plessner's analysis of the so-called *Roman complex*, a concept influenced by Carl Schmitt's *anti-Roman temper*,[22] it was Rome that turned out to be the strongest factor for German consolidation, a catalyst for the development of collective as well as separate consciousness. The dialectical impact of Rome had four different aspects. Firstly, Rome was seen as the expansive empire that Romanised independent Germans. Secondly, Rome was seen as the Papal Church which exercised tyrannical authority over German piety. Thirdly, Rome was seen as the birthplace of Mediterranean humanism which is both topographically and spatially distanced from the northern *barbaricum*. And fourthly, Rome was seen as the lawgiver, and therefore the living embodiment of the universal state of the *respublica christiana* which had the Latin language as its only acceptable medium of communication. These four aspects of dialectical impact constituted the Roman complex of German collective being. Moreover, as clearly testified by Luther, and later by Hegel, the early modern idea of the German nation became an exclusive exponent of genuine Christian qualities (Hegel: 1989, 499–501). These qualities were not determined by the German nation itself and in isolation, but in opposition to what was foreign, namely, the myth of Rome. In brief, for the followers of Luther, being a German meant to speak the vernacular and follow Luther against Rome.

Plessner's typology, however, needs adjustment and further explanation. First of all, the factors identified by Plessner were intended to describe merely the Roman complex of the German nation. In order to extend their functionality to other collective beings, I will use them from now on as general and comprehensive categories of power, faith, value and knowledge. On each level the community sets the boundaries for the appropriate ideas of power, faith, value and knowledge. At the same time, the community ascribes the attribute of exclusive authenticity to its ideas, and in effect enters into polemical, socially-relevant relationship with everything which is different. This relationship, by means of dialectical interaction, that is a constructive opposition of *us* and *them*, petrifies ideas regarding the uniqueness of specific collective being.

According to Plessner, Rome was a relevant factor in the making of the German community. This requires, however, an explanation. From the German perspective, Rome entailed selected aspects of power, faith, value, and knowledge that were foreign or even hostile to Germans. By inverting these properties, Germanness clearly recognised its own set of unique features. It should be emphasised that Rome was not understood as a real, topographically defined place, but as a mythical centre which provided distinctive contents for the collective consciousness, and, thereby, patterns for political conduct as well. Schmitt al-

22 Schmitt: 1996, 7: "the anti-Roman temper as a national or local reaction against universalism and centralism".

ready observed that "the mythical power of this image is deeper and stronger than any economic calculation" (1996, 5). Indeed, for the community identifying itself with such a mythical place, Rome became a nationally integrating factor, the guarantor of Christian unity, and the centre of universal culture (cf. Borowski: 1987, 50; Münkler: 2009, 141–147). Lorenzo Valla's preface to *Elegantiae* was perhaps the most compendious expression of Roman supremacy: "To us belongs Italy, to us belongs France, to us belong Spain, Germany, Hungary, Dalmatia, Illyricum and numerous other nations. For the Roman empire is found where the Roman language exercises its sovereignty".[23] By using the token of linguistic empire, *lingua Romana* as against the expected *lingua Latina*, Valla emphasised the Roman superiority over the whole civilised world in terms of power and knowledge. In similar vein, the *Consilium de emendanda ecclesia*, the report presented to Pope Paul III by the committee under the chairmanship of Gasparo Contarini, underlined the universal order of faith and value established by Rome: "This city of Rome and Roman Church is the mother and master of the other churches. For that reason, especially in Rome, divine worship and moral integrity should flourish".[24]

The myth of *purga Romam, purgatur mundus* was verbalised also by Pope Adrian VI in the instruction which he drafted for the papal nuncio Francesco Chieregati in 1522. I believe this document is the most glaring example of this issue. Adrian VI openly admitted that "many abominable things have occurred in this Holy See, misuses in spiritual matters, transgressions of the commandments, and finally everything was turned into ruin. […] Without exception all of us have strayed from *our* paths. […] We see that entire world ardently desires such a reformation [*reformatio*]".[25] Our paths (*viae nostrae*), a phrase used by Adrian VI, was a highly purposeful and deliberate expression of Roman, and, in fact, anti-Lutheran policy. In comparison with the Lutherans the Roman *via nostra* was the name for the properly conducted renewal of the Christianity under papal auspices, a *via romanitatis*. Born in Utrecht, that is in *Germania*, Adrian VI emphasised that the *secta Lutherana* (a name given to the collective being) brought dishonour upon the German nation, and its glorious, truly Christian, history. Luther did not embody the essence of Germanness, in fact quite the

23 Valla: 1952, 596: "Nostra est Italia, nostra Gallia, nostra Hispania, Germania, Pannonia, Dalmatia, Illyricum, multaeque aliae nationes. Ibi namque romanum imperium est ubicumque romana lingua dominator".

24 Contarini: 1930, 143, l. 18–19: "Haec Romana civitas et ecclesia, mater est et magistra aliarum ecclesiarum; ideo maxime in ea vigere debet divinus cultus et morum honestas".

25 Adrian VI: 1901, l. 14–17, 18–19, 28–29: "in hac sancta sede aliquot iam annis multa abominanda fuisse abusus in spiritualibus; excessus in mandatis et omnia denique in perversum mutata; […] Omnes nos (id est prelati et ecclesiastici) declinavimus unusquisque in vias nostras. […] universum mundum huiusmodi reformationem avidis desiderare videmus".

opposite. “If”, as the Pope observed, “those who hold authority and power in German nation do not strive with all their energy to expel those heresies, they will become unworthy of their own forefathers, the most Christian men, who played a major part in the condemnation of John Hus and the other heretics”.[26]

Obviously neither the *natio Germanica* nor the *deutsche Nation* stood for an empirical being. Since it was founded upon specific convictions about power, faith, value and knowledge, the *natio Germanica* was still merely an effective fiction in the sixteenth century. Its social relevancy consisted in a “society of readers who through reading the same books become a like-minded community”, as Peter Sloterdijk explained his concept of nation as *die wirkungsvolle Fiktion.*[27] According to Adrian VI such ideas were all defined in Roman terms. Regarding the followers of Luther he insisted: “their parents, forefathers have always held to the faith affirmed by the Roman and Catholic Church”.[28] Only under such a condition could *natio Germanica* be a synonym for the German Reich, and hence stand for a constitutionally-validated collective being. Genuine Germans once condemned Hus, recently they approved, as the Pope continues, the imperial edict drawn up for the execution of the apostolic sentence against Luther. In such a way the Roman Pontiff completely inverted the ideas verbalised in the myth of Luther’s Reformation. The privileged role of the Lutherans in Christian as well as German history was questioned and denied. In brief, being a true German meant to follow the Pope against Luther. One may argue now about which version makes sense.

On the eastern side of the Rhine the substance of the myth of *Roma renata* or *purgata* was associated with the negative image of the political, religious and cultural monopoly of Rome. In brief, with the image of Romanisation, which Luther gave expression to both in the address to the nobility of the German nation, and in the image of the Babylonian captivity of the Church, where “by indulgences men are robbed of their faith in God and of their money. […] for the Papacy is a great hunt led by the Bishop of Rome”.[29] In his later writings Luther went further and contrasted Roman abuses with the genuine Christian approach exercised by the German *Volk*. In *On the Councils and the Church*, his major work

26 Adrian VI: 1901, 394, l. 13–17: “qui apud nacionem Germanicam auctoritate et potencia pollent; hereses istas non totis viribus expellere laborant, tum quia degenerabunt a progenitoribus suis, viris christianissimis; qui in Constanciensi concilio ex magna parte interfuerunt condemnacioni Johannis Huss et aliorum hereticorum”.

27 Sloterdijk: 1999, 12: “Was sind die neuzeitlichen Nationen anderes als die wirkungsvollen Fiktionen von lesenden Öffentlichkeiten, die durch dieselben Schriften zu einem gleichgestimmten Bund von Freunden würden?” See also Anderson: 2006, 39–40.

28 Adrian VI: 1901, 394, l. 26–28: “ipsorum parentes et progenitores et ipsimet semper tenuerint fidem, quam ecclesia Romana atque catholica approbat”.

29 Luther: 1888b, 497–498, l. 9, 17–18: “[indulgentiae], quibus et fidem dei et pecunias hominum perderent. […] Papatus est robusta venatio Romani episcopi”.

on ecclesiology, Luther pointed out, through establishing a demarcation line between different, hierarchically juxtaposed forms of divine worship, and using the opposition of *us* and *them*, that *their* means precisely *not ours*. "*Ecclesia Romana sancta* means 'a holy Roman people'; this they also are, since they have created a holiness far greater than Christian holiness, or than the holy Christian people possess. Their holiness is a Roman holiness – *Romanae ecclesiae* – a holiness of the Roman people".[30]

3. Analytical Approach: *Who Are We?* Myth and Identity between *Distinctiveness* and *Selfhood*

Having discussed a handful of historical examples, the functional analysis of myth will be undertaken in order to answer the first of the aforementioned questions, namely *how* the myth impacts on the sense of community.

"Myth", which is all too often used intuitively, functions in scientific vocabulary as a buzzword, which can indeed open every door, but which will inevitably damage every lock. All too often myth stands for falsehood or laxity, and represents an outdated stage of development or an ideologically distorted form of knowledge. Consequently, myth all too often requires revision or even replacement by critical reconsideration. Such connection between myth and trickery, has historical justification and derives obviously from Immanuel Kant's project of instituting "a true reform in the manner of thinking" (*wahre Reform der Denkungsart*), namely the conquest of myth by critical reason. Through the discrediting of prejudices myth loses its epistemic value and stands merely for a harmful prejudice, namely a poetical fiction that is not capable of telling the truth. Through its imaginative force, myth as a form of prejudice seeks to stimulate the aesthetic imagination and causes serious damage to disciplined, scientific cognition (Kant: 1968, 35–36 and Gadamer: 1990, 278–279). All these intellectual sentiments regarding cognitive progress were aptly captured by Wilhelm Nestle in the title of his seminal study on the development of Greek thought – *From Myth to Reason.*

Myth, however, should not be debunked, but first and foremost should be understood. Its pragmatic motivations and conditions should be unveiled. The supposed antithesis of reason and myth, or its epistemic entanglement, have been already questioned by Georges Sorel in his *Reflections on Violence*, first pub-

30 Luther: 1914, 626, l. 1–5: "Ecclesia Romana sancta heisst ein heilig Römisch Volk, Das sind sie auch, Denn sie haben gar viel eine grössere heiligkeiit erfunden, weder der Christen heiligkeit ist, oder das heilge Christlich Volk hat, Denn ire heiligkeit ist eine Römische heiligkeit, Romanae Ecclesiae, des Römischen Volks heiligkeit".

lished in 1908, and masterfully challenged by Robert MacIver, Leszek Kołakowski, Ian Barbour, Hans Blumenberg, George Schöpflin and Miroslav Hroch among others. Therefore the road to reassess myth has finally become wide open. Sorel was the first to indicate the quaint feature of a myth that constitutes its verification method. "Myth cannot be refuted", Sorel reminds us, "since it is, at bottom, identical to the convictions of a group, being the expression of these convictions in the language of a movement". Consequently, the criteria for evaluating myths need to be profoundly changed in order to rehabilitate myth as a valuable scientific tool and indicate their relevant functions: "myths must be judged as a means of acting on the present" (Sorel: 2004, 29, 116).

Kołakowski made another step forward. By way of functional analysis he not only liberated myth from the rules of logic, but also noted that myth has nothing to do with epistemological questions. "The predicates 'true' and 'false' are inapplicable", as he states in *The Presence of Myth*, "here it is not the case of matching a judgment with a situation it describes, but of matching a need with an area which satisfies it. Myth degenerated when it changed into doctrine, that is, a product demanding and seeking proof" (Kołakowski: 2001, 3).[31] Schöpflin establishes a boundary between the supposed and actual area of mythical operation: "myth is about perceptions rather than historically validated truths", and then gives a clear warning that "myth is not identical with falsehood or deception" (Schöpflin: 1997, 19). In a similar manner Blumenberg observed the same constraints and modalities of myth. His reassessment presented in *Work on Myth* was based on an anthropological rather than epistemological understanding. This does not mean, however, that myth is deprived of veracity.

I understand myth as an intellectual and highly purposeful construction. As a narrative determined in terms of a standpoint, myth concentrates on how to generate, maintain and modify the human order of ontologically disintegrated reality. Thus, myth should not be restricted to traditional sacred matters and rituals that are esteemed as divinely justified. Myth is a standpoint lying not within the rules of logic, that is the rules of truthfulness or falsehood, but is based only on the pragmatic category of efficiency. Myth is not an abstract construction. In order to be efficient myth must be verbalised in literature or visual arts, and these verbalisations must remain in circulation within the collective. Myth always tells a story that needs to be retold. The truth of myth is pragmatic, which means that verity is not an intrinsic property of myth. To say that myth is inconsistent with the facts is to misunderstand what myth actually stands for. Principally, myth refers to a practice and conduct, not a cognition. It follows that myth's precision as a supposed historical account is at best of secondary im-

31 On the question of the truth or falsity of myth see also Barbour: 1976, 24; Szacka: 2006, 78–82.

portance. To make this clear I will take advantage of the language introduced by William James.

The pragmatic truth of myth here means the so-called *will to believe*, which can be verified only by way of practical operation. Thus the truth of myth is measured by one's willingness to act, when myth appeals as a real possibility (James: 1897, 2–3). One and the same myth of *Luther's Reformation*, that was verbalised by, among others, Hutten, Bugenhagen and Melanchthon, confirms its efficiency, and consequently, its pragmatic veracity. By following in James' footsteps we can say that when myth is useful then it can be considered true (James: 1907, 204). Man can verbalise myth in literature and visual arts or may use ready-made verbalisations if he finds them useful. Truth is not an inner, static attribute of myth, but an outcome of its relation to the individual or collective user. In other words, this means a measurable impact on human experience, in which myth gives a relevant, purposeful description of historical events or persons, an explanation of current affairs, and finally an indication of the desired goal to achieve (Murray: 1960, 337). Therefore myth is a source of truth completely different from theoretical reason. It informs collective expectations, and by using probable beliefs constitutes a community. Constant verbalisation of myth thus plays a crucial part in the making of collective consciousness. Myth is to be considered useful. For the community must regard its truth as their own and demystify what is foreign. Myth compensates for our deficiencies and binds teleologically the contingent components of human experience with unconditional ideas of power, faith, value, and knowledge. Myth willingly and frequently refers to historical precedent in order to find the proof that can validate present motivations and decisions. Myth helps to domesticate reality, since it provides, as Kołakowski pointed out, "the rules of understanding empirical realities as meaningful" (Kołakowski: 2001, 3).[32]

If we want to speak reasonably of the connection between the word and the reality with reference to myth, it should be noted first that such a relation does not apply to the traditional equation of a statement and its object but only to the conformity of a historical source with its current motivation. With regard to the pragmatic dimension of myth it is reasonable to speak even of the compliance of the historical source with its current motivation. Consequently, as Hroch rightly noticed, to assess myth in a proper manner is to consider it in terms of its current social functions, while subjecting it to logical criteria would be meaningless (2005, 162). Myth is actually more concerned with the present time of its verbalisation than with the past about which it supposedly gives an account. Myth is not a thing of the past. For this reason history retold in myth is subject to several essential and, most often, deliberate modifications, such as: modernisation and

32 A similar conclusion was drawn by Schorer: 1960, 355.

adjustment of the past; passing over details or adding them in; playing up or playing down; manipulating causality; passing binary value judgments; hierarchisation of the whole narrative reality; casual manipulation of individual qualities; personification of driving forces of historical progress; and turning distinguished, historical figures into personifications of particular ideas. Therefore, Hutten, for example, could portray Arminius as a greater chieftain than Alexander the Great, Hannibal and Scipio, and at the same time his deliberate exaggeration did not violate the pragmatic truth of myth. The same may be said of a legendary Hercules turned into the historical *Hercules Germanicus*, or Luther turned into *von Gott gesandten Reformatorn der Kirchen*, and numerous other myths constructed by the Reformation.

Myth always tells a story, and such story is "distinguished by a high degree of constancy in its narrative core and by an equally pronounced capacity for marginal variation". In his *Work on Myth* Blumenberg noticed that periods characterised by high rates of systemic change always need new myths, and strive for their own remythicisations (2001, 40–41). Verbalised around the year 1520, the myth of *Luther's Reformation* was a brand new response to a change that could no longer be handled by the older anti-Roman myths, such as the Germanic myth derived from Tacitus, the myth of Barbarossa, and even the myth of Arminius masterfully retold by Hutten (cf. Münkler: 2009, 37–67, 141–196). Under the influence of the progressive disintegration of the pre-modern Christian community caused by Lutheranism, the Reformation (*reformatio*) itself became a widely disseminated and confessionally diversified historiosophical and social myth.[33] This was the ultimate response. As a myth, the Reformation began to engage various communities against the religious and political chauvinism of Lutheranism, and eventually allowed other collective beings to identify their own privileged place in Christian history. Due to the mythical constellation of Europe on the threshold of the modern period, not one world, but many different worlds existed parallel to each other, each of them claiming to be the only authentic one. For myth, as Blumenberg says, "is not proposed without totality and below the level of a pretension to totality" (2001, 71).

To sum up this recognition of myth I will review the five functions that I consider the most important for the making of the early modern period. Some of these have been identified by the above-mentioned authors, Barbour, Schöpflin and Hroch in particular.[34] From a scientific point of view such a multi-layered,

33 It should be noted that in modern scholarship the notion of Reformation as a myth does not appear very frequently. To the best of my knowledge, Sorel is the one who first spoke of the "remarkable examples of myths" constructed by the Reformation as well as the Catholic image (that is myth) of the Church militant. See Sorel: 2004, 20–21, 24.

34 See Barbour: 1976, 20–22; Schöpflin: 1997, 22–27; Hroch: 2005, 154–155, 162–170.

functional examination of myth can give extremely instructive insights into the way that particular communities understood themselves.

First of all, myth is a story that needs to be understood and purposefully retold (including any of the above-listed modifications) in order to remain useful and pragmatically true. Secondly, myth allows man to domesticate his experience. It provides the basic, binary structure of reality, where opposite ideas of power, faith, value, and knowledge are clearly demarcated. Thereby myth "acts as a means of standardisation". As Schöpflin rightly observes, "through myth, boundaries are established within the community and also with respect to other communities" (1997, 20). Different, often self-contradictory myths of Reformation were verbalised at the time of this groundbreaking historical event, when new forms of individual and collective existence were established or modified. Every myth of Reformation was aimed at establishing the sphere of exclusive property (what is *ours* and typical *for us*, namely what is good and reasonable).

Thirdly, myth instructs people about themselves. Communities understand themselves in relation to the story retold in myth. Such narratives usually refer to historically distant events or persons, but it is the current community that is the principal subject matter of description. By retelling its history the community actually talks about itself. Thus myth endows collective entities with the attribute of consciousness, both self- and collective (that is *us*, and *us among the others*).

Fourthly, myth, as pointed out by Sorel, provides efficient patterns for human conduct. For according to Sorel, myths "allow us to understand the activity, the sentiments and the ideas of the masses as they prepare themselves to enter on a decisive struggle; they are not descriptions of things but expressions of a will to act" (2004, 28).[35] Myth provides, however, not an abstract ideal, but a vivid model for human imitation. Real myth is vivid and impressive, inspiring beings to emotional response and measurable action. Real myth matches their resentments and complexes, expectations and motivations. In consequence it helps to establish a new state of affairs or at least to modify the present state of affairs. Myth instructs us concerning *what* ought to be achieved and *how* it should be achieved. The commonly accepted morality is founded upon the stories retold in real myths, where moral standards and specified value-attitudes are convincingly prescribed.

Fifthly, and finally, these four functions together make up the social dimension of myth. For it essentially promotes the integration of individual entities into a self-conscious community. MacIver noticed that myth not only generates the need for collective life but also enables community to survive in the

35 A little earlier (ibidem, p. 27) Sorel underlines in a similar way the social and, in fact, pragmatic function of myth: "when the masses are deeply moved it then becomes possible to describe a picture which constitutes a social myth".

face of adverse circumstances: "every society is held together by a myth-system, a complex of dominating thought-forms that determines and sustains all its activities. All social relations, the very texture of human society, are myth-born and myth-sustained" (MacIver: 1965, 4). Moreover myth justifies the duties of power, faith, value, and knowledge performed within the community. By expressing a commonly shared set of beliefs, myth becomes a cohesive factor binding a community together, and decisively influencing the making of collective identity.

4. Analytical Approach: Discovering *Selfhood* within the Disintegrated Reality

If these functions of myth involve a consecutive domestication of the constantly and irrevocably changing reality, then the making of *identity* turns out to be an ultimate goal of the work on myth. It should be underlined, however, that this kind of identity does not involve examination of a substance. If so, then identity would have nothing to do with myth, since myth provides different patterns by which man may recognise himself rather than describes what man fundamentally is. For that reason we have to recognise the conditions that forced transition from an inquiry into substance to an introspective, truly early modern need of self-confirmation and self-assertion.

Philosophical reflection dedicated to the problem of identity did not keep up with the actual changes in the methods of apperception which took place in the sixteenth century. According to Plato and Aristotle, identity (ἡ ταὐτότης or τὸ ταὐτόν, literally "sameness", that is something "devoid of variety or change") in its earliest metaphysical form would have been a useless factor for shaping common beliefs. This traditional interpretation of "sameness" was later confirmed by Aquinas, and thereby the "notion of identity" was established for the next 400 years as a binding form of every inquiry into substance. The criterion for the evaluation of meaning became merely the logical opposition of truth and falsehood. The substantial meaning of an entity was static, and could only be true or false according to the accidental properties it bore. The opposite of metaphysical identity is not distinct identity (for instance Lutheran versus Roman Catholic), but difference. The cognitive character of metaphysical identity implied truth as an object of certain knowledge (ἡ ἐπιστήμη) within the universal order of things and names. Consequently there was no room for persuasion which was required only when certain images and beliefs (αἱ δόξαι), that is myths, had to be advocated.

I agree with Robert Spaemann that identity, whether personal or collective, did not emerge as the fundamental and uniquely modern problem until the universal importance of certain concepts and their fixed meanings came to a close. Indeed, as long as universal and normative notions indicating the place of man in the ontological order were available, the apperceptive sense of identity remained dormant. As long as truth was the decisive criterion for assessing human opinions about themselves, and that truth was an object of certain knowledge, the apperceptive sense of identity was simply not needed (Spaemann: 2007, 123–124). I disagree, however, that the conditions listed by Spaemann were not met until the breakthrough caused by the philosophy of Leibniz. Rather, I believe that Spaemann underestimated the impact of late medieval Nominalism upon the sixteenth-century philosophy of man. Since the discursive ambitions and universal order of ontological Realism were devalued, the metaphysical ground justifying the traditional worldview was seriously undermined. Luther's struggles with Aristotelian as well as medieval metaphysics may exemplify the profound change that eventually paved the way for the development of the modern "identity of notion", where *sameness* was replaced by *selfhood.*

Human reason, as Luther insisted, is not capable of understanding the absolute freedom of God. In consequence, the world, from a human-discursive perception, becomes contingent, because reason is unable to find a permanent explanation for the whole order of creatures. Furthermore, claiming that universals are real implies the limitation of God's omnipotence, since then creation would be nothing but a result of imitation and repetition. God's omnipotence neither copies nor imitates, but rather generates unrepeatable beings. Therefore Nominalism casts aside the idolatry of access to objective truth. "Reason", Luther himself declares, "does not learn from aprioric assumptions, but only from experience or empirical evidence".[36] As a result of discursive efforts, truth eventually adopts the attribute of variability. When certain discursive knowledge in terms of a self-revealing reality is no longer available, man eventually loses self-confidence. Sixteenth-century doctrinal struggles demonstrate the truth of this hypothesis.

Within the universal, realistic order of things and names human being was the *ens creatum*, that is created by God as the highest cause, the principle of principleness. Aquinas' *Summa theologiae* leaves no doubt that to recognise humanity, or more precisely to recognise *who I am*, is to recognise by means of discursive reason (*ratio*) man's place in the order of created beings. In such a way man's identity was rationally fixed, because it consisted in being brought before God, and, by the principle of *analogia entis*, in corresponding to the cause of creation. Such identity stands for the correspondence that provides the definite possibilities and ways in which man may recognise himself as an element of

36 Luther: 1926, 175, l. 22–23: "nec ea ipsa ratio novit a priore, sed tantum a posteriore". See Ebeling: 1982, 314–320.

universal order. Thus being *self* means performing duties arising from the place that a particular man occupies. However, it turned out for Luther that the traditional philosophical definition of man as *animal rationale*, confirmed by thirteenth-century scholasticism using discursive reason as its groundwork, possessed only relative relevance, since "this definition defines man only as a mortal and in relation to such existence".[37] Moreover, the principle of *analogia entis* developed by Aquinas, rather blinds a man who seeks God than provides him with a reliable solution.[38] According to Luther, *animal rationale*, or philosophical diagnoses in general, speak neither of original sin which profoundly changed human existence nor about man's actual relation to God and divine grace.[39]

The theological absolutism of late medieval Nominalism pushed man into intellectual aporias regarding God's omnipotence, and in effect deprived him of discursive tools for self-analysis. When the ontological order of unrepeatable beings was no longer seen as comprehensible, profound changes became inevitable. Confronted with a reality that could not be enchained by means of reason, man needed a new form of self-assertion, because from the human perspective the unrepeatableness of divine creation appeared as a set of contingent elements. In *Legitimacy of the Modern Age* Blumenberg showed that the development of the early modern period was determined by the modest desire to self-assert within a limited area, rather than by the claim to give a thorough explanation of reality (1996, 139–259). As an answer to theological absolutism human self-assertion involves making an effort to identify one's own historical situation. Luther clearly stressed that by merely natural abilities a man seeks in vain to bring the whole of God's creation under control.[40]

Since the human being is no longer capable of acting and thinking efficiently within the reality created by God, man has to create his own reality, modelled after its divine pattern, but actually based on human order. Only within such a newly established reality, essentially deprived of God's omnipotence, could man himself finally act and think efficiently, and thereby meet his basic need of self-assertion. In a somewhat gloomy vein, which reminds one of the conclusion

37 Luther: 1926, 175, l. 7–8: "haec definitio tum mortalem et huius vitae hominem definit [hominem, esse animal rationale, sensitivum, corporeum – J.K.]".

38 Luther: 1883b, 354, l. 17–18, 23–24: "Non ille digne Theologus dicitur, qui invisibilia Dei per ea, quae facta sunt, intellecta conspicit. [...] Sapientia illa, quae invisibilia Dei ex operibns intellecta conspicit, omnino inflat, excaecat et indurate".

39 Luther: 1926, 179, l. 3–6, 33–34: "Probe segreganda est philosophia a theologia. Philosophi et Aristoteles non potuerunt intelligere aut definire, quid esset homo theologicus, sed nos Dei gratia, quod bibliam habemus, praestare id possemus. [...] philosophi nihil sciunt de Creatore Deo et homine de gleba terrae facto".

40 Luther: 1883c, 145, l. 11–12: "[Homo] suis naturalibus viribus solis creaturam quamlibet qua utitur vanitati subiicit".

drawn centuries later by dialectical theology, Luther observed that "by nature man is not capable of wanting God to be God [...] man himself wants to be God, and does not want God to be God". Moreover, he conclusively revealed the human need for self-assertion: "If it were possible, man's will would prefer that there would be no law and to be entirely free".[41] Four centuries later Karl Barth confirmed that Luther really hit the nail on the head with his vision of man's disposition toward divine reality: "God himself is not recognised as God, and what is called God is man himself. By living independently, we serve the no-God".[42]

Heidegger captured this distinctive and highly significant change that took place in the understanding of sin's effect upon the human disposition (*Gestelltsein*) toward divine creation. "Luther does not recognize sin as an accumulation of errors, but draws attention to *affectus*, that is, to the way in which man is disposed toward things and terrified by his dependence on them. [...] sin is described as a very specific way of being disposed toward the world".[43] This means that man has to create and constantly try out his own reality where he can finally gain for himself support in the face of insecurity and disintegration.

These struggles led to a profound revaluation of metaphysical foundations. If order, constitutive for man's identity, turned out to be incomprehensible, to assert himself man had to find such order somewhere else. Thus he had to free himself from the aporias of Nominalism and from the external *analogia entis* alike, and return to himself alone. In effect, subjectivism was introduced. The trivial and overused notion of subjectivism requires, however, an explanation. Precisely speaking, subjectivism means that man becomes a subject (*subiectum*, ὑποκείμενον). As ὑποκείμενον, that is "that-which-lies-before" or a "ground which

41 Luther: 1883a, 225, l. 1–2, p. 228, l. 13–14: "Non potest homo naturaliter velle deum esse deum, immo vellet se esse deum et deum non esse deum. [...] Voluntas cuiuslibet mallet, si fieri posset, esse nullam legem et se omnino liberam". Barth: 2010, 67, 69: "Wer glaubt, liebt mit Hiob den Gott, der in seiner unerforschlichen Höhe nur zu fürchten ist, liebt mit Luther den deus absconditus. [...] Wir meinen zu wissen, was wir sagen, wenn wir «Gott» sagen. Wir weisen ihm die höchste Stelle in unsrer Welt zu. Wir stellen ihn damit grundsätzlich auf eine Line mit uns und mit den Dingen. [...] Wir schieben uns zudringlich in seine Nähe und wir ziehen ihn unbedenklich in unsere Nähe. Wir erlauben uns, in ein Gewohnheitsverhältnis zu ihm zu treten. Wir erlauben uns, mit ihm zu rechnen, als ob das nichts Besonderes wäre. Wir wagen es, uns als seine Vertrauten, Gönner, Sachwalter und Unterhändler aufzuspielen. [...] Das ist das Ehrfurchtslose unsres Gottesverhältnisses. Und es ist unbotmäßig. Wir selber sind heimlich die Herren in diesem Verhältnis. Es handelt sich uns nicht um Gott, sondern um unsre Bedürfnisse, nach denen sich Gott zu richten hat".

42 Barth: 2010, 70: "Gott selbst ist als Gott nicht anerkannt und das, was Gott heißt, ist in Wahrheit der Mensch selbst. Wir dienen dem Nicht-Gott, indem wir uns selbst leben".

43 Heidegger: 1996, 29: "Luther sieht hier die Sünde nicht als Anhäufung von Fehlern, sondern er lenkt den Blick auf den affectus, d. h. auf die Weise des Gestelltseins des Menschen zu den Dingen, auf das Entsetztsein vor ihnen, das auf dem Hängen an ihnen entspringt. [...] die Sünde hat ihre Bestimmung in einem ganz bestimmten Gestelltsein zur Welt".

gathers everything onto itself", man eventually becomes the referential centre of the whole ontological order. Man is then finally capable of self-assertion. On account of man, and man only, his identity is established.

This groundbreaking change can be labelled, after Heidegger, as the rise of the "age of the world picture". Let us give the floor to Heidegger himself: "essentially understood *world picture* does not stand for the *picture of the world* but for the world comprehended as a picture. In this perspective being as a whole is in being only insofar as it is set in place by presenting and producing mankind. […] The world picture does not emerge from a formerly medieval to a modern one; rather that the world thoroughly becomes a picture singles out the essence of modern era".[44] The subjectivism, or inwardness, which was essential for the changes caused by Nominalism, is very different from the one we find in Plato or Augustine. Charles Taylor explains its unprecedented specificity: "It does, in a very real sense, place the moral sources within us. Relative to Plato, and relative to Augustine, it brings about in each case a transposition by which we no longer see ourselves as related to moral sources outside of us. […] the order of ideas ceases to be something we *find* and becomes something we *build*" (Taylor: 2001, 143–144). Such inwardness, together with an affirmation of ordinary life, constitutes, according to Taylor, the sources of modern identity.

Heidegger and Taylor mention René Descartes as the figure principally responsible for the making of the modern *subject* or *self*. In fact it was already Luther who undermined the conceptual foundations of metaphysics and largely contributed to the problem discussed by Taylor and Blumenberg. His analysis of the principal concepts of philosophical vocabulary, substance in particular, were seminal efforts to answer the questions posed to man by theological absolutism. His early lectures on Psalms delivered in Wittenberg between the years 1513–1515 provided new standards for understanding *how* man is able to know himself and *how* human being exists (cf. Ebeling: 2006, 92–94; Ozment: 1969, 105–117). Young Luther pointed out that according to Scripture the philosophical meaning of *substantia* is improper. Philosophy speaks of inner nature, while Scripture about something external, something that gives a thing duration, and provides permanence. Man's substance is derived only from his particular existence, that is his way of being. Luther gives a number of examples: a rich man from his particular riches, a healthy man from his particular health.

44 Heidegger: 1977, 89–90: "Weltbild, wesentlich verstanden, meint daher nicht ein Bild von der Welt, sondern die Welt als Bild begriffen. Das Seiende im Ganzen wird jetzt so genommen, daß es erst und nur seiend ist, sofern es durch den vorstellend-herstellenden Menschen gestellt ist. […] Das Weltbild wird nicht von einem vormals mittelalterlichen zu einem neuzeitlichen, sondern dies, daß überhaupt die Welt zum Bild wird, zeichnet das Wesen der Neuzeit aus". See also ibidem, 87–89.

Philosophy proceeds from the phenomenon to the static inner nature (*quidditas*). Scripture does otherwise, for it is not concerned with *quidditates* but only *qualitates*, that is external, dynamic elements and relationships. Biblically speaking, *substantia* does not stand for *essentia*, but rather for *existentia*. It follows that the substance of human being cannot be comprehended by way of logic and metaphysics, but only in its historical development, with all its constantly changing qualities. Only history is able to grasp the diversity of man's manifestations.[45] Consequently, human intellect, as Luther says, is mere *sensualitas*, because *intellectus* is incapable of understanding *spiritualia*.[46] Luther puts it clearly – philosophical deliberations on humanity before God are useless for the answering the question *who am I*.

At the same time the young Luther experienced a profound identity crisis. Within the Roman Catholic doctrine of man, advocated by late medieval theology, he seemed to himself, as Erik Erikson (1993) revealed, sentenced to eternal damnation. It is extremely significant that the crisis experienced by Augustine just before his conversion and baptism had a completely different metaphysical ground. "I would have found it easier to doubt whether I was myself alive than there is no truth", as he admitted in *Confessions* (Augustine: 1991, 124), Luther would possibly have inverted that hierarchy of certitude, by taking human *esse* instead of divine *veritas* as a referential centre, since during his stay in the Augustinian cloister he himself could not comprehend the truth. Descartes actually did so advisedly and confidently.

45 Luther: 1885, 419, l. 25–28, 33–38; 420, l. 1–3: "Substantia in Scriptura metaphorice accipitur tam ex grammaticali quam physicali significatione. Et proprie, non ut philosophi de ea loquuntur, hic accipienda est. Sed pro substaculo seu subsidentia, in qua pedibus stari potest, ut non in profundum labantur et mergantur [...] Sic enim dicitur onme illud, per quod quisque in sua vita subsistit: ut dives subsistit per divitias, sanus per sanitatem, honoratus per honorem, voluptarii per voluptatem. Quia tam diu sunt tales, quam diu ista durant. Et sic substantia proprie magis est qualitas vel extrinsecum quam ipsa essentia rei. Quia Scriptura nihil curat quidditates rerum, sed qualitates tantum. Et sic qualiter unusquisque est et agit, secundum hoc habet substantiam: qua si caret, iam non subsistit. Quare pauper, abiectus, afflictor sui sunt sine substantia. Denique substantia magis de bonis mundi dicitur".

46 Luther: 1885, 176, l. 3–5, 7–10, 12–14, 19–24: "Intellectus in scripturis sanctis potius ab obiecto quam potentia nomen habet, contrario quam in philosophia. Est onim intellectus cognitio vel notitia sensus Christi [...] Et est breviter nihil aliud nisi sapientia crucis Christi, que gentibus stultitia et Iudeis scandalum est, scilicet intelligere, quod filius dei est incarnatus et crucifixus et mortuus et suscitatus propter nostram salutem. [...] Sed quia totum hoc est in fide et non in sensu neque ratione, ideo etiam intellectus hominum in scriptura dicitur sensualitas, eo quod non nisi sensibilia capiat, quantumcunque sit subtilis et acutus et prudens. [...] Intelligere itaque est spiritualia et mysteria salutis et gratie Dei agnoscere, unde usus loquendi obtinuit dicere 'mysteria' redemptionis et incarnationis, eo quod non nisi mysticis pateant et spiritualibus, non autem hominibus, quibus est potius stultitia, quia ipsi sunt stulti equi et muli: ideo primum illos oportet mutari, ut sic mysteria, que sunt eterna, cognoscant".

The philosophical foundations of the modern "identity of notion" were laid by the current which has learned the most from the transformations caused by late medieval and early modern Nominalism, and in effect cared about facts instead of abstractions. This was British Empiricism. *An Essay Concerning Human Understanding* by John Locke is the first philosophical recognition of identity which provides reconsiderations relevant for the description of the phenomena discussed here (1959, 439–470). From the pristine metaphysical identity of substance, Locke marked off so-called *personal identity.* According to Locke, a *person* is a being capable of reflection, namely a being which "can consider itself as itself, the same thinking thing, in different times and places" (1959, 448, 450–451, 466). It follows that, a logical *being the same* was supplemented by an introspective *being self*, exempted from logical, quantitative and qualitative rules.

On the philosophical level identity finally has become capable of asking deliberately the question "what makes my-self?" and able to answer it systematically. Consciousness, according to Locke, is the fundamental building block of *personal identity.* It is consciousness that makes a man what he can call himself. Due to consciousness man is finally able to distinguish himself from other reflective beings. "In [consciousness] alone consists personal identity", as Locke explained (1959, 449). He emphasises that only consciousness sets the limits of *personal identity.* Moreover, consciousness enters into a fundamental relationship with memory. As a correlation of memorised history and an introspective approach, the existence of *personal identity* reaches as far as the consciousness can be extended backwards to past events or ideas. This means that the features describing each *person's* uniqueness are drawn from the collective memory that a person feels a part of (Locke: 1959, 464). Obviously Locke did not use the term *collective memory.* However, his explanations of the historical conditioning of *personal identity* correspond to this notion introduced by twentieth-century sociology. For Locke explains his own findings as follows: "[*personal identity*] extends itself beyond present existence to what is past, only by consciousness, whereby it becomes concerned and accountable; owns and imputes to itself past actions, just upon the same ground and for the same reason as it does the present" (Locke: 1959, 467).

A little later, namely in 1739, David Hume in *A Treatise of Human Nature* took an important step forward regarding "identity of notion". By altering the building block of *personal identity* – memory took the place of consciousness – philosophical reconsiderations regarding this issue entered a new, and in the long run, modern phase. Discussing the question of sources of *personal identity*, Hume concluded: "the memory not only discovers the identity, but also contributes to its production. [...] The case is the same whether we consider ourselves or others. [...] As a memory alone acquaints us with the continuance and extent of this succession of perceptions, 'tis be considered, upon that account chiefly, as the source of personal identity" (Hume: 2007, 170). From now on the making of identity depended mostly on the common history which retold in myth handed down commonly shared patterns of power, faith, value and knowledge.

With British Empiricism concepts of consciousness and memory become functional categories for the identification of development and atrophy of collective being. Paul Ricoeur aptly indicated this pivotal change. In *Oneself as Another* he distinguished two kinds of identity – the first was an old metaphysical notion of *idem*, that is *sameness*, while the second referred to the problem of being self (Ricoeur: 1990, 137–150, 167–198). The latter, discovered by Locke, is the identity of *ipse*, that is *selfhood*. Ricoeur strongly emphasised a distinction between these two kinds: "selfhood is not sameness" (Ricoeur: 1990, 140). Within the universal order of things and names advocated by ontological Realism, such exclusive disjunction would be nothing but nonsense. It is needless to add that the functions of the myth of *Reformation*, or *Luther's Reformation* in particular, consisted in the same introspective recognition of *who are we*, where the story retold in myth binds community together through a common system of identification. Religious community is endowed with such a pattern by myth and doctrine as the building blocks of religious memory. The significance of doctrinal tradition for religious collective memory, as Maurice Halbwachs explained (1925, 147, 149), consists in restoration: the outlining and systematisation of those aspects of the life and early teaching of the Church that the community finds necessary or important to retain.

Despite the fact that neither Locke nor Hume used the notion of myth in the context of identity, their findings regarding the introspective function of memory may offer us an explanation for the complementary interaction of myth and identity. I have already stated that the making of identity is the ultimate goal of work on myth and indicates the pragmatic truth of myth, validated by contemporary motivations rather than history itself. In his *Work on myth* Blumenberg spoke of the absolutism of reality, while in the *Legitimacy of the Modern Age* about theological absolutism. In both cases the creative force of myth was necessary to sustain identity and corresponded to the needs of humanity deprived of a basic moral frame orienting one's action and thinking (cf. Blumenberg: 2001, 269; Taylor: 2001, 28). That frame could only be put in universal terms like *good* and *bad*, so myth, once declared with totality, compensated that loss. By retelling histories through myth man reached a desirable state of self-assertion in a disintegrated, and thus foreign, reality.

Locke noticed that even entities remote in time and space can be united by common consciousness (1959, 464). Self-consciousness is founded upon a conviction that *our* present existence is justified by *our* historical background. The deeper our introspective memory reaches back into antecedents, the more firmly our identity is established (cf. Hroch: 2005, 166–169; Kołakowski: 2005, 208). Barbour accurately reveals this interaction by saying that man "takes his self-identity in part from the past events which he believes have made him what he is. [...] A community is constituted by the key events which it remembers and in which its members participate" (1976, 20). While the origins of religious community is identified by the founding myth, its privileged place in history is justified mostly by the religious memory founded upon doctrinal matters clarified in the different confessions of faith.

Last but not least, early modern identities act on a personal level just as myths act on a collective level. As already stated, the basic relation between myth and identity consists in the integration of individual beings into a self-conscious community. Through myth we can accurately indicate the areas of human conduct where early modern communities were trying to assert themselves. Through myth we can recognise particular modes of self-assertion, namely how man obtains a clear insight into his historical existence. To confirm themselves, communities have to domesticate their experiences, instruct individuals about themselves, and provide patterns for future conduct. All this determines a horizon within which things and names eventually take on fixed meanings, human thoughts and choices are considered good or reasonable (Taylor: 2001, 27–28). Consequently individual being as a part of a community is finally able to gain its proper, historical significance. Only within a community is man endowed with both social duties and guidelines to efficiently carry out his personal obligations. The most important function of community with regard to individuals, as confirmed by Anthony Smith's analyses of national identity, is to save man from personal oblivion and ensure him personal immortality. Community provides a man with "a glorious future similar to its heroic past (Smith: 1991, 160–161).

5. Analytical Approach: Quantitative and Qualitative Attributes

Within the ontologically insecure and changeable order of reality, different identities, that is collective beings endowed with the attribute of self-consciousness, not only existed side by side, but were also reciprocally oriented to one another, as witnessed by the notions of majority (*maior pars*) and minority (*minor pars*). Both *maior* and *minor pars* indicate the mutual and indispensable relationships of feuding early modern communities and as a result reconsideration is required concerning whether these concepts indicate merely a quantitative attribute distinguishing one community from another. Consequently this chapter comments on the third and fourth of the aforementioned issues, namely *how* identity allows us to discuss different but self-conscious communities, that is *how* these communities responded to the *reformatio* idea, whether in their own formulation or that of others, and finally whether *maior-minor* difference was comprehended in terms of quantity or quality.

Already Plessner's analyses of the *Roman complex* prove that a particular community is able to identify itself through interaction with foreigners. Ann Peterson Royce considered such interaction a foundation of being self-conscious within larger communities: "without this contrast, ethnic identity does not exist. The hypothetical group on an island with no knowledge of others is not an ethnic group; it does not have an ethnic identity [...] We define ourselves in large measure in terms of what we are not" (Peterson Royce: 1982, 12).[47] The difference derives only from an interaction that eventually leads to a recognition of self. As a name given to a self-conscious community, Lutheranism is hardly imaginable without Roman Catholicism, post-Tridentine Catholicism and the Catholic Reformation without Christian heterodoxy, the proper without the inappropriate, the majority without the minority – each was sharpened by conflict.

The notion of so-called *counter-identity* has been introduced into scholarship in order to provide a more comprehensive understanding of the changes that contributed to the development of early modern notions of fatherland (*patria*) and nation (*natio*). Orest Ranum, who coined that term, believed that in sixteenth- and seventeenth-century Europe identifying the exclusive qualities and separate ways of a particular community depended on a distinctive set of features of *counter-identities* which "are the opposites of the morally edifying virtues and manners that make up the identity of a *patria* (1986, 65). Ranum's category, functionally analogous to the *Roman complex* described by Plessner, and the concept of interaction indicated by Peterson Royce, is actually a measurable outcome of the transformations discussed above in terms of man's disposition toward disintegrated reality. Like *counter-identity* the same can be said of different types of collective beings, religious communities in particular. Such *counter-identity*, complex and in interaction, always implies a strong hierarchy of collective beings.

The prefix *re-* of "Reformation" indicated not only a descriptive register of the past state of affairs but also an evocative recalling to bygone, but preferable, conditions. It included religious and political ideas as well. Consequently, in the sixteenth century it was a matter of the different understanding of the range and scope of *reformatio*, a concept constantly and frequently used by the feuding parties of Roman Catholicism and the different Protestant denominations. Since *reformatio* was for all of them the name of a properly conducted renewal of Christianity, religious and collective identity became a brand new, recurring

47 See also Hroch: 2005, 153.

theme in discussions between the opposed sides.[48] Each side used the *reformatio* concept either to self-assert their own, positive agenda or to discredit the one promoted by their opponents.

Both self-assertion and disqualification needed a principle that went far beyond historical circumstances or contingent national interest born of objectives determined by particular capabilities. This was possible only by means of indicating the imperishable, divine origin of undertaken actions. Since reality based on the human order was merely modelled after its divine pattern, each idea of power, faith, value and knowledge was ultimately validated by declared supernatural inspiration. In fact, such a rule of conduct practiced by early modern religious communities inevitably meant that man's requirements were of highest importance. "Love of *patria*, in the early-modern period of European societies", Ranum explains, "consisted of believing almost as part of the *credo* that the specific natural resources and morally edifying virtues of a particular native group were gifts from God" (1986, 63). Indeed, we only need to consider one of the copperplates of Thomas Treterus, a secretary of Cardinal Stanislaus Hosius, to see how in practice self-assertion and disqualification were being accomplished. The copperplate *Legatio in Concilio Tridentino* gives a powerful view, where on behalf of the *Sancta synodus* Hosius himself fells personified *haeretica novitas* with a blow of *Sedis Apostolice auctoritas.* Heretical novelty smashed by Hosius is contrasted with nothing other than *Antiquitas* as a cornerstone of Christian *Oecumenica.* Right next to Hosius a group of learned Catholics let free a dove (a depiction of the Holy Spirit) with the inscription *reformatio* (Treterus: 1998, 58). Treterus' image expresses the myth of restoration which was essential for that period. Since *auctoritas* is founded upon *antiquitas* it follows that properly conducted *reformatio* becomes a countermeasure to seditious *novitas.* As such *Legatio in Concilio Tridentino* exemplifies the predominant tendency defining early modern identities – to advocate one's contribution means to indicate by means of myth its divine origin and refuse to acknowledge the part of the other.

This explains why Lutherans were appealing either to Augustine, John Hus, Luther's works and *Augustana* on the theological level, or to Germanic myth, Arminius, Barbarossa, and Luther as a Reformer on the national level. Catholics did exactly the same. The most influential religious orders that originated in the sixteenth century, like the Theatines, Capuchins, and most of all the Jesuits, tended to affirm that a deliberative Catholic renewal had occurred before the Lutheran movement. By suggesting that there were unacceptable incidents in the medieval Church, Catholics were justifying their own positive contribution to the

48 On the conceptual history of reformatio see Wolgast: 1984, 313–360; Strauss: 1995, 1–30; Campi: 2013, 10–16.

history of Christianity. It is worth mentioning that Roman Catholics were still trying to defend their own positive part in the restoration of German Christianity, although the conviction that German means Lutheran almost dominated sixteenth-century imagination. On account of the Germanic chauvinism of Lutherans, distinguished theologians of the Roman Catholic camp were keen to underline that their own reformatory goals were achieved on the territory of German Reich, and most of all served the German welfare – *reformatio in Germania et pro Germania*, as witnessed in one of the documents from the mid-century.[49]

From the Lutheran point of view it seemed a flagrant contradiction to speak of a genuine renewal caused by the Roman Catholic agenda. The antithesis of the Lutheran image of *reformatio* was not only a *deformatio* (a concept used by Catholics as well), but most of all *Gegenreformation*, a notion introduced by the German jurist Johann Stephan Pütter in 1776. According to Pütter's brief explanation, *die catholischen Gegenreformationen* was a common name given to the different strategies aimed by Roman Catholics for political domination over the Lutherans (1776, 10–20). So this concept means exactly what it says, an anti-Reformation devoid of any positive element. In result, as John O'Malley rightly noticed, it "surely captured the sentiments of many oppressed Lutherans" (2000, 20). However, *Gegenreformation* was not only a kind of historical accusation, but first and foremost it conveyed the firm conviction that only the Lutheran movement was responsible for any positive change in religious matters. Early modern reformers were not keen to give the others a share in their own part in Christian restoration.

The categories of *majority* and *minority* derive from the modern subjectivism which was essential for the development of individual and collective inequality, and in the long run for the development of social stratification. As a result of the processes described above that profoundly changed the understanding of the self, the quantitative meaning and function of *majority* and *minority* says very little, if anything at all, about the need for purely human self-assertion as an essential feature of modern humanity. Although in terms of quantity these categories indicate the important problem of confessional coexistence and intermingling (Kooi: 2001, 147–159), they explain neither the reasons for religious uniformity and the sharpness of inter-confessional differences, nor the modes of collective apperception that actually determined what was *majority* and what was *minority*. As testified by accessible sources, collective beings born in the sixteenth

49 Campegius: 1930, 106, l. 11–14: "Cum fieret haec reformatio in Germania et pro Germania, operae pretium fuisset diligenter animadvertere, quibus episcopis eiusmodi permitterentur ordinationes, et nisi illi firmi et constanter semper permansissent in catholica fide, vel summoverentur vel negotium hoc iis demandaretur, qui omni labe caruissent haereticae saltem pravitatis".

century very often estimated their mutual relations by different criteria than population size. Precision was neither the only nor the ultimate criterion, since such evaluative verdicts depended mostly on ideas communities shared about themselves rather than sober, quantitative estimation. Thus *majority* did not always stand for numerical superiority, but it did always imply the relationship of supremacy and subordination.

The mythical groundwork of early modern communities, founded upon binary oppositions (good and bad, for instance), leaves no doubt that majority and minority were a kind of community which were ontologically hardly imaginable. When Adrian VI in his above-quoted instruction spoke of the genuine Germans who approved papal and imperial policy, he used exactly the notion of majority (*maior pars*) (1901, 394, l. 18–19). It ultimately explains the qualitative significance of that concept. Irrespective of population size, majority stood for the collective being endowed with the attribute of self-consciousness, whose identity was described by the specific system of identification consisting of ideas verbalised in myth and doctrinal tradition. When a community in the first person plural deliberately spoke of such ideas as their *own*, they relegated what is other or opposite to an inferior rank, that is to minority status. Particular verdicts actually depended on perspective. According to Melanchthon *boni omnes* praised Luther's efforts; he himself was among the most beautiful multitude of excellent men (*agmen summorum virorum*) elected by God; while according to Roman Catholic officials, *maior eorum pars* approved the sentence against Luther.

Nostra reformatio was both an affirmative, descriptive statement, and an expression of exclusive religious property – *nostra* means exactly neither *vestra* nor *sua*. Again Adrian VI can offer us an extremely instructive insight into the social dimensions of the myth of Reformation: "each community may require its own laws to be obeyed inviolably. [...] Because Luther and his followers condemn the Councils of the holy fathers, burn the sacred canons, bring disorder at their own discretion, and throw the whole world into confusion, it is evident that those who love peace must banish them as enemies of peace and disturbers".[50] By appealing to the exegetical tradition Adrian VI makes it clear that religious memory, objectified in Councils and canons, claims to be fixed once and for all. Moreover, being *nostra*, religious memory, as Halbwachs noticed (1925, 141), obliged other communities to accept its dominant representations in doctrinal documents, otherwise such communities were systematically ignored. *Our* religious memory

50 Adrian VI: 1901, 396–397, l. 34–35, 1–5: "cum tamen unaqueque civitas leges suas inviolabiliter observari exigat; [...] Cum igitur Lutherus et sui concilia sanctorum patrum condemnant, sacros canones conburant et cuncta pro arbitrio suo confundant ac totum mundum perturbent, manifestum est eos tanquam publice pacis inimicos et perburbatores ab omnibus eiusdem pacis amatoribus exterminandos esse".

contrasts *our* own permanence with the instability of others, and in result it relegates them to an inferior rank of minority. When Christianity lost its universal foundation and fell essentially into pieces, this was perhaps the only possible solution for constructive and durable existence.

That is *how* the story of the early modern period can look. The story about man realising that he has no control over the conditions of his existence; the story about the way in which the well-structured medieval hierarchy of beings, founded upon the metaphysical *analogia entis*, came to a close; and finally the story of essentially disintegrated reality. All these stories were retold in the myth of *reformatio* which aimed at human self-assertion.

Bibliography

ADRIAN VI, POPE (1901), Instruktion des Papstes Adrian VI. für Chieregati, in: Deutsche Reichstagsakten, revised edition, vol. 3, Gotha: F.A. Perthes.

ANDERSON, B. (2006), Imagined Communities: Reflections on the Origin and Spread of Nationalism, revised edition, London: Verso.

AUGUSTINE OF HIPPO (1991), Confessions, trans. H. Chadwick, Oxford: Oxford University Press.

BARBOUR, I.G. (1976), Myths, Models and Paradigms: A Comparative Study in Science and Religion, New York: Harper & Row.

BARTH, F. (1998), Ethnic Groups and Boundaries: The Social Organization of Culture Difference, Long Grove, IL: Waveland Press.

BARTH, KARL (2010), Der Römerbrief, 2nd edition (1922), C. van der Kooi/K. Tolstaja (eds.), Zürich: Theologischer Verlag.

BLUMENBERG, HANS (2001), Arbeit am Mythos, 6th edition, Frankfurt am Main: Suhrkamp.

– (1996), Die Legitimität der Neuzeit, revised edition, Frankfurt am Main: Suhrkamp.

BÖCKENFÖRDE, E.-W. (1995), Die Nation – Identität in Differenz, in: Krzysztof Michalski (ed.), Identität im Wandel. Castelgandolfo – Gespräche, Stuttgart: Klett-Cotta, 129–154.

BOROWSKI, ANDRZEJ (1987), Pojęcie i problem renesansu północnego: Przyczynek do geografii historycznoliterackiej humanizmu renesansowego północnego, Krakow: Uniwersytet Jagielloński.

BUGENHAGEN, JOHANNES (1546), Eine Christliche Predigt vber der Leich vnd begrebnis des Ehrwirdigen D. Martini Luthers durch Ern Johan Bugenhagen Pomern Doctor vnd Pfarherr der Kirchen zu Wittemberg gethan. Wittenberg: George Rhaw.

CAMPEGIUS, THOMAS (1930), Iudicium de reformatione Germaniae a. 1548, in: Theobald Freudenberger (ed.), Concilium Tridentinum. Diariorum, actorum, epistolarum, tractatuum nova collectio, vol. 13, Freiburg im Bresgau: Herder.

CAMPI, EMIDIO (2013), Was the Reformation a German Event? in: Peter. Opitz (ed.), The Myth of the Reformation, Göttingen: Vandenhoeck & Ruprecht, 9–31.

CHRZANOWSKI, TADEUSZ (1984), Działalność artystyczna Tomasza Tretera, Warsaw: Państwowe Wydawnictwo Naukowe.

Contarini, Gasparo et al. (1930), Consilium delectorum cardinalium et aliorum praelatorum de emendanda ecclesia S.D. N. Paulo III iubente conscriptum et exhibitum, in: Theobald Freudenberger (ed.), Concilium Tridentinum. Diariorum, actorum, epistolarum, tractatuum nova collectio, vol. 12, Freiburg im Bresgau: Herder.

Ebeling Gerhard (2006), Luther. Einführung in sein Denken, Tübingen: Mohr.

– (1982), Lutherstudien, Bd. 2: Disputatio de homine, Tl. 2: Die philosophische Definition des Menschen. Kommentar zu These 1–19, Tübingen: Mohr.

Erikson, Erik H. (1993), Young Man Luther: A Study in Psychoanalysis and History, New York: Norton.

Gadamer, Hans-Georg (1990), Wahrheit und Methode. Grundzüge einer philosophischen Hermeneutik, Tübingen: Mohr.

Halbwachs, Maurice (1925), Les cadres sociaux de la mémoire, Paris: Librairie Félix Alcan.

Hegel, Georg W.F. (1989), Vorlesungen über die Philosophie der Geschichte, Frankfurt am Main: Suhrkamp.

Heidegger, Martin (1989), Beiträge zur Philosophie (vom Ereignis), Frankfurt am Main: Suhrkamp.

– (1977), Die Zeit des Weltbildes, in: Holzwege, Frankfurt am Main: Suhrkamp.

– (1997), Der europäische Nihilismus, in: Nietzsche, vol. 2, Frankfurt am Main: Suhrkamp.

– (1996), Das Problem der Sünde bei Luther, in: Berndt Jaspert (ed.), Sachgemässe Exegese: Die Protokolle aus Rudolf Bultmanns Neutestamentlichen Seminaren 1921–1951, Marburg: Elwert.

Hroch, Miroslav (2005), Das Europa der Nationen: Die moderne Nationsbildung im europäischen Vergleich, Göttingen: Vandenhoeck & Ruprecht.

Hume, David (2007), A Treatise of Human Nature, A Critical Edition, ed. David F. Norton/ Mary J. Norton, vol. 1, Oxford: Clarendon Press.

James, William (1907), Pragmatism: A New Name for Some Old Ways of Thinking: Popular Lectures on Philosophy, New York: Longmans, Green, and Co.

– (1897), The Will to Believe and Other Essays in Popular Philosophy, New York: Longmans, Green, and Co.

Kant, Immanuel (1968), Beantwortung der Frage: Was ist Aufklärung?, in: Kants Werke, Akademie-Ausgabe, Bd. VIII: Abhandlungen nach 1781, Berlin: Walter de Gruyter.

Kołakowski, Leszek (2001), The Presence of Myth, trans. Adam Czerniawski, Chicago, IL: Chicago University Press.

– (2005), On Collective Identity, in: My Correct Views on Everything, ed. Zbigniew Janowski, South Bend, IN: St Augustine's Press.

Kooi, Christine (2001), Sub Jugo Haereticorum: Minority Catholicism in Early Modern Europe, in: Kathleen M. Comerford/Hilmar M. Pabel (eds.), Early Modern Catholicism: Essays in Honour of John W. O'Malley, S. J., Toronto: University of Toronto Press, 147–162.

Locke, John (1959), An Essay Concerning Human Understanding, ed. Alexander C. Fraser, vol. 1, New York: Dover Publications.

Luther, Martin (1888a), An den christlichen Adel deutscher Nation von des christlichen Standes Besserung. 1520, in: J.K.F. Knaake (ed.), D. Martin Luthers Werke, vol. 6, Weimar: Hermann Böhlau.

– (1888b), De captivitate Babylonica ecclesiae praeludium, in: J.K.F. Knaake (ed.), D. Martin Luthers Werke, vol. 6, Weimar: Hermann Böhlau.
– (1885), Dictata super Psalterium 1513–1516, in: J.K.F. Knaake (ed.), D. Martin Luthers Werke, vol. 3, Weimar: Hermann Böhlau.
– (1926), Die Disputation de homine, in: J.K.F. Knaake (ed.), D. Martin Luthers Werke, vol. 39 I, Weimar: Hermann Böhlau.
– (1883a), Disputatio contra scholasticam theologiam 1517, in: J.K.F. Knaake (ed.), D. Martin Luthers Werke, vol. 1, Weimar: Hermann Böhlau.
– (1883b), Disputatio Heidelbergae habita 1518, in: J.K.F. Knaake (ed.), D. Martin Luthers Werke, vol. 1, Weimar: Hermann Böhlau.
– (1883c), Quaestio de viribus et voluntate sine gratia disputata 1516, in: J.K.F. Knaake (ed.), D. Martin Luthers Werke, vol. 1, Weimar: Hermann Böhlau.
– (1883d), Martin Luther, Resolutiones disputationum de indulgentiarum virtute. 1518, in: J.K.F. Knaake (ed.), D. Martin Luthers Werke, vol. 1, Weimar: Hermann Böhlau.
– (1914), Von den Konziliis und Kirchen, in: J.K.F. Knaake (ed.), D. Martin Luthers Werke, vol. 50, Weimar: Hermann Böhlau.

MacIver, Robert (1965), The Web of Government, New York: Macmillan.

Melanchthon, Phillipp (1843), Oratio in funere D. Martini Lutheri (d. 22. Febr. a Melanthone recitata), in: Karl Gottlieb Bretschneider (ed.), Philippi Melanthonis Opera quae supersunt omnia, vol. 11, Halle: C.A. Schwetschke.

Mertens, Dieter (2004), Die Instrumentalisierung der „Germania" des Tacitus durch die deutschen Humanisten, in: Heinrich Beck (ed.), Zur Geschichte der Gleichung „germanisch - deutsch". Sprache und Namen, Geschichte und Institutionen, Berlin: Walter de Gruyter; 37–102.

Münkler, H. (2009), Die Deutschen und ihre Mythen, Berlin: Rowohlt.

Murray, Henry A. (1960), The Possible Nature of a "Mythology" to Come, in: Henry A. Murray (ed.), Myth and Mythmaking, New York: G. Braziller, 300–353.

O'Malley, John W. (2000), Trent and All That: Renaming Catholicism in the Early Modern Era, Cambridge, MA: Harvard University Press.

Ozment, Steven E. (1969), Homo spiritualis: A Comparative Study of the Anthropology of Johannes Tauler, Jean Gerson and Martin Luther (1509–16) in the Context of their Theological Thought, Leiden: Brill.

Peterson Royce, A. (1982), Ethnic Identity: Strategies of Diversity, Bloomington, IN: Indiana University Press.

Pettegree, Andrew (2015), Brand Luther: 1517, Printing, and the Making of the Reformation, New York: Penguin.

Plessner, Helmuth (1974), Die verspätete Nation: Über die politische Verführbarkeit bürgerlichen Geistes, Frankfurt am Main: Suhrkamp.

Pütter, Johann Stephan (1776), Die Augsburgische Confession in einem neuen Abdrucke und mit einer Vorrede, worinn unter andern der Unterschied der evangelischen Reformation und der catholischen Gegenreformationen wie auch der wahre Grund der evangelischen Kirchenverfassung aus der A.C. selbst erläutert wird, Göttingen.

Ranum, Orest (1986), Counter-Identities of Western European Nations in the Early-Modern Period: Definitions and Points of Departure, in: Peter Boerner (ed.), Concepts of National Identity: An Interdisciplinary Dialogue. Interdisziplinäre Betrachtungen zur Frage der nationalen Identität, Baden-Baden: Nomos, 63–78.

Ricoeur, Paul (1990), Soi-même comme un autre, Paris: Éditions de Seuil.

Schiller, Friedrich (1916), Schillers Gedichtentwurf Deutsche Größe, ed. Friedrich Lienhard, Stuttgart: Greiner & Pfeiffer.

Schmitt, Carl (1996), Roman Catholicism and Political Form, trans. G.L. Ulmen, Westport, CT/London: Greenwood Press.

Schöpflin, George (1997), The Functions of Myth and a Taxonomy of Myths, in: Geoffrey Hosking/George Schöpflin (eds.), Myths and Nationhood, London: Taylor and Francis, 19–35.

Schorer, Mark (1960), The Necessity of Myth, in: Henry A. Murray (ed.), Myth and Mythmaking, New York, G. Braziller, 354–358.

Sloterdijk, Peter (1999), Regeln für den Menschenpark. Ein Antwortschreiben zu Heideggers Brief über den Humanismus, Frankfurt am Main: Suhrkamp.

Smith, Anthony D. (1991), National Identity, London: Penguin.

Sorel, Georges (2004), Reflections on Violence, ed. Jeremy Jennings, Cambridge: Cambridge University Press.

Spaemann, Robert (2007), Das unsterbliche Gerücht. Die Frage nach Gott und die Täuschung der Moderne, Stuttgart: Klett-Cotta.

Strauss, Gerald (1995), Ideas of Reformatio and Renovatio from the Middle Ages to the Reformation, in: T.A. Brady/H.A. Oberman/J.D. Tracy (eds.), Handbook of European History 1400–1600. Late Middle Ages, Renaissance and Reformation, vol. 2: Visions, Programs and Outcomes, Leiden: Brill, 1–30.

Szacka, Barbara (2006), Czas przeszły – pamięć – mit, Warsaw: Wydawnictwo Naukowe Scholar.

Taylor, Charles (2001), Sources of the Self: The Making of the Modern Identity, Cambridge, MA: Harvard University Press.

Treterus, Thomas (1998), Thomae Treteri Theatrum virtutum divi Stanislai Hosii, Krakow: Collegium Columbinum.

Valla, Lorenzo (1952), In sex libros elegantiarum praefatio, in: E. Garin (ed.), Prosatori latini del Quattrocento, Milano: Riccardo Ricciardi.

von Hutten, Ulrich (1860), Arminius: Dialogus Huttenicus quo homo patriae amantissimus patriae laudem celebravit, in: Eduard Böcking (ed.), Ulrichi Hutteni Equitis Germani Opera quae reperiri potuerunt omnia, vol. 4, Leipzig: Teubner.

Wolgast, E. (1984), Reform, Reformation, in: O. Brunner/W. Conze/R. Koselleck (eds.), Geschichtliche Grundbegriffe. Historisches Lexikon zur politisch-sozialen Sprache in Deutschland, vol. 5: Pro-Soz, Stuttgart: Klett-Cotta, 313–360.

Notes on the contributors

Mihály Balázs is Professor Emeritus at the József Attila University in Szeged, Hungary, where he received his doctorate (1981) and taught Old Hungarian and European literature and culture between 1972 and 2018. He has published several books on the Reformation, focusing mainly on Transylvanian Anti-Trinitarianism, and has worked also as an editor of Unitarian and Jesuit primary sources.

Simon J.G. Burton received his PhD in historical theology from the University of Edinburgh in 2011. Following his PhD he took up postdoctoral fellowships at McGill University and the Faculty of "Artes Liberales" of the University of Warsaw, and from 2015–17 was an Assistant-Professor of Early Modern Christianity in Warsaw. He is currently John Laing Senior Lecturer in Reformation History at the School of Divinity of the University of Edinburgh. He is the author of a monograph on Richard Baxter, the celebrated seventeenth-century Reformed theologian, as well as a number of articles and book chapters on late medieval and early modern theology.

Michał Choptiany is an Assistant Professor of Early Modern Intellectual History at the Faculty of "Artes Liberales" of the University of Warsaw. He received his PhD in literary studies from the Jagiellonian University in Cracow in 2013. His research interests include the history of early modern science and scholarship (with particular focus on the intersection of astronomy and historiography), the history of the book and reading, and sixteenth- and seventeenth-century rhetoric and literature.

Alessandra Celati received her PhD in Early Modern History from the University of Pisa in 2016. In 2017 she was awarded a Marie Curie Global Fellowship, which she is currently carrying out between Stanford University and the University of Verona working on the project "Medicine, Heresy and Freedom of Thought: A Network of Dissident Physicians in the Confessional Age". She is currently preparing a monograph entitled *Physicians and heresy in sixteenth-century Venice. The world of Girolamo Donzellini.*

Gábor Ittzés is Associate Professor at Debrecen Reformed Theological University in Hungary. He obtained his PhD in English Literary Studies from Eötvös Loránd University, Budapest, and his ThD in Systematic and Historical Theology from Harvard University. He has widely published on Luther, Melanchthon, the German Reformation, Milton, and religion and culture. His research interests cover a broad range from Milton's *Paradise Lost* to the immortality of the soul in sixteenth-century German theology.

Barbara A. Kaminska is an Assistant Professor of Art History at Sam Houston State University in Huntsville, Texas. She received her MA from the University of Warsaw (2007) and her PhD from the University of California, Santa Barbara (2014). Her research focuses on iconography and the functions of sixteenth-century religious paintings and prints in the Netherlands, early modern festival culture, and art theory.

Jakub Koryl is an Assistant Professor at the Chair of Old Polish Literature of the Faculty of Polish Studies, Jagiellonian University in Cracow, where he also earned his doctorate in literary studies (2012). His dissertation on Polish Erasmianism was awarded a prize by the Polish Prime Minister. His scientific interests include the intellectual and cultural history of the early modern period, the philosophical implications and consequences of Lutheranism, hermeneutics, and phenomenology.

Borbála Lovas is a member of the "Humanism in East Central Europe" Research Group (MTA-ELTE HECE). Following her PhD in European and Hungarian Renaissance Studies at Eötvös Loránd University, Budapest, she has published on the relationship between "popular" and "classical" literature, including Biblical translations, vernacular sermons, and the European printing history of texts from Hungary and Transylvania.

Magdalena Luszczynska is a historian interested in the intersections of religion, science, and politics in early-modern Europe. She holds her PhD from the Hebrew University of Jerusalem. Currently, she is a postdoctoral fellow at the Polonsky Academy for Advanced Study in the Humanities and Social Sciences at the Van Leer Jerusalem Institute. She is the author of a monograph *Politics of Polemic: Marcin Czechowic on the Jews* (De Gruyter, 2018).

Frances Luttikhuizen is an interdisciplinary scholar, a retired educator, teacher-trainer, linguistic consultant, text-book writer, researcher, and lecturer. She holds a PhD from the University of Barcelona. She is a member of the editorial board of *Interdisciplinary Literary Studies* (Penn State Altoona, US) and *Eduforma* (Seville, Spain), and international coordinator for CIMPE (Centro de Investigación y Memoria del Protestantismo Español). Her main fields of interest include the history of translation, applied linguistics, and Spanish Reformation studies.

Christopher Matthews serves as president and professor in the Reina-Valera Theological Seminary in Seville, Spain. His training includes an undergraduate degree in Spanish language from the University of North Carolina and graduate degrees in cross-cultural communications and cross-cultural studies from Wheaton College Graduate School and Gordon-Conwell Theological Seminary.

José Moreno Berrocal holds degrees in Law and Theology. He is a Reformed Baptist pastor in Alcázar de San Juan (La Mancha), Spain. He is also the President of the Evangelical Council of Churches in Castilla La Mancha. His publications include, among others, an introduction to the Spanish Reformation, *La Reforma Ayer y Hoy*, and *La Biblia y Don Quijote* (The Bible and Don Quixote). He has given lectures in Spain, the UK, Portugal, Italy, Argentina, and the USA.

Joanna Partyka is an Associate Professor in Renaissance and Baroque Literature at the Institute of Literary Research, Polish Academy of Sciences in Warsaw. She is a cultural anthropologist and historian of literature and culture. Her main field of interest is the European culture (in particular, Mediterranean culture) of the 16th and 17th centuries analyzed from a comparative perspective. She has published two monographs and more than 70 articles in Polish, Spanish and English. She also translates from Spanish to Polish.

Paweł Rutkowski works as an Assistant Professor in the Institute of English Studies of the University of Warsaw, where he serves as the head of the Department of Cultural Studies. He specializes in the cultural history of early modern Britain with an emphasis placed on its religious and supernatural history. He is the author of the monograph *Kot czarownicy* (*The Witch's Cat*, Kraków 2012) about English witches' familiar spirits and a series of articles on Reformation religion, religious movements, witchcraft, ghosts and animals.

Felicita Tramontana is Marie Curie Fellow in the Centre for the Study of the Renaissance of the University of Warwick and works on geographical mobility in the early modern period, focusing on missionary networks. She has worked extensively on religious conversions in the Middle East, on which she has published "Protestants' Conversion to Catholicism in the Syro-Palestinian Region (17th century)" in *Zeitschrift für historische Forschung* (2014), and the monograph *Passages of Faith. Conversion in the Palestinian countryside* (Harrassowitz Verlag, 2014). Her second monograph focuses on the history of early modern Palestine: *Una terra di intersezioni: Storia e istituzioni della Palestina ottomana* (Carocci, 2015).

Leon van den Broeke is Associate Professor of Religion, Law, and Society/Church Polity and chair of the Centre for Religion and Law at the Faculty of Religion and Theology at the Vrije Universiteit Amsterdam, and Associate Professor of Church Polity and director of the Deddens Church Polity Centre at the Theologische Universiteit Kampen.

Piotr Wilczek is a historian of early modern literature and culture and since 2008 Professor Ordinarius at the Faculty of "Artes Liberales" of the University of Warsaw. He received his PhD (1992) and Habilitation (2001) from the University of Silesia in Katowice. His research interests include Polish Renaissance and Baroque poetry, rhetoric, Anti-Trinitarianism, and the theory and practice of translation. His most recent book is *Polonia Reformata. Essays on the Polish Reformation(s)*, published in 2016 as vol. 36 of the Refo500 Academic Series.

Index of Places

Index of People